MW00826730

Learn, Teach...
Succeed...

With **REA's FTCE Mathematics 6–12**
test prep, you'll be in a class all your own.

Visit our website **www.rea.com**

REA: THE LEADER IN TEACHER CERTIFICATION PREP

3rd Edition

FTCE MATHEMATICS 6-12 (026)

FLORIDA TEACHER CERTIFICATION EXAMINATIONS

Sandra Rush, M.A.

Research & Education Association

Research & Education Association
61 Ethel Road West
Piscataway, New Jersey 08854
Email: info@rea.com

Florida FTCE Mathematics 6–12, 3rd Edition with Online Practice Exams

Printed in the United States of America

Library of Congress Control Number 2018942066

ISBN-13: 978-0-7386-1240-9
ISBN-10: 0-7386-1240-5

The competencies presented in this book were created and implemented by the Florida Department of Education and Pearson Education, Inc. For further information visit the FTCE website at *www.fl.nesinc.com*.

Contents

About Our Author x

About REA x

Chapter 1: Getting Started 1

    How to Use This Book + Online Prep 1

    An Overview of the Test 3

    Studying for the Test 6

    Become Familiar with the Computer and the Calculator 7

    Test-Taking Tips 13

    Before the Test 14

    Diagnostic Test .... *www.rea.com/studycenter*

Chapter 2: Self-Assessment Questions 17

Basic Math Review 21

    Vocabulary 22

    Overview of Number Systems 22

    Number System Properties 25

    Order of Operations 27

    Factors, Multiples, and Primes 28

    Fractions, Decimals, and Percentages 29

    Powers and Roots 34

    Quantity 39

    Chapter 2 Exercises 45

Chapter 3: Self-Assessment Questions 49

Algebra 51

    Expressions 51

    Solving Equations and Inequalities with One Variable 53

    Solving Linear Equations with Two Variables 56

Systems of Linear Equations 66

Ratio, Proportion, and Variations 73

Equations Involving Rational or Radical Expressions 77

Quadratic Equations 79

Solving Quadratic Equations 82

Real-World Quadratic Equations 91

Chapter 3 Exercises 91

Chapter 4: Self-Assessment Questions 95

Advanced Algebra **97**

Nonlinear Inequalities 97

Operations on Complex Numbers 98

Radicals, Powers, Exponents, and Logarithms 100

Polynomials 106

Vectors 113

Sequences and Series 118

Matrices 125

Chapter 4 Exercises 128

Chapter 5: Self-Assessment Questions 131

Functions **133**

Function Definitions 133

Vertical Line Test 134

Types of Functions 135

Inverse Functions 145

Composition of Functions 147

Symmetric Functions 150

Transformation of Functions 151

Chapter 5 Exercises 155

Chapter 6: Self-Assessment Questions 159

Geometry...**161**

    Points, Lines, and Planes 161

    Angles...163

    Lines 165

    Triangles 169

    Quadrilaterals...179

    Polygons 186

    Circles...191

    Composite Figures..201

    Constructions...202

    Three-Dimensional Figures 205

    Chapter 6 Exercises 217

Chapter 7: Self-Assessment Questions 221

Coordinate Geometry..**223**

    The Coordinate Plane 223

    Distance and Midpoint Formulas 223

    Conic Sections..228

    Real-World Application of Conic Sections 235

    Transformations in the Coordinate Plane...240

    Chapter 7 Exercises 247

Chapter 8: Self-Assessment Questions 249

Trigonometry..**251**

    Why Learn Trigonometry?..251

    Basic Trigonometric Vocabulary 252

    Trigonometric Function Values 254

    Inverse Trigonometric Functions...259

    Special Cases..260

    Transformations of Trigonometric Functions...266

Using Trig to Find the Area of a Triangle...270

Chapter 8 Exercises 274

Chapter 9: Self-Assessment Questions...277

Statistics and Probability **279**

Statistics...279

Probability 312

Chapter 9 Exercises 331

Chapter 10: Self-Assessment Questions...333

Calculus **335**

Limits...335

Derivatives and Differentiation 341

First and Second Derivatives 351

Integrals 361

Chapter 10 Exercises 377

Chapter 11: Self-Assessment Questions...379

Mathematical Reasoning **381**

Introduction 381

Arguments 381

Conditional Statements..384

Mathematical Reasoning 386

Mathematical Induction...389

Chapter 11 Exercises 390

Chapter 12: Self-Assessment Questions...393

Instruction and Assessment **395**

Cognitive Development...395

Sequencing Lessons 396

Multiple Representations in Mathematics...397

Problem-Solving Skills..398

Conceptual Misunderstanding..401

Forms of Assessment 403

Chapter 12 Exercises 406

Practice Test 1 *(also available online at www.rea.com/studycenter)* **411**

Answer Sheet 412

Practice Test 1 413

Answer Key 424

Answers and Explanations 425

Practice Test 1 Competency Coverage 434

Practice Test 2 *(also available online at www.rea.com/studycenter)* **435**

Answer Sheet 436

Practice Test 2 437

Answer Key 449

Answers and Explanations 450

Practice Test 2 Competency Coverage 459

Index **461**

About Our Author

Sandra Rush is a bestselling author acclaimed for making mathematics easier to grasp. She has taught math and physics at both the secondary and college levels. As an undergraduate majoring in math at Temple University, Ms. Rush tutored members of the men's basketball team as well as students at Philadelphia public schools, which sparked her interest in teaching. After contemplating a career in the space sciences and receiving her master's degree in ionospheric physics from UCLA, she found fulfillment in teaching in the classroom environment as well as in individual tutoring. Ms. Rush has pursued her academic career in Massachusetts, Colorado, and Arizona. She has written test-preparation guides for all ages, with her approach to books continually informed by her one-on-one tutoring and coaching.

About REA

Founded in 1959, Research & Education Association (REA) is dedicated to publishing the finest and most effective educational materials—including study guides and test preps—for students of all ages.

Today, REA's wide-ranging catalog is a leading resource for students, teachers, and other professionals. Visit *www.rea.com* to see a complete listing of all our titles.

Acknowledgments

In addition to our author, we would like to thank Pam Weston, Publisher, for setting the quality standards for production integrity and managing the publication to completion; Larry B. Kling, Vice President, Editorial, for supervising development; John Paul Cording, Vice President, Technology, for coordinating the design and development of the online REA Study Center; Alice Leonard, Senior Editor, for project management; Laura Schaffer, math educator, Colorado, for writing Chapter 12; Scott Gentile, Mathematics Instructor, Hunter College, New York and Stu Schwartz, teacher of mathematics for reviewing the manuscript; and Kathy Caratozzolo for typesetting this edition.

Getting Started

Congratulations! By taking Florida's FTCE Mathematics 6–12 (026) exam, you're on your way to a rewarding career teaching math. Our book and the online tools that come with it give you everything you need to succeed on this important exam, bringing you one step closer to being certified to teach in Florida. Our test prep package includes:

- an online diagnostic test

- a complete overview of the FTCE Mathematics 6–12 exam

- a comprehensive review of every competency assessed on the exam

- self-assessment questions and end-of-chapter practice

- two full-length practice tests, offered in the book as well as online, where you get the added benefit of timed testing conditions and diagnostic score reporting

HOW TO USE THIS BOOK + ONLINE PREP

REA's third edition of our FTCE Math prep has been completely revised and updated to adhere to the Florida State Board of Education's revisions to the competencies and skills reflected on the exam from September 2018 onward. The revised exam is framed by the Florida Standards, which set foundational expectations for all students in Florida's K–12 schools.

About the Review

The review chapters in this book are designed to help you sharpen the skills needed to pass the FTCE Math test. Each of the skills required for all ten competencies is discussed at length to optimize your understanding.

Keep in mind that your schooling has taught you most of what you need to know to answer the questions on the test. Some of the education classes you took should have provided you with the know-how to understand and make important decisions about professional situations involving young students.

Our review is designed to help you relate the information you have acquired to specific competencies. Studying your class notes and textbooks together with our review will give you an excellent foundation for passing the exam.

About the REA Study Center

The best way to personalize your study plan is to get feedback on what you know and what you don't know. At the online REA Study Center, we give you a diagnostic test as well as two full-length practice tests. Those tests are the same as in the book, but with detailed score reports that pinpoint your strengths and weaknesses.

Before you review with the book, go to the REA Study Center to take the Diagnostic Test. Your score report will identify the areas you should concentrate on. Studying the parts of the book where you're weakest will efficiently focus your study on the areas where you need the most review.

After reviewing with the book, take Practice Test 1 online at the REA Study Center to ensure that you have mastered the material and are ready for test day. Use your score reports to identify any other areas where you need extra study, and read those sections of the review chapters again.

If you are studying and don't have Internet access, you can take the printed versions of the tests. These are the same practice tests offered at the REA Study Center, but without the added benefits of timed testing conditions, automatic scoring, and diagnostic score reports. Because the FTCE is a computer-based exam, we strongly recommend taking both practice tests online to replicate exam-day conditions.

Based on your performance on Practice Test 1, reviewing any topics that require more understanding, prepare to take Practice Test 2, which is intentionally more difficult to ensure you're primed for test day. The actual FTCE test will probably have a difficulty level between those of these two practice tests.

AN OVERVIEW OF THE TEST

What is Tested on the FTCE Mathematics 6–12 Exam?

The Florida Teacher Certification Examination (FTCE) Mathematics 6–12 exam (026) is a computer-based test (CBT) designed for prospective secondary math teachers. The goal of the exam is to evaluate their subject knowledge and the classroom skills they will need to teach mathematics for grades 6 through 12.

The FTCE Mathematics 6–12 exam assesses ten competencies along with the skills aligned to each competency. Below are the competencies used as the basis for the exam, as well as the approximate percentage of the total exam that each competency covers.

These competencies represent the knowledge that teams of teachers, administrators, subject area specialists, and others have determined to be important for beginning teachers who plan to teach mathematics in grades 6–12. Each review chapter discusses a competency in depth and covers the skills that the Florida Department of Education lists for each competency.

Competency	Approximate % of Exam
1. Knowledge of algebra	13%
2. Knowledge of advanced algebra	12%
3. Knowledge of functions	8%
4. Knowledge of geometry	15%
5. Knowledge of coordinate geometry	6%
6. Knowledge of trigonometry	7%
7. Knowledge of statistics and probability	10%
8. Knowledge of calculus	9%
9. Knowledge of mathematical reasoning	5%
10. Knowledge of instruction and assessment	15%

You are expected to pull together strands from these various areas of mathematics, as several of the test questions combine knowledge of more than one of the topics listed above. The test focuses foremost on the test-takers' knowledge and the skills necessary to teach mathematics at the grades 6–12 level. This includes the ability to distinguish patterns, employ logic to arrive at viable solutions, construct simple proofs, and develop and use mathematical models to solve real-world problems. In addition, you may encounter some questions on the test that are being evaluated for future tests and will therefore not affect your score.

What is the Format of the Test?

The FTCE Mathematics 6–12 exam includes 75 scorable multiple-choice questions. Answering the multiple-choice questions is straightforward. Each question will have four choices labeled A, B, C, and D. Mark your answer choice directly below each test item on the computer screen.

You are given two and a half hours to complete the test, but be aware of the amount of time you are spending on each question so you allow yourself time to complete the whole test. Maintain a steady pace when answering questions and use your time efficiently.

When Should the FTCE Exam Be Taken?

Florida law requires that teachers demonstrate mastery of basic skills, professional knowledge, and the content areas in which they are specializing. A Professional Florida Educator's Certificate requires, among other things, that you pass all three parts of the FTCE battery: Professional Education, General Knowledge, and the Subject Area Exam. Temporary Certificates are available to qualified individuals for three years, during which time you may teach while preparing to take the certification tests, including the one corresponding to your area of specialization.

This book helps you prepare for the area of specialization called Mathematics 6–12. Whether you are a student, a graduate of a Florida state-approved teacher preparation program, or an educator who has received certification in another state, you should carefully read the requirements for teaching mathematics in grades 6–12 provided in the Educator Certification pages of the Florida Department of Education website at: *http://www.fldoe.org/*.

How Do I Register for the Test and Is There a Registration Fee?

You may register on the Internet at any time. There are no registration deadlines for the exam, but it is wise to register early for the session you desire, as test sites tend to fill up fast. You must pay a registration fee at the time you register for the exam. Information about FTCE test registration and fees is online at: *http://www.fl.nesinc.com*.

Canceling Test Appointments

You may cancel a test appointment online (*http://www.fl.nesinc.com*) for any reason up to 24 hours before the scheduled test with no additional fees or penalties. If you paid by credit or debit card, your account will be credited within three business days. To cancel an appointment less than 24 hours before the test, call customer service at 413-256-2893 or 866-613-3281 (toll-free) anytime between 8:00 a.m. and 6:00 p.m. Eastern time. Be sure to have your information as originally submitted as well as your test number, date, and time. To reschedule a canceled appointment, go online, log into your account, and follow the instructions. This must be done at least 24 hours before your canceled test time and cannot be done by telephone.

Scoring the Test

There are 75 multiple-choice questions on this test. A question answered correctly is worth one raw point, and your total raw score is the number of questions answered correctly on the full test. The test is scored based on the number of questions you answer correctly, and no points are deducted for wrong answers.

To pass the FTCE Math test, you need to earn a scaled score of at least 200, and your passing status will be reported simply as "Pass" on your score report. Because there is no exact passing percentage across all test forms, the percentage needed to pass the FTCE Math test is best expressed as the *maximum* percentage of correct answers needed to achieve a passing grade. As of fall 2017, that percentage is 67%, or 51 items. We recommend giving yourself a cushion of 75%, which equates with 57 correctly answered items; achieving that level of performance on your REA practice tests will buoy your confidence on test day.

Our online practice tests are scored automatically for you. If you do not get a passing score on the practice tests, review your online score report and study the detailed explanations for the questions you answered incorrectly. Note which types of questions you answered wrong, and re-examine the corresponding review. After further review, you may want to retake the practice tests online.

When Will I Receive My Score Report?

On the score report release date you will receive an email notifying you that your score report is available in your account. This is only if you had provided your email address at the time of registration.

Test scores are released on Tuesdays after 10 p.m. within six weeks of the test date. Your score will be sent directly to the school district, college, or university you indicated when you registered. Your score will also be automatically sent electronically to the Florida Bureau of Educator Certification.

Can I Retake the Test?

If you don't do well on the FTCE, don't panic! You can take it again, and in fact many candidates do. However, you must wait 31 days to retake the exam. You will have to reregister for the test and pay a fee. There is no limit to the number of times you may retest.

STUDYING FOR THE TEST

When Should I Start Studying?

It is never too early to start studying for the FTCE. The earlier you begin, the more time you will have to sharpen your skills. Do not procrastinate. Cramming is not an effective way to study, since it does not allow you the time needed to learn the test material. It is very important for you to choose the time and place for studying that works best for you. Be consistent and use your time wisely. Work out a study routine and stick to it.

When you take the practice tests, simulate the conditions of the actual test as closely as possible. Turn off your electronic devices, and sit down at a quiet table free from distraction.

As you complete each test, review your score reports, study the diagnostic feedback, and thoroughly review the explanations to the questions you answered incorrectly. However, do not review too much at any one time. Concentrate on one problem area at a time by reviewing the question and explanation, and by studying our review until you are confident that you have mastered the material. Give extra attention to the reviews that cover your areas of difficulty, as this will build your skills in those areas.

FTCE Study Schedule

Although our study plan is designed to be used in the six weeks before the exam, it can be condensed or expanded to suit your schedule. Be sure to set aside enough time (at least two hours each day) to study. The more time you spend studying, the more prepared and confident you will be on the day of the test.

Week	Activity
1	Take the Diagnostic test online at the REA Study Center (*www.rea.com/studycenter*). Your detailed report will identify topics where you need the most review.
2–3	Study the review chapters, making sure to answer the Self-Assessment questions at the start of each chapter. These questions will help you determine how well you know the material covered in the chapter. Answering all or some of the questions correctly will help you identify your strengths so you can focus on those topics where you need the most review. The end-of-chapter quizzes will help you gauge your mastery of the topics covered in each chapter.
4	Take Practice Test 1 either in the book or at the REA Study Center. Review your score report and identify topics where you need more review.
5	Reread all of your notes and refresh your understanding of the exam's competencies and skills. Review the information at the testing agency's website *www.fl.nesinc.com*.
6	Take Practice Test 2 either in the book or online at the REA Study Center. Review your score report and restudy the appropriate review section(s) until you are confident you understand the material.

BECOME FAMILIAR WITH THE COMPUTER AND THE CALCULATOR

This book will give you clues about what to expect on the test as far as subject matter is concerned. But even if you are familiar with computers, the ones at the test site have some unique features to navigate through the test that you should know beforehand. Your test session will begin with a tutorial introduction, which will demonstrate these features. These are duplicated here for you. However, even though these features are explained below, be sure to use the tutorial at the beginning of your session and especially try everything it suggests so you have hands-on experience before the test starts. Your time of 150 minutes doesn't begin until the first question on the test, so you won't be penalized by taking the allotted 10 minutes to do the tutorial. Go to *www.fl.nesinc.com/tutorial/standart/12.htm* to see a sample tutorial.

The tutorial is in the form of questions—your answers don't matter here; the only thing that is important is that you can navigate the questions.

- Question number and time display. On each page, the question number appears in the bottom left of the screen and the time remaining appears in the bottom right. By clicking the **Time** button on the toolbar at the top of the screen, you can turn the time display on or off. Some people find it distracting, but it is useful to track the time at certain points during the test.

- Two very important toolbar buttons are **Previous** and **Next**. As you may have guessed, **Previous** takes you to the previous question (it can be clicked several times if you want to go back two or more questions). This is helpful because it is not unusual for your brain to still be working on the last question and all of a sudden you may want to go back and reread the question or change your answer. **Next** takes you to the next question once you have finished answering the present question. The ← and → keys on the computer keyboard function the same way as **Previous** and **Next**, respectively, and may be easier for you to use.

- The **Mark** button keeps track of questions you want to return to later. Just press the **Mark** button while you are in that question, and then press the **Next** button to move on to the next question.

- The **Review** button will list all of the marked questions in a Review Item Display for your further consideration. This is especially helpful as you rework skipped questions in your first round of the test.

You will be given scrap paper, which can be very important as you navigate the questions. Use the paper to note why you marked a certain question so you won't have to take more time to remember this when you use the **Mark** and **Review** buttons. Also, if there are certain formulas or hints that you memorized and may rely on to do particular types of questions, jot them down on the scratch paper before you take the test so they are available to you.

Learn the Calculator

You are expected to know the math to get to the point of calculating the answer. The other chapters in this book will help you to know the math. This section will help you to use the calculator. The calculator provided to you is invaluable to evaluate the four basic functions as well as exponents, roots, trigonometric values, logarithms, and statistical and probability formulas.

Your own calculator is *not* permitted at the testing site for the FTCE Mathematics 6–12 exam. The only approved calculators are those supplied to you during the test. These are Texas Instruments TI-30XIIS scientific calculators. Even if you have a perfectly good handheld calculator with which you are familiar, it would be a good idea to get a TI-30XIIS, if possible, to help you prepare for the test. They are available from online sources, and **used** TI-30XIIS calculators are quite a bit less expensive than new ones.

The manual for the TI-30XIIS, in case you don't have one, is available free of charge at *www.manualsdir.com*. In addition, several online videos on how to use the calculator are available by searching "TI-30XIIS."

The following brief overview of the calculator should answer any questions you might have, but the best way to learn how to use the calculator is hands-on experience.

Important Keys

Each time you use the calculator, take a second or two to (1) Press [ON] to turn it on. The calculator may have "gone to sleep" since the last use. (2) If you want to clear what is in the window, perhaps from a previous problem, press [CLEAR]. (3) Check the lower right corner of the window, which will tell you whether the computer is in degree (DEG) or radian (RAD) mode, and change it, if necessary, by pressing the [DRG] key. The screen will give you a choice, just use the arrow keys to highlight the one you want and don't forget to press [ENTER] so it registers the correct mode. Of course, if you aren't doing a problem that involves geometry or trigonometry, this third step isn't necessary yet.

 The [=] key is the same as the [ENTER] key.

The calculator has a default mode of floating decimals, which means the answer will put the decimal place where it usually belongs, such as 8.3*2.5=20.75, where the decimal point is two places after the decimal point, whereas your input has only one place after the decimal point. This is the mode you want except for scientific notation (discussed later). To check that the calculator is set to this default mode of floating decimals, press [2nd] [FIX] (above the decimal point on the keyboard) and choose F for floating decimal. Be sure to press [ENTER] for it to register.

One of the most important keys on the keyboard is the [2nd] key. (It is even a different color from the others.) It is used to access the functions above the keys, such as percentage, which is above the open parenthesis key; for example, [2nd] [(] gives [%], and [2nd] [ON] has the function OFF, to turn the calculator off.

We concentrate in the following subsections only on the calculator functions needed for the FTCE exam, so if you read this section of the chapter, you will be more comfortable with and less intimidated by the testing center calculator.

Basic Functions

You should be able to do the basic functions on the calculator: add, subtract, multiply, and divide. For example, to find the answer to a problem such as 3 + 5 = ?, you would press the following keys: $\boxed{3}\boxed{+}\boxed{5}\boxed{\text{ENTER}}$. Note that the $\boxed{\text{ENTER}}$ key also has the function "equals." The problem will show at the left side of the top line of the screen, and the answer will appear on the right side of the second line.

- To square a number, use the $\boxed{x^2}$ key; to take the square root, use the $\boxed{\text{2nd}}\boxed{x^2}$ keys.

For 123^2, press $\boxed{1}\boxed{2}\boxed{3}\boxed{x^2}\boxed{\text{ENTER}}$ to get the answer **15129**.

For $\sqrt{15129}$, press $\boxed{\text{2nd}}\boxed{x^2}\boxed{1}\boxed{5}\boxed{1}\boxed{2}\boxed{9}\boxed{\text{ENTER}}$ to get the answer **123**.

- For a power other than squaring, the procedure is similar, using the $\boxed{\wedge}$ key; for the root use the $\boxed{\text{ENTER}}\boxed{\wedge}$ keys.

For 2^4, press $\boxed{2}\boxed{\wedge}\boxed{4}\boxed{\text{ENTER}}$ to get the answer **16**.

For $\sqrt[4]{16}$, press $\boxed{4}\boxed{\text{2nd}}\boxed{\wedge}\boxed{16}\boxed{\text{ENTER}}$ to get the answer **2**.

For a root other than a square root, you must enter the number of the root before pressing $\boxed{\text{2nd}}\boxed{\wedge}$.

Fractions

The key on the computer to use for fractions is labeled $\boxed{A\frac{b}{c}}$. The first time you press this key, the calculator is alerted that the next number is the numerator of a fraction and then when you press this key again the next number is the denominator. The sequence of keystrokes for the number $4\frac{2}{3}$ would be $\boxed{4}\boxed{A\frac{b}{c}}\boxed{2}\boxed{A\frac{b}{c}}\boxed{3}\boxed{\text{ENTER}}$. The upper left display on the calculator (input) looks like

$$4 \lrcorner 2 \lrcorner 3$$

and the lower right display (answer) looks like

$$4 \llcorner 2/3$$

where the symbol $\llcorner$ separates the whole number in a mixed fraction from the fractional part.

1. If you press $\boxed{\text{2nd}}\boxed{A\frac{b}{c}}\boxed{\text{ENTER}}$ at this point, the display will show Ans » $A\frac{b}{c}$ «» $\frac{d}{c}$ on the input (upper left) and the improper fraction 14/3, as the answer (lower right).

2. If you press [2nd] [PRB] [ENTER] at this point, it will show Ans » F » D on the input and the decimal equivalent of that fraction, or 4.666666667, as the answer.

3. If you again press [2nd] [PRB] [ENTER] at this point, it will show Ans D » F on the input, and you will be given 4 ⌣ 2/3 as the answer.

Thus, you will come full circle (mixed fraction → improper fraction → decimal → mixed fraction).

The steps shown above are the basic steps for fractions. For example, if you have a decimal and want to convert it to a fraction, just use Step 3. For example, .25 [2nd] [PRB] [ENTER] will give an answer of $\frac{1}{4}$.

Trigonometry

Before you start any trig calculations, be sure that the calculator is in the correct mode. Use the [DRG] key and the arrows to choose degrees (DEG) or radians (RAD), depending on the problem being solved. Be sure to press [ENTER] after your selection so the calculator is in the chosen mode. Note that pi (π) has a key of its own [π], which should be used whenever an answer involves the calculation of π; however, most trig problems leave the answer in terms of π (4.5π rather than 14.137).

The trig functions [SIN], [COS], and [TAN] are keys on the calculator. The calculations for the inverses [SIN⁻¹], [COS⁻¹], [TAN⁻¹] are accessed by using the [2nd] key with the appropriate function. Note that after entering the function and the value, you must press the [)] key because the functions come with their own built-in open parenthesis for the quantity, but you have to tell where to end the quantity. If you don't put in the end parenthesis, the calculator reads the quantity to be everything to the equal sign, or you may get an error message.

For example, to get a value for sin 30° + 4, you should enter [SIN][30][)][+][4][=] to get the correct answer 4.5. If you forget the end parenthesis and enter [SIN][30][+][4][=], the calculator will give you sin 34° = 0.56. (In this example, if you forget to set the mode to degrees, you might get an answer in radians, sin 34 = 3.01, which should alert you to the fact that you are in the wrong mode since sine θ is confined to $-1 \leq \sin \theta \leq +1$.)

Also, don't forget the [=] key at the end, which is the same as the [ENTER] key, to get the answer. The following examples show how to compute the sine and the arcsin (same as sin⁻¹) functions on the calculator. The same procedures work for cosine and tangent.

- To calculate $x = \dfrac{80}{\sin 50°}$, first be sure you are in DEG mode. Then enter $\boxed{80}\,\boxed{\div}\,\boxed{\text{SIN}}\,\boxed{50}\,\boxed{)}\,\boxed{=}$ to get the correct answer, 104.43. For problems like this one, do not find sin 50° and divide that value into 80. Just enter the fraction $\dfrac{80}{\sin 50°}$. If you round too early in the calculation, such as finding sin 50° and then dividing that into 80, you may encounter rounding errors. The calculator can do several functions (such as division and finding the sine here) in the same problem.

- To find arcsin $\dfrac{9}{35}$, be sure you are in RAD mode. Enter the calculation $\boxed{\text{2nd}}\,\boxed{\text{SIN}}\,\boxed{9}\,\boxed{\div}$ $\boxed{35}\,\boxed{)}\,\boxed{=}$ to get the answer, 0.260, Note that $\boxed{\text{2nd}}\,\boxed{\text{SIN}}$ gives $\sin^{-1}$ (, so you have to enter only the closing parenthesis. In this and similar problems with a fraction, don't waste time finding the decimal equivalent of $\dfrac{9}{35}$ and then using that answer when entering $\sin^{-1}$ for two reasons: (1) the calculator accepts fractions for inverse trig functions (and most everything else as long as you remember to include the fraction in parentheses); and (2) finding the decimal equivalent of a fraction and rounding it in the middle of a calculation can introduce rounding errors in the answer.

Permutations and Combinations

The $\boxed{\text{PRB}}$ key allows you to select permutations, $_nP_r$; combinations, $_nC_r$, or factorial, !. For permutations and combinations, be sure to enter the n value first, then the function by using the arrows, then the r value.

- Permutations: For $_5P_2$, press $\boxed{5}\,\boxed{\text{PRB}}$ then choose $_nP_r$ and enter $\boxed{\text{ENTER}}\,\boxed{2}\,\boxed{=}$. The answer is 20.

- Combinations: For $_8C_3$, press $\boxed{8}\,\boxed{\text{PRB}}$ then choose $_nC_r$ and enter $\boxed{\text{ENTER}}\,\boxed{3}\,\boxed{=}$. The answer is 56.

- Factorial: For $\dfrac{6!}{3!}$, press $\boxed{6}\,\boxed{\text{PRB}}$ then choose ! and enter $\boxed{\text{ENTER}}\,\boxed{\div}\,\boxed{3}\,\boxed{\text{PRB}}$, and again choose ! and enter $\boxed{\text{ENTER}}\,\boxed{=}$. The answer is 120.

The last two keystrokes are actually the same since $\boxed{\text{ENTER}}$ and $\boxed{=}$ are the same key. But you must enter both (the first one completes the ! choice).

- Factorial with division: For $\dfrac{9!}{4!5!}$ on the calculator, enter the following: $\boxed{9}\,\boxed{\text{PRB}}$, then choose ! $\boxed{\text{ENTER}}\,\boxed{\div}\,\boxed{(}\,\boxed{4}\,\boxed{\text{PRB}}$, then choose ! $\boxed{\text{ENTER}}\,\boxed{5}\,\boxed{\text{PRB}}$, and finally choose ! $\boxed{\text{ENTER}}\,\boxed{)}\,\boxed{=}$.

Make sure you choose $\boxed{\text{ENTER}}$ after every choice of ! and be sure to enclose the denominator with parentheses.

Logarithms

- $\boxed{\text{LOG}}$ gives the logarithm (base 10) of a number; for example, $\boxed{\text{LOG}}\boxed{1000}$ gives the answer 3.

- $\boxed{\text{LN}}$ gives the natural logarithm (base e) of a number; for example, $\boxed{\text{LN}}\boxed{7.5}$ gives the answer 2.0149.

- $\boxed{\text{2nd}}\boxed{\text{LOG}}$ results in 10^x, or raises 10 to the power specified, so $\boxed{\text{2nd}}\boxed{\text{LOG}}\boxed{3}$ yields the answer 1000, since $10^3 = 1000$.

- $\boxed{\text{2nd}}\boxed{\text{LN}}$ results in e^x, or raises e to the power specified, so $\boxed{\text{2nd}}\boxed{\text{LN}}\boxed{3}$ yields the answer 20.0855, since $e^3 = 20.0855$.

 Just like the trig functions, $\boxed{\text{LOG}}$ and $\boxed{\text{LN}}$ include an open parenthesis, so you should remember to enter the close parenthesis if you are finding the log or ln of a calculation such as a fraction. (The end parenthesis is not necessary if you are just taking the log or ln of a number with no calculation after it.)

TEST-TAKING TIPS

Taking an important standardized test like the FTCE might make you nervous. These test tips will help alleviate your test-taking anxieties.

Tip 1. Become comfortable with the format of the test. When you are practicing, stay calm and pace yourself. After simulating the test even once, you will boost your chances of doing well, and you will be able to sit down for the actual FTCE exam with much more confidence.

Tip 2. Familiarize yourself with the directions on the test. This will not only save time but will also help you avoid anxiety (and the mistakes anxiety causes).

Tip 3. Read all of the possible answers. Just because you think you have found the correct response, do not automatically assume that it is the best answer. Read through each choice to be sure that you are not making a mistake by jumping to conclusions.

Tip 4. Use the process of elimination. Go through each answer choice and eliminate as many as possible. If you can eliminate two answer choices, you will give yourself a better chance of getting the item correct since there will only be two choices left from which to make your guess. Do not leave an answer blank; it is better to guess than to not answer a question on the FTCE exams as you won't lose points for wrong answers.

Tip 5. Work at a steady pace and avoid focusing on any one question too long. Taking the timed practice tests online at the REA Study Center will help you learn to budget your time, and it's a great way to prepare for the computer-based test.

Tip 6. Since you are taking a computer-based exam, be sure your answer registers before you go to the next item.

Tip 7. Watch for the limiters in a multiple-choice question stem, such as *initial, best, most, not, least, except, required,* or *necessary*. Especially watch for negative words (such as *not*). Double-check yourself by asking how the response you like fits the limitations established by the stem.

Tip 8. Don't let anxiety stifle you. Take a moment to breathe. This won't merely make you feel good. The brain uses roughly three times as much oxygen as your muscles do: Give it what it needs.

BEFORE THE TEST

Check your FTCE registration information to find out what time to arrive at the testing center. Make sure you arrive early. This will allow you to collect your thoughts and relax before the test, and will also spare you the anguish that comes with being late. (If you arrive late, you might not be admitted to the test center.)

Check your admission ticket 24 hours before the test in case there is a change. If there is a change, you will have to print out a new ticket.

Before you leave for the test center, make sure that you have your admission ticket and two forms of identification, one of which must contain a recent and recognizable photograph, your name, and signature (e.g., driver's license). All documents must be originals (no copies). You will not be admitted to the test center and you will forfeit your test fees if you do not have proper identification. (More information about proper forms of ID is listed in the official registration booklet.)

Dress comfortably, so you are not distracted by being too hot or too cold while taking the test.

At the Test Center

It is important that you arrive at the test site alert and well rested. This means planning your trip to the test site beforehand so you are not rushed, including transportation or where you will park your car. Arrive at the testing center 30 minutes before your appointment. If you are late, you may be refused admission, which means you forfeit your fees. An exception to this policy may be granted for illness or injury, in which case you can request a transfer by providing, within

15 calendar days of the missed exam, a signed letter from a medical doctor, physician's assistant, or nurse practitioner on official letterhead stationery. If you have flu-like symptoms, do not report for the test and you can reschedule without additional fees or penalties. No refunds will be given, but you can transfer to another testing date and time with no penalty. If a test site closes due to weather-related or other emergency situations, you will be notified by telephone or email and you can later reschedule your test at no additional cost.

Items Prohibited at the Test Site

The following are prohibited at the test site: smoking of any products, visitors, and weapons of any kind. Do not bring cell phones, smartphones, and other electronic, listening, recording, or photographic devices including anything with an on/off switch, and eyeglasses with communication and recording devices into the testing room. Food and drink, dictionaries, textbooks, notebooks, calculators, briefcases, or packages are also not permitted. If you bring these devices into the testing room, you will be dismissed from the test, your fee will be forfeited, and your test scores will be canceled.

Procedures will be followed to maintain test security. Once you enter the test center you will be signed in by a test administrator who will collect your palm vein image digitally and take your photograph for the purpose of identity verification. Follow all of the rules and instructions given by the test supervisor. If you do not, you risk being dismissed from the test and having your scores canceled.

You will be supplied secure storage at the test site for your personal items. Only materials provided at the test site will be allowed during testing.

Be sure to check the official site in case anything changes (*fl.nesinc.com/FL-DayOfTest.asp*).

After the Test

When you finish your test, hand in your materials and you will be dismissed. Then, go home and relax — you deserve it!

Good luck on the FTCE Mathematics 6–12 (026) Exam!

Before you begin your review, take this short self-assessment to see how well you know the topics covered in this chapter. Answering all or some correctly will help you identify your strengths so you can focus on those topics where you need the most review. Even if you answer all of the questions correctly, we suggest you still review all the examples in the chapter to ensure you're in good shape to move on. Answers are on pages 19 and 20.

1. Which of the following statements is true?

   (A) All integers are rational numbers.

   (B) All whole numbers are natural numbers.

   (C) All integers are natural numbers.

   (D) All rational numbers are natural numbers.

2. What is the sum of $45 + 6{,}390 + 3 + (-479)$?

   (A) 5,958   (C) 5,960

   (B) 5,959   (D) 6,960

3. A certain brand of canned soup usually sells for $1.99 a can. If they are on sale at 3 cans for $4.50, how much would a customer save on 24 cans?

   (A) $36.00   (C) $11.76

   (B) 49 cents   (D) $1.47

4. Arrange the following fractions in order from smallest to largest: $\dfrac{17}{24}, \dfrac{27}{48}, \dfrac{7}{12}, \dfrac{2}{3}, \dfrac{5}{8}$.

   (A) $\dfrac{27}{48}, \dfrac{17}{24}, \dfrac{7}{12}, \dfrac{2}{3}, \dfrac{5}{8}$ (C) $\dfrac{27}{48}, \dfrac{2}{3}, \dfrac{5}{8}, \dfrac{7}{12}, \dfrac{17}{24}$

   (B) $\dfrac{27}{48}, \dfrac{7}{12}, \dfrac{2}{3}, \dfrac{5}{8}, \dfrac{17}{24}$ (D) $\dfrac{27}{48}, \dfrac{7}{12}, \dfrac{5}{8}, \dfrac{2}{3}, \dfrac{17}{24}$

5. Express $\sqrt{-9} + 4i$ as a single term.

   (A) $\sqrt{-11}$

   (B) $7i$

   (C) $\sqrt{-13}$

   (D) They cannot be combined into a single term.

6. Which of the following statements is true?

(A) $|-6| = -6$

(C) $\left|\dfrac{5}{4}\right| \leq \left|\dfrac{20}{16}\right|$

(B) The negative of $|-7| = 7$

(D) $|-5| < 5$

7. A helicopter flying over the Grand Canyon took off from a pad 50 feet above sea level and descended 78 feet into the canyon. At that moment what was its new position relative to sea level?

(A) 78 feet below sea level

(B) 28 feet below sea level

(C) 28 feet above sea level

(D) 128 feet below sea level

8. The quotient of two nonzero rational numbers is

(A) positive if both of the numbers are positive.

(B) positive if both of the numbers are negative.

(C) negative if one of the numbers is positive and one is negative.

(D) All of the above.

9. The part(s) of values in scientific notation is/are

(A) a number with absolute value between 1 and 10.

(B) a power of 10.

(C) Both (A) and (B).

(D) (A) or (B) but not both.

10. The sum of two prime numbers is always

(A) odd.

(C) even.

(B) prime.

(D) None of the above.

1. (A)

    All integers are rational numbers. Rational numbers can be expressed as fractions. All integers can be made into a fraction with a denominator of 1, so answer choice (A) is true. For the rest of the answer choices, you just have to remember that natural numbers are the counting numbers, $\{1, 2, 3, \ldots\}$. They do not include 0, negatives, or fractions, so answer choices (B), (C), and (D) are each false. (See Section 2.2.2)

2. (B)

    You don't have to spend the time adding them—just see how many odd numbers there are in the addition (three), so the answer must be (B) because an odd answer must have an odd number of odd numbers. (Section 2.2.4)

3. (C)

    $11.76. At the original price, 24 cans would cost $47.76. At the sale price, the cost would be $\left(\dfrac{24}{3}\right) \times \$4.50 = \$36.00$. The savings is $\$47.76 - \$36.00 = \$11.76$. Another way to calculate the sale price is to multiply the cost per can by 24: $\left(\dfrac{\$4.50}{3}\right) \times 24 = \$36.00$. (Section 2.6.1)

4. (D)

    Convert all of the fractions to their equivalents with the LCD of 48: $\dfrac{34}{48}, \dfrac{27}{48}, \dfrac{28}{48}, \dfrac{32}{48}, \dfrac{30}{48}$, respectively, which is $\dfrac{27}{48}, \dfrac{28}{48}, \dfrac{30}{48}, \dfrac{32}{48}, \dfrac{34}{48}$ in order from smallest to largest. Then just reduce them back to their original lowest terms for the answer: $\dfrac{27}{48}, \dfrac{7}{12}, \dfrac{5}{8}, \dfrac{2}{3}, \dfrac{17}{24}$. (Section 2.6.2)

5. (B)

    $\sqrt{-9} = \sqrt{9 \times (-1)} = \sqrt{9} \times \sqrt{-1} = 3i$. Then $3i + 4i = 7i$. (Section 2.2.3)

6. (C)

Answer choice (C) is true because the sign is less than or equal to, and the fractions and their absolute values are equal. The sign for answer choice (A) should be >; the answer for (B) should be –7, the negative of 7; and the sign in (D) should be =. (Section 2.2.1; see also Section 3.5.3b)

7. (B)

Consider its starting point as +50 feet and its descent as –78 feet, so the net effect is –28 feet, or 28 feet below sea level. A graph with the x-axis representing sea level helps to visualize this problem. (Section 2.2.1)

8. (D)

(Section 2.3.6)

9. (C)

A typical number in scientific notation is 2.374×10^5, which is a product of a number with absolute value between 1 and 10 and a power of 10. The number part can be negative and the power of 10 also can be a negative. (Section 2.7.1)

10. (D)

To check a statement that uses the word "always," just find one counterexample. The sum (12) of two prime numbers 5 and 7 discounts answer choices (A) and (B). All prime numbers are odd except the prime number 2, so answer choice (C) is true only for primes greater than 2. Therefore, all of the other answer choices have been disproven, and (D) is the correct answer. (Section 2.5)

Basic Math Review

The human brain is marvelous. It stores information that you don't have to figure out — it's just *there*, such as your middle name, how to spell your last name, even your cell phone number. You haven't consciously memorized a lot of information that is stored in your brain. The human brain of a math teacher is extra marvelous because it stores extra information that, again, a math teacher just *knows*. This chapter reviews the math that you should know, as they say, "like the back of your hand." In the following chapters of this book (and, of course, on the exam and in your life as a math teacher), you will be required to recall this information instantaneously when answering questions. Therefore, as you go through this chapter, pay particular attention to anything that seems "new" to you, and especially to the hints that will help your brain to remember without memorization. Most of this chapter will be familiar to you, but you may need reminders of all the information you are assumed to know as a math teacher.

During the exam, you will have two "weapons" in your arsenal: (1) the math that resides in your brain and (2) the calculator. The first of these is absolutely necessary to do well on the exam as well as in the classroom. The second of these is just a helper so you can answer questions quickly — but it depends totally on your math knowledge to function. In fact, many of the exam questions won't require the use of the calculator because you should be able to choose a correct answer with only your knowledge of math.

Therefore, use this chapter as a refresher. Don't skip it because it seems at first glance to present stuff you already know. Some topics may be new and will now become part of your math brain and will be useful for the rest of your life. In particular, be sure you know the math vocabulary presented in **bold** type here and in the rest of this book. In addition, the back of this book has a very useful tool: an index that will help you to find topics quickly and easily.

2.1 VOCABULARY

In addition to knowing what to expect on the exam and how the computer and calculator work, as outlined in the previous chapter, you must know math vocabulary. How can you answer a question if you don't know what it is asking?

As an example, suppose the question is as follows: "Jack claims that since 7 is *prime*, any number with 7 as its *units digit* must be prime. How many *counterexamples* exist between 1 and 100 to disprove Jack's statement?" The answer choices are 4, 5, 17, and 27. If even one of the italicized words in this question is unfamiliar to you, chances are you will get it wrong. It is worth mentioning here that if you misread the question, you may choose 27 as an answer because it is the first nonprime number ending in a 7. The correct answer to the question is 4, which asks how *many* counterexamples exist between 1 and 100. They are 27, 57, 77, and 87, but the question doesn't ask what any of them are, just how many there are.

2.2 OVERVIEW OF NUMBER SYSTEMS

This overview presents math vocabulary and some useful hints. Do not try to memorize these as separate items, but instead follow how each word or concept is related to others. The rules of mathematics do not change—only their contexts might.

2.2.1 The Number Line

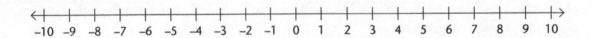

The **number line** actually goes on forever in both directions, as the arrows at the ends indicate. Between the numbers shown on this line are actually infinitely many numbers, such as fractions and decimals. Any number is smaller than all of the numbers to the right of it and larger than any number to the left of it.

You should know the following symbols: = (equal to), < (less than), > (greater than), ≤ (less than or equal to), ≥ (greater than or equal to), ≠ (not equal to).

Hint: To remember whether the symbol means less than or greater than, look at the symbol: the quantity on the smaller side of the symbol (the point) is less than the quantity on the larger side.

Thus,

All positive numbers > Any negative number

All negative numbers < Any positive number

For example, $-6{,}437{,}295 < +34$.

Notice also on the number line that as the numbers get farther from zero, the digits increase. This is obvious on the positive side of the number line, but negative larger digits are less than negative smaller digits. For example, $-983 < -900$ because -983 is farther from 0.

2.2.2 Real Numbers

All **real** numbers are included (but not necessarily labeled) on the number line. Real numbers are either **rational**, which are numbers that can be written as fractions of integers, or not rational (**irrational**), which are equivalent to nonrepeating decimals such as π or the value for $\sqrt{2}$.

All fractions (and thus all rational numbers) also can be written as repeating or terminating decimals, even though the "repeat" may be several numerals long, such as $\frac{12}{13} = .9230769230769230769230\overline{76}\ldots$, so even though a fraction may look strange to you, such as $\frac{137}{143}$, it still is a rational number because it is a fraction. In fact, it is a repeating decimal, $\frac{137}{143} = 0.958041958041\ldots$ with a six-digit repeat (see Section 2.6).

The set of rational numbers is further separated into the set of all **natural** (or **counting**) numbers, $\{1, 2, 3, \ldots\}$. If we add a 0 to the set, then we have the set of all **whole** numbers, $\{0, 1, 2, 3, \ldots\}$, and if we include negative numbers in the set, we get the set of all **integers**, $\{\ldots, -3, -2, -1, 0, 1, 2, 3, \ldots\}$.

What about numbers that aren't real? Not surprisingly, they are called imaginary.

2.2.3 Imaginary Numbers

An **imaginary** number is usually written as bi, where b stands for any number and i is an imaginary unit such that $i^2 = -1$. Since no real number can equal a negative value when it is multiplied by itself, the unit i, with a value of $\sqrt{-1}$ is part of every imaginary number. **Complex** numbers have two parts: a real part (a) plus an imaginary part (bi). All numbers in the following set can be considered to be complex numbers: $\{2, 2 - 3i, 4i\}$.

All real numbers can be thought of as complex numbers with $b = 0$.

The imaginary part of any complex number can be written in terms of i. Therefore, $\sqrt{-9} = \sqrt{9 \cdot (-1)} = 3i$. Imaginary numbers play major roles in complex conjugates and quadratic equations (see Chapter 3, Sections 3.8.2b and 3.9, respectively).

EXAMPLE 2.1

What is $\sqrt{-8}$ in terms of i?

SOLUTION 2.1

$\sqrt{-8} = \sqrt{4 \cdot 2 \cdot (-1)} = 2\sqrt{2}i$.

2.2.4 Odd and Even Numbers

An even number is an integer that is divisible by 2. An odd number is an integer that is not divisible by 2. The odd and even designations hold for positive as well as negative numbers.

If you add two even numbers or two odd numbers, the result is always an even number. However, the sum of an even and an odd number is always odd. It follows that only with an odd number of odd numbers can you get an odd sum. These facts hold for subtraction of two numbers as well.

But what if there are several numbers—will the answer be even or odd? Just count how many odd numbers there are (positive or negative). If there are an even number of them, the answer is even; if there are an odd number of them, the answer is odd. Simple as that. This just tells whether the result is even or odd, not what the result is.

For multiplication of integers, the rule is that if one of the multipliers is even, the product is always even. The only way to get an odd product is to multiply an odd number by an odd number. This is true for a whole string of factors: if any one of them is even, the product is even. Therefore, $7 \times 6 \times 5 \times 4 \times 3 \times 2 \times 1$ must be an even number. If you took out the 4 and 2 and multiplied $7 \times 6 \times 5 \times 3 \times 1$, you still get an even number, although there are more odds than evens. If you now took out the 6 from this product, getting $7 \times 5 \times 3 \times 1$, there would be no evens, and the product would be odd.

Be careful when finding two consecutive even or odd numbers. In both cases, the difference between the numbers is 2, even if they are odd numbers. For consecutive even numbers starting with –6, for example, the numbers are –6, –4, –2, 0, 2, 4, 6, 8, . . . For consecutive odd numbers starting with –7, the numbers are –7, –5, –3, –1, 1, 3, 5, 7, . . .; in other words, you still add 2 to each odd number to get the next odd number.

0 is considered to be an even number.

2.3 NUMBER SYSTEM PROPERTIES

The following properties are true for certain number systems, as indicated.

2.3.1 Closure of Rational and Irrational Numbers

A set of numbers is said to be **closed** for a specific mathematical operation on members of a set if the result is itself a member of the set for all pairs of members in the set.

For example, the set of integers is closed under addition, subtraction, and multiplication, but not division. This is the same as saying that if you add, subtract, or multiply any two integers, you get an integer, but if you divide some integers, for example, $5 \div 7$, the result is a fraction, not an integer. You need only one example not to work to say it lacks closure. This "exception to the rule" is called a **counterexample** and is enough to prove a statement false. Therefore, the set of integers is not closed under division.

The set of rational numbers is closed under addition, subtraction, multiplication, and division (with the exception of division by 0, which is undefined, and therefore neither rational nor irrational). The closure of rational numbers is straightforward. However, the set of irrational numbers is *not* closed for any of the operations. A counterexample for closure of irrational numbers, for example, involves $(2 + \sqrt{3})$ and $(2 - \sqrt{3})$, which are both irrational, but their sum is 4 and their product is 1 (see Chapter 3, Section 3.7.2a), which are both rational.

2.3.2 Transitive Property

The **transitive property** of equality for real numbers states that if the first number is equal to the second number, and the second number is equal to the third number, then the first number is equal to the third number. This is more easily understood with an example: If $4 = \dfrac{8}{2}$, and $\dfrac{8}{2} = \dfrac{16}{4}$, then $4 = \dfrac{16}{4}$.

2.3.3 Addition

An example of the **commutative property of addition** is $3 + 5 = 5 + 3$. The name *commutative* comes from the word *commute*, which means to change position. Changing the position of the numbers in addition does not affect the answer. This property extends to adding any string of numbers:

$$3 + 5 + 6 = 5 + 3 + 6 = 6 + 3 + 5$$

and so on.

Therefore, to add $6 + (-5) + 7 + 5$ you would rearrange, or "commute," the numbers to make the addition easier: $6 + (-5) + 7 + 5 = 6 + 7 + 5 + (-5) = 6 + 7 + 0 = 13$. Note that although subtraction is not commutative, as is shown in Section 2.3.4, this example involved only addition in which one of the numbers happens to be a negative number.

The **associative property of addition** groups numbers by using parentheses, or associates numbers with other numbers in different groups. So we can say, for example:

$$3 + (5 + 6) = (3 + 5) + 6.$$

The **additive identity** (also called the **identity element** for addition) is 0 for all real numbers because $a + 0 = a$ for all a. The identity property can be stated as "when a number and the additive identity (0) are added, the result is the original number."

The **inverse** of an operation on a number "undoes" the operation on that number and the result is the identity element for that operation, which we just saw is 0 for addition. Addition and subtraction are inverse operations, so, with a standing for any number, the **additive inverse** of a is $-a$, and $a + (-a) = 0$. Similarly, the inverse of subtraction is addition, so the additive inverse of $-a$ is a, and $-a + a = 0$.

2.3.4 Subtraction

Because the order in which the numbers appear in subtraction can make a difference (that is, which number is subtracted from which), the operation of subtraction isn't associative or commutative. For example, $7 - 4 \neq 4 - 7$ and $(5 + 2) - 3 \neq 3 - (5 + 2)$.

2.3.5 Multiplication

Just as for addition, multiplication can be done in any order (called the **commutative property of multiplication**). So $3 \times 8 = 8 \times 3$. And $3 \times 5 \times 2$ is the same as $3 \times 2 \times 5$ or $5 \times 3 \times 2$ or any other order of these three numbers. The products are the same.

Also similar to addition, the associative property allows us to "group" numbers in multiplication. This grouping has the name **associative property of multiplication**, and it makes finding the product easier. To multiply $25 \times 7 \times 4$, if we group the 25 and 4 first, we get $(25 \times 4) \times 7$, which is $100 \times 7 = 700$. Compare this solution to multiplying $(25 \times 7) \times 4 = 175 \times 4$, or worse yet, $25 \times (7 \times 4) = 25 \times 28$.

Another property of multiplication is that $6(3 + 4) = (6 \times 3) + (6 \times 4)$. This is called the **distributive property** of multiplication over addition because multiplication by 6 is "distributed" to each number being added in the parentheses. (Of course, this particular problem is easily done from the beginning as $6 \times 7 = 42$, but not all calculations are that simple, especially in algebra.)

Sometimes we can recognize a common factor in an addition problem for which the reverse of the distribution property presented above can be useful. Suppose Leroy bought 12 pencils for 6 cents each, and when he told his mother about his purchase, she thought it was such a bargain that she bought 88 more for the class. How much did they spend together? One way to do the problem is a straightforward sum: $6(12) + 6(88)$, which will give the answer although it involves some unnecessary multiplication. The reverse of the distribution property, however, gives $6(12) + 6(88) = 6(12 + 88) = 6(100) = 600$ cents $= \$6.00$, which is much easier.

When a number is multiplied by its **multiplicative identity**, the result is the original number. The multiplicative identity is 1 for all real numbers, and thus $a \times 1 = a$ for all a.

As was stated above for addition, the **inverse** of an operation "undoes" the operation and the result is the identity element for that operation (which is 1 for multiplication). Multiplication and division are inverse properties, so the multiplicative inverse of a is $\dfrac{1}{a}$, and $a \times \left(\dfrac{1}{a}\right) = 1$.

2.3.6 Division

Just as for subtraction, where the order of the terms makes a difference, order makes a difference for division. Obviously, the answer for $6 \div 2 = 3$ is different from the answer for $2 \div 6 = \dfrac{2}{6} = \dfrac{1}{3}$. The commutative and associative properties don't work for division. The inverse of division is multiplication, so the inverse of $\dfrac{1}{a}$ is a, and $\dfrac{1}{a}(a) = 1$.

2.4 ORDER OF OPERATIONS

Before we tackle algebra, it is important to address the **order of operations**, which usually doesn't get as much prominence in textbooks as it deserves. Unless the order of operations is followed, though, all the work done to get to the correct equation may be for naught. That is because many answers are incorrect, even after doing the difficult parts, simply because the test-taker did not follow this basic rule. Calculations must follow the order listed below, without exceptions, to come to the correct answer, whether the problem is a string of numbers connected by operations or an algebra problem or any calculation that involves multiple operations. Simplify the problem by following these steps *in this order*:

- *Parentheses:* Parentheses say "do me first." In other words, evaluate what is in the parentheses ( ) or brackets [ ] or braces { }, working from the inside out, until they are all gone.

- *Exponents:* Evaluate any part of the expression that contains exponents next.

- *Multiplication and Division:* Do any multiplication and/or division in order from left to right.

- *Addition and Subtraction:* Do any addition and/or subtraction in order from left to right.

The order of operations is often remembered by the mnemonic word **PEMDAS**, in which each letter stands for one of the above operations in order. (A **mnemonic** is a method to help memory—it doesn't even have to be a real word.) A mnemonic sentence for the same order of operations is the sentence "**P**lease **E**xcuse **M**y **D**ear **A**unt **S**ally," which uses the first letter of each word. You just need to remember what operations they stand for.

So even if the string of operations doesn't have parentheses or exponents or division or subtraction, for example, $7 \times 2 + 4 \times 2$, PEMDAS tells us to do the multiplication first, and then the addition:

$$7 \times 2 + 4 \times 2 = 14 + 8 = 22.$$

If the operations were done left to right as they appear, without regard to the order of operations, the *incorrect* answer would be $7 \times 2 + 4 \times 2 = 14 + 4 \times 2 = 18 \times 2 = 36$.

2.5 FACTORS, MULTIPLES, AND PRIMES

Counting numbers are the set of numbers that we use to learn how to count: 1, 2, 3, 4, 5, and so on. They are also called **natural numbers** or **positive integers**. Some of these numbers can be expressed as a multiplication of other counting numbers, which are called **factors** of that number. For example, the three sets of factors of 12 are 2 and 6, 3 and 4, and 1 and 12, and some of these factors can be factored as well, such as $12 = 2 \times 2 \times 3$.

Likewise, every number has an infinite number of **multiples**, which are the numbers obtained when the number is multiplied by integers. For example, the multiples of 3 are 3, 6, 9, 12, 15, 18, . . .

A **prime** number is not divisible by any positive number except 1 and itself. The first several prime numbers are 2, 3, 5, 7, 11, 13, 17, and 19—no positive numbers divide into any of these numbers. The opposite of prime is **composite**, meaning the number is divisible by three or more numbers, including 1 and itself. The numbers that divide evenly into a number are called **factors** of that number. (Note that the number 1 is considered to be neither prime nor composite, and the number 2 is the only even prime because it is divisible only by 1 and itself.)

The composite factors of a composite number can themselves be factored, and this factoring can be performed over and over until there are no more composite factors. This is the operation called **prime factorization**—when all of the factors of the original number are prime numbers. Let's look at the number 24, which has factors of 1, 2, 3, 4, 6, 8, 12, and 24. But the prime factors of 24 are only 2 and 3. That's because the other factors, 4, 6, 8, and 24, can themselves be factored and factored again until all that is left are 2's and 3's.

2.6 FRACTIONS, DECIMALS, AND PERCENTAGES

Now let's consider the numbers between the integers on the number line. These are decimals, fractions, and percentages, which are all closely related. For example, to say that 5 is half of 10 can also be represented as $.50 \times 10$, $\frac{1}{2} \times 10$, or 50% of 10, respectively. All of the properties of numbers pertain to these types of numbers as well, so this section concentrates only on new vocabulary.

Fractions consist of two parts, the **numerator** (on the top) and the **denominator** (on the bottom). All fractions can be converted into **decimals** by simply dividing the numerator by the denominator. **Rational decimals** either **terminate**, such as $\frac{1}{2} = .5$, or **repeat**, such as $\frac{1}{3} = .33\overline{3}$. The bar over the last 3 indicates that the 3 is repeated forever. Sometimes the repeating part of the decimal is more than just the last number. For example, any fraction with 7 in the denominator is a decimal with a group of several repeating numbers, such as $\frac{1}{7} = 0.142857\overline{142857}$. Sometimes it may not be easy to see the repeat pattern; here, it didn't occur until the seventh decimal place.

EXAMPLE 2.2

What are the next three digits in the decimal equivalent of $3\frac{1}{13} = 3.\overline{076923}$?

SOLUTION 2.2

076. The bar over $\overline{076923}$ means these six digits are repeated over and over. If you used your calculator before you thought about what was being asked, you would have answered 077 because the calculator rounds the answer, but the problem asks for the next three digits only (not rounded), which is another sequence of 076923, so the answer is 076.

 The denominator of a fraction can never be zero because division by zero is impossible.

Fractions are **reducible** if the numerator and denominator have factors in common that can cancel out. For example, $\frac{16}{24}$ can be reduced because 2 is a common factor (since both parts are even numbers): $\frac{16}{24} = \frac{\cancel{2} \times 8}{\cancel{2} \times 12} = \frac{8}{12}$. But the same is true for $\frac{8}{12} = \frac{\cancel{2} \times 4}{\cancel{2} \times 6} = \frac{4}{6}$, and yet again, $\frac{4}{6} = \frac{\cancel{2} \times 2}{\cancel{2} \times 3} = \frac{2}{3}$. How much easier would this have been if we recognized that 8 was a common factor in the first place: $\frac{16}{24} = \frac{\cancel{8} \times 2}{\cancel{8} \times 3} = \frac{2}{3}$.

The cancellation of common factors from the numerator and denominator of a fraction works only with multiplication. For example, $\frac{8+2}{8+3} = \frac{\cancel{8}+2}{\cancel{8}+3} = \frac{2}{3}$ is incorrect.

The word *decimal* comes from the Latin word that means "10." Our counting system as well as our monetary system are based on the number 10. Decimals indicate parts of units, with placeholders of tenths, hundredths, thousandths, and so on. The decimals appear after a decimal point (.) and get smaller as the numbers go to the right, starting at tenths, then hundredths, thousandths, etc. Note that there is no corresponding "unit" designation after the decimal point.

A **mixed number** consists of an integer part and a fractional or decimal part. For example, the mixed number $17\frac{2}{3}$ is read as "seventeen and two-thirds," and the mixed number 365.421 is usually read as "three hundred sixty-five point four, two, one." Sometimes the decimal portion is read as a whole number (421 here) with the designation of the smallest measure (thousandths), read as "three hundred sixty-five and four hundred twenty-one thousandths."

To convert decimals to fractions, just divide the numbers by the smallest decimal measure, which is thousandths here. For example, $.421 = \frac{421}{1000}$, which may not necessarily be reducible.

Fractions and decimals can be converted to **percentages**. The word *percent* comes from per hundred because "cent" refers to 100 (100 cents in a dollar, 100 years in a century, etc.). So a percentage is just a way to express a fraction with 100 as the denominator. In fact, the percent sign (%) came into use as a shorthand for 1/100, with the two 0's in the % sign being the two 0's in the number 100.

To convert a fraction to a percentage, convert it first to a decimal. To convert a decimal to a percentage, the decimal movement is to the right. For example, .23 is 23%, .675 is 67.5%, and .04 is 4%.

Hint: If you remember that .50 is 50%, you shouldn't get confused about which direction to move the decimal point.

Converting percentages to decimals just involves dropping the percent sign and moving the decimal point in the percentage two places to the left: two places because hundredths has two placeholders, to the left because the decimal equivalent is 100 times smaller than the percentage number. Confusion may arise when you have to fill in "phantom" places with zeros, such as in 3%, which equals .03, or when the percentage is itself a decimal, such as 1.2%, which is .012. But the rule doesn't change—move the decimal point two places to the left when converting percentages to decimals.

To convert a percentage to a fraction, drop the percent sign and multiply by $\frac{1}{100}$. Therefore, 20% means $20 \times \frac{1}{100} = \frac{20}{100} = \frac{1}{5}$, and 100% means $100 \times \frac{1}{100} = \frac{100}{100} = 1$, the whole thing.

Two percentage-type problems that make their way into most tests deal with percentage increase and percentage decrease. For these types of problems, construct a fraction and convert it to a percentage. The fraction has the increase (or decrease) in the numerator. The percentage (increase or decrease) depends on the original price in both cases:

An increase in price from $100 to $120 is $20, or $\frac{\text{change}}{\text{original}} = \frac{20}{100} = 20\%$ increase.

A decrease in price from $120 to $100 is also $20, but $\frac{\text{change}}{\text{original}} = \frac{20}{120} = 16.7\%$ decrease.

A decrease of 20% from the price of $120 would come out to $24, not $20.

2.6.1 Multiplying and Dividing Fractions

This section and the next one on addition and subtraction of fractions are brief primers on operations on fractions. **Multiplication of fractions** is the easiest of these operations, so let's start with that. Division of fractions is similar to multiplication.

Generally, when you multiply two or more fractions, you multiply the numerators to get the numerator of the answer, and then you multiply the denominators to get the denominator of the answer.

Multiplication of fractions is simplified by using **cancellation**, similar to reducing fractions discussed above, except in cancellation, any factor in the numerator of any fraction that is a common factor of a value that is in the denominator of any fraction can be canceled by dividing that common value into both until it cannot be reduced any further.

For example, $\dfrac{24}{35} \times \dfrac{5}{36} = \dfrac{\overset{2}{\cancel{24}}}{35} \times \dfrac{5}{\underset{3}{\cancel{36}}} = \dfrac{2}{\underset{7}{\cancel{35}}} \times \dfrac{\overset{1}{\cancel{5}}}{3} = \dfrac{2}{7} \times \dfrac{1}{3} = \dfrac{2}{21}$. In this example, 12 is a common factor of 24 in the numerator and 36 in the denominator, and 5 is a common factor of 5 in the numerator and 35 in the denominator. If, instead of 12 being recognized as a common factor the common factor used was 6, it would be obvious that the remaining numerator and denominator would be even and thus have 2 as a common factor. Cancellation might take a few easy steps—but it's better than multiplying lots of numbers out unnecessarily. A lot of cancellation can be done mentally.

The important part of cancellation is that the common factor must be a factor in the numerator *and* the denominator, and you can cancel it only once. This procedure is also called **simplifying the fraction**.

Multiplication of **mixed numbers** that have an integer part and a fraction part often is easier if you convert the mixed numbers to improper fractions. **Improper fractions** are fractions with a numerator greater than the denominator, such as $\dfrac{3}{2}$. The method for the conversion is essentially to convert the whole number part into a fraction with the same denominator as the fraction part and then add this result to the fraction. Thus, $3\dfrac{1}{4} = \dfrac{12}{4} + \dfrac{1}{4} = \dfrac{13}{4}$. The middle step of this conversion is usually incorporated into a one-step procedure by just multiplying the whole number by the denominator and adding it to the numerator to get the numerator of the improper fraction: $3\dfrac{1}{4} = \dfrac{12+1}{4} = \dfrac{13}{4}$, where the middle part is usually done mentally.

Division of fractions is the same as multiplying by the **reciprocal** (the fraction formed by flipping the numerator and denominator). This is easy to remember if you think of dividing, let's say, a dozen doughnuts between two hungry football players—it's the same as multiplying 12 by the reciprocal of 2, or $12 \div 2 = 12 \times \dfrac{1}{2} = 6$. Therefore, to divide by a fraction, just flip it over and multiply. Remember to first convert any mixed number to an improper fraction.

EXAMPLE 2.3

What is the value of $2\dfrac{6}{7} \div 1\dfrac{3}{7}$?

SOLUTION 2.3

$$2\dfrac{6}{7} \div 1\dfrac{3}{7} = \dfrac{20}{7} \div \dfrac{10}{7} = \dfrac{20}{7} \times \dfrac{7}{10} = \dfrac{20 \times 7}{7 \times 10} = \dfrac{\overset{2}{\cancel{20}} \times \overset{1}{\cancel{7}}}{\underset{1}{\cancel{7}} \times \underset{1}{\cancel{10}}} = \dfrac{2 \times 1}{1 \times 1} = \dfrac{2}{1} = 2$$

Whew! That example seems like a lot of math because it involves knowing not only to convert mixed numbers to improper fractions, and knowing to use the reciprocal of the divisor, but also factoring and canceling. However, many of the steps should have been done mentally, so actually there would be only one step written out before getting the answer. Or perhaps you recognized that the first mixed number is twice the second mixed number and eliminated the tedious math altogether.

2.6.2 Adding and Subtracting Fractions

This section is just a brief review of the basics of adding and subtracting fractions.

The most important rule about **adding or subtracting fractions** is that the denominators of the terms must be the *same*. Then you simply add or subtract the numerators and keep the denominators the same. For example, $\frac{1}{7} + \frac{4}{7} = \frac{5}{7}$ and $\frac{7}{8} - \frac{2}{8} = \frac{5}{8}$.

If the denominators are not the same, you must find the **common denominator**, which is based on two facts:

1. Any number divided by itself equals 1.

2. Multiplication by 1 doesn't change the value.

For example, $\frac{1}{7} + \frac{2}{5} = \frac{1}{7}\left(\frac{5}{5}\right) + \frac{2}{5}\left(\frac{7}{7}\right) = \frac{5}{35} + \frac{14}{35} = \frac{19}{35}$. In this calculation, the common denominator of 35 was found by multiplying the denominators together, which works every time. Then each term is multiplied by a fraction with the same numerator and denominator (so it is equal to 1 and doesn't change the value of the term) so that the denominators of both terms will equal the common denominator. Thus, the term with 7 in the denominator is multiplied by $\left(\frac{5}{5}\right)$ and the term with 5 in the denominator is multiplied by $\left(\frac{7}{7}\right)$.

The most efficient common denominator is known as the **lowest common denominator** (LCD), which is the lowest number all denominators can divide into. For example, to add $\frac{5}{27} + \frac{7}{54}$, a common denominator is, of course, 27×54, but the *lowest* common denominator is just 54. Both 27 and 54 divide evenly into 54, or said another way, both 27 and 54 are factors of 54. Then we have $\frac{5}{27} + \frac{7}{54} = \frac{5}{27}\left(\frac{2}{2}\right) + \frac{7}{54} = \frac{10}{54} + \frac{7}{54} = \frac{17}{54}$. Subtraction of fractions is done the same way:

EXAMPLE 2.4

Evaluate $\frac{5}{27} - \frac{7}{54}$ and give your answer in lowest terms.

SOLUTION 2.4

$$\frac{5}{27} - \frac{7}{54} = \frac{5}{27}\left(\frac{2}{2}\right) - \frac{7}{54} = \frac{10}{54} - \frac{7}{54} = \frac{3}{54} = \frac{1}{18}$$

Notice that the answer here is simplified at the end because 3 is a common factor of the numerator and denominator, so it can be canceled.

2.7 POWERS AND ROOTS

Powers have to do with multiplication. They are a shorthand for repeated factors. **Exponents** indicate the power, or the number of repeated factors. We can write $2 \times 2 \times 2 \times 2 \times 2 \times 2 \times 2 \times 2$ as 2^8, which we say is "2 to the eighth power." The 8 is an exponent and the 2 is called a **base**.

 2^8 means there are eight 2's multiplied together. This is NOT the same as 2 multiplied by itself eight times—if you count, there are only seven "×" signs.

Two particular powers are quite important: 2 and 3. An exponent of 2 is almost always called **squared** rather than "to the second power," and an exponent of 3 is almost always called **cubed** rather than "to the third power." Exponents are used a lot in algebra, the topic of Chapters 3 and 4. We discuss the basics of exponents here.

The powers of 0 and 1 are special. Anything to the 0 power equals 1. *Anything.* So $10^0 = 1$ and $524^0 = 1$ also. Anything to the first power is itself. That makes sense from the definition of power. So $10,524^1 = 10,524$, and $0^1 = 0$.

 0^0 is **indeterminate** because 0^0 can't equal 1 and 0 at the same time. (The value of 1 is due to $n^0 = 1$ for all values of n, and the value of 0 is due to the definition of powers of 0, or $0^n = 0$ for all n.). The word "indeterminate" is used in math when something has one value at one time and also has another value and they can't both be true at the same time.

To save time during the exam, become familiar with the following powers, but don't necessarily take the time to memorize them because you can always figure them out by multiplication or by using the calculator.

$$2^2 = 4 \quad 2^3 = 8 \quad 2^4 = 16 \quad 2^5 = 32 \quad 2^6 = 64 \quad 3^2 = 9 \quad 3^3 = 27$$
$$4^2 = 16 \quad 5^2 = 25 \quad 6^2 = 36 \quad 7^2 = 49 \quad 8^2 = 64 \quad 9^2 = 81 \quad 10^2 = 100$$

Powers have the following properties.

1. *Product of powers property:* To multiply two quantities with the same base, add their exponents: $2^2 \times 2^3 = 2^{2+3} = 2^5$.

2. *Power of a power property:* To find a power of a power, multiply the exponents: $\left(2^2\right)^3 = 2^{2 \times 3} = 2^6$.

3. *Power of a product property:* To raise a product to a power, raise each factor to that power: $(2 \times 3)^2 = 2^2 \times 3^2$.

4. *Quotient of powers property:* To divide two quantities with the same base, subtract the exponents: $\dfrac{2^5}{2^2} = 2^{5-2} = 2^3$.

5. *Power of a quotient property:* To raise a quotient to a power, raise each factor to that power: $\left(\dfrac{2^3}{3^2}\right)^4 = \dfrac{\left(2^3\right)^4}{\left(3^2\right)^4} = \dfrac{2^{12}}{3^8}$.

6. *Negative exponent property:* A base with a negative exponent is the equivalent of the reciprocal of that base with a positive exponent: $2^{-3} = \dfrac{1}{2^3}$.

(Hint:) The examples for each of the six power rules involve the numbers 2 and 3 as bases. This is a helpful way to remember the rules because the lower powers of 2 and 3 are familiar to you. If you momentarily forget what to do with the exponents in, for example, rules 1 and 2, just use 2 as a base to remind you whether to add or multiply the exponents. So use $2^2 \times 2^3 = 2^{2+3} = 2^5$, which is the same as $4 \times 8 = 32 = 2^5$, so to multiply two quantities with the same base, add their exponents (rule 1). Likewise, use $(2^2)^3 = 2^{2\times3} = 2^6$, which is the same as $4^3 = 64 = 2^6$, so to find a power of a power, multiply the exponents (rule 2) to remind you whether to add or multiply the exponents.

2.7.1 Scientific Notation and Orders of Magnitude

Scientific notation makes working with very large and very small numbers much simpler. Scientific notation uses powers of 10 to rewrite numbers that are either too big or too small to be conveniently written as decimals. A number in scientific notation consists of the product of a number with only one digit before the decimal point times a power of 10. The number part is a decimal whose absolute value is between 1 and 10 (including 1 but not including 10). **Absolute value** is indicated by two vertical bars | |. The value of the expression inside the absolute value signs is changed to a positive value. For example, $|-6| = 6$, and $|3 + 4 - 2 - 8| = |-3| = 3$.

The two steps to convert to scientific notation are:

1. To make the numerical part have only one digit before the decimal point, move the existing decimal point left or right.

2. The power of 10 part, which indicates how many places the decimal point was moved from its original position, is found by counting the number of spaces the decimal point was moved. If the decimal point is moved to the left, the power of 10 is positive; if the decimal point is moved to the right, the power of 10 is negative.

For example, we can write the distance from Earth to the sun, which is 93,000,000 miles, as $9\underset{\uparrow}{,}3000000.\underset{\uparrow} = 9.3 \times 10^7$, where the little arrows show that the original decimal point at the end of the whole number 93,000,000 is moved seven spaces to the left to go between the 9 and 3 since the absolute value of the number part must be <10, and it is 9.3.

Likewise, very small numbers such as the weight of an electron, which is .00055 atomic mass units (or amu, where 1 amu is roughly the mass of a proton or neutron), can be written as $.\underset{\uparrow}0005\underset{\uparrow}5 = 5.5 \times 10^{-4}$, where, again, the little arrows show that the original decimal point is moved, this time four spaces to the right to go after the first 5 since the number part must be <10, and it is 5.5.

> **Hint:** Another way to figure the sign of the power of 10 is to ask yourself whether the original number is more or less than the range 1 to 10. If it is more, the exponent of 10 is positive (e.g., $93,000,000 = 9.3 \times 10^7$); if it is less, the exponent of 10 is negative (e.g., $.00055 = 5.5 \times 10^{-4}$).

One advantage of having numbers in scientific notation is that they make comparisons of **orders of magnitude** easy to see. If numbers differ by one order of magnitude, one of them is about ten times the quantity of the other. If values differ by two orders of magnitude, they differ by a factor of about 100. So when comparing very large or very small numbers, comparing the powers of 10, even ignoring the number part of the scientific notation, gives a good idea of the order of magnitude, or how much the two numbers differ.

EXAMPLE 2.5

Compare the distance of a light-year (5,859,000,000,000 miles) to the distance from the Earth to the sun (93,000,000 miles), giving your answer in orders of magnitude.

SOLUTION 2.5

Compare their sizes in scientific notation to get an order of magnitude. Convert 5,859,000,000,000 miles and 93,000,000 miles, or 5.859×10^{12} to 9.3×10^7, from which we can see that the light-year is 5 orders of magnitude (or the order of $10^5 = 10,000$ times) greater than the Earth's distance from the sun, which wasn't as obvious just by looking at the two numbers not in scientific notation.

In general, an increase of n orders of magnitude is the equivalent of multiplying a quantity by 10^n. Thus, 1234 is one order of magnitude larger than 123.4, which in turn is one order of magnitude larger than 12.34.

Similarly, a decrease of n orders of magnitude is the equivalent of multiplying a quantity by 10^{-n}. Thus, .5678 is one order of magnitude smaller than 5.678, which in turn is one order of magnitude smaller than 56.78.

The numbers 942 and 672 are on the same order of magnitude (2), even though they clearly are not equal.

2.7.2 Radical Expressions

Radicals are inverses of powers. Remember that the inverse of an operation "undoes" the operation. Whereas powers are indicated by an integer exponent, radical expressions are indicated by a radical sign, $\sqrt[n]{\ }$, where n can be any positive number. Therefore, if $4^3 = 64$, then $\sqrt[3]{64} = 4$. The 4 can even have a fractional exponent, such as in $4^{\frac{1}{2}}$ or $(1 - a)^{\frac{2}{3}}$, as explained below.

The radical expression $\sqrt[n]{a}$, the nth root of a, consists of the **radical sign**, $\sqrt{\ }$; the **radicand**, a; and the **index**, n. Square roots are often indicated by a radical sign without an index.

For even or odd n, if a is positive, the value of the radical is positive: $\sqrt{16} = 4$ and $\sqrt[3]{27} = 3$. If n is odd and a is negative, the value of the radical is negative: $\sqrt[3]{-8} = -2$, since $(-2) \times (-2) \times (-2) = -8$. However, if a is negative, any root for which the index n is an even number will produce an imaginary answer involving $i = \sqrt{-1}$; for example, $\sqrt{-9} = 3i$. If $a = 0$, the value of the radical is 0.

A **fractional exponent** indicates a root, with the denominator being the root and the numerator being the power. For example, $4^{\frac{1}{2}} = \sqrt{4^1} = \sqrt{4} = 2$ and $8^{\frac{2}{3}} = \sqrt[3]{8^2} = \sqrt[3]{64} = 4$.

2.7.3 Common Radicals

To save time during the test, become familiar with the following radicals, but don't necessarily take the time to memorize them because you can always use your calculator. The square roots that equal whole numbers are square roots of **perfect squares**, defined as numbers for which the square root is an integer, such as 25, since $\sqrt{25} = 5$.

$$\sqrt{4} = 2 \quad \sqrt{9} = 3 \quad \sqrt{16} = 4 \quad \sqrt{25} = 5 \quad \sqrt{36} = 6 \quad \sqrt{49} = 7 \quad \sqrt{64} = 8 \quad \sqrt{81} = 9 \quad \sqrt{100} = 10$$

$$\sqrt[3]{8} = 2 \quad \sqrt[3]{27} = 3 \quad \sqrt[4]{16} = 2 \quad \sqrt[5]{32} = 2 \quad \sqrt[6]{64} = 2$$

The square roots of numbers between the perfect squares 1, 4, 9, 16, 25, 36, 49, 64, 81, and 100 are not integers and in fact are irrational numbers.

2.7.4 Simplifying Radical Expressions

The rules for simplifying radical expressions are based on the inverses of the rules for powers.

1. *Product of roots property:* To multiply two quantities with the same index, multiply their radicands: $\sqrt{20} \times \sqrt{5} = \sqrt{20 \times 5} = \sqrt{100} = 10$.

2. *Root of a product property:* If the radicand can be factored, the root of the radicand is equal to the product of the roots of the factors. The indices must match:
$$\sqrt{36} = \sqrt{4 \times 9} = \sqrt{4} \times \sqrt{9} = 2 \times 3 = 6, \text{ or } \sqrt{200} = \sqrt{100 \times 2} = \sqrt{100} \times \sqrt{2} = 10\sqrt{2}.$$

   Or a combination of rule 1 and rule 2 above:
$$\sqrt[4]{32} \times \sqrt[4]{8} = \sqrt[4]{256} = \sqrt[4]{16 \times 16} = \sqrt[4]{16} \times \sqrt[4]{16} = 2 \times 2 = 4.$$

3. Multiplication of radicals: Use the commutative property to rewrite the multiplication:
$$3\sqrt{20} \times 4\sqrt{5} = (3 \times 4)\left(\sqrt{20} \times \sqrt{5}\right) = 12\sqrt{100} = 12(10) = 120.$$

4. Quotient of roots property: To divide two quantities with the same index, divide their radicands: $\dfrac{\sqrt{50}}{\sqrt{2}} = \sqrt{\dfrac{50}{2}} = \sqrt{25} = 5$.

5. Root of a quotient property: If the radicand can be written as the division of two numbers, the root is equal to the quotient of the roots of the numerator and denominator: $\sqrt[3]{\dfrac{8}{27}} = \dfrac{\sqrt[3]{8}}{\sqrt[3]{27}} = \dfrac{2}{3}$.

6. Division of radicals (the indices must match): $\dfrac{8\sqrt{15}}{4\sqrt{5}} = \dfrac{8}{4} \times \dfrac{\sqrt{15}}{\sqrt{5}} = 2\sqrt{3}$.

7. Addition and subtraction of radicals: To add or subtract radicals, the radicands and indices have to be the same. $6\sqrt{2} + 3\sqrt{2} = 9\sqrt{2}$.

$3\sqrt{2} - 2\sqrt{5}$ cannot be combined because the radicands are not the same.

Many radical expressions can be simplified by combining the rules. For example, even though the expression $3\sqrt{2} + 5\sqrt{32}$ looks at first to be an addition of unlike radicals, which cannot be done (according to rule 7), it actually can be simplified by using rule 2 first and then rule 7:

$$3\sqrt{2} + 5\sqrt{32} = 3\sqrt{2} + 5\sqrt{16 \times 2}$$
$$= 3\sqrt{2} + 5\sqrt{16} \times \sqrt{2}$$
$$= 3\sqrt{2} + 5 \times 4 \times \sqrt{2}$$
$$= 3\sqrt{2} + 20\sqrt{2}$$
$$= 23\sqrt{2}$$

Here, every step is shown, but most steps are done mentally. Notice on the third and fourth lines that the multiplication is done before the addition, following the Order of Operations (PEMDAS, see Section 2.4).

Hint: The square root of a sum is not the sum of the square roots. Write the squares of 1, 2, and 3 to show that $\sqrt{1 + 4 + 9} \neq \left(\sqrt{1} + \sqrt{4} + \sqrt{9}\right)$ because $\sqrt{14} \neq 6$. (In fact, using these numbers is an easy way to remember this rule—it's equal only for multiplication, not addition.)

2.7.5 Approximating Radicals

The values of radicals of perfect squares, such as $\sqrt{4}$ and $\sqrt{49}$, are familiar, but what about others that may be irrational or rational, such as $\sqrt{7}$ or $\sqrt{110}$? Sure, we can use our calculators to get the value, but we should know enough to at least approximate the values. This approximation is based on the fact that we can establish a range of values from the radicals of perfect squares above and below the radical of interest.

We can approximate $\sqrt{7}$ by knowing it must be between $\sqrt{4}$ and $\sqrt{9}$, which, of course, means between 2 and 3. So our first approximation of $\sqrt{7}$ is that it is greater than 2 but less than 3. If we want to be even more specific, we can select a best-guess answer to the tenths place by surmising that since 7 is closer to the upper limit 9 than it is to the lower limit 4, $\sqrt{7}$ is closer to 3 than it is to 2. In fact, since 7 is $\frac{3}{5}$ (= .6) of the way closer to 9, let's use 2.6 as our first guess. We calculate $(2.6)^2$ = 6.76 to see how close we are, and then we calculate $(2.7)^2 = 7.29$. By using this same best-guess method, we try $2.65^2 = 7.02$ and $2.64^2 = 6.97$. So we can say that, to the nearest tenth, $\sqrt{7} \approx 2.6$.

2.8 QUANTITY

Any **quantity** has two parts: the numerical part and the **unit**, or dimensional, part. For example, 8 hours has the numerical part 8 and the unit *hours*. Often, the quantity has the unit as a rate, such as manufacturing 24 widgets in an 8-hour day, written as $\dfrac{24 \text{ widgets}}{8 \text{ hours}}$, which simplifies to $\dfrac{3 \text{ widgets}}{1 \text{ hour}}$, or 3 widgets per hour.

2.8.1 Dimensional Analysis

Dimensional analysis allows **unit conversion** to an equivalent unit of measure based on known equivalencies such as 1 minute = 60 seconds, 1 foot = 12 inches, 1 pound = 16 ounces, and so on. Dimensional analysis sets these equivalencies up as ratios (or fractions) that equal 1. Thus, when any dimension is multiplied by any of these equivalences, the value is unchanged, even though the numerical part and unit change. The rules on fractions are also the rules used in dimensional analysis.

A typical problem in dimensional analysis asks: "How many seconds are there in a week?" To find the answer, figure out what unit(s) you want to end up with. In this case, for example, it is seconds per week, or $\dfrac{\text{seconds}}{\text{week}}$. Write down the dimensional ratios you know that relate to the problem. There are two methods to start the problem.

For the first method, pick a starting ratio (see Section 3.5.1) that you know as a fact. In this case, you may start with the fact that 1 week has 7 days, which can be written as either $\dfrac{1 \text{ week}}{7 \text{ days}}$ or $\dfrac{7 \text{ days}}{1 \text{ week}}$. Both of these equal 1, so choose the one that allows you to cancel out any units you don't want and still be left with "week" in the denominator. Continue in this manner until you are left with only the units you do want. The unit conversion here is from weeks to seconds. The solution for this problem looks like this:

$$\frac{7 \text{ days}}{1 \text{ week}} \times \frac{24 \text{ hours}}{1 \text{ day}} \times \frac{60 \text{ minutes}}{1 \text{ hour}} \times \frac{60 \text{ seconds}}{1 \text{ minute}}$$

$$= \frac{7 \times 24 \times 60 \times 60 \text{ seconds}}{1 \text{ week}} = 604{,}800 \; \frac{\text{seconds}}{\text{week}}$$

In the second method, you start with the ratio $\dfrac{60 \text{ seconds}}{1 \text{ minute}}$, and the math goes in reverse of the first method with the same result.

The above example of finding how many seconds in a week shows **quantitative reasoning**, which is defined as using basic mathematical skills, understanding elementary mathematical concepts, and having the ability to model and solve problems with quantitative methods. In short, quantitative reasoning is equivalent to "doing math correctly." In fact, **problem solving** can be thought of similarly. All of the math that you encounter involves quantitative reasoning and problem-solving skills. Even though a person can be taught the various algorithms for doing math, the skill to solve any math problem can be acquired only by experience. Practice, practice, practice!

2.8.2 Measurement

Basically, there are two systems of units in use in the United States: (1) the **US standard** (or customary) **system** and (2) the **metric system**, also known as the International System of Units (SI). The metric system is used outside of the United States and in the scientific, medical, and international trade communities; the US standard system is the primary system used in the United States.

Since the system in common use in the United States is the US standard system, let's start with that. The US system is based on a British system that dates back to centuries before the United States even became a nation. The conversion numbers within the US system can be unwieldy and not necessarily easy to remember (for example, 1 mile = 5280 feet, 1 yard = 3 feet, 1 foot = 12 inches).

Measurement in the US system is basically of three kinds:

- **Length**, such as inch, foot, yard, and mile.

- **Weight**, such as ounce, pound, and ton.

- **Volume**, such as cubic inches, cubic feet, and cubic yards; also, teaspoons, tablespoons, cups, pints, quarts, and gallons (the latter two are used for liquid measures as well as for agricultural products, such as a quart of strawberries).

Volume (the amount of space an object takes up) is technically different from **capacity** (the amount of space that is available), although the two terms are sometimes used interchangeably.

  Fluid ounces are not units of weight, but of capacity.

The metric system, in contrast, is based on the number 10:

- length, based on the meter, m.

- weight, based on the gram, g.

- volume, based on the cubic meter (m^3, volume) and the liter (l, capacity).

The names of these basic units are then combined with prefixes that tell how many times 10 the value is:

- milli-, meaning one-thousandth.

- centi-, meaning one-hundredth.

- kilo-, meaning times one thousand.

- mega-, meaning times one million.

- giga-, meaning times one billion.

Measurements in the metric system consist of combining the prefixes with the basic units, yielding measurements such as centimeters, kilograms, or milliliters. Some common metric combinations are

- millimeter (mm) = one-thousandth of a meter, so 6 mm = .006 m

- centimeter (cm) = one-hundredth of a meter, so 6 cm = .06 m

- kilometer (km) = a thousand meters, so 6 km = 6×10^3 m

- a cubic centimeter (cc) is equivalent to a milliliter (ml), so 6 cc = 6 ml = .006 l

- milligram (mg) = one-thousandth of a gram, so 6 mg = .006 g

- kilogram = one thousand grams, so 6 kg = 6×10^3 g

It is important to have a sense of the size of these units, such as knowing that the length of a piece of writing paper should be measured in inches (or maybe feet) rather than yards or miles. Or that the weight of a baseball is measured in ounces (or fractions of a pound), but never in tons, and that your weight can be measured in kilograms (a kilogram is a little more than two pounds). Or that a bathtub has a capacity of about 200 liters (a liter is a little more than a quart).

A good way to get a sense of metric units is to become aware of the metric units for the everyday things you use or food you eat. Almost everything sold in the United States has its metric equivalent written on the package. Some examples may help in remembering metric units:

- Length

  ▶ A meter is a little more than a yard.

  ▶ A millimeter is the size of a pin head.

  ▶ A centimeter is less than four-tenths of an inch, since a common conversion is 1 inch = 2.54 centimeters.

  ▶ A kilometer is about five-eighths of a mile, or a little more than a half mile.

- Weight

  ▶ A gram is about the weight of a paper clip.

  ▶ A milligram is so tiny that you cannot see it; capsule pills often contain 1000 mg.

  ▶ A kilogram is a little more than 2 pounds, which is the weight of a pineapple, for example.

- Volume

  ▶ A liter is about a quart.

  ▶ A cubic centimeter is about the size of a sugar cube.

2.8.3 Base 2 Number System

We are familiar with the decimal number system, which is based on 10 and has ten digits, 0 through 9. Reading from right to left, the numbers before the decimal point are powers of 10, starting with 10^0. For example, $6274 = (6 \times 10^3) + (2 \times 10^2) + (7 \times 10^1) + (4 \times 10^0) = 6000 + 200 + 40 + 7$, but we just automatically say "six thousand two hundred seventy-four" without even thinking of how we got this expression.

In number systems with bases other than 10, the procedure is similar. For example, the binary (base 2) number system has only two digits, 0 and 1, so the binary number 1001, expressed as 1001_2, is equivalent to the decimal number 9 as follows: $1001_2 = (1 \times 2^3) + (0 \times 2^2) + (0 \times 2^1) + (1 \times 2^0) = 8 + 0 + 0 + 1 = 9_{10}$. However, we express 1001_2 simply as "1-0-0-1 base 2."

 Base 2 is used in digital electronics, where the two "bits," 0 and 1, represent "off" or "on," respectfully. The simplicity of this system allows for the incredibly high speed of digital computations.

When adding binary numbers (similar what we do in the decimal system), when the sum is 2, put a 0 in the total and "carry" 1 to the next column (the binary system uses only 1's and 0's). For example, 1001 + 101 would look like:

$$10^101$$

$$+1\ 01$$

$$1\ 1\ 1\ 0$$

2.8.4 Rounding

Rounding an answer comes up frequently with decimals, although any number can be rounded. As an example, when something costs $24.95, we often say it costs $25. In this case, we rounded off to the nearest unit (dollar).

The method for **rounding** is to look at the next digit after the place value that we want to round. If it is less than 5, we just drop that digit and all the ones to the right (inserting zeros if necessary). If it is 5 or more, we add "1" to the digit to be rounded. This method works whether the number is a whole number or a decimal number. You just have to know which digit is being rounded.

For example, 1,346 rounded to the nearest hundred would be 1,300 because we look at the 4—the digit to the right of the "hundreds" digit 3. Since 4 < 5, we leave the 3 alone and fill in zeros for the rest of the placeholders. It is important to look only at the number *one digit to the right* of the one to be rounded and ignore the others to the right of it. A common mistake in rounding off is to start at the rightmost digit instead of the digit just one place to the right of the one being rounded.

For example, to round 1,346 to the nearest hundred, if we started at the 6 and rounded the 4 up to 5 (since 6 > 5), we would have 1,350, and then the answer we would get for the nearest hundred would be 1,400, not the correct answer of 1,300 that we got above.

When dividing decimals, carry out the division to the next digit after the one to be rounded. For example, if we were dividing $125.32 by 7, the answer, according to the calculator, would be $17.90285714; however, because this is money we would look only at $17.902 (ignoring the other numbers) and round to the nearest cent, or $17.90. If the question had asked for the answer to the nearest dollar, we would carry the division only to $17.9 and then round up to $18.

Be careful when rounding, though. If you round early in a calculation, the answer may end up being way off. In fact, these type of errors are so common that they have a name, **rounding errors**. A well-known example of this type of error is provided by the Vancouver stock exchange index. When it began in 1982, the index was given a value of 1000.000. After 22 months of computing the index and rounding to three decimal places at each change in market value, the index stood at 524.881 despite the fact that its true value should have been 1009.811. Needless to say, that stock exchange index is no longer in existence.

2.8.5 Estimation

Estimation is a rough calculation of the value, number, or quantity. It is "good enough," "close enough," and works if you don't need the exact answer. However, it is useless if it has no valid basis or is too broad, such as, "I estimate the population of the city to be more than a thousand."

Often, estimation is based on rounding to the nearest hundred, thousand, and so on, and is expressed in terms such as "not more than" or "approximately." Estimation is helpful when taking a test because even using a calculator, mistakes can be made in entering the data. If you can estimate what the answer should be—even what is called a "ballpark" estimation (in the vicinity of the correct answer)—you can catch errors before they catch you.

Estimation is related to rounding. For example, if you want to buy 7 items that cost $2.95, you can quickly estimate the cost by rounding $2.95 to $3.00, and know that the total will be around $21.00. This is only one example of the usefulness of estimation. Now, the accuracy of an estimation is something else.

Chapter 2 Exercises

Answers are on the following pages.

1. How many different prime factors does 36 have?

    (A) 2

    (B) 3

    (C) 4

    (D) 7

2. Jason was paying $80 a month for cell service, but his last bill was $110. What is the percent increase in his monthly bill?

    (A) 25.5%

    (B) 27%

    (C) 35%

    (D) 37.5%

3. Which of the following represents the decimal system number 13 in the base-2 system?

    (A) 1010

    (B) 1001

    (C) 1111

    (D) 1101

4. The number 18.

    (A) is real.

    (B) is complex.

    (C) is rational.

    (D) is all of the above.

5. Choose the appropriate word to complete the sentence: If $n < -n$, then n must be a _____ number. (Nonnegative and nonpositive here include 0, whereas negative and positive do not.)

    (A) positive

    (B) negative

    (C) nonnegative

    (D) nonpositive

6. In building a model car, Joshua spent three and a half hours assembling the body, one and a half hours attaching the wheels and other parts, and an hour and a half painting it. How much time in all did Joshua spend on the car?

   (A) Six and a half hours

   (B) Six hours and 30 minutes

   (C) 390 minutes

   (D) All of the above

7. The quotient when a rational number is divided by a nonzero rational number is NOT:

   (A) a positive number if both numbers are positive.

   (B) a positive number if both numbers are negative.

   (C) 0 if the dividend is 0.

   (D) an irrational number.

8. Exactly how many point(s) on the number line correspond to any given real number?

   (A) 0

   (B) 1

   (C) 2 (positive and negative)

   (D) Depends on the real number.

9. The method of simplifying a fraction such as $\dfrac{16}{24}$ is also called

   (A) cancellation of common terms.

   (B) cancellation of common factors.

   (C) $\dfrac{2}{3}$.

   (D) $\dfrac{4}{6}$.

10. In the summer, a farmer sold 4,837 cows, 7,952 chickens, and 1,848 more rabbits than chickens. If these are the only animals sold, how many farm animals did he sell in the summer?

    (A) 14,637

    (B) 22,589

    (C) 9,800

    (D) 19,474

Chapter 2 Answers and Explanations

1.   (A)

To find the prime factors of a number, check which prime numbers from 2 up to that number divide evenly into it. Every time you get a composite number, break that number down to its primes also. You can do this mentally with the following method: picture a tree diagram like the one here.

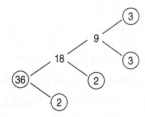

$36 = 2 \times 2 \times 3 \times 3$, so you might be inclined to say there are 4 prime factors, but the question asks for different prime factors, so there are only two: 2 and 3. If you counted all factors (prime or not), the answer would be 7, but that includes composite factors (such as 18), which themselves have prime factors of 2 and 3.

2.   (D)

Percent increase means how much the increase is over the original price. So the calculation for the percent increase is $\dfrac{change}{original} = \dfrac{110 - 80}{80} = 37.5\%$.

3.   (D)

The place values for the binary (base 2) system are 2^3, 2^2, 2^1, 2^0, or 8, 4, 2, 1. Rather than evaluating all of the answer choices in the decimal system, evaluate the largest of the choices (1111 = 15), and subtract 13 from that. Then you just have to change whatever 1's equal 2 and replace them by 0's, or change 1111 to 1101.

4.   (D)

Answer choice (D) is true for all of the above descriptions. The number 18 is real because it is an integer. It is complex because all real numbers can be thought of as complex numbers ($a + bi$) with $b = 0$. It is rational because all integers can be written as fractions with a denominator of 1.

5.   (B)

A number n is less than its opposite only if the number n is a negative number. For example, let n be -3; then the inequality is $-3 < -(-3)$, which is the same as $-3 < +3$ which is true. If n is allowed to be 0 (nonpositive, choice (D)), the less than sign must be changed to a less than or equal to ($\leq$) sign.

6.　(D)

Joshua spent $3\frac{1}{2} + 1\frac{1}{2} + 1\frac{1}{2} = 6\frac{1}{2}$ hours on the car, but remember to read all of the answer choices. They are all different ways to say $6\frac{1}{2}$ hours. (Remember 1 hour = 60 minutes.)

7.　(D)

Since a rational number is defined as a number that can be expressed as a ratio of whole numbers, all quotients of a division of two rational numbers are, by definition, rational. Even if the division is $7.234 \div 3.4$, this is the same as (by multiplying both numerator and denominator by 1000), $7234 \div 3400$, a ratio of whole numbers.

8.　(B)

The number line is composed of infinitely many points, each corresponding to only one real number.

9.　(B)

Like *factors* in the numerator and denominator can be canceled to simplify fractions. Cancellation of like *terms* is not allowed because you can get something like $\frac{16}{24} = \frac{\cancel{12} + 4}{\cancel{12} + 12} = \frac{4}{12}$, which is incorrect. The last two answer choices are wrong because the question asked for the method, not the value.

10.　(B)

Just add the number of animals, realizing that there are $(7{,}952 + 1{,}848)$ rabbits.

Before you begin your review, take this short self-assessment to see how well you know the topics covered in this chapter. Answering all or some correctly will help you identify your strengths so you can focus on those topics where you need the most review. Even if you answer all of the questions correctly, we suggest you still review all the examples in the chapter to ensure you're in good shape to move on. Answers are on the following page.

1. Which of the following is FALSE?

   (A) $(a + b)c = ac + bc$

   (B) $(a + b) \div c = \dfrac{a}{c} + \dfrac{b}{c}$

   (C) $c(a + b) = ac + bc$

   (D) $c \div (a + b) = \dfrac{c}{a} + \dfrac{c}{b}$

2. William spends one-sixth of his monthly salary on food. If he spends \$458 on food each month, what is his annual salary?

   (A) \$2,748

   (B) \$5,496

   (C) \$30,338

   (D) \$32,976

3. Find the equation of the line passing through the point (0, 4) with a slope of –5.

   (A) $y = 5x - 4$

   (B) $y = -5x + 4$

   (C) $y = -5x - 4$

   (D) $y = 5x + 4$

4. The graph of the quadratic equation $-2x^2 + 5x - 1 = 0$

   (A) opens downward.

   (B) opens upward.

   (C) has a vertex at the lowest point of the graph.

   (D) is tangent to the x-axis.

5. Two lines, $3x - y + 3 = 0$ and $6x - 2y + 6 = 0$, are graphed on the same coordinate system. What can be said about their intersection?

   (A) They are coincident so they have the same graph.

   (B) All the points of the first line are also points of the second line.

   (C) They have an unlimited number of points in common.

   (D) All of the above.

1. (D)

    Answer choice (D) is false because division is not distributive. In fact, division is not com-mutative either, so although answer choice (B) is correct (because c is in the denominator), answer choice (D) is not. Answer choices (A) and (C) correctly use the distributive property as well as the commutative property of multiplication. (Section 3.1.2)

2. (D)

    If one-sixth of William's monthly salary is $458, he makes $6 \times \$458 = \$2,748$ per *month*, but the question asks for his annual salary, which is 12 times that, or $32,976. (Section 3.5.2)

3. (B)

    The given point (0, 4) shows the y-intercept to be 4 since $x = 0$ on the y-axis. The slope is given as –5, so just use the slope intercept form of a line: $y = mx + b = -5x + 4$. (Section 3.3.1)

4. (A)

    The graph of a quadratic equation is always a parabola. Whether it opens up or down depends on the sign of the coefficient of x^2: + for upward and – for downward. It opens downward because the coefficient of x is negative. But before you answer (A), check answer choices (C) and (D) to eliminate them. Since it opens downward, the vertex is at the highest point of the graph, and since it has two unequal roots (the discriminant $\neq 0$), it crosses the x-axis at two different points. (Section 3.8.3)

5. (D)

    If the second equation is divided by 2, the result is the first equation, so the graphs are depen-dent, meaning they graph to the same line. All of the infinite number of points on one line are also on the other. (Section 3.4)

Competency 1: Algebra

3.1 EXPRESSIONS

Algebra involves **equations** or **inequalities**, which can be thought of as the sentences of algebra. Equations, in turn, involve **expressions**, which are equivalent to phrases in any language. The difference between equations and expressions is whether there is a verb. Complete sentences must have verbs. The verbs in mathematical statements are the relation symbols. These statements or expressions are not given to you algebraically in many cases; instead, you are given information and you have to "translate" that information into expressions to make up the equations to solve problems.

Examples of expressions are "a number less than 15," and "7 less than a number." Neither of these expressions contains a verb so they are not equations. They can become equations, however, with the inclusion of a relation, such as "What number *is* 8 less than 15?" and "What value *is* 7 less than 24?" As shown below, these two equations are $x = 15 - 8$ and $y = 24 - 7$.

3.1.1 Translating Words into Algebraic Expressions

The following list shows how expressions translate into symbols to write algebraic equations (or inequalities). These are the more common words and phrases; the context of the question may give hints for others.

1. The words *is* (or any variation of it), *cost*, and *is the same as* mean equals and should be substituted by an equal sign (=).

2. The words *what* or *how much* (or a similar question) mean the unknown, so replace them with a variable—it can be x, y, or whatever you choose. The equation you construct will find the value for this variable.

3. *Sum*, *plus*, *in all*, or *combined* mean addition (+).

4. *Difference*, *less than*, *how much more*, *exceeds*, or *minus* mean subtraction (−).

5. *Product*, *times*, *area*, or *of* (e.g., *half of*) mean multiplication (×).

6. *Quotient*, *distribute*, or *per* mean division (÷).

7. *Decreased by* often indicates subtraction (−).

8. *Increased by* often indicates addition (+).

9. *At least* or *not less than* indicates equal to or more than (≥).

10. *At most* or *no more than* indicates equal to or less than (≤).

11. *Equals*, *less than*, and *more than* indicate =, <, and >, respectively.

 Any letter (or even a word) can be used as the unknown in algebra. This is usually the answer to "what," "how much," or similar wording.

3.1.2 Relations of Expressions to Numbers

Algebraic expressions are any combinations of numbers and variables, such as $3x$, $3x + 4y$, $5xy$, or $6a + 5b - 4c$. The numbers in front of the variables are called **coefficients**, and each part of the expression (separated by + or − signs) is a **term**. To combine algebraic terms, they must be **like terms**, meaning that they have the same variables to the same powers. For example, $3x$ and $5x$ can be added ($3x + 5x = 8x$) or subtracted ($3x - 5x = -2x$) because they both have x to the first power (remember, we don't have to write the exponent 1). But we cannot add or subtract $3x$ and $5xy$ or $3x$ and $3x^2$ because the variables are not identical.

Expressions have the same properties as numbers do because expressions actually are describing numbers. These properties include the commutative property of addition and multiplication, the associative property of addition and multiplication, the distributive property of multiplication, the identity property, and the inverse property (see Chapter 2, Section 2.3). Likewise, the basic arithmetic operations of addition, subtraction, multiplication, and division as well as factoring and PEMDAS (see Chapter 2, Section 2.4) hold for expressions. Again, the rules don't change, only the circumstances in which they are used.

For example, we can rewrite the expression $(x + 3) + 2(y - 6)$ as $2(y - 6) + (x + 3)$ by using the commutative property of addition. Then, by using the distributive property, we can get rid of the parentheses by multiplying the first part of this sum by 2 to get $2y - 12 + x + 3$ and finally by using the associative and commutative properties of addition we get $x + 2y - 9$. So the original expression $(x + 3) + 2(y - 6)$ becomes $x + 2y - 9$.

Since expressions are actually taking the place of numbers, **rational expressions** have the same properties as rational numbers. Rational expressions are expressions that can be written in fraction form, where the numerator and denominator are themselves expressions, such as $\frac{x+3}{x-2}$. Rational expressions are closed under addition, subtraction, multiplication, and division, just as rational numbers are, which means if we add (or subtract, multiply, or divide) two rational expressions, the result is also a rational expression. The restriction that the denominator cannot equal zero also holds.

3.2 SOLVING EQUATIONS AND INEQUALITIES WITH ONE VARIABLE

When we use connecting verbs between two expressions or between an expression and a value, we end up with an equation or inequality. Usually in equations with only one variable we are answering a "what" or "how many" question, and we use a letter to represent that unknown. If we can manipulate the equation so that the unknown is alone on one side of the equal sign, usually by using the inverse property and applying it to both sides of the equation, we can end up with our answer, the value of the unknown.

If you add something to one side, you must also add it to the other side. The same is true for subtracting, multiplying, dividing, taking roots, or raising to powers. Working with any of these operations in an equation usually depends on inverses (see Chapter 2, Section 2.3).

EXAMPLE 3.1

Solve for x: $3x + 7 = 13$

SOLUTION 3.1

$3x + 7 - 7 = 13 - 7$ Use subtraction (inverse of addition) for the 7.

$3x = 6$ Simplify.

$\dfrac{3x}{3} = \dfrac{6}{3}$ Use division (inverse of multiplication) for the coefficient 3.

$x = 2$ Simplify.

Both sides of an equation are equal (thus, the word *equation*). To keep this equality, whatever is done to one side of the equation must be done to the other.

As stated above, equations are expressions with a verb, so equations are complete sentences, just written in algebraic symbols with letters for the unknown quantities. Often the question in an algebraic problem asks, "What *is* . . .?" "How many *are* . . .?" "The amount left *was* . . .?" and so forth. These all involve various forms of the word "is," which stands for the equal sign.

For example, "What is the difference between 32 and 28?" translates into the equation $x = 32 - 28$. This same question could have been posed as "Chary needs 32 ounces of liquid for a recipe, but she has only 28 ounces. How many more ounces does she need?" The equation is the same, but more thinking is involved.

Equations can take information from more than one sentence in a problem. For example, "Jordan has 7 marbles. He gives 3 to a friend. How many marbles does Jordan have left?" These three sentences end up with one equation: $7 - 3 = m$, where m is the number of marbles Jordan has left.

Constraints can be thought of as a restriction on the value of a variable. Constraints are indicated by using inequalities or interval notation. The inequality $-5 < x \leq 4$ means "all values of x greater than -5 and less than or equal to 4."

In **interval notation** $(-5, 4]$ is the same thing as $-5 < x \leq 4$. It simply shows the upper and lower bounds of the interval. An *open* constraint, indicated by a parenthesis, means up (or down) to the value indicated (the same as $<$ and $>$). A *closed* constraint, indicated by a bracket, means to also include that value (the same as $\leq$ and $\geq$). Intervals can be completely closed, completely open, or a combination, as we have here. Graphically, an open constraint is indicated by an open circle.

In reality, a line contains an infinite number of points, and for the majority of them x is not an integer. For linear equations, x can take on any real value, denoted as $(-\infty, \infty)$. Whenever interval notation to $-\infty$ or ∞ is indicated, parentheses are used because the variable cannot actually reach infinity.

Inequalities are solved the same as equalities (equations) except for one important difference: When you multiply or divide an inequality by a negative number, the inequality sign is reversed.

EXAMPLE 3.2

Solve for x: $2x > 4$.

SOLUTION 3.2

$$\frac{2x}{2} > \frac{4}{2}$$

$$x > 2$$

EXAMPLE 3.3

Solve for x: $-2x > 4$.

SOLUTION 3.3

$$\frac{-2x}{-2} < \frac{4}{-2}$$

$x < -2$. Note the reversal of the inequality sign.

EXAMPLE 3.4

Graph the solution to $-2x > 4$ (Example 3.3).

SOLUTION 3.4

EXAMPLE 3.5

Cassandra wants to spend no more than $100 ordering shirts from an online company. The company charges a $5 shipping fee for any order and $15 per shirt. What is the inequality for all possible numbers of shirts x that Cassandra can buy?

SOLUTION 3.5

$5 + 15x \leq 100$. The words "no more than $100" translate into ≤ 100.

(Hint:) Example 3.5 asks only for the inequality—don't spend time solving for x if the question doesn't ask for it.

3.3 SOLVING LINEAR EQUATIONS WITH TWO VARIABLES

The examples in the last section solved equations with one unknown to the first power, so the answer is one number. Equations with two unknowns, usually designated x and y, each to the first power, are known as **linear equations** because the unknown values that make these types of equations true form a line when graphed on an xy-coordinate system. There are two basic ways to solve linear equations:

- Algebra, by using basically the same rules as were used for equations with one variable.

- Graphing, where every point on the line is a solution to the equation.

3.3.1 Algebra

Remember, that addition and subtraction are inverses; multiplication and division are inverses; and in higher-order equations, powers and roots are inverses (see Chapter 2, Section 2.3). For the solution of a linear equation, we want one variable (usually y) alone on one side of the equal sign and the other unknown (usually x) and numbers on the other side. To do that, we use inverses. Whatever you do to one side of an equation must be done to the other side.

EXAMPLE 3.6

Consider the equation $2(2y +1) = 3x - 10$. Find the equation for y in terms of x.

SOLUTION 3.6

$4y + 2 = 3x - 10$	First, use the distributive property to get rid of the parentheses.
$4y + 2 - 2 = 3x - 10 - 2$	Next, to get y on one side of the equation, add -2, the inverse of $+2$, on both sides.
$4y = 3x - 12$	Combine the constant terms.
$\dfrac{4y}{4} = \dfrac{3x - 12}{4}$	Finally, to get y alone, divide by 4, the inverse of multiplying by 4.
$y = \dfrac{3x}{4} - \dfrac{12}{4} = \dfrac{3x}{4} - 3$	Simplify the equation.

Every step of the solution to Example 3.6 is spelled out here, but most of the steps are usually done mentally.

3.3.2 Graphing on the Coordinate Plane

One method of solving a linear equation with two variables is to graph its line. Any point on the line that represents a linear equation is a solution to the linear equation. The values of the point (x, y) don't have to be integers, but for every x there is one and only one value of y that is a solution to the linear equation.

Equations with two unknowns are usually graphed on the coordinate system called the **Cartesian coordinate system**. The **domain** axis (usually the *x*-axis) runs horizontally and the **range** axis (usually the *y*-axis) runs vertically. The axes (plural of axis) divide the coordinate system into four **quadrants**, usually labeled counterclockwise with Roman numerals from the upper right quadrant. The point where the axes meet is called the **origin**.

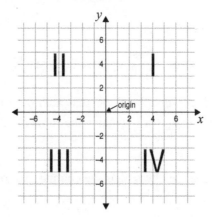

We can locate points (called **coordinates**) and the lines and curves that these points form on the Cartesian coordinate system. The coordinates are of the form (x, y) or (domain, range), and because order makes a difference in how we write coordinates, they are also called **ordered pairs**. The coordinates of the origin are usually (0, 0). Note that in Quadrant I, all x and y values are positive; in Quadrant II, x is negative and y is positive; in Quadrant III, x and y are both negative, and in Quadrant IV, x is positive and y is negative.

 Hint: You don't have to memorize these, just remember that + is up and to the right of the origin, as you are used to.

For example, the ordered pair $(x, y) = (4, 3)$ is plotted as a point 4 units to the right of the origin and 3 units up from it. Each labeled point is unique, meaning in this case there is only one point that can be labeled (4, 3). The point $(-4, 3)$ would be in Quadrant II.

3.3.2a Slope-Intercept Form

One method to graph an equation in two variables on the coordinate plane uses the slope-intercept form of the equation. Example 3.6 showed that the equation $2(2y + 1) = 3x - 10$ can also be written as $y = \dfrac{3x}{4} - 3$, which is in the form $y = mx + b$, with the slope $m = \dfrac{3}{4}$, and the y-intercept $b = -3$. Now let's discuss what each of these values means and how to graph the equation using the slope-intercept form.

The **slope** of a line tells us about the relationship between x and y, such as how quickly y changes in relation to x (or the rate of change of the relationship). Formally,

$$\text{slope} = \frac{\text{change in } y}{\text{change in } x},$$

which is sometimes stated as

$$\text{slope} = \frac{\text{rise}}{\text{run}} \text{ or "rise over run."}$$

If you pick any two points on a line to find the slope, that fraction (the slope) doesn't change value; the ratio of the change in y to the change in x remains the same all along the line.

 Remember that the slope always has the change in y, or the rise, as the numerator.

The slope of a line can be positive or negative. If the slope is positive, the line goes up to the right; if it is negative, the line goes down to the right. If the line is parallel to the x-axis, y doesn't change, so the slope of a horizontal line is 0. If the line is parallel to the y-axis, x doesn't change, but since division by 0 is undefined, so is the slope of a vertical line. The magnitude of the slope gets larger for steeper slopes.

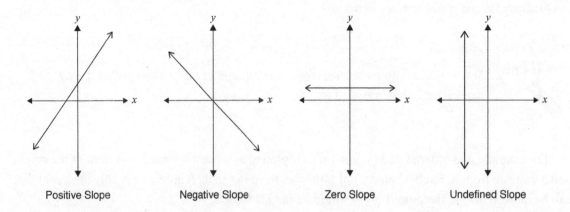

Positive Slope   Negative Slope   Zero Slope   Undefined Slope

Obviously, many lines can have the same slope (see the graphs below of $y = x + 5$ (top line), $y = x$ (middle line), and $y = x - 4$ (bottom line), which each have a slope of 1). Then what distinguishes the graph of one line from another? The answer is where it crosses the y-axis, the point called the **y-intercept**. That pins down exactly where the line is graphed.

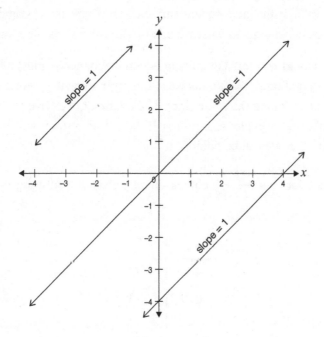

 The value of x at the y-intercept is always 0.

For $y = \dfrac{3x}{4} - 3$, the slope is $\dfrac{3}{4}$, which means for every change of 3 units for y, the change in x is 4. The slope is positive, so it goes up to the right. We also found that the y-intercept occurs at the point with coordinates $(0, -3)$. Therefore, the graph of our original equation, $2(2y + 1) = 3x - 10$, is as shown below. First, the point of the y-intercept is graphed, and then points that are 3 units in the y-direction and 4 units in the x-direction are graphed and finally the line connecting the points is drawn.

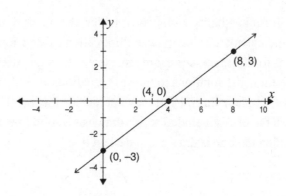

3.3.2b Table of Values

Another method for graphing a linear equation on the coordinate system is to use a **table of values**. Usually, the x value is the independent variable, which means we can plot a bunch of (x, y) points, with the y values depending on what we choose (arbitrarily) as the x value.

How many points should we plot? For a linear equation, connecting just two points will make a line, but to make sure one of those two points wasn't in error somehow, plot a third point. All three points should be **collinear** (along the same line). If they aren't, we have to go back and find and correct the error. A safety net is to plot four points. If there is an error, it will show up as a point not on the line that contains the other three points.

The table of values for $y = \dfrac{3x}{4} - 3$ comes directly from substituting each x value into the equation.

x	y
4	0
0	-3
2	$-1\dfrac{1}{2}$
-2	$-4\dfrac{1}{2}$

The corresponding points to plot on the graph are thus $(4, 0)$, $(0, -3)$, $(2, -1\frac{1}{2})$, $(-2, -4\frac{1}{2})$. The graph looks exactly like the one we found through the slope-intercept method.

3.3.3 Constraints

3.3.3a Graphing Inequalities

Remember that for a linear inequality with two variables, the rule is to treat it as an equality but reverse the inequality if the calculation involves multiplication or division by a negative number. Now, whereas the solutions to a linear equation are represented by a line with every point on the line being a solution to the equation, the solutions to linear inequalities are only the points that make the inequality true, which is a half-plane that may or may not include the line. If the inequality indicates "or equal to" ($\leq$ or $\geq$), then the line is included and is drawn as a solid line; if the inequality doesn't include the line ($<$ or $>$), then the line is drawn as a dashed line.

The graph of the solution of a linear inequality has only two steps:

1. Graph the inequality as if it had an equal sign. Then make the line dashed or solid, according to the inequality sign (dashed if the sign is < or >; solid if it is ≤ or ≥).

2. Choose a point on either side of the line. (Usually the origin (0, 0) is a good choice since the math is easier.) If that ordered pair makes the inequality true, shade that side of the line; if not, shade the other side.

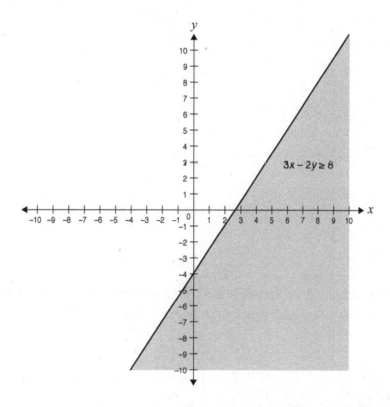

Graphically, a **constraint** on a linear equation confines the graph to just part of the coordinate plane. It may truncate (or end) the graph at a certain point or confine it to certain quadrants. Let's look at the graphs of two examples.

EXAMPLE 3.7

Plot the graph of $y = x + 2, x > 3$.

SOLUTION 3.7

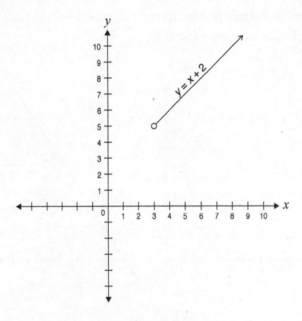

The constraint here is $x > 3$, so the graph will appear only in the first quadrant because if $x > 3$, then $y > 5$. A typical table of values for this graph is shown below.

x	y
4	6
5	7
6	8

Note that we didn't use any values outside of the constraint. The graph ends (or begins) at the point (3, 5), and we make an open circle at that point. The open circle says that the line gets as close as possible to (3, 5), but the actual point is not part of the graph. If it were, the circle at (3, 5) would be filled in. Note that we draw a circle because a point cannot be drawn that would show whether it was filled in or not, but the circle is supposed to represent just one point.

EXAMPLE 3.8

Graph $y = 2x - 1$, $(x, y) \leq 0$.

SOLUTION 3.8

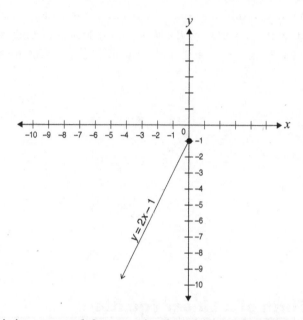

The equation is in $y = mx + b$ form, so the slope is 2 and the y-intercept is at $(0, -1)$. The constraint $(x, y) \leq 0$ means $x \leq 0$, $y \leq 0$, so the graph appears only in the third quadrant, which is the only quadrant for which x and y are both less than 0. The "or equal to" part of the constraint means that the point on the axis that forms the boundary of Quadrant III is included. Note that it has a solid dot.

3.3.3b Absolute Value

A special kind of constraint is the absolute value. **Absolute value** is used for expressing distance, and is indicated by two vertical bars | |. The value of the expression inside the absolute value signs is changed to a positive value. For example, $|-6| = 6$, and $|3 + 4 - 2 - 8| = |-3| = 3$.

When absolute value appears in an equation or an inequality, we must evaluate the expression inside the absolute value signs as a negative as well as a positive quantity, so we end up with two separate equations. This can be seen when solving the simple equation $|x| = 4$. The value of x can be either positive or negative, yielding two answers: $x = 4$ or -4. Likewise, $|3x - 2| = 7$ has two solutions, one for $(3x - 2)$ being positive, or simply $3x - 2 = 7$, and one for the case when $(3x - 2)$ is negative, which is the equation $-(3x - 2) = 7$, or $-3x + 2 = 7$, which is completely different than the positive case.

To solve any equation involving absolute value, isolate the absolute-value expression and then split the equation into two possible cases and solve each independently.

To graph an equation or inequality involving absolute value, graph the two independent equations (or inequalities) on one coordinate graph. The result is a mirror-image across a vertical line creating a V-shaped curve with the vertex of the V being the lowest or highest point. For example, for $y = |x| + 3$, graph $y = x + 3$ and $y = -x + 3$, both of which have a y-intercept of 3. The graph is

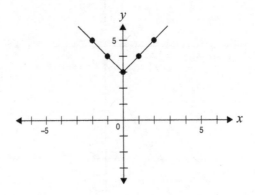

3.3.4 Standard Form of a Linear Equation

We already discussed the slope-intercept form, $y = mx + b$, where m is the slope and b is the y-intercept of the line. The **standard form** of a linear equation looks different. It is $Ax + By = C$, where A, B, and C can be any numbers, such as $-4x + 2y = 9$, where $A = -4$, $B = 2$, and $C = 9$. We recognize this as a linear equation because it involves two variables raised to the first power. Use basic algebra to change any linear equation into slope-intercept form or standard form.

To write an equation in standard form, use inverses (to switch sides) plus the properties of expressions to have the x and y terms on the left side and the number term on the right side. To write an equation in slope-intercept form, put the y term alone on one side.

EXAMPLE 3.9.

Write $2 - 4x = 2y - 7$ in standard form.

SOLUTION 3.9

Use the following steps:

1. Move the y term to the left side of the equation by using inverses to switch sides:

$$-4x - 2y + 2 = -7$$

2. Move the constant term (2) to the right side of the equation:

$$-4x - 2y = -7 - 2 = -9$$

3. Multiply through by −1 to make the coefficient of x positive (optional):

$$4x + 2y = 9$$

 Hint: Sometimes multiplying an equation by −1 is handy to eliminate working with a lot of minus signs; this is especially true when all the terms in a linear equation are negative.

EXAMPLE 3.10

Write $2 - 4x = 2y - 7$ in slope-intercept form.

SOLUTION 3.10

Use the following steps:

1. Move the y term to one side of the equation by doing whatever algebra is needed (e.g., using inverses or switching sides):

$$4x + 2y = 9$$

$$2y = -4x + 9$$

2. Now get y alone by using the multiplicative inverse, dividing both sides by 2, the coefficient of y.

$$\frac{2y}{2} = \frac{-4x + 9}{2}$$

$$y = \frac{-4x}{2} + \frac{9}{2}$$

3. Simplify the equation.

$$y = -2x + \frac{9}{2}$$

This equation has a slope of −2 and a y-intercept of $\left(0, \frac{9}{2}\right)$.

3.4 SYSTEMS OF LINEAR EQUATIONS

Systems of equations refer to a group of two or more equations that share one solution. Since they all have the same solution at the same time, they are often called **simultaneous equations**. An important rule with systems of equations is that you must have as many equations as variables. If the variables in the equations are x and y, you need two equations to find the one ordered pair that is a solution for both. If the variables in the equations are x, y, and z, you need three equations to find the one set of values for x, y, and z that is a solution to all three equations.

Any point on a line is a solution to the equation of that line. When two lines cross, they intersect in only one point, and that point is a solution to both equations. Likewise, if three lines intersect in only one point, that ordered pair is a solution for all three lines. We use this fact to solve systems of linear equations—to find the one ordered pair that works for all linear equations involved.

Every system of equations falls into one of the following categories:

- **Consistent equations**. These are equations whose graphs intersect at a common point, the solution for all of the equations. These can be solved algebraically and graphically, as well as by using matrices.

- **Inconsistent equations**. These are equations whose graphs are parallel lines. This means they never intersect, so there is no one solution that holds for all of the equations. For example, $x + 7y = 6$ and $x + 7y = 10$ are parallel lines (they have the same slope, which is $-\frac{1}{7}$, but different y-intercepts). Notice that they are inconsistent because $x + 7y$ cannot have two different values, 6 and 10, at the same time.

- **Dependent equations**. These are equations whose graphs are the same line. One equation is actually equal to the other equation multiplied (or divided) by the same quantity on both sides. Since they are the same line, they have an infinite number of matching ordered pairs, so they have an infinite number of solutions, just like any single line. For example, $x + y = 3$ and $2x + 2y = 6$ are dependent equations because the second equation is just twice the first equation.

3.4.1 Solving Systems of Equations by Substitution

Among the several ways to solve systems of equations, substitution is the most straightforward, especially for two equations and two unknowns. The method involves the following steps:

1. If possible, you can rewrite one of the equations so that one variable is written in terms of the other.

2. Substitute this value in the other equation and solve the resulting equation.

3. Substitute the value of the variable found in step 2 into one of the original equations and solve the resulting equation for the other variable.

EXAMPLE 3.11

Solve the system of equations $x - 2y = -7$ and $7x + 5y = 8$.

SOLUTION 3.11

The first equation can be rewritten as $x = 2y - 7$. If we substitute that value for x in the second equation, we get

$$7(2y - 7) + 5y = 8,$$

which is now one equation with one unknown, so it is solvable as follows.

$$14y - 49 + 5y = 8$$
$$19y = 57$$
$$y = 3$$

To get the value for x, substitute $y = 3$ into either of the original equations:

$$x - 2y = -7$$
$$x = 2y - 7$$
$$x = 2(3) - 7 = -1$$

Thus, the solution is $(-1, 3)$.

In Example 3.11, if instead we had used the second equation to find x, we would get the same result, but it would be less straightforward and involve working with fractions since both variables have coefficients.

Coin problems may seem complicated until you realize that the value for each denomination should be written in the same units, usually cents. So n nickels are worth $5n$ cents, d dimes are worth $10d$ cents, and q quarters are worth $25q$ cents. Usually the total number of coins is given as well as a value for the worth of all coins together, and thus you have two simultaneous equations, one for the number and the other for the value of all the coins.

EXAMPLE 3.12

A purse contains 3 more nickels than dimes. The value of the coins is $1.95. How many coins of each type are there?

SOLUTION 3.12

Since there are two unknowns, there should be two equations. First, for the *number* of coins, 3 more nickels than dimes means $n = d + 3$. Now, for the *value* (in cents): $5n + 10d = 195$. So these are the two simultaneous equations, and we can substitute the first equation into the second to get numbers for n nickels and d dimes.

$$5(d + 3) + 10d = 195$$

$$5d + 15 + 10d = 195$$

$$15d = 180$$

So there are $d = 12$ dimes, and thus $n = d + 3 = 15$ nickels.

 Hint: In coin problems, write the equation for the number of coins separately from the equation for the value. It is only in the value equation that we use 5 for nickels, 10 for dimes, etc.

3.4.2 Solving Systems of Equations by Addition or Subtraction

Substitution doesn't always work so easily for solving simultaneous equations, but addition or subtraction of the two equations will always work. Efficiently solving systems of equations by addition or subtraction requires practice, but it works every time and doesn't involve fractions, which is a good thing, but sometimes happens with the substitution method. This method involves the following properties:

- The algebraic associative, commutative, and distributive properties.

- Equals added to or subtracted from equals are equal. In other words, if $a = b$, and $c = d$, then $a + c = b + d$ and $a - c = b - d$, where a, b, c, and d can stand for either numbers or equations.

- If an equality is multiplied through by the same number on both sides, the result is also an equality.

The addition or subtraction method is illustrated in Example 3.13.

EXAMPLE 3.13

Use the addition or subtraction method for the same set of equations used in Example 3.11:

$$x - 2y = -7$$
$$7x + 5y = 8$$

SOLUTION 3.13

The solution involves the following steps:

1. If necessary, multiply one or more of the equations by numbers that will make the coefficients of one of the unknowns in the resulting equations numerically equal.

2. Then subtract the equations. The result is one equation with one unknown.

3. Solve that equation and, as was done in the third step of the substitution method, substitute the value into the other equation(s) to find the other unknown(s).

So we multiply the first equation by 7 and subtract the second equation from it to eliminate the x's.

$$
\begin{array}{r}
7x - 14y = -49 \\
-(7x + 5y = 8) \\
\hline
-19y = -57 \\
y = 3
\end{array}
$$

Note that the first equation could have been multiplied through by -7, and then the two equations would be added. The rest of this solution is the same as was found by substitution, and the result is the same, $(-1, 3)$.

3.4.3 Solving Systems of Equations by Graphing

Graph each equation on the same set of axes. The ordered pair of the point of intersection of the drawn lines is a simultaneous solution for the equations, which corresponds to the answer that would be found analytically. This method takes more time and is less accurate than analytical solution protocols if the solution involves numbers that are not integers, as seen in the following graph.

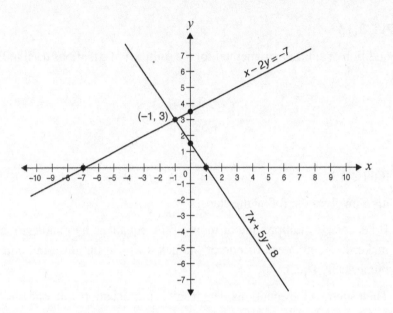

3.4.4 Solving Systems of Equations by Using Matrices

Solving systems of equations by using **matrices** is related to solution by addition or subtraction because the elements in the matrix are the values of A, B, and C in the standard form of the equations that are manipulated in the addition/subtraction method. Although the explanation seems lengthy, the solution is actually short and usually easy because it involves only 2×2 matrices. Matrices of other dimensions are discussed in Chapter 4, Section 4.7.

A **matrix** is simply a way to organize data in columns and rows. A matrix can easily be evaluated by finding its **determinant**, a special number that can be calculated from a **square matrix**, which has the same number of rows and columns. The determinant is useful for solving systems of equations.

The determinant of a matrix has the same elements as the matrix, and its value is found by multiplying the elements in the main diagonal, which starts at the upper left corner, and then subtracting the product of the elements in the second diagonal. This specific order is important because subtraction is not associative—it makes a difference which value is subtracted from which value. Always start at the upper left corner.

 Hint: The order of the diagonals used to evaluate the determinant is the same order as used for cross-multiplication in proportions (see Section 3.5.2): start with the upper left element ↘ and then the upper right element ↙ thus forming an **X**.

Since linear equations have only two variables, we will be working with two equations, and 2×2 (read as "two-by-two") matrices. We will evaluate three determinants that come from the A, B, and C values in the equations when they are written in standard form, $Ax + By = C$.

EXAMPLE 3.14

Let's use the equations that we solved by substitution, the addition and subtraction method, and graphically in Sections 3.4.1–3.4.3. They are already in standard form.

$$x - 2y = -7$$
$$7x + 5y = 8$$

SOLUTION 3.14

The first determinant, let's call it det D, is the one formed only by the coefficients of x and y in the equations. Next to det D, write a column of the C values, called a column matrix because its values form a column only one element wide. We will be working with det D, and using the column matrix only for constructing the other two determinants for x and y from our system of equations, called det D_x and det D_y.

$$\det D = \begin{vmatrix} 1 & -2 \\ 7 & 5 \end{vmatrix} \qquad \text{column matrix} = \begin{bmatrix} -7 \\ 8 \end{bmatrix}$$

The second determinant, det D_x, is formed by replacing the x coefficient values in det D with the column matrix values. Similarly, the third determinant, det D_y, is formed by replacing the y coefficient values in det D with the column matrix values.

$$\det D_x = \begin{vmatrix} -7 & -2 \\ 8 & 5 \end{vmatrix}$$

$$\det D_y = \begin{vmatrix} 1 & -7 \\ 7 & 8 \end{vmatrix}$$

Now we are ready to get values for x and y that are solutions to both equations. The way to do this is to evaluate the following determinants by using the difference of the **X** multiplications:

$$x = \frac{\det D_x}{\det D} = \frac{\begin{vmatrix} -7 & -2 \\ 8 & 5 \end{vmatrix}}{\begin{vmatrix} 1 & -2 \\ 7 & 5 \end{vmatrix}} = \frac{(-35 - (-16))}{(5 - (-14))} = \frac{-19}{19} = -1$$

$$y = \frac{\det D_y}{\det D} = \frac{\begin{vmatrix} 1 & -7 \\ 7 & 8 \end{vmatrix}}{\begin{vmatrix} 1 & -2 \\ 7 & 5 \end{vmatrix}} = \frac{(8 - (-49))}{(5 - (-14))} = \frac{57}{19} = 3$$

We get the same answer as before (–1, 3), except this time we used the "magic" of matrices and their determinants. It's not truly magic because it is based on math, but it seems like it is. The name for this method is **Cramer's Rule**, and it simply states that

$$x = \frac{\det D_x}{\det D} \text{ and } y = \frac{\det D_y}{\det D},$$

where D is the determinant of the coefficients of the left sides of the equations, D_x is det D with the x coefficients replaced by the C values in the column matrix, and D_y is det D with the y coefficients replaced by the C values in the column matrix.

 For a set of equations to be solved by using Cramer's Rule, D must not equal 0 since division by zero is not allowed. Any matrix for which $D = 0$ is not **invertible**. So the first step in solving a system of equations by Cramer's Rule is to evaluate the determinant D. If it equals 0, it is not invertible. Stop right there — it cannot be solved by using Cramer's Rule.

Matrices may be used to solve any system of equations that have as many equations as unknowns, thus forming a square matrix. The method is identical to what is shown above for a 2×2 matrix, except that evaluating a higher order matrix is a little more involved than multiplying in an "X" format.

3.4.5 Systems of Linear Inequalities

The graphical area for solutions to systems of inequalities is restricted to the overlap, or intersection, of the shaded areas of each inequality. To graph the solution of a system of linear equalities, graph each inequality, including the shading, on the same coordinate system. Remember to make the line dashed or solid, according to its inequality sign; shade above (for > or ≥) or below (for < or ≤) the line. The result for the simultaneous system of the equations is the area of overlap. So for $3x - 2y \geq 8$ and $2x + y > 3$, the answer would be the darker shaded area on the right side of the graph below.

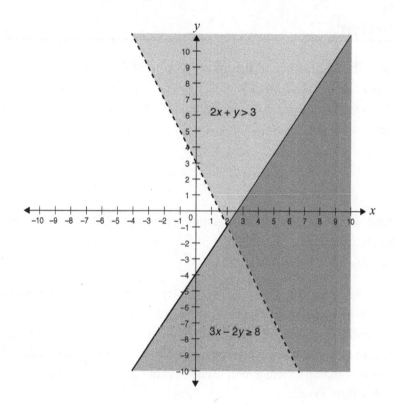

3.5 RATIO, PROPORTION, AND VARIATIONS

Relationships between two or more quantities result in equations such as those already discussed in this chapter. Examples of these relationships include ratio, proportion, and several types of variation.

3.5.1 Ratio

A **ratio** is a way of comparing two quantities. Ratios can be expressed as fractions, decimals, or by two numbers separated by a colon. For example, let's say the ratio of the length to the width of a bathmat is 3 feet to 2 feet. This can be written as $\frac{3}{2}$, 1.5, 3:2 (read as "3 to 2"), or even that the length is 1.5 times the width.

As an example, Bill's age is triple his son Will's age. The ratio of Bill's age to Will's age is 3 to 1, or $\frac{3}{1}$. The ratio of Will's age to Bill's age is $\frac{1}{3}$. It is very important to state the ratio in the correct order. It would make no sense in this case to say that the ratio of the son's age to the father's age is 3:1.

3.5.2 Proportion

A **proportion** is the equivalence of two ratios. For example, let's say that we know the ratio of Bill's age to Will's age is 1:3 and that Will is 10 years old, and we want to know Bill's age. A proportion would answer this question by putting the ratio we know equal to the ratio that has the unknown. It is important to put "like" quantities in like places in a proportion.

$$\frac{3}{1} = \frac{\text{Bill's age}}{10} = \frac{x}{10}$$

On the left-hand side of this proportion, the numbers represent Bill's age on top and Will's age on the bottom. So the right-hand side should be the same: Bill's age on top and Will's age on the bottom. We'll call Bill's age x because it is unknown.

We want to get the unknown value that we are trying to find (x) alone on one side of the equation. This is done by **cross-multiplication**, which ends up with a short equation in which the unknown has a multiplier. Just like it sounds, cross-multiplication means multiplying in the shape of an **X**, where the two multiplications equal each other. Then we divide both sides of that equation by the multiplier of the unknown (remember, division is the inverse of multiplication), and we get the unknown quantity right away.

$$\frac{3}{1} \diagup \frac{x}{10}$$

$$3 \times 10 = x \times 1$$
$$x = 30.$$

Often, however, the numbers aren't as simple as this.

3.5.2a Means and Extremes of a Proportion

In any proportion of the form

$$\frac{a}{b} = \frac{c}{d}$$

b and c are called the **means** of the proportion, and a and d are called the **extremes** of the proportion. A basic property of a proportion is that the product of the means is equal to the product of the extremes, or $a \times d = b \times c$, as shown above with cross-multiplication.

To check whether two fractions are equal (or proportional), set them up as a proportion, multiply the means and multiply the extremes. If these two results don't match, the fractions are not equal.

In a true proportion, the product of the means equals the product of the extremes.

3.5.2b Variation

Another type of relationship between two variables that involves proportions is called **variation**. Three types of variation are of interest here: direct, inverse, and joint.

With **direct variation**, the product is a constant; when one variable increases, the other increases in proportion so that the ratio between the variables is unchanged. The general equation for direct variation between two variables is

$$y = kx,$$

where x and y are the variables and k is the **constant of variation**, also called the **constant of proportionality**. A classic example of direct variation is speed and distance. The formula for distance is $d = rt$, where r is speed, and t is time. In the same amount of time (so t takes the place of the constant k), we intuitively know that if you go faster, you go farther, so as r increases, so does d.

EXAMPLE 3.15

The growth of a particular strain of bacteria varies directly with the temperature. When the temperature is 100 degrees, there are 20 million bacteria. How many millions of bacteria are there are when the temperature is 150 degrees?

SOLUTION 3.15

Using direct variation, we first have to find the constant of variation, k, in the relationship $B = kT$, which we can find from the given information that at a temperature (T) of 100 degrees, there are 20 million bacteria (B). Since the question asks for *how many millions* of bacteria there would be, we can use 20 (millions of bacteria) in our calculation. Therefore,

$$k = \frac{B}{T} = \frac{20}{100} = 0.2.$$

Then the final equation to find how many millions of bacteria there are when the temperature is 150 degrees is $B = kT = (.2)(150) = 30$. The answer is 30 rather than 30 million because the question asks *how many millions* of bacteria there would be.

Example 3.15 brings up several facts:

1. In many cases, you first have to find the constant of variation before you find the answer.

2. Here we used T and B instead of x and y. We can use any letters as the variables.

3. Instead of using 20,000,000, we just used 20, but we must remember that the answer is in millions of bacteria. It just makes the calculation easier.

Note that Example 3.15 could also have been set up as a proportion problem:

$$\frac{100}{20 \text{ million}} = \frac{150}{B}$$
$$100B = 3000 \text{ million}$$
$$B = 30 \text{ million}.$$

With **inverse variation**, when one variable increases, the other decreases in proportion so that the product of the variables is unchanged. The general equation for inverse variation between two variables is

$$y = \frac{k}{x}, \text{ or } xy = k,$$

where k, again, is the constant of variation. So the bigger x becomes, the smaller y becomes, and vice versa. An example of an inverse relation is the amount of gas used to heat a home versus the temperature outside. As the temperature falls, the amount of gas used increases.

EXAMPLE 3.16

A paving company wants to estimate how long it will take to do a job. On a similar job, 10 workers took 3 days. If the company has only 5 workers available for the new job, how long will it take them to complete it?

SOLUTION 3.16

Using inverse variation, we first have to find the constant of variation, k, in the relationship $T = \frac{k}{W}$. We can find k from the given information that it took 10 workers (W) 3 days (T), so $T = \frac{k}{W} \rightarrow k = WT = 10(3) = 30$. Then for the new job,

$$T = \frac{k}{W} = \frac{30}{5} = 6 \text{ days.}$$

Joint variation problems are similar to direct variation problems but they involve three variables and a constant of variation. The general form of joint variation is $a = kbc$, where variable a varies jointly with variables b and c. The constant of variation is k. The steps to solve a problem involving joint variation are similar to the steps for direct variation:

- Write the equation in the form $a = kbc$. Choose letters for the variables that make sense for the problem. Read the problem carefully to determine whether there are any other changes in the joint variation equation, such as squares, cubes, or square roots.

- Use the information given in the problem to find the value of k.

- Rewrite the equation, substituting the value of k and the new information given in the problem.

- Include units in your answer.

3.6 EQUATIONS INVOLVING RATIONAL OR RADICAL EXPRESSIONS

3.6.1 Rational Equations

For equations that contain at least one fractional expression, known as rational equations, no matter whether the unknown quantity is in the denominator or not, we should "clear the equation of fractions." Thus, the original rational equation is transformed into an equivalent equation without fractions. This procedure is the same as that used for fractions in general, and usually involves multiplying every term in the equation by a common multiple of the denominators and simplifying the result. It is best to use the least common multiple (LCM), which is the *smallest* expression (it can be just an integer) that is a multiple of all of the denominators.

EXAMPLE 3.17

Solve for x: $\dfrac{x}{3} - \dfrac{x+4}{6} = 3$.

SOLUTION 3.17

The LCM for this equation is 6, since it is a multiple of both 3 and 6. Multiply *all* of the terms by 6 and simplify the resulting equation. (Many of these steps can be done mentally. Don't forget to also multiply constants by the LCM.)

$$6\left(\frac{x}{3}\right) - 6\left(\frac{x+4}{6}\right) = 6(3)$$
$$2x - (x+4) = 18$$
$$2x - x - 4 = 18$$
$$x - 4 = 18$$
$$x = 22$$

Sometimes the unknown is in a denominator, but the rules don't change. Many times, there is no least common multiple for the denominators, so the common denominator is just the product of the denominators. In fact, Example 3.17 would yield the same result if $3(6) = 18$ were used for the common denominator.

EXAMPLE 3.18

Solve for z: $5 + \dfrac{16}{z - 4} = -\dfrac{1}{3}$.

SOLUTION 3.18

Here, the common denominator is the product of the two denominators, or $3(z - 4)$. Don't multiply this out yet because the factors make the fraction reducing easier. Multiply every term by $3(z - 4)$ to get:

$$(3)(z - 4)(5) + 3(z - 4)\frac{16}{(z - 4)} = 3(z - 4)\left(-\frac{1}{3}\right).$$

And now simplify the equation by canceling like factors:

$$(3)(z - 4)(5) + 3(z - 4)\frac{16}{(z - 4)} = 3(z - 4)\frac{-1}{3} = 15(z - 4) + 3(16) = -(z - 4),$$

which yields an equation with no fractions when simplified:

$$15z - 60 + 48 = -z + 4$$
$$16z = 16$$
$$z = 1.$$

3.6.2 Radical Equations

Radical equations are equations containing at least one radical expression, which is any expression containing a radical symbol $\left(\sqrt{}\right)$ that contains a variable. To solve a radical equation, isolate the radical on one side of the equation with all other terms on the other side and then raise both sides of the equation to the power of the radical. Often this is just a square root, but it can be a cube root, or any root.

EXAMPLE 3.19

Solve $6 + \sqrt{x - 2} = 10$ for x.

SOLUTION 3.19

Isolate the radical on one side of the equation to get $\sqrt{x-2} = 10 - 6$. Square both sides: $x - 2 = 4^2$. Solve for x: $x = 18$.

Check the answer: $6 + \sqrt{18 - 2} = 6 + \sqrt{16} = 6 + 4 = 10$.

When you square terms in a radical equation you sometimes get a solution to the squared equation that is not a solution to the original equation; these are called **extraneous solutions**. Extraneous solutions usually occur when squaring both sides of the original equation produces a squared term, such as x^2. Nevertheless, it is important to always check your answer in the original equation.

3.6.3 Combination Rational and Radical Equations

Before even trying to solve an equation that has a radical in the denominator, first remove the radical from the denominator (this is called **rationalizing the fraction**). To do this, multiply the entire original fraction by a fraction whose numerator and denominator are the conjugate of the original denominator. A **conjugate** in math is formed by changing the sign between two terms, and it refers only to **binomials** (expressions with two terms). For example, the conjugate of $x + y$ is $x - y$. See Section 3.7.2b for the method of multiplying complex conjugates.

Generally in algebra, radicals should not appear in the denominator of a fraction.

3.7 QUADRATIC EQUATIONS

3.7.1 Basics of the Quadratic Equation

A **quadratic equation** is an equation of the **second degree**, meaning the unknown is squared and there is no higher power of the unknown. The **general form of a quadratic** is $ax^2 + bx + c = 0$ where a and b are numerical coefficients, c is a constant, and x is the unknown variable. Examples of quadratic equations are $x^2 + x - 6 = 0$, $x^2 - 9 = 0$, and $x^2 - 3x = 0$.

Binomials are the sum or difference of two terms, such as $x + 3$ or $3y - 4$. When two binomials with the same unknowns to the first power are multiplied together, the result is a quadratic expression. This multiplication has a lot of uses and implications.

3.7.2 Multiplying Binomials

3.7.2a F-O-I-L Method

Let's use the two binomials $(x + 6)(2x + 3)$ to illustrate the multiplication of binomials. One way to do this is by longhand using the distributive property—multiply $(2x + 3)$ by x and then multiply $(2x + 3)$ by $+6$ and combine like terms. Thus,

$$(x + 6)(2x + 3) = x(2x + 3) + 6(2x + 3) = 2x^2 + 3x + 12x + 18 = 2x^2 + 15x + 18,$$

which is a **trinomial** (three terms).

A similar method, called the **F-O-I-L method**, is easier to remember. F-O-I-L is a **mnemonic**, with the letters in F-O-I-L standing for:

First-Outside-Inside-Last

This means that when we multiply two binomials, such as $(x + 6)(2x + 3)$, we multiply the **F**irst terms, then the **O**utside terms, then the **I**nside terms, and finally the **L**ast terms. The following example of F-O-I-L uses our specific binomials because it is easier to understand that way, but F-O-I-L works for two binomials with any coefficients and any constants but usually with the same unknowns. The explanation below seems long, but it is the same method as the distributive one above, only easier to remember, and it should eliminate confusion about what terms to multiply together.

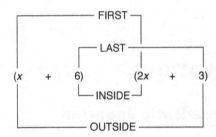

The first terms (F) are x and $2x$, the outside terms (O) are x and 3, the inside terms (I) are 6 and $2x$, and the last terms (L) are 6 and 3. When we multiply each of them, in F-O-I-L order, we end up with the product of the two binomials. Here, multiplication of the first terms yields $2x^2$, multiplication of the outside terms yields $3x$, multiplication of the inside terms yields $12x$, and multiplication of the last terms yields 18. Then when we add it all up, we get the quadratic $2x^2 + 15x + 18$.

EXAMPLE 3.20

Multiply $(x - 7)$ and $(2x + 1)$ using the F-O-I-L method.

SOLUTION 3.20

$$(x - 7)(2x + 1) = 2x^2 + x - 14x - 7 = 2x^2 - 13x - 7.$$

If the two binomials have the same first terms, and the second terms differ only in sign, then the outer and inner products cancel each other out and the answer is only the difference of the F and L terms. For example, $(3x + 5)(3x - 5) = 9x^2 - 15x + 15x - 25 = 9x^2 - 25$. So if you recognize two binomials as the sum and difference of the same terms, you can write the answer directly, eliminating the inner and outer products, $(3x + 5)(3x - 5) = 9x^2 - 25$. Remember that in the product of the sum and difference of the same real terms, the last term is always negative.

3.7.2b Multiplying Complex Conjugates

Complex conjugates are pairs of complex numbers such that the real parts are the same and the complex parts differ only in sign, such as $a + bi$ and $a - bi$. Since both terms are binomials, this is just a special case of multiplying binomials, discussed above. When a complex number is multiplied by its conjugate, the complex parts cancel each other out. The longhand version is as follows:

$$(a + bi)(a - bi) = a(a) + a(-bi) + bi(a) + bi(-bi) = a^2 - abi + abi - b^2i^2 = a^2 + b^2.$$

The answer is the difference of F and L in the F-O-I-L calculation, but watch out! Those last terms contain $i^2 = -1$, so the last term of the multiplication of complex conjugates is positive because a negative (from F-O-I-L) times a negative (from i^2) equals a positive. Therefore,

$$(a + bi)(a - bi) = a^2 + b^2.$$

This fact is similar to rationalizing a fraction (Section 3.6.3), which involved removing the radical from the denominator of a fraction. Since a complex number involves a radical, $i = \sqrt{-1}$, it also has to be rationalized because radicals should not appear in the denominator of a fraction (see also Section 4.2.2).

EXAMPLE 3.21

Rationalize the fraction $\dfrac{3}{1 + \sqrt{2}}$.

SOLUTION 3.21

To eliminate the radical in the denominator, multiply the entire fraction by a fraction with the conjugate of the radical in both the numerator and denominator (so it is equal to 1), as follows:

$$\frac{3}{1 + \sqrt{2}} = \frac{3}{1 + \sqrt{2}} \times \frac{1 - \sqrt{2}}{1 - \sqrt{2}} = \frac{3 - 3\sqrt{2}}{1 - 2} = \frac{3 - 3\sqrt{2}}{-1} = -3 + 3\sqrt{2}$$

EXAMPLE 3.22

Rationalize the fraction $\dfrac{2 - 3i}{1 + 4i}$.

SOLUTION 3.22

Multiply the numerator and denominator of the fraction by a fraction with the complex conjugate of the denominator in its numerator and denominator:

$$\frac{2 - 3i}{1 + 4i} \times \frac{1 - 4i}{1 - 4i} = \frac{(2 - 3i)(1 - 4i)}{1^2 + 4^2} = \frac{2 - 8i - 3i + 12i^2}{17} = \frac{2 - 11i - 12}{17} = -\frac{10}{17} - \frac{11i}{17}$$

 With a *complex* conjugate, we still have an *i* term, but it is only in the numerator.

3.7.3 Binomial Theorem

The **binomial theorem,** stated in general terms, is:

$$(x + y)^n = x^n + \frac{n}{1}x^{n-1}y + \frac{n(n-1)}{1 \times 2}x^{n-2}y^2 + \frac{n(n-1)(n-2)}{1 \times 2 \times 3}x^{n-3}y^3 + \ldots + y^n,$$

where *n*, a positive integer, is the power of the binomial. This formula, called the **binomial formula,** may look complicated, but it finds any power of a binomial without multiplying at length. So for $(x + y)^2$, $n = 2$, and we can immediately write

$$(x + y)^2 = x^2 + 2xy + y^2.$$

 The square of a binomial has only three terms because all the terms with $(n - 2)$ are zero. Likewise, the cube of a binomial has only four terms because all the terms with $(n - 3)$ are zero. And so on.

3.8 SOLVING QUADRATIC EQUATIONS

As stated previously, a **quadratic equation** is an equation in which the unknown is squared and there is no higher power of the unknown. It is okay if there are no lower powers of the unknown (in other words, no "*x*" term and/or no "pure number" term is okay).

Quadratic equations always have two solutions for the value of x (even though at times they are the same value twice). The general form of a quadratic equation is $ax^2 + bx + c = 0$, where b and c can be any numbers, even 0. If $a = 0$, though, the equation is no longer a quadratic—according to the definition, there has to be an x^2 term. If $a = 0$, it is a linear equation.

A quadratic equation can be solved by factoring, using the quadratic formula, or graphically.

3.8.1 Factoring

The algebraic solutions to a quadratic equation are usually found by writing the quadratic expression on one side of the equal sign and 0 on the other. To make calculations easier, be sure to clear the equation of fractions, if there are any, by multiplying through by a common denominator.

If we can find two factors for a quadratic expression, the solution to the quadratic equation is found by setting each of the factors equal to 0 and solving for the unknown variables. Each of the factors will contain the unknown to only the first power (e.g., x). Solving each of these gives two **roots** (solutions, or zeros) for the quadratic equation.

 The algebraic solutions to a quadratic equation are based on a simple fact: if two factors are multiplied together and the product is 0, then either one or both of the factors must equal 0. There aren't any two nonzero numbers whose product is 0. Period.

Four methods to solve a quadratic equation by factoring include the following:

1. **Difference of two squares**. If the quadratic equation is the difference of two squares (a perfect square, a minus sign, and another perfect square, such as, $x^2 - 25 = 0$), the factors are two binomials that are the sum and difference of the square roots $[x^2 - 25 = (x - 5)(x + 5) = 0]$. If we set each factor equal to 0, we get, $x = +5$ or $x = -5$, written as $x = \pm 5$, since $\pm$ means plus or minus.

   If $b = 0$ in the general equation and it isn't obvious that the equation is the difference of two squares, simply isolate x^2 on one side of the equal sign and then take the square root of each side of the equation. This is the basic reasoning for method #4, completing the square.

   EXAMPLE 3.23

   What are the roots of $9x^2 - 8 = 0$?

   SOLUTION 3.23

   Rewrite $9x^2 - 8 = 0$ with x^2 alone on one side: $x^2 = \dfrac{8}{9}$. Therefore, $x = \pm\sqrt{\dfrac{8}{9}} = \pm\dfrac{2\sqrt{2}}{3}$.

2. **Common factor**. The common factor method involves recognizing that there is a common factor in each term, for equations without the constant (c) term. Factor out the common factor, and the binomial that is left is the other factor. Set the factors equal to 0 to find the values for the unknown.

EXAMPLE 3.24

Solve the equation $3x^2 = 9x$ for x.

SOLUTION 3.24

Rewrite the equation as $3x^2 - 9x = 0$. Because this quadratic doesn't have a c term, it should have a common factor involving x. Indeed, the common factor is $3x$, and if this is factored out of both terms, the result is $3x(x - 3) = 0$, which results in solutions of $3x = 0$ and $x - 3 = 0$, or $x = 0, 3$.

3. **Factoring into Binomials**. Factoring a quadratic equation of the general form $ax^2 + bx + c = 0$ involves finding two binomials that are factors of the quadratic. This is the reverse, of course, of finding the product of two binomials by the F-O-I-L method. This involves finding factors of the product ac that add up to b. This method is essentially by trial and error because ac can have many pairs of factors that all have to be checked to see if they add up to b. Don't forget to consider all of the combinations, including positives and negatives (for example, 15 has factors of –1 and –15, –3 and –5, 1 and 15, and 3 and 5; and the number 24 has many more pairs of factors. If $a \neq 1$, remember to factor a as well). Use the reverse of the distributive law to find the two factors of the quadratic. Once you have the two binomial factors, the solutions are found by setting each binomial equal to 0.

Not all factors of quadratics are whole numbers, and sometimes $a \neq 1$, so the factors may not work out right away. Don't waste time. Just use another method, such as the quadratic formula (Section 3.8.2), which always works.

EXAMPLE 3.25

Solve the equation $x^2 - 2x = 15$ for x by factoring into binomials.

SOLUTION 3.25

- First, write the equation in the general form of $ax^2 + bx + c = 0$ by moving the 15 to the left side of the equation: $x^2 - 2x - 15 = 0$.

- Find two numbers whose product is –15 and sum is –2. The possibilities for a product of –15 are 3 and –5, –3 and 5, 1 and –15, and –1 and 15.

- Only the first of these (3 and -5) has a sum of -2, so the quadratic has the factors $(x + 3)(x - 5) = 0$. Set each of these factors equal to 0 and solve independently.

- The solutions are $x = -3$ or $x = 5$.

EXAMPLE 3.26

Solve the equation $x^2 - 10x + 25 = 0$ for x.

SOLUTION 3.26

If the last term is a perfect square, start with the square roots for the factors because the two solutions may be equal. The factors in Example 3.26 are $(x - 5)(x - 5) = 0$, and the roots are $x = 5$ and $x = 5$ (called a **double root**).

EXAMPLE 3.27

Solve the equation $3x^2 + 5x - 8 = 0$ for x by factoring into binomials.

SOLUTION 3.27

Find two numbers whose product is -8 and, since $a \neq 1$, also find two numbers whose product is 3. The possibilities for factors of c are 1 and -8, -1 and 8, 2 and -4, and -2 and 4. Now find the factors of a, which are just 1 and 3 or -3 and -1. Finally, determine which combinations of these roots will give a sum equal to b, or $+5$. For example, choosing 3 and 1 for a, and 2 and -4 for c, the factors of the quadratic would be $(3x + 2)(x - 4)$, which would give $-10x$ for the middle term, so they don't work out. Neither would several other combinations—the only one that works out is $(3x + 8)(x - 1)$, but it may take a long time to find it.

The quadratic has the factors $(3x + 8)(x - 1) = 0$. Set each of these factors equal to 0 and solve independently. $3x + 8 = 0$ gives $x = -\dfrac{8}{3}$, and $x - 1 = 0$ gives $x = 1$, so the solutions are $x = -\dfrac{8}{3}$, $x = 1$.

Method #3 above may sound a little different from other methods for factoring a quadratic into binomials, but it has the advantage of finding the factors more quickly than traditional trial-and-error methods when $a = 1$. However, when $a \neq 1$, the quadratic formula (see Section 3.8.2) is usually the best way to find the roots of a quadratic equation.

4. **Completing the Square.** Basically, this is a method to "force" an equation into a form that essentially is the equality of two squares, which is solved by taking the square root of each side. This method actually works for any quadratic, but it can be more cumbersome than the three preceding methods. However, it is useful in some situations.

This method involves several steps but it isn't difficult. Follow the steps to solve the equation $3x^2 + 2x - 1 = 0$ by completing the square.

a. Make sure the coefficient of the square term is 1. If it isn't, divide the equation through by the coefficient of the square term. Be sure to do this to every term.

b. Put the constant by itself on the other side of the equal sign.

c. Take half the coefficient of the first-degree term and square it, and add it to both sides of the equation.

d. Express the left-hand side as the square of a binomial and simplify the right-hand side.

e. Take the square roots of both sides of the equation (not forgetting the plus or minus) and solve the resulting equations.

EXAMPLE 3.28

Find the roots of $3x^2 + 2x - 1 = 0$ by completing the square.

SOLUTION 3.28

Follow the five steps listed to complete the square:

a. Dividing $3x^2 + 2x - 1 = 0$ by 3 gives $x^2 + \dfrac{2}{3}x - \dfrac{1}{3} = 0$.

b. $x^2 + \dfrac{2}{3}x = \dfrac{1}{3}$

c. $\left(\dfrac{1}{2} \times \dfrac{2}{3}\right)^2 = \dfrac{1}{9}$, and adding $\dfrac{1}{9}$ to both sides of the equation gives

   $\left(x^2 + \dfrac{2}{3}x + \dfrac{1}{9}\right) = \dfrac{1}{3} + \dfrac{1}{9}$.

d. $\left(x + \dfrac{1}{3}\right)^2 = \dfrac{4}{9}$

e. $x + \dfrac{1}{3} = \dfrac{\sqrt{4}}{\sqrt{9}} = \pm\dfrac{2}{3}$, so $x = \left(\pm\dfrac{2}{3}\right) - \dfrac{1}{3}$, or $x = \dfrac{1}{3}, \ -1$.

No matter what method you use, be sure to check your answers by substituting the roots, or the values found for x, into the original equations.

3.8.2 Quadratic Formula

The **quadratic formula** can find the roots for *all* quadratic equations and, although the formula looks complicated, it is in many cases easier than other factoring methods. *All* quadratic equations of the form $ax^2 + bx + c = 0$ can be solved by using the quadratic formula.

$$x = \frac{-b \pm \sqrt{b^2 - 4ac}}{2a}$$

Note the following details about this useful formula:

- The value of a cannot be 0, because if $a = 0$, the equation would be linear and not quadratic, and also because division by 0 is undefined.

- The formula contains a $\pm$ sign, which gives the two roots that all quadratic equations have.

- The formula involves a square root. The value under the square root sign, $b^2 - 4ac$, is called the **discriminant**, which describes the roots, so often it is a first step when solving quadratic equations.

- If $b^2 - 4ac > 0$, both roots are real and easily found by using the quadratic formula. The graph of this function crosses the x-axis at exactly two places.

EXAMPLE 3.29

Solve the equation $3x^2 + 5x - 8 = 0$ for x by using the quadratic formula. This is the same equation as in Example 3.27, but see how this answer is easier.

SOLUTION 3.29

In general form, $ax^2 + bx + c = 0$, this equation has $a = 3$, $b = 5$, and $c = -8$. Then

$$x = \frac{-b \pm \sqrt{b^2 - 4ac}}{2a} = \frac{-5 \pm \sqrt{5^2 - 4(3)(-8)}}{2(3)} = \frac{-5 \pm \sqrt{25 + 96}}{6} = \frac{-5 \pm 11}{6}$$

So, the answer is $x = \dfrac{-16}{6}, \dfrac{6}{6}$ or $x = -\dfrac{8}{3}, 1$. This is the same result as in Example 3.27 but there is no trial and error involved.

- If $b^2 - 4ac = 0$ (that is, if $b^2 = 4ac$), the two roots are real and identical and equal to $\dfrac{-b}{2a}$. When two roots are identical, they are called **double roots**. An example of this case is the quadratic equation $x^2 - 6x + 9 = 0$, with a double root of $+3$. The graph of this function touches the x-axis at only one point (it is **tangent** to the x-axis).

EXAMPLE 3.30

Solve the equation $x^2 - 10x + 25 = 0$ for x. This is the same equation as in Example 3.26.

SOLUTION 3.30

In general form, $ax^2 + bx + c = 0$, this equation has $a = 1$, $b = -10$, and $c = 25$. Then

$$x = \frac{-b \pm \sqrt{b^2 - 4ac}}{2a} = \frac{-(-10) \pm \sqrt{(-10)^2 - 4(1)(25)}}{2(1)} = \frac{10 \pm \sqrt{100 - 100}}{2} = 5 \pm 0$$

Indeed, this double root of 5 can be found immediately by computing $\dfrac{-b}{2a} = \dfrac{-(-10)}{2(1)} = 5$.

- If $b^2 - 4ac < 0$, the roots are not real; they are **imaginary**, or **complex**. Complex roots always come in pairs, so if one root is $6 + 3i$, the other root is $6 - 3i$, its **complex conjugate**. This type of function, when graphed, does not cross the x-axis.

EXAMPLE 3.31

Solve $5x^2 + 4x + 1 = 0$ for x.

SOLUTION 3.31

In general form, $ax^2 + bx + c = 0$, this equation has $a = 5$, $b = 4$, and $c = 1$. Then

$$x = \frac{-b \pm \sqrt{b^2 - 4ac}}{2a} = \frac{-(4) \pm \sqrt{(4)^2 - 4(5)(1)}}{2(5)} = \frac{-4 \pm \sqrt{16 - 20}}{10}$$

$$x = \frac{-4 \pm \sqrt{-4}}{10} = \frac{-4 \pm 2i}{10} = \frac{-2}{5} \pm \frac{i}{5}$$

In addition,

- If $b^2 - 4ac$ is a perfect square, the roots are rational, and if $b^2 - 4ac$ is not a perfect square, the roots are irrational.

EXAMPLE 3.32

Solve $2x^2 - 6x + 3 = 0$ for x.

SOLUTION 3.32

In general form, $ax^2 + bx + c = 0$, this equation has $a = 2$, $b = -6$, and $c = 3$. Then

$$x = \frac{-b \pm \sqrt{b^2 - 4ac}}{2a} = \frac{-(-6) \pm \sqrt{(-6)^2 - 4(2)(3)}}{2(2)} = \frac{6 \pm \sqrt{36 - 24}}{4}$$

$$x = \frac{6 \pm \sqrt{12}}{4} = \frac{6 \pm 2\sqrt{3}}{4} = \frac{3 \pm \sqrt{3}}{2}$$

 Do not mix up factors and roots. The roots are the values that make the factors equal zero.

Important things to watch out for when using the quadratic formula include:

- When determining what a, b, and c are, remember to write the quadratic terms in descending powers of the unknown and to include their signs.

- The factor $2a$ divides into the whole numerator, not just one of the terms. A common mistake is to divide it only into the square root term and to forget about the $-b$ term that is also in the numerator.

- Following the order of operations, check out the discriminant first. That will tell whether the roots are real or imaginary.

- The quadratic equation gives roots, not factors, so if you are using the quadratic equation as a tool for factoring, the last step after finding the roots is to then write the factors. For example, if the roots of an equation are 3 and –4, the factors are $(x - 3)$ and $(x - (-4)) = (x + 4)$.

 All quadratic equations can be solved by using the quadratic formula, which is important enough to memorize.

3.8.2a Graphical Solutions

The graph of a quadratic equation is a **parabola** (U-shaped graph) of the form $y = ax^2 + bx + c$ with the following properties:

1. The parabola opens upward if $a > 0$ and downward if $a < 0$.

2. The real solutions to the quadratic equation (there are two, or there may be one double root) are the points where the graph crosses the x-axis (at $y = 0$). These points are called the **zeros** of the quadratic equation, or the x values for which the quadratic equation has a value of zero.

3. The highest (or lowest) point of the quadratic is called the **vertex**, whose x-coordinate is given by $\left(\dfrac{-b}{2a}\right)$.

4. The quadratic is symmetric around the vertical line that goes through the vertex. This line is therefore called the **axis of symmetry**.

Examples of two parabolas are given below.

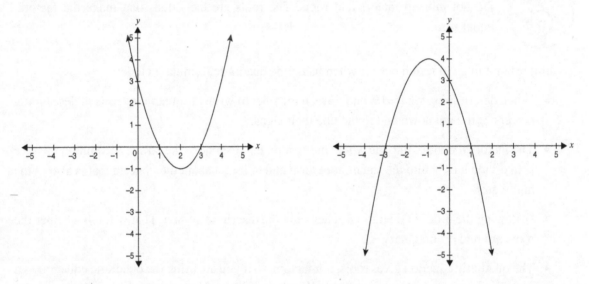

These graphs could have been sketched directly from their equations. For the left graph, $y = x^2 - 4x + 3$, the graph is U-shaped and the lowest point, the vertex, has an x value of $x = \dfrac{-b}{2a} = \dfrac{-(-4)}{2(1)} = 2$. The vertex point is found by substituting this value into the quadratic equation and solving for y: $y = 2^2 - 4(2) + 3 = 4 - 8 + 3 = -1$. So the vertex is $(2, -1)$. The axis of symmetry is around the line $x = 2$. An easy point to find is at $x = 0$, where $y = 3$, or at $(0, 3)$. Since the graph is symmetric around $x = 2$, another point on the graph is $(4, 3)$. This gives a rather good sketch of the parabolic curve, and we can visually estimate the zeros, or solutions, at $(1, 0)$ and $(-3, 0)$.

The right-hand graph, $y = -x^2 - 2x + 3$, opens downward because a is negative, the x value at the vertex is $x = \dfrac{-b}{2a} = \dfrac{-(-2)}{2(-1)} = -1$ and the y value at the vertex is $y = -(-1)^2 - 2(-1) + 3 = 4$. Therefore, the vertex is $(-1, 4)$ and the axis of symmetry is $x = -1$. Some easy points to find are the y-intercept when $x = 0$, $(0, 3)$, and its symmetric point $(-2, 3)$.

3.9 REAL-WORLD QUADRATIC EQUATIONS

The best example of an everyday quadratic is the position formula and its variations, such as figuring out how far a baseball will go knowing its original height h_0 (the height of the bat), the initial velocity v (velocity of the swing), and the effect of gravity a. A quadratic formula such as $h = h_0 + vt + at^2$ will tell the position of the ball at any time t. But that's not the only motion that depends on a variation of this distance formula: the speed of a roller coaster, the landing of a rocket, and the trajectory of a golf ball are just some examples of real-world experiences that depend on the quadratic equation. Other examples include finance, such as the rise and fall of profits from sales using a profit function, or other variables for which a maximum or minimum value is to be determined. See Chapter 7, Section 7.4.1 for more everyday examples.

Chapter 3 Exercises

Answers are on the following pages.

1. Manuel buys a car for $19,620 at a "10% off" sale. How much did he save?

    (A) $21,800

    (B) $2,180

    (C) $21,582

    (D) $1,962

2. Solve the quadratic equation for d: $d^2 - \dfrac{9}{16} = 0$.

    (A) $\dfrac{3}{4}$

    (B) $-\dfrac{3}{4}$

    (C) $\pm\dfrac{3}{4}$

    (D) $-\sqrt{\dfrac{9}{16}}$

3. Which of the following addition problems is INCORRECT?

 (A) $\left(\dfrac{1}{3}+\dfrac{1}{4}\right)+\dfrac{1}{5}=\dfrac{1}{5}+\left(\dfrac{1}{3}+\dfrac{1}{4}\right)$

 (B) $(0.5+1.3)+(-0.7)=0.5+(1.3+(-0.7))$

 (C) $4\dfrac{1}{3}+3\dfrac{1}{3}=(4+3)\times\dfrac{1}{3}$

 (D) $\left(\dfrac{7}{8}+\left(-\dfrac{7}{8}\right)\right)+0=0$

4. The qth root of a^p is written as

 (A) $a^{\frac{p}{q}}$

 (B) $\sqrt[q]{a^p}$

 (C) $\left(\sqrt[q]{a}\right)^p$

 (D) All of the above.

5. What is the value of s^2-3s+4 when s is the value given by the proportion $\dfrac{6}{20}=\dfrac{s-1}{10}$?

 (A) 0

 (B) 4

 (C) 8

 (D) 32

Answers and Explanations

1. **(B)**

First, realize that answer choices (A) and (C) cannot be correct because the question isn't what the original price was, but what Manuel saved. Since this is 10% off, he paid 90% of the original price, so the equation is $19{,}600=.90x$ or $x=\$21{,}800$, so he saved 10% of that, or $2,180. Answer choice (D) is 10% of the sale price, not the original price.

2. **(C)**

This quadratic is the difference of two squares, since 9 and 16 are both perfect squares. One way to solve for d is to use the difference of squares formula, which results in $\left(d+\dfrac{3}{4}\right)\left(d-\dfrac{3}{4}\right)=0$, or $d=\pm\dfrac{3}{4}$. Alternatively, clear the equation of fractions by multiplying through by 16 to get $16d^2-9=0$, which is clearly the difference of two squares, which factors into $\left(4d+3\right)\left(4d-3\right)=0$, or $d=\pm\dfrac{3}{4}$. A third method to solve this problem is to say $d^2=\dfrac{9}{16}$ and use square roots.

3. (C)

Answer choice (C) may look like the distributive property, but it isn't, and it is false. Answer choice (A) is true by the commutative property, answer choice (B) is true by the associative property, and answer choice (D) is a combination of the additive inverse and additive identity.

4. (D)

All of the above. Each answer choice is read as "the qth root of a^p."

5. (C)

For the given proportion $\dfrac{6}{20}=\dfrac{s-1}{10}$, s is found by cross-multiplication: $20(s-1)=60$, or $s=4$. Substituting $s=4$ into the expression s^2-3s+4 yields $(4)^2-3(4)+4=16-12+4=8$.

Before you begin your review, take this short self-assessment to see how well you know the topics covered in this chapter. Answering all or some correctly will help you identify your strengths so you can focus on those topics where you need the most review. Even if you answer all of the questions correctly, we suggest you still review all the examples in the chapter to ensure you're in good shape to move on. Answers are on the following page.

1. What is the common ratio for the sequence 5, 12.5, 31.25, 78.125 . . . ?

   (A) 0

   (B) 2.5

   (C) −2.5

   (D) 1

2. Express $\log_4 a + \log_4 b - \log_4 c$ as a single logarithm.

   (A) $\log_4(a + b - c)$

   (B) $\log_4 \dfrac{ab}{c}$

   (C) $\log_4(a + b) - \log_4 c$

   (D) $\dfrac{\left(\log_4 a\right)(\log_4 b)}{\log_4 c}$

3. If a root of a rational equation with real integer coefficients is $(a + bi)$, another root is

   (A) a.

   (B) b.

   (C) $(a - bi)$.

   (D) Cannot tell without more information.

4. Solve for x: $x^4 = 81$.

   (A) ±2

   (B) ±3

   (C) ±4

   (D) ±9

5. What is the product of $(3 + 4i)$ and $(2 - 5i)$?

   (A) −14 + 7i

   (B) 26 − 7i

   (C) −14 − 7i

   (D) 26 + 7i

1. (B)

The common ratio of a geometric sequence can be found by dividing any term by the term before it, such as $\frac{12.5}{5} = 2.5$. If the numbers are more complicated (for example, suppose this sequence started with 31.25 instead of 5), this problem could also be solved by elimination. Geometric sequences never have a ratio of 0 or 1, and if the ratio is negative, every other number in the geometric sequence changes sign. Therefore, the only viable answer is (B) 2.5. (Section 4.6.3)

2. (B)

The rules for multiplication and division of logarithms are that (1) the log of a product is equal to the sum of the logs of its factors and (2) the log of a quotient is equal to the log of the dividend minus the log of the divisor. Working backward from the answer choices to the given logarithm shows that only (B) follows these rules. (Section 4.3.3a)

3. (C)

Whenever a complex number is a root of a rational function with real coefficients, its complex conjugate is also a root of that polynomial. The complex conjugate of $(a + bi)$ is $(a - bi)$. (Section 4.4.2b)

4. (B)

You can find the correct choice by substituting x with the answer choices. Another way is $\sqrt{x^4} = \sqrt{81}$, or $x^2 = \pm 9$, or $x = \pm 3$. (Section 4.3.2)

5. (B).

Use FOIL: $(3 + 4i)(2 - 5i) = (3)(2) + (3)(-5i) + (2)(4i) + (4i)(-5i) = 6 - 15i + 8i - 20i^2 = 6 - 7i + 20$ since $i^2 = -1$. (Section 4.2.2)

Competency 2: Advanced Algebra

4.1 NONLINEAR INEQUALITIES

Chapter 3 covers related algebraic and graphical presentations of the parabola, a nonlinear equation. For a nonlinear inequality, use steps similar to those outlined in Chapter 3 for linear inequalities:

- Algebraically, treat the inequality as an equality, remembering the inequality sign changes when multiplying or dividing by a negative.

- Graphically, graph the inequality as if it has an equal sign. Then make the graph line dashed or solid, according to the inequality sign (dashed if it is < or >; solid if it is ≤ or ≥). Choose a point on either side of the curve. (Usually the origin $(0, 0)$ is a good choice since the math is easier.) If that ordered pair makes the inequality true, shade that side of the curve; if not, shade the other side.

EXAMPLE 4.1

Graph $y > x^2$.

SOLUTION 4.1

Follow the instructions above to graph $y > x^2$. For $y = x^2$, we recognize that this is a parabola that opens upward (since a, the coefficient of x^2, is positive), has its vertex at $(0, 0)$, and the axis of symmetry is the y-axis. (See Chapter 3, Section 3.8.3.) Since the inequality is >, the parabola is dashed, and the shading is as shown because $y > x^2$ is true for the points within the parabola. The graph is shown on the next page.

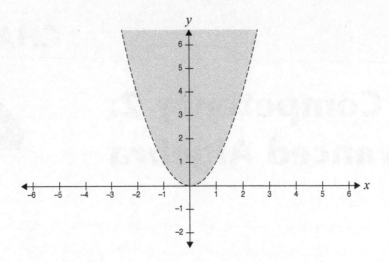

4.2 OPERATIONS ON COMPLEX NUMBERS

4.2.1 Addition and Subtraction

When adding two complex numbers, merely add the real parts for the real part of the answer, and add the imaginary parts for the imaginary part of the answer, remembering to retain the symbol i.

$$(a + bi) + (c + di) = (a + c) + (b + d)i$$

EXAMPLE 4.2

Evaluate $(7 + 5i) + (4 - 2i)$.

SOLUTION 4.2

$$(7 + 5i) + (4 - 2i) = (7 + 4) + (5 - 2)i = 11 + 3i.$$

Likewise for subtraction, transforming it into addition by using the opposites of both parts of the second quantity. (This is similar to $10 - (-7) = 10 + (+7) = 17$.)

$$(a + bi) - (c + di) = (a + bi) + (-c - di) = (a - c) + (b - d)i.$$

EXAMPLE 4.3

Evaluate $(8 + 2i) - (4 - 3i)$.

SOLUTION 4.3

$(8 + 2i) - (4 - 3i) = (8 + 2i) + (-4 + 3i) = (8 - 4) + (2i + 3i) = 4 + 5i$.

4.2.2 Multiplication and Division

When multiplying two complex numbers, use the same technique as for binomials, remembering that $i^2 = -1$. In other words, use F-O-I-L.

EXAMPLE 4.4

Evaluate $(3 - 4i)(2 + 5i)$.

SOLUTION 4.4

$(3 - 4i)(2 + 5i) = (3)(2) + 3(5i) + (-4i)(2) + (-4i)(5i) = 6 + 15i - 8i - 20i^2 = 26 + 7i$,

where the term $-20i^2 = (-20)(-1) = +20$.

To divide two complex numbers, convert the problem to a multiplication problem by writing it as a fraction and then multiplying both numerator and denominator by the **complex conjugate** of the denominator (also known as **rationalizing the fraction**). This transforms the problem into a fraction with a complex number on top and a real number on the bottom, which is divided into each part of the numerator.

EXAMPLE 4.5

Divide $6 - 2i$ by $4 + i$.

SOLUTION 4.5

Write the problem as a fraction: $\dfrac{6 - 2i}{4 + i}$. Multiply top and bottom by $4 - i$, the complex conjugate of $4 + i$:

$$\frac{6 - 2i}{4 + i} \times \frac{4 - i}{4 - i} = \frac{24 + 6(-i) + (-2i)(4) + (-2i)(-i)}{16 - i^2} = \frac{24 - 6i - 8i + 2i^2}{16 - (-1)} =$$

$$\frac{22 - 14i}{17} = \frac{22}{17} - \frac{14}{17}i$$

4.2.3 Graphing Complex Numbers

Graphically, complex numbers use the coordinate plane, but the usual *x*-axis is the *Re*-axis (real axis) and the *y*-axis is the *Im*-axis (imaginary axis), and a complex number is plotted as a point in this new (complex) coordinate system.

4.3 RADICALS, POWERS, EXPONENTS, AND LOGARITHMS

4.3.1 Radical Equations

An equation that has one or more unknowns under a radical is called a **radical equation**. Chapter 3 (Section 3.6.2) presented radical equations in which the index was 2 (square root). Working with a radical equation with an index greater than 2 is similar. Isolate the radical term on one side of the equation and move all of the other terms to the other side. Then raise both sides of the equation to a power equal to the index of the radical. As with square roots, it is important to check the answer because extraneous values are possible when working with roots and powers, especially because the radicand cannot be negative for even roots. For example, if the equation contained the radical $\sqrt[4]{x-3}$, the answer cannot include any value of *x* that is less than 3.

4.3.2 Equations Involving Powers and Exponents

Equations that involve the unknown raised to a power were discussed in Chapter 3 and will be addressed in this chapter in Section 4.4 on polynomials. However, it is possible for an equation to have the exponent contain the unknown. The general form of an **exponential equation** is $y_n = a^{nx}$, where the constant ratio *a* can be any number except 1, and *n* is the number of the term.

Whereas linear functions grow by equal differences over equal intervals, exponential functions grow or decay by *powers* over equal intervals. Therefore, exponential equations grow or decay much faster than linear equations. You can recognize an exponential equation by noticing that as one unknown varies by a constant term, the other variable increases or decreases very fast, the graph always goes through the value $y = 1$, and the graph gets very close to the *x*-axis but doesn't cross it.

For example, compare the first few values of *y* for $x = \{2, 3, 4, 5\}$ for the linear equation $y = 2x$ versus the increasing exponential equation $y = 2^x$ and compare the linear equation $y = \frac{1}{2}x$ versus the decreasing exponential equation $y = \left(\frac{1}{2}\right)^x$. The exponential equations change much more rapidly.

x	$y = 2x$	$y = 2^x$	$y = \frac{1}{2}x$	$y = \left(\frac{1}{2}\right)^x$
2	2	4	1	$\frac{1}{4}$
3	4	8	$1\frac{1}{2}$	$\frac{1}{8}$
4	6	16	2	$\frac{1}{16}$
5	8	32	$2\frac{1}{2}$	$\frac{1}{32}$

The graphs below are decreasing exponentially (dashed line) and increasing exponentially (solid line). Notice that they both cross the y-axis at $(0, 1)$ because $y = a^x$ always equals 1 at $x = 0$. Also, because a^1 always equals a, the graph of any exponential equation $y = a^x$ passes through the point $(1, a)$. If a is a real number greater than 1, the domain of $y = a^x$ is $(-\infty, \infty)$, and the range is $(0, \infty)$.

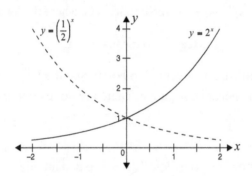

Exponential equations always follow the properties of exponents (powers) shown in Chapter 2, Section 2.7, except now the exponent, or power, is x. Therefore, using b as the base, we have the similar properties listed below.

- $b^{x+c} = b^x b^c$ To multiply two quantities with the same base, add their exponents.

- $(b^c)^x = (b^x)^c = b^{cx}$ To find a power of a power, multiply the exponents.

- $(ab)^x = a^x b^x$ To raise a product to a power, raise each factor to that power.

- $\dfrac{a^{cx}}{a^{dx}} = a^{cx-dx}$ To divide two quantities with the same base, subtract the exponents.

- $\left(\dfrac{a}{b}\right)^x = \dfrac{a^x}{b^x}$ To raise a quotient to a power, raise each factor to that power.

- $b^{-cx} = \dfrac{1}{b^{cx}}$ A base to a negative exponent is equivalent to the reciprocal of the base with a positive exponent.

- $b^x = 1$ if $x = 0$.

EXAMPLE 4.6

In a biological experiment, 10 organisms are isolated, and each of them produces 10 new organisms each hour (this is hypothetical), so that at the first hour, there are 100 similarly prolific new organisms. How many new organisms are present in the ninth hour?

SOLUTION 4.6

At the beginning, call it hour 0, 10 organisms are present and then at the beginning of hour 1, $10 \times 10 = 10^2$ new organisms are present, and so on through 9 hours. The exponential formula would be $y = 10^{x+1}$, where y is the number of new organisms at hour x. Therefore, in hour 9, the number of new organisms is $10^{10} = 10{,}000{,}000{,}000$, or 10 billion.

4.3.3 Logarithmic Equations

Exponents and logarithms (logs) are inverse functions, where the logarithm (or log) is defined as

$$\log_a x = b \text{ means } a^b = x,$$

where $a > 1$. If a is not specified, it is assumed to be 10, and the log is known as the **common log**. For $y = \log_a x$, the x value can never be negative. There are no restrictions on y.

EXAMPLE 4.7

Express the logarithmic equation $\log_5 125 = 3$ exponentially.

SOLUTION 4.7

Use the definition $y = \log_b x$ if and only if $b^y = x$. Then $\log_5 125 = 3$ means $5^3 = 125$.

4.3.3a Properties of Logarithms

The properties of logarithms come directly from the properties for exponents:

- The sum of logarithms with equal bases is equal to the logarithm of the product. Since logarithms are inverses of exponents (just as $\log_a b + \log_a c = \log_a (bc)$), the sum of logarithms with equal bases is equal to the logarithm of the product. For example, $\log_a b + \log_a c = \log_a (bc)$. The reverse is also true; that is, the logarithm of a product is equal to the sum of the logarithms with the same base, or $\log xy = \log x + \log y$.

EXAMPLE 4.8

Rewrite as a single logarithm: $\log_2 x + \log_2 7 + \log_2 y$.

SOLUTION 4.8

Since the sum of logs equals the log of the product, $\log_2 x + \log_2 7 + \log_2 y = \log_2 7xy$.

Hint: You probably can do log base 2 in your head since you should know at least the first five exponents of 2, because $\log_2 x = n$ means $2^n = x$.

- The difference of logarithms with equal bases is equal to the logarithm of the quotient. Therefore, $(\log a - \log b) = \log\left(\dfrac{a}{b}\right)$. The reverse is also true; that is, the logarithm of a quotient is equal to the difference of the logarithms with the same base. Therefore, $\log\left(\dfrac{a}{b}\right) = (\log a - \log b)$.

EXAMPLE 4.9

Rewrite as a single logarithm: $\log_4 5 - (\log_4 8 + \log_4 2)$.

SOLUTION 4.9

$$\log_4 5 - (\log_4 8 + \log_4 2) = \log_4\left(\frac{5}{8+2}\right) = \log_4\left(\frac{5}{10}\right) = \log_4\left(\frac{1}{2}\right)$$

- $n\log_a x = \log_a x^n$ and the reverse $\log_a x^n = n\log_a x$. This fact follows from the fact that a times a logarithm is equal to the logarithm added to itself n times (e.g., $3\log x = \log x + \log x + \log x$), and the sum of n logarithms with the same base becomes ($\log x + \log x + \log x = \log(x \times x \times x) = \log x^3$), the logarithm to the power of n. The reverse is also true.

Because exponents and logs are inverse functions, they cancel each other out. So $\log_3 3^5 = 5$ because it is asking "3 raised to what power equals 3 to the 5th power?" If translated from logs to exponents, it would look like: $\mathbf{3}^x = 3^5$. (The boldface type distinguishes that the 3 is the log index here.) Likewise, $4^{\log_4 x} = x$. In other words, exponential and logarithmic functions with the same base (e.g., $y = a^x$ and $y = \log_a x$) are inverses of each other, which underscores a fundamental logarithmic fact:

$$\log_a a^n = n$$

EXAMPLE 4.10

Simplify the expression $\log_4 4^3$.

SOLUTION 4.10

If we rewrite this expression equal to an unknown b, the problem is asking for b. Using the definition of logarithms, $\log_a x = b$ means $a^b = x$, $\log_4 4^3 = b$ means $4^b = 4^3$, which means $b = 3$. So $\log_4 4^3 = 3$.

Therefore, to solve simple logarithmic equations, we can rewrite the equation as an exponential equation. To find $\log_5 x = 3$, solve $5^3 = x = 125$, and $\log_{10} x = -2$ becomes $10^{-2} = x = \dfrac{1}{10^2} = \dfrac{1}{100}$. If the solution gives more than one value for x, use only the positive value.

EXAMPLE 4.11

Solve for x: $\log_x 4 = 2$.

SOLUTION 4.11

$\log_x 4 = 2$ becomes $x^2 = 4$, or $x = \sqrt{4} = 2$.

4.3.3b Graphing Logarithmic Equations

The basic curve of a log equation is similar to an exponential curve (see Section 4.3.2), with a vertical asymptote of the y-axis. Graphing a log function involves three main steps:

1. Write the equivalent equation in exponential form using the definition $\log_a x = b$ means $a^b = x$.

2. Make a table of points (assign values to y in this case and solve for x).

3. Plot the points and connect them with a curve.

EXAMPLE 4.12

Graph the function $y = f(x) = \log_4 x$.

SOLUTION 4.12

In exponential form, $y = \log_4 x$ is $4^y = x$. Make a table of points (assign values to y in this case and solve for x) and connect them with a curve. Remember that you are still graphing x vs. y.

y	−1	0	1	2
x	$\frac{1}{4}$	1	4	16

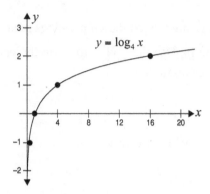

4.3.3c Basics of Logarithm Values

Logarithms do not have to be whole numbers. From the definition of logarithms as the inverse of exponents, logarithms clearly can be any number. It is important to know what the numbers stand for. For example, $\log 8 = 0.903$ (according to the calculator), means $10^{0.903} = 8$. If we examine 0.903, we see that the number before the decimal point (called the **characteristic** of the log) is between 0 and 1, which means the value of the number is between $10^0 = 1$ and $10^1 = 10$, which is correct (it is 8). The numbers after the decimal point (.903), called the **mantissa**, identify the numerical value between 1 and 10. The characteristic merely tells the limits of the power, so if $\log 8 = 0.903$, then $\log 80 = 1.903$, which says the numerical value is 8, but the "1." in 1.903 shows it is between 10 and 100 (between 10^1 and 10^2), so it is 80. In summary, the log has two parts that identify its value: the mantissa identifies the numerical value (8, here) and the characteristic identifies the placement of the decimal point (which shows whether it is 8, 80, or 8,000, for example).

EXAMPLE 4.13

If $\log (728.2) = 2.862$, what is $\log 7.282$?

SOLUTION 4.13

Look at the mantissa of the log, which is .862; this number will be the mantissa of all numbers with the digits 7282, and the characteristic just tells us whether it is 7.282, or 72.82, or 7,282, etc. Here the characteristic should be 0, since the number is between 1 (or 10^0) and 10 (or 10^1), and the answer is 0.862. Check it out on your calculator.

The base of a **natural logarithm** (ln) is e, called **Euler's number**, instead of 10. In other words, $\ln = \log_e$. The value of e is programmed into the calculator. **Exponential growth** and **exponential decay** use natural logs, and are given in terms of e as e^x. For example, a typical function that uses natural logs involves compounded interest, where the amount accrued is $A = Pe^{rt}$, where P is the initial principal amount, r is the interest rate, and t is the time in years.

 Logarithms to base e are treated the same as logs to any other base with $\log_e$ denoted by the abbreviation ln. Use the $\boxed{\text{LN}}$ button on the calculator to enter the value for which you want the natural log.

EXAMPLE 4.14

Solve the equation $\ln(e^3 \cdot e^{5x}) = 13$ for x.

SOLUTION 4.14

Rewrite the problem as $\ln(e^3 \cdot e^{5x}) = \ln(e^{5x+3}) = 13$. From the fact that natural logs and the exponential e are inverse functions, this becomes $5x + 3 = 13$, so $x = 2$.

 You are expected to know the relationship that is the definition for logs: $\log_a x = b$ means $a^b = x$ and $\ln x = c$ means $e^c = x$.

4.4 POLYNOMIALS

A **polynomial** is defined as an expression of more than two algebraic terms that contain different powers of variable(s). Thus, a quadratic is a type of polynomial of degree 2. The **degree** of a polynomial is the largest sum of the exponents of the variables in any term. Coefficients are not considered in determining degree.

 Watch out! An expression may not be in lowest terms. For example, $4x^6 - (2x^3)^2 + x$ has degree 1, not 6, because the $4x^6$ terms cancel out: $4x^6 - 4x^6 + x = x$. Also, the term that determines the degree may not be the first term of a polynomial.

EXAMPLE 4.15

What is the degree of the polynomial $x^2y + x^2 + y$?

SOLUTION 4.15

The degree is the highest total power of any term. In the first term, $(x^2y \equiv x^2y^1)$ the power is $2 + 1 = 3$, so the expression has a degree of 3. Note the use of the equivalence symbol $\equiv$, which means "is identical to."

Although polynomials can contain more than one variable, as in Example 4.15, the polynomials discussed from here on contain only one variable.

4.4.1 Polynomial Identities

It is useful to know the following polynomial identities, some of which you already know. The ones for cubic polynomials will become more familiar as you use them.

$$(a + b)(c + d) = ac + ad + bc + bd$$
$$a^2 - b^2 = (a + b)(a - b)$$
$$a^3 + b^3 = (a + b)(a^2 - ab + b^2)$$
$$a^3 - b^3 = (a - b)(a^2 + ab + b^2)$$

The first identity is the distributive law. If we substitute $(a + b)$ instead of $(c + d)$ into that identity, we get

$$(a + b)^2 = a^2 + 2ab + b^2.$$

Likewise, if we substitute $(x + a)$ and $(x + b)$ instead of $(a + b)$ and $(c + d)$, respectively, into the first identity, we get

$$(x + a)(x + b) = x^2 + (a + b)x + ab.$$

4.4.2 Roots of a Polynomial

4.4.2a Fundamental Theorem of Algebra

The **Fundamental Theorem of Algebra** states:

Any polynomial of degree n has n roots.

So we automatically know that the total number of roots equals the degree of the polynomial. Finding the actual roots of a polynomial of degree $n > 2$ is not as straightforward as finding the roots of a quadratic, however, for which $n = 2$.

 Quadratics are equations of degree 2 with two roots, which are both real or both imaginary.

4.4.2b Complex Roots of a Polynomial

Every **complex root** of an equation (of the form $a + bi$) is accompanied by its **conjugate** ($a - bi$), the result of changing the sign in the middle of two terms. So if there is one complex root to an equation, there are automatically two. Because complex roots never appear alone, a polynomial can have any even number of complex roots up to n, the degree of the polynomial, including 0 complex roots. To determine what these roots actually are, use information from Descartes' Rule of Signs.

4.4.2c Descartes' Rule of Signs

Use **Descartes' Rule of Signs** to determine how many of the roots can be positive real numbers and how many can be negative real numbers, and therefore determine how many complex roots there can possibly be. This rule doesn't involve any real math — just an ability to count sign changes. Count the number of times the sign changes between successive terms in the original equation — that number is the maximum number of *positive* real roots. For the maximum number of *negative* real roots, rewrite the equation with x replaced by $-x$ and count the sign changes between terms. Subtract 2 or a multiple of 2 from the maximum number of real roots found this way to account for the number of possible complex roots since complex roots come in pairs.

For example, the equation $x^3 + 4x^2 + 3x - 2 = 0$ has exactly three roots (since the highest power is 3). There is only one sign change, from $+3x$ to -2, so there is a maximum of one positive real root. Replacing x with $-x$, we get $(-x)^3 + 4(-x)^2 + 3(-x) - 2 = 0$, with two sign changes, so there is a maximum of two negative real roots. Therefore, $x^3 + 4x^2 + 3x - 2 = 0$ has either one real positive root and two real negative roots, or one real positive root and two complex roots.

4.4.2d Factor Theorem

For the Factor Theorem, we use the notation $f(x)$ instead of y for the polynomial because we are discussing functions (see Chapter 5 for a complete discussion of functions). The function notation $f(x)$ is generally read as "f of x." It does not mean to multiply $f \times x$, even though it looks the same. Also, the letter f doesn't have to be used; we could just as well have used $g(x)$ or any other letter, just as we could use any letter for x. However, we use $f(x)$ here.

The **Factor Theorem**, which we have used without naming it, can be stated in two equivalent ways:

For a polynomial $f(x)$, if $f(c) = 0$, then $(x - c)$ must be a factor of $f(x)$,

or

if $(x - c)$ is a factor of a polynomial $f(x)$, then $f(c) = 0$.

EXAMPLE 4.16

For $f(x) = x^2 - x - 12$, if $f(4) = 0$, $(x - 4)$ is a factor of $f(x)$. What are the roots of $f(x)$?

SOLUTION 4.16

If $(x - 4)$ is a factor, 4 is one root. There are several ways to find the other root. If we divide $f(x)$ by $(x - 4)$, the quotient is the other factor. Or we can use the reverse of F-O-I-L.

1. By division: Long division gives us

$$
\begin{array}{r}
x + 3 \\
x - 4 \overline{) x^2 - x - 12} \\
\underline{x^2 - 4x} \\
+3x - 12 \\
\underline{+3x - 12} \\
0
\end{array}
$$

So the other factor is $(x + 3)$, and the other root is -3.

2. By using the reverse of F-O-I-L: $x^2 - x - 12 = (x - 4)(x + ?)$, from which we get that the other factor is $(x + 3)$, and the other root is -3.

4.4.2e Synthetic Division

Now, let's do the same division in Example 4.16 ($x^2 - x - 12$ divided by $x - 4$) using **synthetic division**. One of the rules for synthetic division is that the divisor must be a first-degree (linear) expression with 1 as the coefficient for x. So you can use synthetic division to divide by $x - 4$ (as shown below), or by any binomial such as $x + 6$, but not by $x^2 - 2$ nor by $2x + 5$. (However, in the last case, you can use $x + \dfrac{5}{2}$ instead to make the coefficient of x equal to 1.) The steps for synthetic division follow.

1. Set the original divisor equal to 0, (set $x - 4 = 0$), and solve for x. In Example 4.16 ($x^2 - x - 12$ divided by $x - 4$), once we set $x - 4 = 0$, we know our "synthetic divisor" will be 4.

We use the factor (e.g., $x - 4$) in long division, but use the root of the factor (e.g., 4) in the easier synthetic division.

Next, we find the "synthetic dividend,"

2. Make sure the terms are in descending powers and merely write *only the coefficients* of all the terms in the polynomial, along with their signs, using 0 for any missing power.

For our example, then, we have the following set-up for synthetic division:

$$4 \,\big|\; 1 \quad -1 \quad -12$$

3. Bring down the first number (1) into the first column of the dividend, multiply it by the synthetic divisor (4), and put that value (4) in the next column.

4. Add the numbers in the next column, multiply this sum (3) by the synthetic divisor, and put that value (+12) in the next column, and add that column.

$$
\begin{array}{r|rrr}
4 & 1 & -1 & -12 \\
& \downarrow & 4 & +12 \\
\hline
& 1 & 3 & 0
\end{array}
$$

The last number, 0 here, is the remainder.

If the remainder equals 0, the divisor *is a root* of the original equation. Not only that, but the numbers in that last row are the coefficients of the other factor of the original polynomial, or 1 3 0 translates into $x + 3$.

The quotient of long division by a root is the "other factor" if the remainder is 0.

If the remainder in the synthetic division isn't 0, that divisor isn't a root of the original equation, but it provides valuable information, according to the Remainder Theorem.

4.4.2f Remainder Theorem

The **Remainder Theorem** states:

> When a polynomial is divided by a binomial $(x - c)$
> the remainder equals the value of the polynomial at $x = c$.

In other words, the value of $f(x)$ at any point c, designated as $f(c)$, is simply the remainder when $f(x)$ is divided by $(x - c)$. For this division, use synthetic division. This theorem is a useful shortcut to find the value of a polynomial at any value of x just by looking at the remainder when synthetically dividing the polynomial by the given binomial factor without having to substitute the value into the polynomial and do all the arithmetic.

EXAMPLE 4.17

If $f(x) = x^3 + 3x^2 - 10x - 24$, find $f(2)$.

SOLUTION 4.17

One way to find the answer is to substitute 2 for x in the equation, do the powers, multiplication, addition, and subtraction (notice the Order of Operations) to get the value, or we can just do synthetic division, to get –24 as the answer in much less time.

$$
\begin{array}{r|rrrr}
2 & 1 & 3 & -10 & -24 \\
 & \downarrow & 2 & 10 & 0 \\
\hline
 & 1 & 5 & 0 & -24
\end{array}
$$

So $f(2) = -24$.

4.4.3 Pascal's Triangle

Pascal's triangle provides another useful "shortcut." When we square a binomial such as $(x + 3)$, we can use F-O-I-L to get $(x + 3)^2 = x^2 + 6x + 9$. But not all binomials are so simple, and we may want to raise the binomial to the fifth power. Luckily, the binomial theorem is simplified by looking at a very interesting triangle called **Pascal's triangle** (named after seventeenth-century French mathematician, Blaise Pascal, although it had been used hundreds of years before Pascal by mathematicians in China, India, Persia, and Europe). The first part of Pascal's triangle looks like the following:

$$
\begin{array}{ccccccccccc}
 & & & & & 1 & & & & & \\
 & & & & 1 & & 1 & & & & \\
 & & & 1 & & 2 & & 1 & & & \\
 & & 1 & & 3 & & 3 & & 1 & & \\
 & 1 & & 4 & & 6 & & 4 & & 1 & \\
1 & & 5 & & 10 & & 10 & & 5 & & 1
\end{array}
$$

We can continue to add rows to this triangle because the method is that all the edges are 1's, and all the numbers in the middle are the sums of the two numbers above them. You should see that the next row in the triangle above would be

$$
\begin{array}{ccccccc}
1 & 6 & 15 & 20 & 15 & 6 & 1
\end{array}
$$

Hint: If you remember that Pascal's triangle starts with 1 $\overset{1}{}$ 1 and each succeeding row starts and ends with a 1 and is formed by adding the two numbers from the row above it, you can always construct the triangle, especially when confronted with a binomial raised to any power.

Pascal's triangle is a very powerful tool. Among other uses, it determines the coefficients that arise in **binomial expansions**. The first row of the triangle is row 0, the next is row 1, then row 2, etc. These row numbers correspond to the power of a binomial. The second number of each row tells which row it is. For example, the 5th row is 1 $\underline{5}$ 10 10 5 1, and gives the coefficients of the terms in a binomial raised to the 5th power.

For an example, let's consider the expansion $(x + y)^3 = x^3 + 3x^2y + 3xy^2 + y^3$. First, notice that the coefficients of the terms are 1, 3, 3, 1, which is row 3 in Pascal's triangle. The second step in writing the expansion of $(x + y)^3$ using Pascal's triangle to fill in the powers of the variables of the binomial (here, they are x and y). Start with the highest power of x, which is 3 here, and the lowest power of y, which is 0 (remember that $y^0 = 1$). Then just decrease the x power and increase the y power in each term. The sum of the exponents in each term equals the power of the binomial. This is better shown by example, using the same binomial, $(x + y)$.

1. Since this is a third-order binomial, go to row 3 on Pascal's triangle, 1 3 3 1, which also shows that there will be four terms, $(x + y)^3 = 1\_\_\_\_ + 3\_\_\_\_ + 3\_\_\_\_ + 1\_\_\_\_$.

2. Now fill in the blanks with x's, starting with x^3 and going down, and y's, starting with y^0 and going up. (Notice that the sums of the exponents always add to 3 in this example.)

$$(x + y)^3 = 1x^3y^0 + 3x^2y^1 + 3x^1y^2 + 1x^0y^3$$

3. Simplify the answer by getting rid of the 1's and 0's as exponents. In reality, you wouldn't even be writing these anyway: $(x + y)^3 = x^3 + 3x^2y + 3xy^2 + y^3$.

This method works with any binomial to any power. Just substitute the first term for x and the second term for y. This will take two steps: (1) writing the expansion according to the rules for Pascal's triangle, and (2) simplifying each term. There is no adding of like terms or multiple multiplications by the binomial. All you have to do is follow the steps.

EXAMPLE 4.18

Find $(2x - 3)^4$ by using Pascal's triangle.

SOLUTION 4.18

This binomial has a coefficient in the first term and a negative second term, so it is as complicated as you would encounter on a test.

Row 4 is 1 4 6 4 1, so the solution would start as follows, substituting $(2x)$ for x and (-3) for y in the steps using Pascal's triangle:

$$(2x - 3)^4 = 1(2x)^4 + 4(2x)^3(-3) + 6(2x)^2(-3)^2 + 4(2x)(-3)^3 + 1(-3)^4$$

Notice that the coefficients are 1 4 6 4 1, so there are five terms. The first term has $(2x)$ to the 4th power and each succeeding term has $(2x)$ to one lower power; also, the first term has (-3) to the 0 power (since that equals 1, we don't have to write it) and each succeeding term has (-3) to one higher power. Now we just have to do the multiplication term by term in each of the five terms:

$$(2x - 3)^4 = 16x^4 + (4)(8)(-3)x^3 + (6)(4)(9)x^2 + (4)(2)(-27)x + 81$$
$$= 16x^4 - 96x^3 + 216x^2 - 216x + 81$$

Pascal's triangle can also be used to find a specific term in the expansion of a binomial, which is usually what is asked on a test. Just find the position in the triangle, which gives the coefficient, and then use the same process as above in the expansion, and you will have the powers needed for that specific term. Then rather than doing the tedious evaluating to get the term, you will only have to simplify what Pascal's triangle indicates for the particular term.

EXAMPLE 4.19

What is the third term of the expansion of $(x - y)^5$?

SOLUTION 4.19

First, go to the third term of row 5 of Pascal's triangle, which is 10. That is the coefficient. Since this is the third term, the power of x is 3, and the power of $(-y)$ is 2 because the exponents must add up to 5. Thus, the third term of $(x - y)^5$ is $10x^3y^2$. Notice that the minus sign that belongs to y disappears because $(-y)$ is to an even power. How much simpler this is than doing the multiplication longhand, combining like terms, and then counting over to the third term!

4.5 VECTORS

4.5.1 Definition

So far, the quantities we have worked with are **scalar** quantities, which are quantities that have only magnitude. **Vectors** are quantities that have both **magnitude** and **direction**. A couple of examples will illustrate the difference between scalar and vector measurements.

The first involves a prison escapee. A helicopter pilot spots the suspect and radios in the information to the police on the ground. The information is, "He is in a blue van going 50 miles per hour." Is this information helpful? Not really. Rather than that scalar description, the vector description of "50 miles per hour traveling northeast from the prison" tells the police where to go. Ongoing transmissions to the police on the ground have to include direction to be useful.

Next, consider measurements of the wind if you are in a sailboat. You would likely want the measure to include both the speed and the direction. Knowing just the speed (a scalar) doesn't help you to know how to set the sails. You must also know the direction of the wind, a vector quantity. This information can make the difference between a pleasant ride and a harrowing one.

4.5.2 Graphing Vectors

Because direction is so important with vectors, they are well illustrated with graphs, in which the vector is shown as an arrow. The length of the arrow from the base (**tail**) to the point (**head**) indicates its magnitude, and the position of the arrow indicates its direction. On a graph, the direction is usually measured from the positive *x*-axis; on a compass it is measured relative to north. The vector shown below is represented as $\overrightarrow{AB}$, with the tail mentioned first and the arrow above the letters indicating that it is a vector.

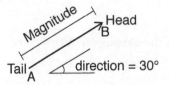

In text, a vector is given as a pair of numbers written either horizontally (A, B) or vertically $\begin{pmatrix} A \\ B \end{pmatrix}$, sometimes with square brackets. A indicates horizontal distance and B indicates vertical distance from a point (often $(0, 0)$), just like ordered pairs, but the vector is actually the line from the starting point to the vector "head." Either capital or lowercase letters are used.

An important property of vectors is that they do not have an assigned location per se. As long as the direction and length of the arrow is maintained, we can move it anywhere we want without changing it. Getting back to the sailboat example, the wind will have the same magnitude and direction anywhere in the vicinity of the sailboat. Therefore, the vectors shown in the figure below are all considered to be equivalent—they all have the same magnitude and direction. The only distinction is the location of the tail (or head). This property of vectors allows addition or subtraction of two vectors graphically.

The triangle method of adding or subtracting vectors involves moving one of the vectors so that a third side of a triangle can be formed, and it is this third side that is the resulting vector. Another method that can be used is the parallelogram method, which involves duplicating the two vectors and placing them so they form a parallelogram. The diagonal of this parallelogram is the resulting vector. This involves a little more work than the triangle method, although they are essentially the same. The triangle method is used in this chapter.

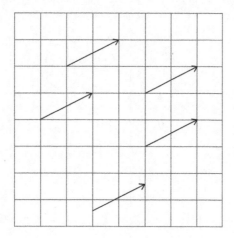

4.5.3 Vector Addition

4.5.3a Algebraically

Algebraically, vectors are added separately element by element, and the result is a new vector with new elements. This is similar to adding complex numbers, where the real and imaginary parts are added separately. Therefore, if we add $\vec{A} = (4, 1) + \vec{B} = (-1, 2)$, we get a new vector, $\vec{A} + \vec{B} = (4 - 1, 1 + 2) = (3, 3)$. Algebraically, that's all there is to it, but it is difficult to visualize what this means unless we add the vectors graphically.

4.5.3b Graphically

Graphically, when we add two vectors, we position the tail of the second at the head of the first and then create a new vector starting from the tail of the first and ending at the head of the newly positioned second vector.

Let's consider the same vectors as above, $\vec{A} = (4, 1)$ and $\vec{B} = (-1, 2)$. First plot their points individually, just as we plotted points on the coordinate plane (see Chapter 3, Section 3.3.1). Now, draw the two vectors individually. Then, using the fact that vectors can be moved anywhere as long as the magnitude and direction aren't changed, let's move vector $\vec{B}$ so that it starts at the head of vector $\vec{A}$. Then we draw the new vector, $\vec{A} + \vec{B}$, the head of which has coordinates (3, 3).

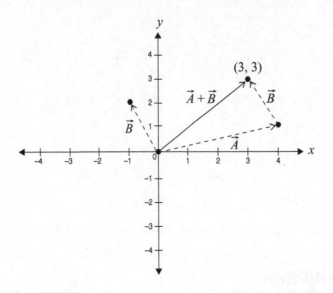

4.5.4 Vector Subtraction

4.5.4a Algebraically

Algebraically, vector subtraction is the same as adding the negative of the vector being subtracted. Since subtraction is not commutative, the two vectors cannot be switched. Vector subtraction means the values of the elements of the subtracted vector are negated (e.g., (2, 3) becomes (–2, –3)) and the direction of the vector is reversed (the head and tail are switched). Add the original first vector and this negated vector separately element by element, just like in addition, and the result is a new vector with new elements $\left(\vec{A} - \vec{B} = \vec{A} + (-\vec{B})\right)$.

Using the original vectors from above, $-\vec{B} = (1, -2)$. When we subtract the second vector from the first, $\vec{A} = (4, 1) + -\vec{B} = (1, -2)$, we get a new vector, $\vec{A} - \vec{B} = (4 + 1, 1 - 2) = (5, -1)$. Algebraically, that's all there is to it, but again, it is difficult to visualize what this means unless we show it graphically, as shown below.

4.5.4b Graphically

Again, let's graph the same vectors. First plot their points individually (as we did above) and draw the two vectors individually. To make $\vec{B}$ a negative vector, switch the head and tail. The new vector is $-\vec{B} = (1, -2)$. Then graphically add the first vector $\vec{A}$ and the negative vector $-\vec{B}$. Then, using the fact that vectors can be moved anywhere as long as the magnitude and direction aren't changed, let's move vector $-\vec{B}$ so that it starts at the head of vector $\vec{A}$. Then we can draw the new vector, $\vec{A} - \vec{B}$, the head of which has coordinates (5, –1).

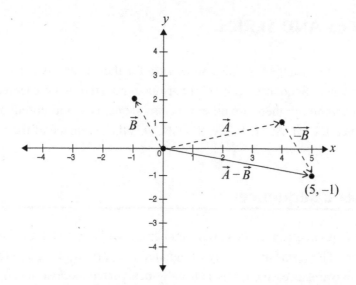

The processes of addition and subtraction of vectors are summarized in the figures below. Notice that the tails of the vectors $\vec{Y}$ and $-\vec{Y}$ start at the heads of the original vector $\vec{X}$.

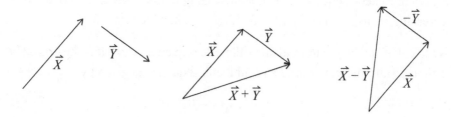

4.5.5 Multiplying a Vector by a Scalar

Multiplying a vector by a scalar (other than 1) simply changes its magnitude only. Its direction does not change. Although a negative vector looks like the original vector is multiplied by −1, its orientation (angle it makes with the *x*-axis) is not changed, only the direction of the vector as it is flipped. The following illustration shows the effects of multiplying a vector by a scalar—if the scalar is <1, the vector is shortened; if it is >1, the vector is lengthened. The scalar can be any number, not just integers.

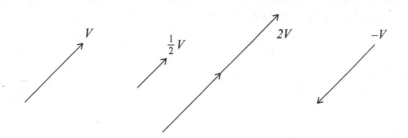

4.6 SEQUENCES AND SERIES

A **sequence** is a set of things that have some rule for their order. A **series** is the sum of a finite numerical sequence. Sequences can be of various types; the two presented here are arithmetic and geometric, although there are other types of sequences, and not all are numeric. For example, the sequence J, F, M, A, M, J, J, A, S, O, N, D is the sequence of the first letters of the months of the year.

4.6.1 Arithmetic Sequence

An **arithmetic sequence** is a sequence of numbers in which a fixed number is added from each term to the next. The terms are usually designated as $a_1, a_2, a_3, \ldots$, and the **constant difference** between any two successive terms is usually designated as d, so $d = a_n - a_{n-1}$, where n is any positive integer greater than 1. An arithmetic sequence is also known as an **arithmetic progression**.

Examples of arithmetic sequences include increasing terms, such as 2, 4, 6, 8, 10, . . . in which $d = 2$; or decreasing terms, such as 21, 18, 15, 12, 9, . . ., in which $d = -3$.

It is easy to calculate the nth term of an arithmetic sequence, since it is the original term with d added $n - 1$ times. Thus, the nth term of an arithmetic sequence is given by

$$a_n = a_1 + (n - 1)d.$$

What this formula is saying is that if we take the first number in the sequence, we can find any other term in the sequence by multiplying the common difference by one less than the position of the term we are finding. We subtract 1 because we already are adding the first term by including a_1 in the formula. So to find the tenth term of the sequence 10, 12, 14, 16, 18, . . ., $a_{10} = 10 + 9(2) = 28$. This checks out by counting ten terms of the sequence starting with the number 10 and counting by twos, but for other sequences and higher terms, it's better to just rely on the formula.

Since the terms of an arithmetic sequence change steadily, if we graph the placement of a term versus the value of the term, we get a straight line with a positive slope for $d > 0$ and a negative slope for $d < 0$.

EXAMPLE 4.20

Find b_{13} in the arithmetic sequence in which $b_1 = -4$ and $b_4 = -13$.

SOLUTION 4.20

To find the value of any term in an arithmetic sequence, we use the formula $a_n = a_1 + (n-1)d$. Here the a's are replaced by b's, but any letter can be used to name the terms. To find b_{13}, we need to find d, so we use the nth-term formula for the 4th position: $b_4 = b_1 + (n-1)d = -13 = -4 + (4-1)d$, so $d = -3$. Then use the formula for the 13th position, b_{13} with $d = -3$.

$$b_{13} = b_1 + (13-1)(-3) = -4 + (12)(-3) = -40$$

 To find n, the number of terms in the sequence, subtract the first term index from the last term index (in the example above, that would be $13 - 1 = 12$), but add 1 to include the first term in the count. As a reminder that you should add the 1, keep in mind the number of terms from a_1 to a_3—it's 3, not 2.

 When solving for n, be sure your answer is a positive integer. There is no such thing as a fractional or negative number of terms in a sequence!

EXAMPLE 4.21

Insert the three terms of the arithmetic sequence between 5 and 21.

SOLUTION 4.21

In an arithmetic sequence, this would be the three terms that complete the sequence 5, ___, ___, ___, 21. The first term is $a_1 = 5$ and the 5th term is $a_5 = 21$. We have to find the common difference, d, to find the missing terms. Using the formula $a_n = a_1 + (n-1)d$ for the five terms, we have $21 = 5 + (5-1)d$, or $d = \dfrac{21-5}{5-1} = \dfrac{16}{4} = 4$, so the missing terms are 9, 13, and 17.

An application of an arithmetic sequence in the world of finance is *simple interest*. Suppose P = the original principal, r = annual interest rate, t = time in years, and A = amount. Then $A = P + Prt$. The corresponding values of the amount for 1 year, 2 years, 3 years, and 4 years, are $P + Pr$, $P + 2Pr$, $P + 3Pr$, and $P + 4Pr$, which is an arithmetic sequence in which the first term is $P + Pr$ and the common difference is Pr.

For example, if $200 is deposited into a bank in which the annual simple interest rate is 4.5%, what would be the amount after 9 years? Simply plug the numbers into the formula, where $P = \$200$, $r = 4.5\% = .045$, and $t = 9$ years. Then the amount $A = \$200 + (\$200)(0.045)(9) = \$281$. If the question asked how much interest would be earned, the answer would be $281 – $200 = $81.

For simple interest problems, the amount of interest is $I = Prt$, which is the amount added to the initial deposit P to find the total amount: $A = P + Prt$.

4.6.2 Arithmetic Series

An **arithmetic series** is just the sum of a certain number of terms of an arithmetic sequence, usually designated as S_n. The formula is based on the average value between the first and nth term multiplied by n, or

$$S_n = \left(\frac{a_1 + a_n}{2}\right)(n) = \frac{n(a_1 + a_n)}{2}.$$

It looks like we don't even have to know d to use this formula, but if we aren't given the value for a_n, we'll need to know d to find a_n. For example, to answer the question, "What is the sum of the sequence of five numbers 11, 13, 15, 17, 19?" you would just substitute the numbers into $S_n = \frac{n(a_1 + a_n)}{2}$ to get $\frac{5(11 + 19)}{2} = 75$. Yes, you can just add up these numbers to get 75 as well, but the next examples show how the formula for a series works faster than brute force.

EXAMPLE 4.22

Find the sum of the first 10 terms of an arithmetic progression when the first term is 5 and the tenth term is –13.

SOLUTION 4.22

Use the formula $S_n = \frac{n(a_1 + a_n)}{2} = \frac{10(5 + (-13))}{2} = -40$.

EXAMPLE 4.23

Find the sum of the first seven even integers greater than 10.

SOLUTION 4.23

This is the same as asking for the sum of the first seven integers of the sequence 12, 14, 16, ... So what is the seventh integer in this series? (Yes, we can count to find it here, but not every problem would be that simple.) We have to use the $a_n = a_1 + (n - 1)d$ formula for that, where a_n is what we are finding, $a_1 = 12$, $n = 7$, and $d = 2$. So we do have to know d to find an arithmetic sequence sometimes, even though it isn't in the formula for the series. Then we have $a_7 = a_1 + (n - 1)d = 12 + 6(2) = 24$ and the sum is $S_n = \dfrac{n(a_1 + a_n)}{2} = \dfrac{7(12 + 24)}{2} = 126$.

4.6.3 Geometric Sequence

A **geometric sequence** is a sequence with a constant **ratio** between any two consecutive terms. This ratio is called the **common ratio**. The terms are usually designated as $a_1, a_2, a_3, \ldots$, and the constant ratio between successive terms is usually designated as r, such that $r = \dfrac{a_n}{a_{n-1}}$, where n is any positive integer greater than 1. A geometric sequence is also known as a **geometric progression**.

The common ratio r can never be 0 or 1. If r is a fraction less than 1, the geometric sequence gets smaller. If r is negative, any two successive terms have opposite signs.

Examples of geometric sequences include increasing terms, such as 2, 4, 8, 16, 32, . . . in which $r = 2$, or decreasing terms, such as in the sequence 243, 81, 27, 9, 3, . . ., in which $r = \dfrac{1}{3}$.

No term in a geometric sequence can ever be 0 because we cannot divide by 0.

To calculate the nth term of a geometric sequence, multiply the original term by r to the $(n - 1)$st power. The exponent of r is n is diminished by 1 because the first term is already in the equation. Thus, the nth term of a geometric sequence is given by

$$a_n = a_1 r^{n-1}.$$

To recognize a sequence as a geometric sequence, keep dividing successive terms to find r. Once there is a different value for r, you need not go any further—it is not a geometric sequence because the ratio has to be the same between *any* two successive numbers.

To find a specific term in a given geometric sequence, you must know the first term and the common ratio between successive terms.

EXAMPLE 4.24

Find the fifth term of the geometric sequence $\frac{1}{4}$, 1, 4, 16, ...

SOLUTION 4.24

First find the common ratio by dividing any term by the one before it. Here it is $r = \frac{1}{\frac{1}{4}} = \frac{4}{1} = \frac{16}{4} = 4$. Using the formula for the nth term of a geometric sequence, the fifth term is $a_n = a_1 r^{n-1} = a_5 = \frac{1}{4}(4)^4 = 4^3 = 64$. Of course, since the common ratio is 4 in this particular sequence, a quicker solution is that the fifth term has to be 4 times the fourth term, or $4(16) = 64$.

EXAMPLE 4.25

The fourth term of a geometric sequence is $\frac{1}{2}$ and the seventh term is $\frac{1}{16}$. What is the first term?

SOLUTION 4.25

The sequence is ___, ___, ___, $\frac{1}{2}$, ___, ___, $\frac{1}{16}$. We can work backward to find the first term if we know the value of r. To find r, we use the equation $a_n = a_1 r^{n-1}$ but we need a "first" term, so we make the first term of the sequence $\frac{1}{2}$. Then $a_1 = \frac{1}{2}, n = 4$, and $a_4 = \frac{1}{16}$. Note that $n = 4$ because we are momentarily shifting over to making $\frac{1}{2}$ the first term, and $\frac{1}{16}$ becomes the fourth term. Once we find r, it will be the r for the original sequence and we can go back to the original sequence. Thus, $a_n = a_1 r^{n-1} = \frac{1}{16} = \frac{1}{2} r^3$, so $r^3 = \frac{1}{8}$ and $r = \frac{1}{2}$. Now, we just work backward multiplying by 2 (or dividing by $\frac{1}{2}$) to find the actual first term, 4. The sequence is 4, 2, 1, $\frac{1}{2}$...

4.6.4 Geometric Series

A **geometric series**, usually designated as S_n, is the sum of the first n terms of a geometric sequence. For a finite geometric series, this sum is given by

$$S_n = \frac{a_1(1 - r^n)}{1 - r}$$

An **infinite geometric series** is one for which $n \to \infty$. Its value depends on the value of r. Remember that r can never be 0, or 1.

- $S_\infty = \dfrac{a_1}{1 - r}$ for an infinite geometric series with $-1 < r < 1$ (i.e., r is a fraction or 0).

- $S_\infty = \infty$ for an infinite geometric series with $r > 1$.

- S_∞ doesn't exist if $r \leq -1$.

EXAMPLE 4.26

Find the sum of the first four terms in the sequence 256, –64, 16, –4, ...

SOLUTION 4.26

We can easily find that $r = \dfrac{-4}{16} = -\dfrac{1}{4}$. Then, since this is a finite sequence, the equation to use is $S_n = \dfrac{a_1(1 - r^n)}{1 - r} = \dfrac{256\left(1 - \left(-\frac{1}{4}\right)^4\right)}{1 - \left(-\frac{1}{4}\right)} = \dfrac{256(1 - \frac{1}{256})}{\frac{5}{4}} = \dfrac{255}{1.25} = 204$.

 Hint: Use the distributive rule in Example 4.26 to evaluate $256\left(1 - \dfrac{1}{256}\right) = 256 - 1 = 255$.

Just as the arithmetic sequence is useful for *simple interest* problems, the geometric sequence is useful for **compound interest** problems. The equation for $P(t)$, the compounded amount after t years, is given by

$$P(t) = P_0\left(1 + \frac{r}{n}\right)^{nt}$$

where P_0 = original principal, r = annual interest rate, n = number of compounding periods per year, and t = total number of years.

The corresponding values of the amount for 1 year, 2 years, 3 years, 4 years, ... are given by $P_0\left(1+\dfrac{r}{n}\right)^n, P_0\left(1+\dfrac{r}{n}\right)^{2n}, P_0\left(1+\dfrac{r}{n}\right)^{3n}, P_0\left(1+\dfrac{r}{n}\right)^{4n}$ .... This is a geometric sequence in which the first term is $P_0\left(1+\dfrac{r}{n}\right)^n$ and the common ratio is $\left(1+\dfrac{r}{n}\right)^n$.

EXAMPLE 4.27

If \$600 is deposited into a bank in which the interest rate is 8% compounded quarterly, what is the amount after five years?

SOLUTION 4.27

Quarterly compounding means there are four compounding periods per year and a total of $(5)(4) = 20$ compounding periods in five years. Thus, for $t = 5$,

$$P(t) = P_0\left(1+\frac{r}{n}\right)^{nt} = P(5) = (\$600)\left(1+\frac{0.08}{4}\right)^{20} \approx \$891.57.$$

 Hint: You probably need to use your calculator for compound interest problems.

EXAMPLE 4.28

A person will need \$5000 in 3 years to help pay off a car loan. To the nearest dollar, how much money should be deposited into a bank in which the interest rate is 10% compounded monthly?

SOLUTION 4.28

\$3709. Monthly means there are twelve compounding periods per year, so there are a total of $(12)(3) = 36$ compounding periods in three years. Then $\$5000 = P_0\left(1+\dfrac{0.10}{12}\right)^{36} \approx 1.3482 P_0$, and thus $P_0 \approx \$3709$.

 NOTE Be sure to know whether the sequence is arithmetic or geometric before you start to answer any question. If that isn't stated explicitly, you may have to check successive numbers to find whether there is a common difference (arithmetic) or ratio (geometric).

Hint: If you have to identify a sequence and the numbers increase or decrease rapidly, your first guess should be a geometric sequence, so check for common ratios first. Otherwise, common differences (for an arithmetic sequence) are quicker to find.

4.7 MATRICES

4.7.1 Matrix Notation

A **matrix** is simply a way to organize data in columns and rows. A **matrix** is denoted by square brackets around the **elements**, or entries, which make up the matrix. The number of rows and columns of a matrix are called its **dimensions**. The number of rows is the first dimension, and the number of columns is the second dimension, so $\begin{bmatrix} 5 & 7 \\ -3 & 0 \\ \frac{2}{3} & 1 \end{bmatrix}$ is a 3×2 matrix, and $[4 \quad 3 \quad 20 \quad 2a]$ is a 1×4 matrix. These two matrices (plural of matrix) show that the elements can be integers or fractions (even decimals), positive or negative, or even unknowns.

A square matrix (number of rows = number of columns) is a special matrix because it can be evaluated by its **determinant**. For example, the determinant of $\begin{bmatrix} 1 & 3 \\ 4 & 2 \end{bmatrix}$ has the same elements as the matrix and is written between two vertical lines, not brackets, to indicate that it is being evaluated:

$$\begin{vmatrix} 1 & 3 \\ 4 & 2 \end{vmatrix}$$

The value of a 2×2 determinant is found by multiplying the elements on the main diagonal, which starts at the upper left corner, and then subtracting the product of the elements in the other diagonal. This specific order is important because subtraction is not commutative — it makes a difference which value is subtracted from which value. Always start at the upper left corner. The value for the determinant $\begin{vmatrix} 1 & 3 \\ 4 & 2 \end{vmatrix}$ is $(1)(2) - (3)(4) = 2 - 12 = -10$. Simultaneous equations can be solved by using matrices, as shown in Chapter 3, Section 3.4.4.

Hint: The order of the diagonals used to evaluate the determinant is the same order as we used for cross-multiplication in proportions.

NOTE: Even though the determinant symbols look like absolute value signs, determinants are not absolute values, and their values can be negative.

4.7.2 Operations on Matrices

4.7.2a Matrix Addition and Subtraction

Matrix addition and subtraction is similar to vector addition and subtraction. In fact, vectors are presented as matrices with either one row or one column.

Addition and subtraction of matrices can be done only between matrices with the same dimensions, and is done element by element for elements in the corresponding positions. The result is a new matrix of the same dimensions in which each element is the sum of the corresponding elements of the previous matrices. Whereas the commutative property of addition allows the matrices to be presented in any order, this property does not hold for subtraction, so it is important to indicate which matrix is being subtracted. For example,

$$\begin{bmatrix} 1 & -2 \\ 0 & 23 \\ 2 & 2 \\ 3a & c \end{bmatrix} + \begin{bmatrix} 7 & 4 \\ 3 & -18 \\ 4 & -4 \\ b & -6 \end{bmatrix} = \begin{bmatrix} 8 & 2 \\ 3 & 5 \\ 6 & -2 \\ 3a+b & c-6 \end{bmatrix} \text{ and } \begin{bmatrix} 7 & -2 \\ 0 & 19 \\ 2 & 5 \\ 3a & b \end{bmatrix} - \begin{bmatrix} 7 & 1 \\ 4 & 18 \\ 6 & -2 \\ a & -5 \end{bmatrix} = \begin{bmatrix} 0 & -3 \\ -4 & 1 \\ -4 & 7 \\ 2a & b+5 \end{bmatrix}$$

4.7.2b Multiplication of a Matrix by a Scalar

Each element of a matrix is multiplied by the scalar. For example,

$$6\begin{bmatrix} 1 & 2 \\ -3 & -4 \end{bmatrix} = \begin{bmatrix} 6 & 12 \\ -18 & -24 \end{bmatrix}$$

4.7.2c Matrix Multiplication by a Matrix

Although most multiplications are commutative, multiplication is *not commutative* for matrices. Two matrices, $\vec{S}$ and $\vec{T}$, can be multiplied only if the number of columns in $\vec{S}$ equals the number of rows in $\vec{T}$. If not, they just cannot be multiplied, and their multiplication is "not defined."

You can check quickly whether a given multiplication is defined. Write the matrix dimensions of each matrix next to each other. If the middle numbers match, the product is defined, and in fact the two outer numbers will give the dimensions of the product. For example, to check whether

$$\begin{bmatrix} 3 & 4 \\ 2 & 1 \\ 0 & -1 \end{bmatrix} \text{ and } \begin{bmatrix} -3 & 2 \\ 1 & -2 \end{bmatrix}$$ can be multiplied, just write their dimensions (row × column):

$$(3 \times 2) \qquad (2 \times 2).$$

Sure enough, the middle numbers match, so they can be multiplied, and the result will be a 3 × 2 matrix, shown by the outer numbers.

Let's do the multiplication. It is just a little tricky, but easy when you get the hang of it.

$$\begin{bmatrix} 3 & 4 \\ 2 & 1 \\ 0 & -1 \end{bmatrix} \begin{bmatrix} -3 & 2 \\ 1 & -2 \end{bmatrix} = \begin{bmatrix} 3(-3)+4(1) & 3(2)+4(-2) \\ 2(-3)+1(1) & 2(2)+1(-2) \\ 0(-3)+-1(1) & 0(2)+-1(-2) \end{bmatrix} = \begin{bmatrix} -5 & -2 \\ -5 & 2 \\ -1 & 2 \end{bmatrix}$$

All of this can be done mentally, rather than writing on paper, once the pattern is established. The clue is where to place each of the computed elements. The pattern shows up if we look at the first numbers in each element—they are the column elements in the left matrix. And the numbers in parentheses are the row elements of the second matrix.

4.7.3 Matrix Applications

Matrix mathematics has many applications, among them a systematic way for mathematicians, scientists, and engineers to represent groups of equations. Matrix arithmetic embedded in graphic processing algorithms are mainstays in video games. For example, in the Cartesian x-y plane, the matrix $\begin{bmatrix} 1 & 0 \\ 0 & -1 \end{bmatrix}$ reflects an object vertically. In a video game, this would render the upside-down mirror image of a dungeon reflected in a lake. Computer animation is based on matrix mathematics.

Many Internet and computer programming companies also use matrices as data structures to track user information, perform search queries, and manage databases. In the world of information security, many public key cryptosystems are designed to work with matrices over finite fields, in particular those that are designed with speed of decryption as a goal. In fact, one of the most important uses of matrices is encryption of message codes, including sensitive and private data. Matrices also are the base elements for robot movements.

So even though we are surrounded by applications of matrix mathematics, few of us recognize it or consciously apply it in our day-to-day lives.

Chapter 4 Exercises

Answers are on the following pages.

1. Which of the following cannot possibly be a root of the polynomial

    $x^4 - x^3 + 2x^2 - 4x - 8 = 0$?

    (A) ± 2

    (B) ± 4

    (C) 0

    (D) ± 8

2. What is the third term of $(a + b)^4$?

    (A) $6a^2b^2$

    (B) $6a^3b$

    (C) $4a^2b^2$

    (D) $4a^3b$

3. The expansion of the logarithmic expression $\ln x^2 y^3$ is

    (A) $(2 \ln x)(3 \ln y)$.

    (B) $(2 \log x)(3 \log y)$.

    (C) $2 \ln x + 3 \ln y$.

    (D) $5 \ln (x + y)$.

4. What is the result of the following matrix multiplication?

$$\begin{bmatrix} a & b \\ c & d \\ e & f \end{bmatrix} \times \begin{bmatrix} 1 & 0 & 0 \\ 0 & 1 & 0 \\ 0 & 0 & 1 \end{bmatrix}$$

(A) $\begin{bmatrix} a & b \\ c & d \\ e & f \end{bmatrix}$

(B) $\begin{bmatrix} b & d & f \\ a & c & e \end{bmatrix}$

(C) $\begin{bmatrix} a & c & e \\ b & d & f \end{bmatrix}$

(D) Cannot be done.

5. Which of the following is a geometric sequence?

(A) 2, 4, 8, 16, 30, 32, . . .

(B) 2, 4, 6, 8, 10, 12, . . .

(C) 2, 4, 8, 16, 32, 64, . . .

(D) 2, 4, 8, 10, 20, 40, . . .

Answers and Explanations

1. (C)

If a root equaled 0, the equation would read $-8 = 0$, which is impossible. That answers the question of what value of x cannot be possible right away. Although answer choices (A), (B), and (D) could be roots, it is not necessary to check them out.

2. (A)

Using Pascal's triangle, the coefficients of the 4th power of the binomial $(a + b)$ are 1, 4, 6, 4, 1, so the third term has a coefficient of 6, which eliminates answer choices (C) and (D). The power of a starts at 4, the power of the binomial, and goes down by 1 for each term, so the power of a in the third term is a^2, which means answer choice (A) is correct.

3. **(C)**

Use the definition that $\ln x^a$ means $a \ln x$, and that the logarithm of a product is the sum of the logarithms.

4. **(D)**

Matrix multiplication is possible only if the number of columns in the left matrix equals the number of rows in the right matrix.

5. **(C)**

Remember that every term must to be multiplied by a common ratio (here, 2) to get the next term. That is true in answer choice (A) for only the first four terms. Answer choice (B) is an arithmetic sequence. Answer choice (D) has a common ratio of 2, except for from 8 to 10, where the difference, not ratio, is 2. Be sure to check all the numbers in each choice until there is, or is not, a common ratio.

Before you begin your review, take this short self-assessment to see how well you know the topics covered in this chapter. Answering all or some correctly will help you identify your strengths so you can focus on those topics where you need the most review. Even if you answer all of the questions correctly, we suggest you still review all the examples in the chapter to ensure you're in good shape to move on. Answers are on the following page.

1. $f(x) = \dfrac{x}{x^2 - 1}$ is

   (A) an even function.

   (B) an odd function.

   (C) neither an even nor an odd function.

   (D) both an even and an odd function.

2. A functional relation may be expressed in all but which of the following ways:

   (A) by an equation.

   (B) as a number line.

   (C) by a graph.

   (D) by a table of values.

3. What is the notation for the inverse of $f(x)$?

   (A) $f'(x)$

   (B) $\dfrac{1}{f(x)}$

   (C) $f^{-1}(x)$

   (D) $-f(x)$

4. The composition $(f \circ g)(x)$ means $f(g(x))$. If $f(x) = x + 2$ and $g(x) = x^2 - 2$, then $f \circ g(x) =$

   (A) $x^2 + x.$

   (B) $x^2.$

   (C) $(x + 2)^2 - 2.$

   (D) $x^2 + 4x + 2.$

5. An example of a periodic function does NOT include:

   (A) tides.

   (B) a bouncing ball.

   (C) side-to-side motion of a pendulum.

   (D) planetary rotation (the time of day).

1. (B)

$f(-x) = \dfrac{-x}{x^2 - 1} \neq F(x)$, so it isn't even, but $-f(x) = -\dfrac{x}{x^2 - 1} = f(-x)$, so it is odd.
(Section 5.6)

2. (B)

A number line does not show a relation between two variables, which is what a function is. (Section 5.3)

3. (C)

Answer choice (A) is the first derivative of $f(x)$; (B) is the reciprocal of $f(x)$; and (D) is the opposite of $f(x)$. Answer choice (C), $f^{-1}(x)$, is the standard notation for the inverse of $f(x)$. It is not the same as answer choice (B). (Section 5.4)

4. (B)

Answer choice (B) is $(f \circ g)(x) = f(g(x)) = (x^2 - 2) + 2 = x^2$, which is correct. Answer choice (A) is the sum of the two functions, and answer choices (C) and (D) are equivalent, but they are answers for $(g \circ f)(x)$. (Section 5.5)

5. (B)

Periodic functions are defined by motion that repeats itself after equal intervals of time. This is the case for each of the answer choices except a bouncing ball (B) because due to gravity and other forces on the ball, the height of the ball decreases, as does the time between bounces. (Section 5.3.8)

CHAPTER 5

Competency 3: Functions

5.1 FUNCTION DEFINITIONS

A **relation** is a set (collection) of **elements** called **ordered pairs** in the form (x, y), for example. The order within each element makes a difference—the element $(2, 3)$ is not the same as $(3, 2)$. For each ordered pair of a relation, the first part of the element (usually x) is a member of the set called the **domain**; and the second part (usually y) is a member of the set called the **range**, which is the same definition that is used, for example, in graphing a linear equation, in which each coordinate is given in (x, y), or (domain, range), order.

The elements in a relation can be written in set notation, indicated by braces. For example, relation A can be defined as $A = \{(5, 7), (5, 1), (a, b), (\text{bee}, \text{hive})\}$. Notice that the elements can consist of numbers, letters, or even "things." There is no repetition of elements in a relation, so if we want to add another element to set A, it can't be the same as the four elements already in the set. Set A is a relation, but it's *not* a function. Let's see why.

A **function** is a special kind of relation. In a function, each different element in the domain has exactly one element in the range assigned to it. That means elements in the range can be repeated in a function, but elements in the domains cannot. So set A shown above is not a function because in the domain 5 is repeated and it has two values in the range. Set $B = \{(5, 7), (7, 5), (a, b), (\text{bee}, \text{hive})\}$ and set $C = \{(5, 7), (6, 7), (7, 7), (8, 7)\}$ are functions. No two elements have the same first coordinate in either set, and that's all that matters.

Many functions are equations for which all of the solutions are ordered pairs. For example, for the equation $y = x + 2$, if we restrict the set of elements for the domain to be $\{-2 \le x \le 1\}$, then the set of elements for the solution is $\{(-2, 0), (-1, 1), (0, 2), (1, 3)\}$. Since this equation is clearly a function (because for every x, there is only one y), we use the function notation $f(x)$ for y.

$f(x) = \{x + 2 : -2 \leq x \leq 1\}$ has the same meaning as $y = \{x + 2 : -2 \leq x \leq 1\}$ but emphasizes that $x + 2$ is a function of x. The colon is read as "such that."

Likewise, x is just a placeholder that shows where the input goes and what happens to it. Anything, usually letters, can be used for the input. So $f(x) = x^2 + x + 1$ is the same as $f(q) = q^2 + q + 1$ or even $f(\text{pig}) = (\text{pig})^2 + (\text{pig}) + 1$, which doesn't make much sense. The variable (x, q, pig) just tells where to put the values, so if we substitute $x = 2$ into $f(x) = x^2 + x + 1$, we get $f(2) = 2^2 + 2 + 1 = 7$.

For a relation to be a function, it doesn't have to be in the $f(x)$ format—it just has to have only one output for each input. An example of a function is buying cookies at a price of 50 cents each. Two cookies cost \$1.00, 4 cost \$2.00, and so on. The cost is a *function* of the number of cookies bought because for every number of cookies there is only one cost. In function notation, this would be cost × (number of cookies) = \$0.50 × (number of cookies), or $C = .50n$, where C is the cost in dollars and n is the number of cookies.

The values of the domain and range of a function may be limited to a specific interval. For example, the domain of $f(x) = \sqrt{x}$ is limited to $x \geq 0$ because the square root of a negative number isn't real. The range of $f(x) = \sqrt{x}$ is $f(x) \geq 0$ because we consider only positive square roots. As discussed in Chapter 3, **interval notation** is a pair of numbers that are the endpoints of the interval with a parenthesis and/or bracket to show whether the endpoint is excluded or included in the interval. A parenthesis shows that the endpoint is not included, and a bracket shows that it is. For example, for the interval $-3 < x \leq 7$, interval notation is $(-3, 7]$, showing that the -3 is not included but 7 is. If there is no restriction, use ∞ or $-\infty$ as the endpoint, but use a parenthesis with infinity because there is no real endpoint—it goes on forever. For $f(x) = \sqrt{x}$, the domain is $[0, \infty)$ and the range is also $[0, \infty)$.

5.2 VERTICAL LINE TEST

Many equations are functions, which can easily be seen when they are graphed. This is not to be interpreted as saying that graphing many functions is easy because some are indeed difficult. Here we concentrate on the graphs of relations that can easily be recognized as functions (or nonfunctions). Remember that the criterion is that for every input there is one and only one output. Commonly, when $y = f(x)$, this translates into "for every x there is one and only one y." Some common graphs can be seen clearly as functions because they don't "double back."

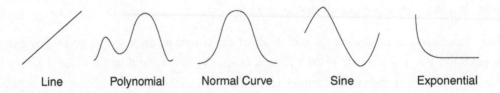

Line   Polynomial   Normal Curve   Sine   Exponential

Other graphs are certainly not functions:

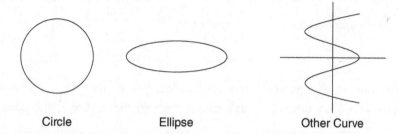

Circle   Ellipse   Other Curve

In fact, if you have the graph of a relation, an easy test, called the **vertical line test**, determines whether it is a function. If every vertical line that can be drawn through the graph has only one point of intersection with the graph, it is a function. If there are two or more points of intersection, it isn't a function. That's all there is to it. To illustrate, imagine a series of vertical lines (parallel to the *y*-axis) through all of the graphs shown above.

5.3 TYPES OF FUNCTIONS

5.3.1 Linear Functions

For a linear equation, for every *x*, there is one and only one value of $f(x)$, so a linear equation (except x = constant) is always a function. The graph of a linear equation is a straight line, and we can easily see that a linear equation is a function because it certainly passes the vertical line test.

5.3.2 Quadratic Functions

As shown in Chapter 4, the second-degree functions called **quadratic functions** graph as **parabolas**. All parabolas are basically U-shaped, opening up or down, and have one lowest (or highest) point called the **vertex**. Parabolas may or may not have *x*-intercepts, but they will always have a single *y*-intercept. The **domain** of a quadratic equation is all real numbers.

The general form of a parabola, $f(x) = ax^2 + bx + c$, gives information about the shape of the parabola. The sign of *a* determines whether the parabola opens up (positive *a*) or down (negative *a*). For any quadratic function $f(x)$, the *x*-coordinate of the vertex is the value $x = -\dfrac{b}{2a}$, and the *y*-coordinate is the corresponding value $y = f\left(-\dfrac{b}{2a}\right)$. Thus, the vertex is the point

$$\text{vertex} = \left(-\frac{b}{2a}, f\left(-\frac{b}{2a}\right)\right)$$

Hint: Once the x value at the vertex, $x = -\dfrac{b}{2a}$ is found, simply use that x value in the equation to find the y value at the vertex.

The axis of symmetry of a parabola is a vertical line that divides the parabola into two congruent halves. The axis of symmetry always passes through the vertex of the parabola; it is the vertical line $x = -\dfrac{b}{2a}$. In other words, to sketch the graph of a parabola, put it in the general form $f(x) = ax^2 + bx + c$, determine whether the parabola will open up $(\cup)$ or down $(\cap)$ by the sign of a, and draw the parabola by using the following points.

1. The vertex is point $\left(-\dfrac{b}{2a}, f\left(-\dfrac{b}{2a}\right)\right)$.

2. The y-intercept is always the point $(0, c)$, since $f(0) = a(0)^2 + b(0) + c = c$.

3. The x-intercept(s), if there are any, are the solutions to $f(x) = 0$, or $ax^2 + bx + c = 0$. These are also called the **zeros** of the function. They are the real solutions to the quadratic formula, as seen in Chapter 3, Section 3.8.2.

4. The line $x = -\dfrac{b}{2a}$ is the axis of symmetry. Since a parabola is symmetric around this axis, any point that is found on one side of the axis of the parabola has a mirror image on the other side.

EXAMPLE 5.1

What is the vertex of the parabola $f(x) = 2x^2 - x - 1$?

SOLUTION 5.1

The x value of the vertex of a parabola of the form $f(x) = ax^2 + bx + c$ is given by $x = -\dfrac{b}{2a}$. For this parabola, $a = 2$, $b = -1$, $c = -1$, so the x value of the vertex of this parabola is $x = -\dfrac{-1}{2(2)} = \dfrac{1}{4}$. The corresponding y value is $f\left(\dfrac{1}{4}\right) = 2\left(\dfrac{1}{4}\right)^2 - \left(\dfrac{1}{4}\right) - 1 = \dfrac{2}{16} - \dfrac{4}{16} - \dfrac{16}{16} = -\dfrac{18}{16} = -\dfrac{9}{8}$. The vertex is thus $\left(\dfrac{1}{4}, -\dfrac{9}{8}\right)$.

5.3.3 Polynomial Functions

A **polynomial function** of degree n is of the form

$$f(x) = a_n x^n + a_{n-1} x^{n-1} + \ldots + a_1 x + a_0,$$

where all a_i are real numbers and $a_n \neq 0$. The **domain** of polynomial functions is all real numbers $(-\infty, \infty)$, but the **range** and the **roots** of a polynomial depend on the equation $a_n x^n + a_{n-1} x^{n-1} + \ldots + a_1 x + a_0 = 0$. The graph crosses the y-axis when $x = 0$, so the y-intercept is $y = a_0$. Chapter 4 (Section 4.4.2) shows the method for finding the real roots of a polynomial.

The only general statements that can be made for a polynomial are:

- The domain is all real numbers $(-\infty, \infty)$.

- The y-intercept is $y = a_0$.

- The general shape of the graph of a polynomial, where a_n represents the coefficient of the highest power of x, is as shown below. The graph within the dotted line portions may increase, decrease, or both, depending on the equation.

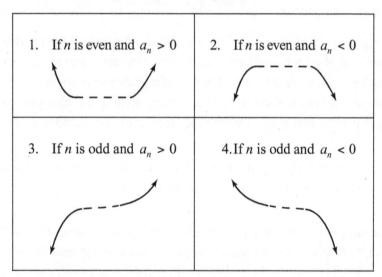

1. If n is even and $a_n > 0$
2. If n is even and $a_n < 0$
3. If n is odd and $a_n > 0$
4. If n is odd and $a_n < 0$

- Any real roots (values for which $x = 0$) can be described (but not actually found) by using Descartes' Rule of Signs. Any complex roots come in pairs, $c + di$ and $c - di$. The actual roots are often not easy to find (see Chapter 4, Section 4.4.2c).

5.3.4 Rational Functions

A **rational function** is the quotient of two polynomials. Rational numbers, which can be written as fractions, include all integers, since integers can be written with a denominator of 1. In addition, the denominator cannot equal 0. The same is true for rational functions, for which the numerator and denominator are usually, but not exclusively, polynomials of degree 2 or more. The following discussion involves only these types of rational functions, which take the form of

$$f(x) = \frac{a(x)}{b(x)} = \frac{a_m x^m + a_{m-1} x^{m-1} + \ldots + a_1 x + a_0}{b_n x^n + b_{n-1} x^{n-1} + \ldots + b_1 x + b_0}$$

Rational functions may have asymptotes. **Asymptotes** are lines to which a curve gets closer and closer but never crosses. On the graph of a curve that has asymptotes, the asymptotes are not part of the curve but they may be drawn in as dashed lines to show that the curve gets close to that particular line. A rational function may have several **vertical asymptotes** but only either one or no **horizontal asymptote** (values that the function approaches as the variable in the function approaches $+\infty$ or $-\infty$) or one or no **slant asymptote** (an oblique, or slanted, line (such as $y = x$) similar to the horizontal asymptote).

Vertical asymptotes of a rational function, if any exist, occur wherever the denominator equals zero and the numerator does not equal zero. To find the vertical asymptote(s), solve the equation formed when the denominator equals zero. However, if both denominator and numerator equal zero at some point, there is a hole in the graph, or a missing point in an otherwise continuous graph. When graphing, remember that vertical asymptotes consist of x-values that are not allowed.

 Remember that the degree of the polynomials discussed here is the largest exponent of the x variable in any term (see Chapter 4, Section 4.4).

There can be one or no horizontal asymptotes. To determine whether the rational function has a horizontal asymptote, look at the degrees of the numerator and denominator:

- If the degree of the numerator is higher than the degree of the denominator, there is no horizontal asymptote.

- If the degree of the numerator is lower than the degree of the denominator, the horizontal asymptote is the line $y = 0$ (the x-axis).

- If the degree of the numerator is the same as the degree of the denominator, the horizontal asymptote is the line $y = \frac{a_m}{b_n}$, where a_m is the coefficient of the highest power variable in the numerator and b_n is the coefficient of the highest power of that same variable in the denominator.

EXAMPLE 5.2

Does the function $\dfrac{x^3 - 2x + 3}{x^5 + x^4 - 3x^3}$ have a horizontal asymptote?

SOLUTION 5.2

Yes, the degree of the numerator is 3 and the degree of the denominator is 5, so the horizontal asymptote is the line $y = 0$ (the x-axis).

EXAMPLE 5.3

Does the function $\dfrac{x^5 + x^4 - 3x^3}{x^3 - 2x + 3}$ have a horizontal asymptote?

SOLUTION 5.3

No, because the degree of the numerator (5) is higher than the degree of the denominator (3).

A slant asymptote is any asymptote that is neither vertical nor horizontal. A rational function in which the degree of the numerator is one greater than the degree of the denominator has a slant asymptote, which is found by painstakingly using polynomial long division, ignoring any remainder.

Rational functions can have at most only one horizontal *or* one slant asymptote, independent of whether the function has any vertical asymptotes. An exponential function is an example of a function with one horizontal asymptote (see Chapter 4, Section 4.3.2). Note that the horizontal or slant asymptote indicates how the curve behaves as the variable in the function approaches $+\infty$ or $-\infty$. It is possible for the curve to cross the asymptote at other locations, as shown in the figures below, in which $g(x)$ crosses a horizontal asymptote (left figure) and a slant asymptote (right figure).

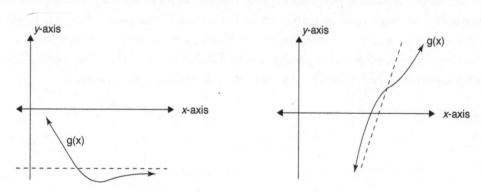

5.3.5 Piecewise Functions

Just as the name implies, **piecewise functions** are pieces of different functions defined for a particular scenario. They are graphed all on one graph. An example of a piecewise function is:

$$f(x) = \begin{cases} x^2 - 2, & \text{for } x < 1 \\ -2x + 4, & \text{for } x \geq 1 \end{cases}$$

which looks like

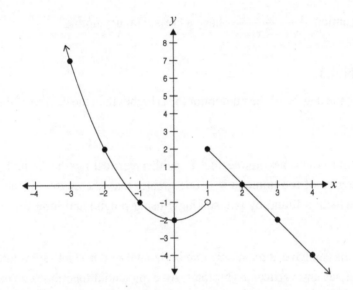

From the graph, this piecewise relationship is indeed a function because for every x there is only one y. For this function we must determine which interval x falls into, and then determine $f(x)$ accordingly. For example, for $x < 1$, the graph is simply $f(x) = x^2 - 2$; and for $1 \leq x \leq 4$, the graph is $f(x) = -2x + 4$. (Each piece is independent of the others, but they may share an endpoint—which they do not here—in which case the graph may be continuous at that point.) At $x = 1$, however, the graph is discontinuous because the two relationships don't have the same $f(x)$ value there. At $x = 1$, one function includes that point and one doesn't. Note that $f(x) = -x^2 - 2$ is an open point of the graph at $x = 1$, although $f(x) = -2x + 4$ does have a value at $x = 1$, and that point is solid.

5.3.6 Step Function

The step function has constant values that vary between given intervals. It is a special type of piecewise function that has a countable number of pieces. Its name comes from the appearance of the function as a set of stairs when graphed. A common step function is a taxi fare that jumps up every 0.2 mile. The graph of cost versus time in Example 5.4 illustrates a step function.

EXAMPLE 5.4

A handyman's fee is based on the length of time that he works:

- 1 hour or less costs $50

- From 1 to 2 hours costs $80 total, or an additional $30

- Over 2 hours costs $80 plus $20 per 15-minute interval above 2 hours.

What is the function for this fee schedule?

SOLUTION 5.4

$$f(t, \text{ in hours}) = \begin{cases} \$50 & \text{if } t \leq 1 \\ \$80 & \text{if } 1 < t \leq 2 \\ \$80 + \$80\left(\dfrac{t-2}{4}\right) & \text{if } t > 2 \end{cases}$$

5.3.7 Absolute Value Function

A well-known example of a piecewise function is the absolute value function. When we speak of an absolute value function, it is important to know whether we mean the absolute value of the function itself or a function that contains an absolute value term. An absolute value function that is the absolute value of the function itself can be written as the piecewise function

$$f(x) = |x| = \begin{cases} x & \text{for } x \geq 0 \\ -x & \text{for } x \leq 0 \end{cases},$$

which is continuous because at $x = 0$, both functions have the same value. An example of a function that contains an absolute value is $f(x) = |x| + 3$.

The shape of an absolute value function is a V that is symmetric around a vertex. The general form of an absolute value function is $f(x) = |x - h| + k$, where (h, k) is the vertex. Therefore, for $f(x) = |x| + 3$, the vertex is at $(0, 3)$ and we can construct a table of values around that point by choosing *x* values 1 and 2 units above it and below it. Put the vertex in the middle of the five values and fill in the others to get:

x	*y*
2	5
1	4
0	3
–1	4
–2	5

The symmetric shape is becoming evident. The graph looks like

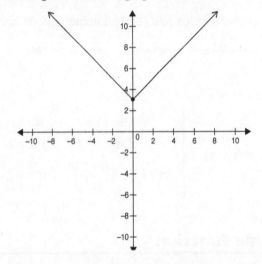

Remember that absolute value changes the value of the expression inside the absolute value signs to a positive value. Therefore, consider that $f(x) = |x| + 3$ has two conditions, one for $x \geq 0$ and one for $x \leq 0$. Therefore, we have the piecewise function

$$f(x) = |x| + 3 = \begin{cases} x + 3 & \text{if } x \geq 0 \\ -x + 3 & \text{if } x \leq 0 \end{cases}.$$

The graph will be the same as we found above. In fact, graphing the function of any absolute value of x ($f(|x|)$) reflects the points to the left of the axis of symmetry of the original function $f(x)$ across the *y*-axis, so they correspond to the points of the original function $f(x)$, which are retained. The **axis of symmetry** of an absolute value function is the vertical line through the vertex (similar to the axis of symmetry of a parabola). If there was a *y*-intercept of $f(x)$, it is also the *y*-intercept of $f(|x|)$.

If the absolute value is preceded by a minus sign, such as in $f(x) = -|x + 1|$ the graph is in the shape of an upside-down V since now the *y* values of all the points of $f(x) = |x + 1|$ are negatives.

In contrast, the absolute value of an entire function, $|f(x)|$, retains the points of the original function that were above the x-axis, but flips the points that were below the x-axis to above the x-axis so they become a mirror reflection across the x-axis. ($f(x) \rightarrow |f(x)|$). This produces graphs such as those shown below.

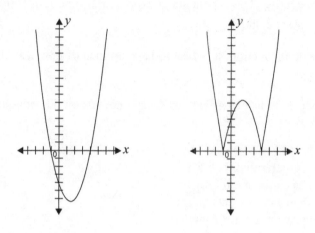

5.3.8 Periodic Functions

Periodic functions repeat on a set interval. One complete repetition of the output values of a periodic function is called a **cycle**. The **period** is the horizontal length of one cycle. Examples of periodic functions are sound waves, tides, and heartbeats. Periodic functions are useful because the period determines the value of the function anywhere in the domain. The period is the smallest repeat value for the function. In other words, if a function has period n, then $f(x) = f(x + n)$ over the entire domain of the function. A typical periodic function is shown in the figure below.

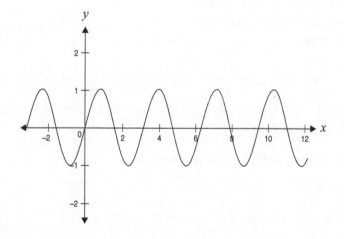

All trigonometric functions are periodic (see Chapter 8, Section 8.3). Chapter 8, Section 8.6.1 presents in detail transformations on the basic sine function.

5.3.9 Exponential Functions

An **exponential function** is a function of the form $f(x) = b^x$, where b is a fixed number called the **base**, and x can be any real number. The base has certain restrictions: $b > 0$ and $b \neq 1$. The exponent can be positive or negative. The exponents in exponential functions follow all of the rules for exponents shown in Chapters 2 and 4.

To graph an exponential function, it is best to have an idea of how it will look. Features of all exponential graphs include:

- Whether the function indicates growth or decay depends on the value of the base, b.

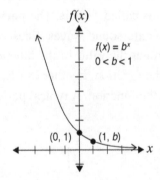

A base greater than 1, $b > 1$, indicates exponential growth, or an increase as x gets larger and approaches a horizontal asymptote of the x-axis as x gets smaller.

A base less than 1, $0 < b < 1$ (remembering the restrictions that $b > 0$ and $b \neq 1$), indicates exponential decay, or a decreasing function. The value of the function gets smaller and approaches a horizontal asymptote of the x-axis as x gets larger.

- The domain of $f(x) = b^x$ is all real numbers, and the range is all positive real numbers.

- The graph of $f(x) = b^x$ must pass through the point (0, 1) because any number, except zero, raised to the zero power is 1.

- The y-intercept of the graph $f(x) = b^x$ is always 1.

- At $x = 1$, $f(1) = b$

- The graph of $f(x) = b^x$ always has a horizontal asymptote at the x-axis.

5.4 INVERSE FUNCTIONS

Inverse functions behave the same way as other inverses; that is, an inverse function undoes the action of the function. An inverse function of $f(x)$ is denoted $f^{-1}(x)$, and it is found by switching the x to y and y to x in the original function, and then solving for y. In other words, if $f(x)$ is a function that maps x to y, then the inverse function $f^{-1}(x)$ maps y back to x. Graphically, $f^{-1}(x)$ is a reflection of $f(x)$ across the line $y = x$.

Note that not all inverses of functions are also functions. A function $f(x)$ has an inverse *function* only if for every y in its range there is only one value of x in its domain. Any function whose inverse is also a function is termed a **one-to-one function**, and it is said to be **invertible**, that is, no y-coordinates are ever repeated.

A function is invertible if it passes the "**horizontal line test**," which says that any *horizontal* line can cross the graph at no more than one point. Its inverse will be a function because it will pass the vertical line test that determines functions. Note that the horizontal line test is done on the original function and it is used to determine whether the inverse of that function is also a function. Thus, we can tell whether the inverse of a function is a function without even having to graph its inverse just by checking to see whether any horizontal line crosses the graph in more than one place.

 Parabolas aren't invertible functions because they don't pass the horizontal line test—every line parallel to the x-axis that goes through a parabola does so in two places.

 Use the horizontal line test on a function to check whether it is invertible. If it is not, its inverse is not a function.

To algebraically generate the inverse of a function $f(x)$:

1. Replace "$f(x)$" with y.

2. Solve the resulting equation for x as a function of y.

3. Switch the variables x and y.

4. Solve this new equation for y as a function of x, if possible.

5. The result is the inverse of $f(x)$, designated as $f^{-1}(x)$.

EXAMPLE 5.5

Does the inverse of $f(x) = 5x - 2$ exist? If so, what is it?

SOLUTION 5.5

The original function passes the horizontal line test, so the inverse exists. To find the inverse, follow the steps:

1. Replace "$f(x)$" with y: $y = 5x - 2$

2. Solve for x: $x = \dfrac{y + 2}{5}$.

3. Switch x and y: $y = \dfrac{x + 2}{5}$.

4. Solve for y: the new function is $y = f^{-1}(x) = \dfrac{x + 2}{5}$. This is the inverse of $f(x)$.

EXAMPLE 5.6

Find the inverse function of $f(x) = x^2 + 1$, if it exists.

SOLUTION 5.6

It doesn't exist. This graph doesn't pass the horizontal line test (this is true for all parabolas), so the inverse is not a function.

If we restrict the domain in Example 5.6 to the part of the graph that has an inverse (it passes the horizontal line test), we can find an inverse function within that same constraint, as seen in Example 5.7.

EXAMPLE 5.7

Find the inverse function of $y = x^2 + 1$, $x \le 0$, if it exists.

SOLUTION 5.7

1. The graph passes the horizontal line test and does have an inverse function.

2. Solve $y = x^2 + 1$, $x \le 0$ for x: $x^2 = y - 1$, or $x = -\sqrt{y - 1}$.

3. Since the domain is limited to negative numbers the sign before the square root is only negative.

4. Switch x and y to get $y = -\sqrt{x - 1}$, $x \ge 1$, so every x value will have only one y value, and the inverse exists and is a function. Note that the restriction $x \ge 1$ must be included to avoid the square root of a negative number.

Compare Example 5.7 to Example 5.6. The difference between them is that the domain has been restricted to $x \leq 0$. This restriction makes the graph look like the following:

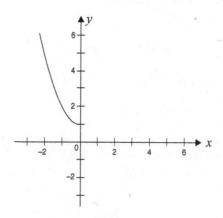

The inverse of this function is also a function because this graph passes the horizontal line test. Here is the graph for this function and its inverse (dashed curve)

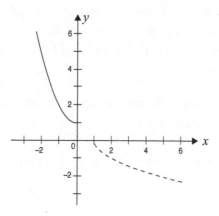

5.5 COMPOSITION OF FUNCTIONS

Simply put, the **composition of functions** is applying one function, let's call it $f(x)$, to the output of another function, let's call that one $g(x)$. The symbol for the composite function would then be $f(g(x))$ or sometimes $(f \circ g)(x)$. In other words, a **composite function**, also called a **function of a function**, is one in which the output of one function, $g(x)$, becomes the input for another, $f(x)$. Work from the innermost function outward. To evaluate the composition $f(g(x))$, it is obvious that we cannot evaluate $f(x)$ without knowing $g(x)$. So first find what $g(x)$ is and then replace the x in the $f(x)$ expression with the expression for $g(x)$; then simplify the result.

The key to understanding the composition of functions is remembering that x is just a placeholder for the input.

EXAMPLE 5.8

If $f(x) = 2x$, what is $f(3x - 1)$?

SOLUTION 5.8

Replace the x in $f(x) = 2x$ with $g(x) = 3x - 1$ to get $f(3x - 1) = 2(3x - 1) = 6x - 2$.

EXAMPLE 5.9

If $f(x) = 2x$ and $g(x) = 3x - 1$, find $g(f(x))$.

SOLUTION 5.9

This example has the same functions as Example 5.8 but this time we have to know $f(x)$ first so we can replace the x in $g(x)$ with that expression. Since $f(x) = 2x$, $g(x)$ now becomes equal to $g(f(x)) = g(2x) = 3(2x) - 1 = 6x - 1$.

$f(g(x))$ usually gives a different answer than $g(f(x))$, so don't get mixed up. Composition is not commutative.

A check on inverses is to verify that $f(f^{-1}(x)) = f^{-1}(f(x)) = 0$. Let's check Example 5.5, in which $f(x) = 5x - 2$ and $f^{-1}(x) = \dfrac{x + 2}{5}$.

$$f(f^{-1}(x)) = 5\left(\frac{x + 2}{5}\right) - 2 = x + 2 - 2 = x$$

$$f^{-1}(f(x)) = \frac{(5x - 2) + 2}{5} = \frac{5x - 2 + 2}{5} = x$$

Values that result from the composition of two functions can also come from a table of the functions.

EXAMPLE 5.10

Given the table below, find $f(g(x))$ for $x = 6$.

x	f(x)	g(x)
0	2	1
2	4	2
4	6	3
6	8	4
8	10	5

SOLUTION 5.10

First we have to find a value for $g(6)$ from the table, which is 4, and substitute that (4) into $f(x)$, which is $f(4) = 6$. So the answer is that for $x = 6$, as given in the table, $f(g(x)) = 6$.

EXAMPLE 5.11

Using the table in Example 5.10, what is the value of $(g \circ g)(x)$ when $x = 6$?

SOLUTION 5.11

From the table, $g(6) = 4$. Then $g \circ g(6) = g(4) = 3$.

The **domain of any function**, including composites, is the set of all possible values of the independent variable that will make the function real. The domain of a composite function is the intersection of the domain of the composite, $f(g(x))$, and the domain of the second function, $g(x)$.

EXAMPLE 5.12

If $f(x) = \dfrac{x}{x+1}$ and $g(x) = \dfrac{4}{x}$, what is the domain of $f(g(x))$?

SOLUTION 5.12

$f(g(x)) = \dfrac{\frac{4}{x}}{\frac{4}{x}+1} = \dfrac{4}{4+x}$. The domain of the composite $f(g(x)) = \dfrac{4}{4+x}$, is all real x except $x = -4$, which would make the denominator equal zero. The domain of the second function, $g(x) = \dfrac{4}{x}$, is all real x except $x = 0$. Therefore, the domain of the composite function is all real x except $x = -4$ and 0.

In Example 5.12, $x = -1$ is not restricted because it affects only $f(x)$, and that function will change when the composition is completed.

EXAMPLE 5.13

If $f(x) = x^2$ and $g(x) = \sqrt{x}$, what is the domain of their composite, $f(g(x))$?

SOLUTION 5.13

The composite function is $f(g(x)) = \left(\sqrt{x}\right)^2 = x$. Usually the domain of x is all real numbers, but the domain of $g(x) = \sqrt{x}$ is all real positive numbers $x \geq 0$ since square roots of negative numbers aren't real. The domain of the composite $f(g(x))$ has to be the intersection of these two domains, so it is all nonnegative real numbers, or $x \geq 0$.

5.6 SYMMETRIC FUNCTIONS

Symmetric functions are reflected around a specific line or point. They can be of two different types, even or odd, or they can be neither, determined by the following rules.

- **Even**: $f(-x) = f(x)$ for all x. The graphs of even functions are symmetric about the y-axis (like a reflection), and functions that are symmetric about the y-axis are even functions. But watch out—an even exponent does not always make an even function—for example, $(x + a)^2$ is *not* an even function because $f(x) = x^2 + 2ax + a^2$ but $f(-x) = x^2 - 2ax + a^2$.

- **Odd**: $f(-x) = -f(x)$ for all x. Odd functions are symmetric with respect to the origin. But watch out again—an odd exponent does not always make an odd function; for example, $(x + a)^3$ is *not* an odd function because $f(-x) = -x^3 + 3x^2a - 3xa^2 + a^3$ but $-f(x) = -x^3 - 3x^2a - 3xa^2 - a^3$.

- **Neither odd nor even**. A function does not have to be even or odd, and in fact most functions are neither. For example, $f(x) = x^3 - x + 1$ is neither because $f(-x) = -x^3 + x + 1$, which equals neither $f(x)$ nor $-f(x) = -x^3 + x - 1$.

Unlike the case for adding odd and even numbers, the sum of two even functions is even, the sum of two odd functions is odd, and the sum of an even function and an odd function is neither, except for $y = 0$. The products also are different from those for numbers: the product of two even functions or two odd functions is always even, and the product of an even and an odd function is always odd.

EXAMPLE 5.14

Is the function $f(x) = \dfrac{3x}{x^2 - 2}$ even or odd?

SOLUTION 5.14

$f(-x) = \dfrac{-3x}{x^2 - 2} = -f(x)$, so it is odd.

5.7 TRANSFORMATIONS OF FUNCTIONS

Transformation is the general term for manipulating a point, a line, or a shape. A **transformation of a function** involves a change of variables or coordinates in which a function of new variables or coordinates is substituted for each original variable or coordinate. In the following discussion of these transformations, the symbol → means "transforms to," and the function is a curve in the *xy*-plane. Transformations of geometric shapes are done similarly, as shown in Chapter 7, Section 7.5.

Transformations of functions can be done in four specific ways:

- Translation

- Dilation (or Compression)

- Reflection

- Rotation

Two transformations can be carried out on one function by doing one transformation and then performing the other transformation on the result.

 If a change is made to the variable, be sure to make that change for every appearance of that variable in $f(x)$. For example, if $f(x) = x^2 + 3x + 5$, then $f(\mathrm{F}x) = (\mathrm{F}x)^2 + 3(\mathrm{F}x) + 5$ and $f(x + \mathrm{C}) = (x + \mathrm{C})^2 + 3(x + \mathrm{C}) + 5$.

5.7.1 Translation

Adding (or subtracting) a constant to (or from) *a function* $f(x)$ shifts the graph vertically but does not change its shape or size. Adding a positive constant A ($f(x) \to f(x) + \mathrm{A}$) shifts every unit up A units; likewise, subtracting a positive constant B ($f(x) \to f(x) - \mathrm{B}$) shifts it down B units.

Adding a positive constant to *a variable* within the function ($f(x) \to f(x + \mathrm{C})$) moves the function to the left (contrary to what instinct might tell you because it shifts –C units); subtracting a positive constant from the variable ($f(x) \rightarrow f(x - D)$) moves the function to the right because it shifts $-(-D) = +D$ units. Again, the size and shape of the function are unchanged.

The table below summarizes the effect of translation on the function $f(x)$ and its coordinates.

Translation	Impact on Coordinates	Impact on function $y = f(x)$
$\lvert h \rvert$ units horizontally Positive h indicates movement to the right Negative h indicates movement to the left	$(x, y) \rightarrow (x + h, y)$	$y = f(x - h)$
$\lvert k \rvert$ units vertically Positive k indicates movement up Negative k indicates movement down	$(x, y) \rightarrow (x, y + k)$	$y = f(x) + k$

Do not confuse adding a positive constant *to a function*, ($f(x) \rightarrow f(x) + A$), which shifts the function up, with adding a constant *to the variable* in a function $f(x)$, which shifts the graph horizontally to the left. And the same holds for the opposite: subtracting a positive constant from a function shifts the function down and subtracting a positive constant from a variable in a function shifts the graph horizontally to the right.

5.7.2 Dilation and Compression

Dilation of a function means it has been stretched away from an axis. All the distances on the coordinate plane are lengthened by multiplying either all x-coordinates (horizontal dilation) or all y-coordinates (vertical dilation) by a factor $E > 1$.

Compression of a function means it has been squeezed toward an axis. All the distances on the coordinate plane are shortened by multiplying either all x-coordinates (horizontal compression) or all y-coordinates (vertical compression) by a factor $0 < E < 1$.

This is a little more difficult to envision than translation because the shape is being changed, as shown in the graphs below. If the left graph is the original graph, vertical *dilation* will change it to look like the right graph. Alternatively, if the right graph is the original graph, vertical *compression* will change it to look like the left graph.

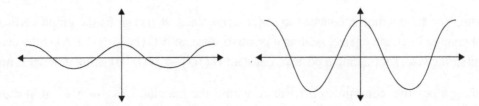

In summary, for curves along the *x*-axis, multiplying a function $f(x)$ by a constant E compresses the graph (makes it squatter) if $0 < E < 1$, or stretches the graph (makes it taller) if $E > 1$, but the *x*-values are unchanged. This is shown in the graphs below, in which the middle curve is the original curve, and it is multiplied by 3 to get the top curve and multiplied by 0.5 to get the bottom curve. Note that the *x* values don't change in a vertical dilation or compression; only the *y* values do.

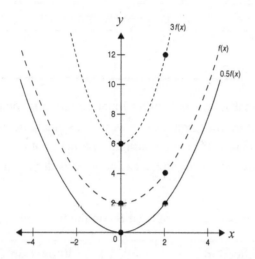

Likewise, for curves along the *y*-axis, multiplying *x* by a constant $F(f(x) \rightarrow f(Fx))$ compresses the graph (makes it narrower) if $F > 1$, or stretches the graph (makes it wider) if $0 < F < 1$, but the *y*-values are unchanged.

 In the *y*-direction, larger values of the constant cause more compression in the *x*-direction. In the *x*-direction, larger values of the constant cause more compression in the *y*-direction.

5.7.3 Reflection

Reflection of a function means reflecting the function over an axis or a line (such as $f(x) = x$) to form a mirror image. Multiplying a function $f(x)$ by −1 reflects its graph across the *x*-axis $(f(x) \rightarrow -f(x))$. Multiplying *x* by −1 reflects the graph across the *y*-axis $(f(x) \rightarrow f(-x))$. Switching *x* and $f(x)$ for a function (the inverse, $f(x) \rightarrow f^{-1}(x)$; see Section 5.1) reflects the graph of the function across the line $y = x$.

The table below summarizes the effect of reflection on the function $f(x)$ and its coordinates.

Reflection	Impact on Coordinates	Impact on function
Reflection over x-axis	$(x, y) \to (x, -y)$	$y = -f(x)$
Reflection over y-axis	$(x, y) \to (-x, y)$	$y = f(-x)$
Reflection over $y = x$	$(x, y) \to (y, x)$	$y = f^{-1}(x)$

5.7.4 Rotation

Rotation of a function that results in another function requires rotating the original function. Rotation by 180° is achieved by changing x to $-x$ as well as changing $f(x)$ to $-f(x)$. If a function is rotated by an angle other than 180°, the resulting graph may not be a function because it won't pass the vertical line test. This can be visualized easily by considering the rotation of a parabola by only 90°.

The table below summarizes the effect of rotation on the function $f(x)$ and its coordinates.

Reflection	Impact on Coordinates
Clockwise rotation 90° about the origin	$(x, y) \to (y, -x)$
Rotation 180° about the origin	$(x, y) \to (-x, -y)$
Clockwise rotation 270° about the origin or counterclockwise by 90°	$(x, y) \to (-y, x)$

5.7.5 Transformation Combinations

Two transformations can be carried out on one function by doing one transformation and then performing the other transformation on the result. For example, multiplying $f(x)$ by -2 will flip its graph upside down *and* stretch it in the y-direction.

EXAMPLE 5.15

What happens in the transformation of $f(x) = (x)^2$ to $g(x) = (-x)^2$?

SOLUTION 5.15

Nothing. Changing x to $-x$ flips $f(x)$ left and right, but it can't be seen because x^2 is an even function—it is symmetrical about the y-axis.

Summary Table of Transformations of $f(x)$

Translation	$f(x) \rightarrow f(x) + C$	$C > 0$ moves $f(x)$ up C units
		$C < 0$ moves $f(x)$ down C units
	$f(x) \rightarrow f(x + C)$	$C > 0$ moves $f(x)$ left C units
		$C < 0$ moves $f(x)$ right C units
Dilation or Compression	$f(x) \rightarrow Cf(x)$	$C > 1$ stretches $f(x)$ vertically by a factor of C
		$0 < C < 1$ compresses $f(x)$
	$f(x) \rightarrow f(Cx)$	$C > 1$ compresses $f(x)$ vertically by a factor of $\dfrac{1}{C}$
		$0 < C < 1$ stretches $f(x)$
Reflection	$f(x) \rightarrow -f(x)$	Reflects $f(x)$ about x-axis
	$f(x) \rightarrow f(-x)$	Reflects $f(x)$ about y-axis

Chapter 5 Exercises

Answers are on the following pages.

1. The surface area of a sphere S is a function of its radius r such that $S = f(r) = 4\pi r^2$. What would $r = f(S)$ be equal to?

    (A) $f(S) = \dfrac{1}{4\pi} S$

    (B) $f(S) = \dfrac{S}{4\pi}$

    (C) $f(S) = \dfrac{1}{2} \sqrt{\dfrac{S}{\pi}}$

    (D) $f(S) = 2\sqrt{\dfrac{S}{\pi}}$

2. The graph of the function $y = f(x) = x^2$ has symmetry

    (A) about the y-axis (even function).

    (B) about the x-axis.

    (C) about the origin (odd function).

    (D) It has no symmetry.

3. Which of the following functions has an inverse?

    I.   A vertical parabola ($y = ax^2 + bx + c$)

    II. A straight line ($y = mx + b$)

    III. An exponential function ($f(x) = b^x$)

    IV. A periodic function ($y = \sin x$)

(A) I and III

(B) II and III

(C) I, II, and IV

(D) All have inverses.

4. Describe the transformations that turn $f(x) = x^2$, is $g(x) = 2(x + 3)^2 + 4$. Describe the transformation. (Choose *all* that apply.)

(A) It stretches $f(x) = x^2$ by 2 units vertically.

(B) It shifts $f(x) = x^2$ to the left 3 units.

(C) It shifts $f(x) = x^2$ up 4 units.

(D) All of the above.

5. The domain and range of the parabola $f(x) = x^2 + 4x + 4$ are

(A) Domain: $-\infty < x < \infty$; Range: $y \geq 0$.

(B) Domain: $-\infty < x < \infty$; Range: $y > 0$.

(C) Domain: $-\infty < x < \infty$; Range: $y \leq 0$.

(D) Domain: $-\infty < x < \infty$; Range: $y < 0$.

Answers and Explanations

1.   (C)

Solve the original equation, $S = f(r) = 4\pi r^2$ for r. $r^2 = \dfrac{S}{4\pi}$, or $r = \sqrt{\dfrac{S}{4\pi}} = \sqrt{\dfrac{1}{4}\left(\dfrac{S}{\pi}\right)} = \dfrac{1}{2}\sqrt{\dfrac{S}{\pi}}$.

Note that we don't consider the negative root because the radius cannot be negative.

2.   (A)

For symmetry around the y-axis, $f(-x) = f(x)$: $f(-x) = (-x)^2 = x^2 = f(x)$. Yes.

Functions cannot have symmetry around the x-axis because it would violate the vertical line test.

For symmetry around the origin, $f(-x) = -f(x)$: $f(-x) = (-x)^2 = x^2$, but $-f(x) = -x^2$. No.

3.   (B)

Of the choices, only a straight line and an exponential function pass the horizontal line test, so only II and III can have inverses.

4.   (D)

The stretch is caused by the coefficient 2 and the shift is caused by adding 3 to x^2, and it is to the left because 3 is positive. The shift is up 4 units because 4 is added to the function.

5.   (A)

The domain of any quadratic equation is $-\infty < x < \infty$ because any real value of x will yield a real value of $f(x)$. Consider the values of a, b, and c when the equation is put in the form $y = ax^2 + bx + c$. The range is all y-values above (if $a > 0$) or below (if $a < 0$) the vertex $\left(f\left(-\dfrac{b}{2a} \right) \right)$, including the value at the vertex. For the given equation, $a > 0$ and since $-\dfrac{b}{2a} = -\dfrac{4}{2} = -2$, $f\left(-\dfrac{b}{2a} \right) = f(-2) = (-2)^2 + 4(-2) + 4 = 0$, so the range is $y \geq 0$.

Before you begin your review, take this short self-assessment to see how well you know the topics covered in this chapter. Answering all or some correctly will help you identify your strengths so you can focus on those topics where you need the most review. Even if you answer all of the questions correctly, we suggest you still review all the examples in the chapter to ensure you're in good shape to move on. Answers are on the following page.

1. In scalene triangle ABC, $\angle A = 60°$. Which of the following statements must be true? (Choose *all* that apply.)

    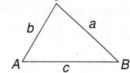

    (A) Side $b = \dfrac{1}{2}c$.

    (B) If $\angle B = 35°$, then $\angle C = 85°$.

    (C) $\angle B = 30°$.

    (D) If $\angle B = 35°$, then side c is the longest side.

2. Which of the following properties is NOT true for the diagonals of a square $ABCD$?

    (A) $BD = AC$.

    (B) BD is perpendicular to AC.

    (C) BD is parallel to AC.

    (D) BD bisects AC.

3. State the circumference of a circle of radius 4 inches in terms of π.

    (A) 4π inches   (C) 8π inches

    (B) 4π square inches   (D) 8π square inches

4. Which of the following quadrilaterals is not a special kind of parallelogram?

    (A) Square   (C) Rectangle

    (B) Rhombus   (D) Kite

5. Lines j and k are parallel. Lines m and n are also parallel. Angle 10 is NOT supplementary to which of the following angles?

    (A) $\angle 11$

    (B) $\angle 3$

    (C) $\angle 15$

    (D) $\angle 6$

    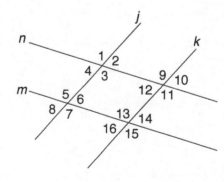

1.   (B) and (D)

For answer choices (B) and (D), if $\angle B = 35°$, then $\angle C = (180° - (60° + 35°)) = 85°$, and since $\angle C$ is the largest angle, the longest side is opposite it, so side c is the longest side. Answer choices (A) and (C) are true only if $\angle C$ is a right angle, but the exercise doesn't state that $\triangle ABC$ is a scalene right triangle, so we cannot assume it is. (Section 6.4)

2.   (C)

The diagonals intersect, so they cannot be parallel to each other. All of the other properties listed are true. (Section 6.5.5)

3.   (C)

Since $C = 2\pi r$, the circumference is $C = 2\pi(4) = 8\pi$ inches. Circumference is length, not area. (Section 6.7.2)

4.   (D)

A parallelogram has two pair of parallel sides. A kite has two nonadjacent pair of equal sides that are not parallel. The other answer choices are special parallelograms. (Section 6.5)

5.   (D)

When two parallel lines are crossed by a transversal, the resulting angles are either equal or supplementary. Angle 10 is supplementary to angles 1, 3, 5, 7, 9, 11, 13, and 15, which all are corresponding angles equal to each other, so if one is supplementary to $\angle 10$, they all are. Angles 9 and 10 are supplementary because they form a straight line. Note that two supplementary angles total 180°; they do not have to be adjacent. (Section 6.3.1)

CHAPTER

Competency 4: Geometry

6

6.1 POINTS, LINES, AND PLANES

6.1.1 Dimensions

The "building blocks" that define the dimensions of the figures that are the basis of Euclidean geometry (plane and solid geometry) are the point (no dimensions), line (one dimension: length), plane (two dimensions: length and width), and so-called solids (three dimensions: length, width, and depth). Three-dimensional figures do not have to be solid—a basketball is three-dimensional and certainly not solid.

6.1.2 Points

Let's start with the most basic geometric object—the **point**. A true point actually has no dimensions (no length, no width, no height). That brings two questions to mind: (1) What good are points? (2) How can we draw them?

Points are used for defining positions. For example, we talk about the position of a point when plotting ordered pairs on a graph. Even though a point has no dimensions, it is real, it isn't invisible, and it's really useful. Points are the building blocks of all other geometric objects. We draw a point as a dot, which even if we use the sharpest pencil, still looks like it has a tiny length and width or maybe looks like a really small circle, but in reality a point is dimensionless.

6.1.3 Lines

A **line** connects two points. A line is actually a string of an infinite number of points together. Lines can be straight or curved. A line is visible, and it has one dimension—length. Between any two points on a line, there is always another point, and so on and so on, so even though you don't see them individually, there are an infinite number of points on a line.

 (Hint:) To get an idea of the infinite number of points on a line, draw a six-inch line segment and label the endpoints *A* and *B*. Put a mark at the halfway point, 3 inches from either end. From that point, make a mark halfway to point *B*, then halfway again, and again, and again. Even though the distance to *B* is getting smaller and smaller, there is always a point that will be in the middle of the remaining distance, and you never get to point *B*.

When you are plotting points on a Cartesian coordinate system to define a straight line, you can get a line by connecting just two points, but it is important to plot a third point because if you made a mistake with the two points, the third point won't line up with them and you'll know you have to check your math. Points that align on a straight line are described as **collinear** points.

When we talk about lines, we should be precise about what kind of line we mean.

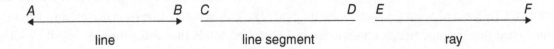

A straight line goes on forever in two directions. Of course, when we draw a line, we can't draw out to outer space, so we indicate that it goes on forever by putting an arrowhead on both ends, and by referring to it as $\overleftrightarrow{AB}$. Often, though, we are using **line segments**, which have endpoints and a definite length. Segments are usually named by their endpoints, such as line segment $\overline{CD}$ for the one pictured above. A **ray** is a special type of line that has an **endpoint** on one "end" and an arrowhead on the other, indicating that it has an endpoint on only one end and it isn't ending in the other direction, like $\overrightarrow{EF}$, shown above. If two or more lines of any kind intersect, their intersection is a **point**.

6.1.4 Planes

A sheet of paper is a pretty good approximation of a **plane**. It has length and width, but appears to have no depth (or height). It is a flat, two-dimensional surface that extends infinitely far in all directions, just like a line extends infinitely far in two directions.

A plane can be determined by three noncollinear points, or a line and a point not in the line (the plane is the platform they all rest on). Points and/or lines that are all in the same plane are termed **coplanar**. An example of noncoplanar points (there would have to be at least four) would be three points on the base of a Pyramid and the fourth point at the tip. An example of noncoplanar lines can be seen easily by looking at the edges of a box. Noncoplanar lines are termed **skew** lines.

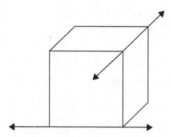

Don't be fooled into thinking any two lines define a plane (meaning both lines rest on the same plane). Often they do, but if you draw a line on a piece of paper and then think of your pencil as a line and hold it above the paper so it isn't parallel with the line you drew, there cannot be a plane that contains both that line and your pencil.

6.2 ANGLES

If we connect two rays at their endpoints, we form an **angle**. The place where the two endpoints meet is called the **vertex** of the angle. The sides of the angle, being rays, go off into space unless we put an endpoint on one or both of them.

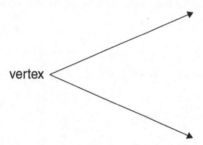

vertex

What distinguishes one angle from another is how wide open it is. The measurement of an angle is based on 360°, which is how many degrees there are in a circle. Indeed, if an angle has 360°, the sides would be on top of each other and they would no longer look like an angle, they would look like a ray.

6.2.1 Types of Angles

An angle that measures 90° is a **right** angle. The rays of a right angle are perpendicular to each other. Any angle that is less than 90° is called **acute**, and any angle greater than 90° and less than 180° is called **obtuse**.

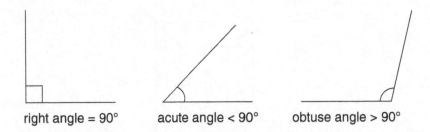

right angle = 90°   acute angle < 90°   obtuse angle > 90°

An angle of exactly 180° is called a **straight angle** because the rays form a straight line. An angle that is greater than 180° but less than 360°, is called a **reflex** angle.

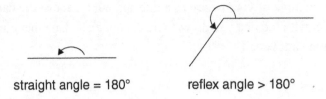

straight angle = 180°   reflex angle > 180°

6.2.2 Angle Relationships

Relationships between angles mostly have to do with their measurements. **Adjacent angles** share a side. Any two angles that total 180° are called **supplementary**, and they need not be adjacent. If they are adjacent, their outer sides form a straight line. Likewise, any two angles that total 90° are called **complementary**, and they need not be adjacent. If they are adjacent, their outer sides form a right angle.

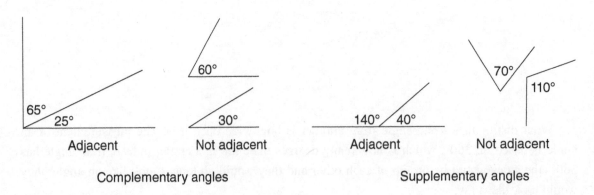

65°   25°   60°   30°   140°   40°   70°   110°

Adjacent   Not adjacent   Adjacent   Not adjacent

Complementary angles   Supplementary angles

When two lines intersect, the nonadjacent angles opposite each other are termed **vertical angles**. Vertical angles always have the same measure. Actually, two intersecting lines form two pairs of vertical angles and four pairs of supplementary angles, as shown in the figure below. The vertical angle pairs are $\angle A = \angle C$ and $\angle B = \angle D$. The supplementary angles are $\angle A$ and $\angle B$, $\angle B$ and $\angle C$, $\angle C$ and $\angle D$, and $\angle D$ and $\angle A$.

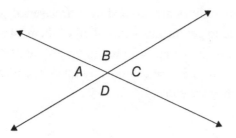

6.3 LINES

6.3.1 Parallel Lines

Two lines that never meet are called **parallel** lines. If parallel lines are crossed by another line, which is called a **transversal**, eight angles are formed.

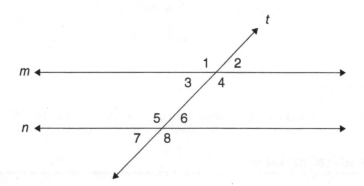

As was just shown in Section 6.2.2, when two lines cross, the angles formed are either **supplementary** or **vertical angles**. The supplementary angle pairs are adjacent angles. In the figure above, the supplementary angles are $\angle 1$ and $\angle 2$, $\angle 3$ and $\angle 4$, $\angle 5$ and $\angle 6$, $\angle 7$ and $\angle 8$, and also $\angle 1$ and $\angle 3$, $\angle 2$ and $\angle 4$, $\angle 5$ and $\angle 7$, $\angle 6$ and $\angle 8$. The vertical angle pairs, which are equal, are $\angle 1 = \angle 4$, $\angle 2 = \angle 3$, $\angle 5 = \angle 8$, $\angle 6 = \angle 7$.

From these relationships, we can see, for example, that $\angle 1 = \angle 5$; these are called **corresponding angles** because they are in corresponding positions (upper left angles) on the two parallel lines (the others are $\angle 2 = \angle 6$, $\angle 3 = \angle 7$, and $\angle 4 = \angle 8$). Likewise, since all of the angles formed by the three lines are either equal or supplementary to each other, we can see that $\angle 1 = \angle 8$ and $\angle 2 = \angle 7$. These angles are called **alternate exterior angles** because they are on *alternate* sides of the transversal and *exterior* to the parallel lines. Similarly, the pairs $\angle 3 = \angle 6$ and $\angle 4 = \angle 5$, are called **alternate interior angles** because they are *interior* to the parallel lines and on *alternate* sides of the transversal of the two parallel lines. The equal angles can be visualized quite readily.

Therefore, when two parallel lines are crossed by a transversal, we need the measure of only one of the eight angles formed to get the measures of all of them, since all of the angles are either supplementary or are vertical (equal) angles. In the figure of parallel lines *m* and *n*, for example, if we know the measure of $\angle 1$ is 105°, we can quickly know the measures of all the other angles formed by the transversal—they are either 75° or 105°.

EXAMPLE 6.1

In the figure of two parallel lines cut by a transversal *t* below, if the measure of $\angle h$ = 67°, what is the measure of $\angle a$?

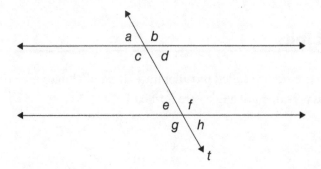

SOLUTION 6.1

$\angle a$ and $\angle h$ are alternate exterior angles, so they are equal, and $\angle a = 67°$.

6.3.2 Perpendicular Lines

Perpendicular lines are two lines that intersect at a right (90°) angle. Since vertical angles are equal, two perpendicular lines form four 90° angles. Right angles play a prominent role in finding the areas of closed figures, as will be seen in the remainder of this chapter. The areas of most figures depend on knowing the altitude of the figure. The **altitude** of a two-dimensional figure, for example, is defined as a line that is perpendicular to one side of the figure and ends at the opposite angle (vertex). The altitude of a three-dimensional figure is similarly perpendicular to one plane and ends at an opposite vertex, or it can be the perpendicular distance between the two sides (e.g., for a cylinder, as shown in Section 6.10.2).

6.3.3 Slopes of Parallel and Perpendicular Lines

Remember from Chapter 3, Section 3.3.2a, that the slope of a straight line ($y = mx + b$) tells its orientation—how the vertical values change in relation to the horizontal values. Slope m is determined by $\dfrac{\text{change in } y}{\text{change in } x}$, or as $m = \dfrac{\Delta y}{\Delta x}$.

The figures below show the slopes of parallel lines (lines that have the same slopes), perpendicular lines (slopes of the lines are negative reciprocals of each other), and nonperpendicular intersecting lines.

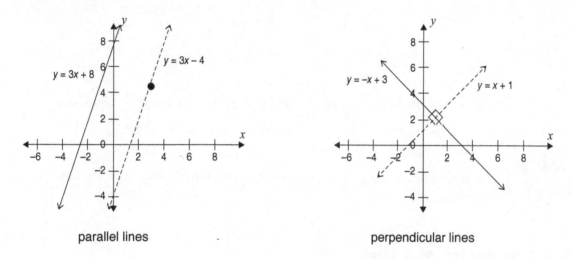

parallel lines   perpendicular lines

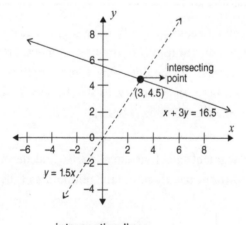

intersecting lines

If you know the slopes of two lines, you don't even have to graph them to see whether they are parallel or perpendicular. Put the equations of the lines in slope-intercept form ($y = mx + b$), and compare the m values.

- Lines with the same slope are all parallel.

- The slopes of perpendicular lines are negative reciprocals of each other.

- If neither of the above are true, two coplanar lines are nonperpendicular intersecting lines.

EXAMPLE 6.2

Are the two lines given by $3x + 4y = 6$ and $3y - 4x = 7$ perpendicular?

SOLUTION 6.2

Put each equation in slope-intercept form:

$$3x + 4y = 6 \qquad\qquad 3y - 4x = 7$$
$$4y = 6 - 3x \qquad\qquad 3y = 4x + 7$$
$$y = -\frac{3}{4}x + \frac{6}{4} \qquad\qquad y = \frac{4}{3}x + \frac{7}{3}$$
$$y = -\frac{3}{4}x + \frac{3}{2}$$

The slope of the first line is $-\dfrac{3}{4}$ and the slope of the second line is $\dfrac{4}{3}$, which are negative reciprocals, so the lines are perpendicular. The answer is "yes."

 For perpendicular lines, the slopes are not just reciprocals, they must also have opposite signs.

6.3.4 Midpoint of a Line

Line segments can be divided into equal parts. If a line segment is divided into two equal parts, the point where they meet is called the **midpoint** of the line segment. That point is exactly halfway between the endpoints of the segment. Midpoints play a prominent role in finding the areas of closed figures as well as other attributes in geometry, as will be seen in the remainder of this chapter. Midpoint formulas are presented in Chapter 7, Section 7.2.3.

 To divide a line segment into four equal parts, find the midpoint using the much easier midpoint formula, and then find the midpoints of the two half-line segments.

6.3.4a Dividing a Line Segment by Using Ratios

To divide a line segment so that the parts are in the same ratio as another line segment, use perpendicular lines. The geometry for this will be evident in Section 6.4.6, but for now it is sufficient to know that the following is possible. Say, for example, that we have a board with marks for where we want to attach hooks (not necessarily equally spaced). Then we discover that this board is too long (or too short), so we buy another board of the correct length but we still want the hooks to be marked with the same spacing ratio between the hooks. This can be done as shown in the figure below.

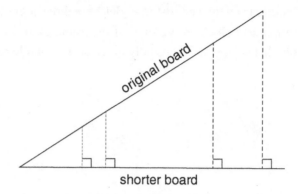

shorter board

6.4 TRIANGLES

Triangles are the basic building blocks of plane geometry. They are formed when three line segments form a **closed** figure. A closed figure is totally enclosed by lines or contours. You can think of a closed figure as a corral with no open gate. Geometrically, there is no line or curve that forms the figure that isn't connected to another line that forms the figure.

Triangles are the most important shapes in plane geometry because all closed figures composed of lines can shown to be made up of adjacent triangles. In addition, triangles are rigid. Once you have three sides attached in a triangle shape, you cannot change it. You cannot make one of the sides longer, and you cannot make any of the angles larger without changing at least one of the other sides and angles.

For example, consider two straight line segments of specific lengths that are connected at a specific angle. There is one, and only one, triangle that can be formed. Try that with any other closed plane figure, and it can collapse. For example, if you push on any side of a given triangle △ you cannot change its shape, but if you push on any side of a square, ☐ it can collapse into a parallelogram (for example, pushing on the left side, it becomes ▱). This is true for any polygon except a triangle. Now suppose you draw a diagonal in the square ◩ and try again to push on the left side. Since it is now two triangles, the square will maintain its shape. That is why bridges and other constructions are often made up of triangles.

A useful fact that has to do with a triangle's rigidity is that if only three measurements in a triangle are known, the remaining measurements can be determined by using trigonometry, discussed in Chapter 8. The exceptions are (1) if only the three angles are known, triangles of different sizes can be formed, and they are similar triangles (same shape, differing only in size, as discussed in Section 6.4.6); and (2) if two sides and an angle (not the one between the sides) are known, there can be two possible triangles.

The name "triangle" comes from the fact that triangles have three angles. The sides of a triangle are designated by their endpoints (which are vertices of the triangle), or by a lowercase letter that matches the angle opposite that side, which is usually given as a capital letter.

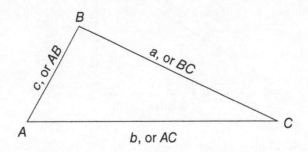

Three more of the many useful facts about triangles are:

- The sum of the angles in a triangle is 180°.

- The longest side is opposite the largest angle, and the smallest side is opposite the smallest angle.

- The sum of the lengths of any two sides of a triangle must be greater than the length of the opposite side.

If the third fact isn't true, we don't have a triangle (the two sides won't meet), as illustrated below. Another way to look at this fact is that the difference between the lengths of any two sides of a triangle must be less than the length of the shortest side.

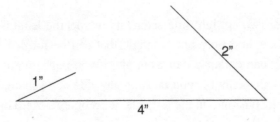

If all you know are the lengths of two sides of a triangle and nothing about the angles, you don't necessarily know the third side of the triangle—it actually could be anything, depending on the angle between the two sides.

6.4.1 Types of Triangles

6.4.1a Classification by Sides

Triangles can be classified by their side measurements.

- **Isosceles:** A triangle with two equal side lengths. The two equal sides are called the **legs**, and the third side is called the **base**.

- **Equilateral**: A triangle in which all three side lengths are equal. The name comes from the two parts of the word: *equi* (equal) and *lateral* (sides).

- **Scalene**: A triangle in which all the side lengths are different.

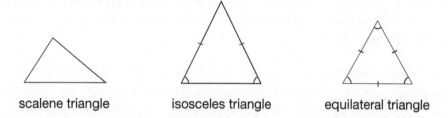

scalene triangle   isosceles triangle   equilateral triangle

In the figures in this book, if two or more sides are equal, they will be marked with the same tick marks (either single, double, or triple). If angles are equal, they will be marked with the same angle marks. Right angles are marked with a small box.

6.4.1b Classification by Angles

Triangles are also classified by their angle measurements. The **base angles** in an isosceles triangle are equal. These are the angles that are across from the equal sides. An equilateral triangle is also called an **equiangular** triangle because if all three sides are equal, so are all three angles. The two parts of the word *equiangular* are: *equi* (equal) and *angular* (angles). The angles in an equilateral triangle are each 60° because there are three of them and they have to add up to 180°.

- **Equiangular**: All the angles are equal to 60°.

- **Acute**: All the angles are acute angles.

- **Right**: One of the angles is a right angle. This is such an important kind of triangle that it deserves a section in this book all its own (Section 6.4.2).

- **Obtuse**: One of the angles is an obtuse angle. There can be only one obtuse angle in a triangle because it uses up more than 90° of the total 180° in a triangle.

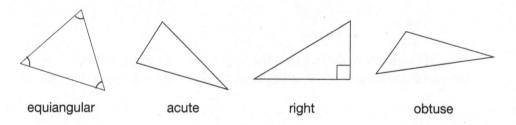

equiangular   acute   right   obtuse

6.4.2 Right Triangles

Right triangles are a special class of triangles because they are so common in our everyday life. They get their name from the fact that one of the angles is a right angle (90°), which means that two of the sides are perpendicular. Everyday examples of right triangles include a ladder propped against a house (the house is perpendicular to the ground) or a shadow cast by a tree (the tree is perpendicular to the ground).

In a right triangle, you need to know only one of the other two angles to figure out the third angle. The right angle is 90°, so since the measures of the three angles in a triangle add up to 180°, the other two angles must add up to 90°. For example, in a right triangle with one angle of 30°, the third angle is found by subtracting that angle from 90°, so we get $90° - 30° = 60°$. This quick subtraction from 90° applies only to *right* triangles.

The sides of a right triangle are special, too. Knowing two sides and being able to find the third side isn't possible with any other triangle, unless you also know one of the angles. But in a right triangle, you certainly know one of the angles—it is 90°.

6.4.2a Pythagorean Theorem

The formula for finding the third side of a right triangle if you know any of the other two sides is based on the **Pythagorean Theorem**, which states:

> In a right triangle, the square of the hypotenuse is equal to
> the sum of the squares of the other two sides.

The **hypotenuse** of a right triangle is the side opposite the 90° angle. It is the longest side. The **legs** are the other two sides, and they aren't necessarily equal.

The **converse** (see Chapter 11, Section 11.3.1) of the Pythagorean Theorem is also true:

> Whenever the sum of the squares of two sides of a triangle is equal to
> the square of the third side of the triangle, the triangle is a right triangle.

or

> If the square of the length of the longest side of a triangle is equal to
> the sum of the squares of the other two sides, then the triangle is a right triangle.

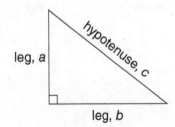

The formula for the Pythagorean Theorem is thus written as

$$c^2 = a^2 + b^2,$$

which is referred to as the **Pythagorean formula**, and commonly also called the Pythagorean Theorem.

It is a good idea (and a time-saver on the test) if you know at least one of the **Pythagorean triples**. These are the lengths of the sides of right triangles that are whole numbers, and thus don't involve a lot of math (such as finding square roots of numbers that aren't perfect squares). The most popular is easy to remember. It is known as the **3-4-5 right triangle**. Since $3^2 + 4^2 = 5^2$, the sides of this right triangle are indeed 3, 4, and 5.

Any triangle whose sides are a multiple of the 3-4-5 right triangle (such as 6-8-10 or 9-12-15) is also a right triangle. So if we know that the two legs of a right triangle are 6 and 8, we automatically know the third side is 10. Other Pythagorean triples are not as easy to remember as the 3-4-5. They include 5-12-13 and 8-15-17, and, of course, any multiples of them, as well as many other less-used triples.

EXAMPLE 6.3

A ladder 10 feet long is propped 8 feet up on a house. How close to the foundation of the house is the base of the ladder? (Not drawn to scale.)

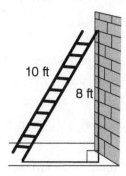

10 ft

8 ft

SOLUTION 6.3

Since the house and its foundation form a right angle, we can use the Pythagorean Theorem, so $c^2 = a^2 + b^2$, or $10^2 = 8^2 + b^2$, and $b^2 = 36$. Thus, b, which is the distance from the house to the base of the ladder, is 6 feet. This is double a 3-4-5 right triangle, so its sides are 6-8-10.

EXAMPLE 6.4

To drive to the ball game after work, Nick drives 8 miles north and then 15 miles west. How many miles is a straight line from Nick's workplace to the ball field?

SOLUTION 6.4

A sketch of the problem shows that it forms a right triangle in which the distance from work to the ball field is the hypotenuse. Use the Pythagorean Theorem: $c^2 = 8^2 + 15^2$. So the ball field is $\sqrt{289} = 17$ miles from Nick's workplace. This is an 8-15-17 right triangle.

6.4.2b Ratios of Sides of Right Triangles

In addition to knowing Pythagorean triples, which saves time when doing problems involving right triangles, two other right triangles whose sides have memorable ratios are the 30°-60°-90° triangle and the 45°-45°-90° triangle.

- In the 30°-60°-90° triangle, the length of the side opposite the 30° angle is half the hypotenuse and the length of the side opposite the 60° angle is the shortest side times $\sqrt{3}$. So the ratio of the sides of any 30°-60°-90° right triangle is fairly easy to remember; it is 1-2-$\sqrt{3}$. So if you know that one angle of a right triangle is 30° and it has a hypotenuse of x units, you automatically know that the length of the shortest side (side opposite 30°) is $\frac{x}{2}$ units, and the length of the other side is $\frac{x}{2}\sqrt{3}$ units.

- In a 45°-45°-90° triangle the legs are equal because it is not only a right triangle, but also an isosceles triangle. The sides of this triangle also have a memorable ratio: 1-1-$\sqrt{2}$. So if you know one angle of a right triangle is 45° and one of the legs is y units long, the other leg is also y units long, and the hypotenuse is $y\sqrt{2}$ units long.

 For both the 30°-60°-90° (or 1-2-$\sqrt{3}$) triangle and the 45°-45°-90° (or 1-1-$\sqrt{2}$) triangle, you need be given only one angle measurement and one side length to be able to find all of the other measurements of the triangle. Just remember which side is the hypotenuse (the longest side).

6.4.3 Perimeter of a Triangle

The **perimeter** of a triangle is simply the sum of the side lengths. If the triangle is an isosceles triangle, two lengths will be the same. If it is an equilateral triangle, the perimeter is three times the length of one side, since they are all the same. For a right triangle, we may have to calculate the third side by the Pythagorean formula before we can add the three sides. For any triangle with sides, a, b, and c, the perimeter (P) is given by

$$P = a + b + c.$$

6.4.4 Area of a Triangle

The **area** of a triangle is one-half the base times the height (altitude) of the triangle. You can choose any of the three sides to be the **base**. The **height**, or **altitude**, is a line that goes through a vertex and is perpendicular to the opposite side. For an isosceles triangle, it is easiest if the base is the unequal side, and for a right triangle it should be one of the legs because the two legs already are perpendicular, so one could be the base and then the other would be the height. But any side in any triangle can be chosen as the base.

The tricky part to finding the area is determining the height of the triangle. The figures below show the heights for right, acute, obtuse, and equilateral triangles. Note that for equilateral triangles (as well as isosceles triangles), the height divides the base into two equal segments, and for the obtuse triangle, the height may actually be measured outside the triangle itself.

For isosceles and equilateral triangles the height can be found by using the Pythagorean formula because the sides will be given and the height forms a right triangle.

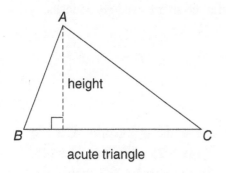

acute triangle

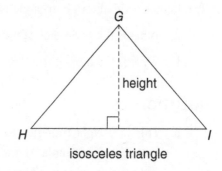

isosceles triangle

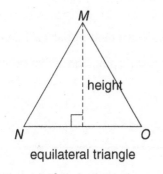

equilateral triangle

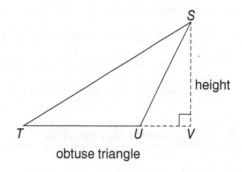

obtuse triangle

The formula for the area A of a triangle, where b is the base and h is the height to that base, is

$$A = \frac{1}{2}bh$$

Where did the $\frac{1}{2}$ come in? For any triangle, we can flip it across any of the sides and end up with a four-sided figure in which the sides across from each other are equal. The area of this new four-sided figure (a parallelogram; see an example below) is simply its base times its height (perpendicular distance between the two bases; see Section 6.5.2). The two triangles are identical. The area of either triangle is one-half the area of the four-sided figure. So when you calculate the area of a triangle, don't forget the $\frac{1}{2}$.

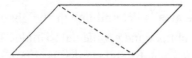

Triangle flipped on its longest side.

EXAMPLE 6.5

The longest side of a right triangle is 13 inches and the shortest side is 5 inches.

    a. What is the perimeter of the triangle?

    b. What is the area of the triangle?

SOLUTION 6.5

    a. This is a right triangle, so the longest side is the hypotenuse. Use the Pythagorean formula to find the third side: $169 = 25 + b^2$. Then $b^2 = 144$, and the third side is 12 inches. (Or recognize this as a 5-12-13 Pythagorean triple.) The perimeter is then the sum of the sides, or $13 + 5 + 12 = 30$ inches.

    b. The legs of the right triangle are 5 and 12, as determined in part a. Then the area is $\frac{1}{2}(5)(12) = 30$ square inches. (It is just a coincidence that both answers here are the same numerically.)

6.4.5 Congruent Triangles

Congruent figures are exactly the same size and shape. Their orientation may be different, but their sizes (sides and angles) are correspondingly equal. The "correspondingly" refers to which sides are between which angles. The symbol for congruence is ≅. It is easy to see that $\triangle ABC \cong \triangle DEF$, but not as straightforward to see that $\triangle ABC \cong \triangle GHI$, or that $\triangle ABC \cong \triangle JKL$.

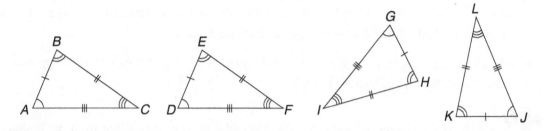

 The angles and sides of congruent triangles appear in *corresponding* places when written out. For example, $\triangle ABC \cong \triangle DEF$ means that $\angle A = \angle D$, $\angle B = \angle E$, and $\angle C = \angle F$, and $AB = DE$, $AC = DF$, and $BC = EF$.

As a consequence of the rigidity of a triangle, there is one and only one triangle that can be drawn if two angles and the distance between them are known. As another example, if the lengths of two sides and the measure of the angle between them are known, the measures of the third side and the other two angles are fixed. The figure on the left below shows that if the lengths of sides DE and DF and $\angle D$ are known, there is only one way to form a triangle (draw EF). Likewise, if one side and two angles in a triangle are known, the lengths of the other two sides are predetermined. If we extend the two partial sides in the figure on the right below, they will meet at a point (let's call it T) that depends on $\angle R$ and $\angle S$. Thus, there is one and only one triangle that can be drawn if two angles and the distance between them are known.

It makes sense, then, that if two angles and the distance between them are identical in two triangles, the triangles must be congruent. The same is true for a number of relationships between two triangles, as noted below, where S = side and A = angle. For example, ASA stands for two angles and the side between them. If the two angles and included side of one triangle are identical to two angles and the included side of another triangle, the two triangles are congruent.

For two triangles to be congruent, one of the following must be true.

- **SSS**: The three sides of one triangle are equal to the three corresponding sides of another triangle.

- **SAS**: Two sides and the angle between them of one triangle are equal to the corresponding two sides and angle between them of another triangle.

- **ASA**: Two angles and a side of one triangle are equal to the corresponding two angles and side of another triangle. (Note that the side doesn't have to be between the angles. This is sometimes called **AAS** if the side is not between the angles).

- **HL**: In a right triangle, if the hypotenuse and either of the legs are equal to the hypotenuse and either of the legs of another triangle.

 HL is a variation of SSS, since the third sides must also be equal from the Pythagorean formula.

If the three angles of one triangle are equal to the corresponding three angles of another triangle and nothing is said about the sides, the triangles are not necessarily congruent. However, they are similar, the subject of the next section.

6.4.6 Similar Triangles

Similar figures have equal corresponding angles, but the lengths of the corresponding sides are *proportional*, and not necessarily equal. The symbol for similarity is ~. Therefore, in the figure below, $\triangle ABC \sim \triangle DEF$, but $\triangle ABC$ is clearly not congruent to $\triangle DEF$.

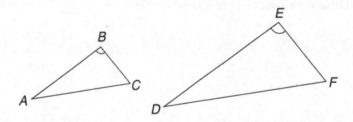

Since these two triangles are similar, we can deduce that $\angle A = \angle D$, $\angle B = \angle E$, and $\angle C = \angle F$, as well as that $\dfrac{AB}{DE} = \dfrac{BC}{EF} = \dfrac{CA}{FD}$. In fact, we didn't even need the figures to state these equalities and proportionalities—we needed only to follow the corresponding places of the letters in $\triangle ABC \sim \triangle DEF$. And since the corresponding sides are in corresponding places when we write $\triangle ABC \sim \triangle DEF$, it is *not* true that $\triangle ABC \sim \triangle EDF$.

6.4.6a Proportions in Similar Triangles

The sides are not the only proportional parts of similar triangles. The altitudes to any side are also proportional (as long as we have the correct corresponding sides).

We already know that if two angles of one triangle are equal to two corresponding angles of another triangle, the triangles are similar because if we know two angles of a triangle, there is only one measure left for the third angle. We can also prove two triangles are similar by proving two of the corresponding sides of each of the two triangles are proportional as long as their included angles are equal.

6.4.6b Scale Factors

Because all similar triangles have the same shape, the only thing that is different from one triangle to a similar triangle is its size. Imagine two triangles, one with a side of 1 inch and the other with a corresponding side of 2 inches. The **scale factor** between these two triangles is 2, the ratio of the sides. What about the areas of the two triangles? Since area involves the product of two dimensions ($\frac{1}{2}$ × base × height), and each linear measure in the smaller triangle is scaled by 2 in the larger triangle, the area is enlarged 2×2, or 4 times.

 If two two-dimensional figures have the same shape and are linearly scaled by a factor of x, their areas are scaled by a factor of x^2. The fact that area measures are given in square units will remind you to square the scale factor. Likewise, the volumes of similar three-dimensional figures (such as spheres or cubes) scaled by a factor of x have volumes scaled by a factor of x^3 (see Section 6.10).

6.5 QUADRILATERALS

Quadrilaterals (*quadri* = four and *lateral* = side) are four-sided closed figures. Squares and rectangles are familiar figures, but there are infinitely many other quadrilaterals. Their only requirement is that they be closed and have four sides. Typical quadrilaterals are the following:

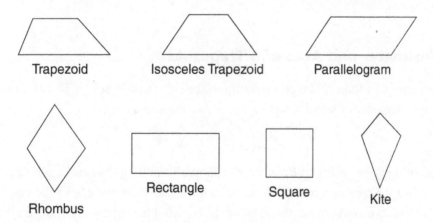

Trapezoid   Isosceles Trapezoid   Parallelogram

Rhombus   Rectangle   Square   Kite

Three facts are true of all quadrilaterals:

- The sum of the **interior angles** in a quadrilateral is 360°, and the sum of the exterior angles in a quadrilateral is 360°.

- The perimeter of a quadrilateral is the sum of the lengths of the four sides. So if the four sides have lengths a, b, c, and d, the perimeter is

$$P = a + b + c + d$$

- In general, the areas of many quadrilaterals (exceptions are trapezoids (see Section 6.5.1a), kites, and irregularly shaped quadrilaterals) are based on the product of one side (called the *base*) times the *height*, the perpendicular distance to the opposite side. For a quadrilateral with base b and height h, the area is

$$A = bh$$

Five quadrilaterals are special due to certain facts about their angles and side lengths, as shown next.

6.5.1 Trapezoid

A **trapezoid** is a quadrilateral with only one special fact: two of the sides are parallel. They don't have to be equal.

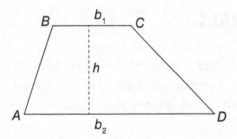

6.5.1a Perimeter and Area of a Trapezoid

The *perimeter* of a trapezoid is just the sum of the sides ($AB + BC + CD + DA$, here). So for a trapezoid with four sides of lengths, say, e, f, g, and h, the perimeter is

$$P_{\text{trapezoid}} = e + f + g + h$$

The area of a trapezoid is still based on the simple formula of base × height (also called altitude), but to find the area of a trapezoid, we have to consider the average of the two bases as the base in this calculation. Otherwise, the area would be two different numbers, depending on which of the parallel sides is considered to be the base. The height is defined as the perpendicular distance between the bases. The average of the two bases is their sum divided by 2. So the "base" to use in the general formula for the area of a trapezoid is $\frac{1}{2}(b_1 + b_2)$, where b_1 and b_2 are the lengths of the two parallel sides. Thus, the area of a trapezoid is given by

$$A_{\text{trapezoid}} = \frac{1}{2}(b_1 + b_2)h.$$

6.5.1b Isosceles Trapezoids

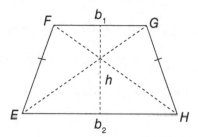

If the two nonparallel sides of a trapezoid are equal, the trapezoid has a special name: isosceles, just as for triangles. An **isosceles trapezoid** has two parallel sides (*FG* and *EH* in the figure above), and the other two sides are equal (*EF = HG*). The trapezoid is often drawn with the longest parallel side at the bottom of the figure, and the base angles (the angles on either side of it) are equal ($\angle E = \angle H$), although it is also true that the other two angles are equal ($\angle F = \angle G$). In addition, for an isosceles trapezoid, the *diagonals* (here they would be *FH* and *GE*) are of equal length.

6.5.2 Parallelogram

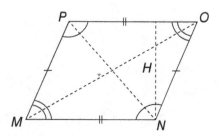

A **parallelogram** is a quadrilateral with two pair of parallel (and equal) sides, as the name implies. In this case, it is a step up from the trapezoid because the other two sides are also parallel. Parallelogram *MNOP* looks a little "busy," but it shows the following properties of parallelograms:

- Opposite sides (*MN* and *PO* as well as *MP* and *NO*) are equal and parallel.

- Opposite angles are equal ($\angle M = \angle O$ and $\angle P = \angle N$).

- The height *H* is perpendicular to both parallel sides ($H \perp MN$ and $H \perp PO$).

- The diagonals (*MO* and *PN*) bisect each other.

- The pairs of adjacent angles ($\angle M$ and $\angle N$, $\angle N$ and $\angle O$, $\angle O$ and $\angle P$, and $\angle P$ and $\angle M$) each add up to 180°, which means they are **supplementary** to each other.

6.5.2a Perimeter of a Parallelogram

The *perimeter* of a parallelogram is still the sum of the lengths of all four sides. So the perimeter of parallelogram *MNOP* is

$$P_{\text{parallelogram}} = MN + NO + OP + PM$$

Since the sides opposite each other are equal, the perimeter can be rewritten as

$$P_{\text{parallelogram}} = 2MN + 2NO = 2(MN + NO)$$

Thus, the perimeter of a parallelogram is twice the sum of the two unequal sides.

6.5.2b Area of a Parallelogram

The *area* of a parallelogram is given by the general formula of base × height, where the height is perpendicular to the base:

$$A_{\text{parallelogram}} = bh$$

For parallelogram *MNOP*, $A_{\text{parallelogram}} = (MN) \times H$.

6.5.3 Rhombus

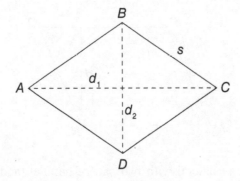

A **rhombus** has all of the properties of a parallelogram plus:

- The sides are all equal ($AB = BC = CD = DA$) = s.

- The diagonals of a rhombus bisect each other (as they did for the parallelogram), but now they also are perpendicular to each other ($d_1 \perp d_2$).

6.5.3a Perimeter of a Rhombus

In the figure of the rhombus above, the *perimeter* can be written as

$$P_{\text{rhombus}} = (AB + BC + CD + DA) = 4s$$

where s is the length of a side.

6.5.3b Area of a Rhombus

Likewise, the *area* of the rhombus is given by

$$A_{\text{rhombus}} = bh = sh,$$

where any of the sides s can be used as the base, and the height drawn to each side is the same. An easier formula for the area of a rhombus involves the lengths of the diagonals:

$$A_{\text{rhombus}} = \frac{1}{2}\left(d_1 \times d_2\right).$$

6.5.4 Rectangle

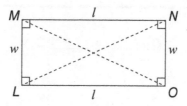

A **rectangle** is a parallelogram with four equal angles (but not necessarily four equal sides), so it has all of the properties of a parallelogram plus:

- All four angles are equal. In the figure of the rectangle above, $\angle L = \angle M = \angle N = \angle O$.

- Since the angles of any quadrilateral always add up to 360°, each of the four angles is 90°, or a right angle.

- The diagonals of a rectangle are equal. They bisect each other (as they did for the parallelogram), but they are not necessarily perpendicular to each other—that was true only for the rhombus.

- A rectangle can be bisected (cut into two equal halves) in several ways (by a diagonal or by a line through the midpoints of the sides), and the area of each half will always be equal, even though the halves may have different shapes.

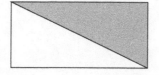 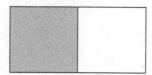 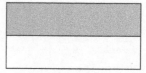

For rectangle *LMNO*, the vertex *L* in the lower left corner was chosen as the starting point. The rectangle could also be called *MNOL*, or *NOLM*, or *OLMN*, as long as the order of the letters matches the order in the figure. This is true for all closed polygons. Also, any letters can be chosen.

6.5.4a Perimeter of a Rectangle

The *perimeter* of a rectangle is written as usual as the sum of the lengths of the sides. Here, *l* is the length and *w* is the width, as shown on the figure.

$$P_{rectangle} = 2l + 2w = 2(l + w)$$

6.5.4b Area of a Rectangle

Because all the angles are right angles, all sides *l* (length) are perpendicular to sides *w* (width), so they are the base and height, and the *area* of the rectangle is

$$A_{rectangle} = lw = bh$$

6.5.5 Square

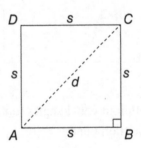

Now we come to the most restrictive quadrilateral—the square. A **square** is a parallelogram with

- Four equal angles *and* four equal sides. (It can also be thought of as a rhombus with four equal angles or a rectangle with four equal sides.)

- A square has all of the properties of the other parallelograms described above:

Property of the square:	Same as property for:
Opposite sides are parallel	Parallelogram
All sides are equal	Rhombus
All angles are equal	Rectangle
Diagonals bisect each other	Parallelogram
Diagonals are perpendicular to each other	Rhombus

6.5.5a Perimeter of a Square

Since a square is a rectangle with equal sides, its perimeter is

$$P_{square} = 4s.$$

6.5.5b Area of a Square

Since a square is a rectangle with equal sides, its area is

$$A_{square} = s^2.$$

EXAMPLE 6.6

What is the value of x in the quadrilateral shown below?

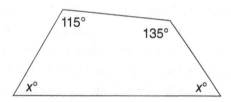

SOLUTION 6.6

All of the angles in a quadrilateral total 360°. So we have

$$135° + 115° + x + x = 360°$$
$$2x = 110°$$
$$x = 55°$$

EXAMPLE 6.7

Which of the following rectangles have the same perimeter? (The figures are not drawn to scale; use the given measurements.)

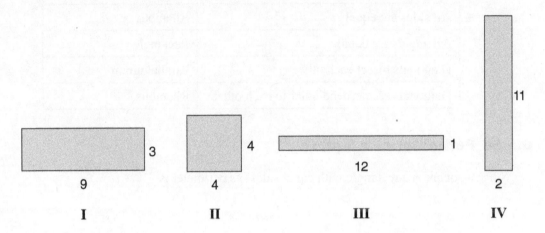

I   II   III   IV

SOLUTION 6.7

The perimeter of a rectangle is $P = 2(l + w)$. For figure I, $P = 24$; for II, $P = 16$; for III, $P = 26$; and for IV, $P = 26$. So rectangles III and IV have the same perimeter.

6.6 POLYGONS

Polygons are closed, straight-line figures. Each angle of a polygon is referred to as a **vertex**. Polygons are named for the number of their sides, which also happens to be the number of vertices (plural of vertex). An aerial view of the government building called the Pentagon shows that it has five equal sides. A cell in a beehive and the cross-sections of most wooden pencils are six-sided hexagons. **Interior angles** are the angles formed by any two adjacent sides. **Exterior angles** are the angles between any side of a shape and a line extended from the next side. At every vertex, the interior and exterior angles are supplementary, as shown below.

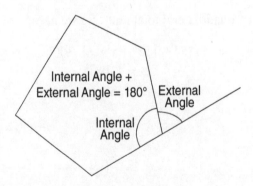

The sum of the interior angles in a polygon increases as the number of sides increases. The formula for the total number of interior degrees in a polygon is given by $(n-2)180°$, where n is the number of sides of the polygon. The number of sides and the sum of the interior angles for certain polygons is given in the following table. Note that the sum of the interior angles increases with the number of sides, whereas the sum of the exterior angles is always 360°, no matter how many sides the polygon has.

 For all quadrilaterals, the sum of the interior angles is 360° and the sum of the exterior angles is also 360. $(4-2)180° = 2 \times 180° = 360°$.

 You can always figure out the sum of the interior angles because it increases by 180° for each side, and you know the sum for the triangle and quadrilateral already.

Name of Polygon	Number of Sides	Sum of Interior Angles
Triangle	3	180°
Quadrilateral	4	360°
Pentagon	5	540°
Hexagon	6	720°
Heptagon	7	900°
Octagon	8	1080°
Nonagon	9	1260°
Decagon	10	1440°
n-gon	n	$(n-2)180°$

6.6.1 Regular Polygons

Most polygons we see, such as stop signs or the markings on a soccer ball, are **regular polygons**, meaning all the sides (and angles) are equal. Equilateral triangles and squares are examples of regular polygons of three and four sides, respectively. But closed figures don't have to be regular. You can draw a figure of connected straight lines that aren't all the same length, and it is still a polygon.

6.6.2 Perimeter of a Polygon

The *perimeter* of any polygon is the sum of the lengths of the sides—just add them up. It follows that the perimeter of a regular polygon is the length of a side multiplied by how many sides there are. For an irregular polygon, if any of the sides are unknown, they can be found by dividing the polygon into triangles and using the Pythagorean Theorem or trigonometry (see Chapter 8) to find the missing side.

6.6.3 Area of a Polygon

The *area* of an irregular polygon is more complicated. It can be found by dividing the polygon into a number of triangles and adding up their areas. But finding the area of a scalene triangle can be complicated, too.

The area of a regular polygon, however, is derived from the fact that any regular polygon is made up of identical isosceles triangles, for which we can more easily determine the area. An example is a regular hexagon, shown below.

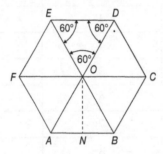

The area of this figure is 6 times the area of each triangle because it is a regular hexagon and the triangles are all equilateral. The formula for the area of a triangle involves not only the base (which is the side of the hexagon), but also the height to the base (here, *ON*), or a perpendicular line from the center of the hexagon to a side. This line is called the **apothem**. So the area of any regular polygon is given by

$$A_n = n\left(\frac{1}{2}bh\right) = \frac{1}{2}ap,$$

where *a* is the apothem and *p* is the perimeter, which is equal to *n* times any side.

Thus, the tricky part of finding the area of a regular polygon is finding the apothem. We concentrate on only one of the triangles, and find the apothem in the same manner as when we found the height of any isosceles triangle in Section 6.4.4. The triangles in a regular polygon are all isosceles, and the apothem divides the base in half. In addition, we also know the central angle of the triangles that form the polygon, which is $\dfrac{360°}{n}$, where n is the number of sides of the polygon, and $360°$ is the sum of the degrees of the central vertices. So, for example, finding the apothem reduces to finding the height ON of the right triangle on the right-hand side of triangle AOB, which is one of the triangles of an n-sided regular polygon with side length s. This may involve trigonometry (see Chapter 8).

To find the area of a regular hexagon with side length 8, however, we use the fact that the triangles that form a regular hexagon are all equilateral, so the apothem would be the altitude of half of one of the equilateral triangles ($\triangle ONB$ in the figure above), or a 30°-60°-90° right triangle with hypotenuse 8 and base 4. We can just use the Pythagorean formula to find the apothem, a.

$$8^2 = a^2 + 4^2, \text{ so } a^2 = 48 \text{ and } a = \sqrt{48} = 4\sqrt{3}$$

(Or, remembering that the ratio of the sides of any 30°-60°-90° right triangle, is 1-2-$\sqrt{3}$, the apothem is the shortest side times $\sqrt{3}$, or $4\sqrt{3}$.)

Thus, the area of the hexagon is

$$A_n = \frac{1}{2}ap = \frac{1}{2}\left(4\sqrt{3}\right)(6 \times 8) = 96\sqrt{3}$$

Can you see that if this was a pentagon, even if we knew each side length was 8, we wouldn't necessarily know the distances AB or BC without trigonometry?

EXAMPLE 6.8

Each side of the Pentagon building is 921 feet. What is the perimeter of the Pentagon, assuming it is a regular polygon?

SOLUTION 6.8

Since the Pentagon has five sides, its perimeter is 5 times the length of a side, or 5 × 921 feet = 4,605 feet.

6.6.4 Diagonals of Polygons

A diagonal of a polygon is a line from any vertex to another vertex. The number of diagonals from any vertex is three fewer than the number of sides because the lines to the two adjacent vertices are not diagonals (they are sides of the polygon), and there is no line drawn from a vertex to itself. Therefore, the formula for the number of diagonals from any vertex of a polygon of n sides is $n - 3$. For a pentagon, each vertex has $(5 - 3) = 2$ diagonals, as shown below.

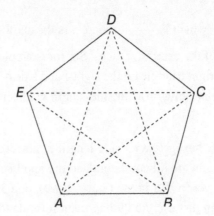

That would lead you to believe that a pentagon has 10 diagonals (2 for each of 5 vertices). However, a diagonal from vertex A to vertex C would be the same as one from C to A, so we must divide this result by 2 to eliminate all of the duplicates. Therefore, the total number of diagonals for any n-sided polygon is given by $\dfrac{n(n-3)}{2}$. For a pentagon, this would be $\dfrac{5(2)}{2} = 5$, as shown above. But don't be fooled into thinking the number of diagonals is always the number of sides. (Think of a quadrilateral; it has only two diagonals, not four.)

 For convex polygons, all diagonals are inside the figure. A diagonal can be outside of the polygon if the polygon is **concave** (one of the angles is greater than 180°).

convex

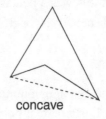

concave

6.6.5 Congruent and Similar Polygons

As is the case for congruent triangles, two polygons are **congruent** if all of the pairs of corresponding angles and corresponding sides are equal. And as is the case for similar triangles, two polygons are **similar** if all the pairs of corresponding angles are equal and pairs of corresponding sides are *proportional* (have the same ratios), meaning the figures have the same shape but not necessarily the same size.

Therefore, all squares are similar to all other squares because they all have 90° angles and the sides of any square are equal, so the ratios between the sides of two squares will be constant.

 If the sides of two squares are in the ratio of $\dfrac{s_1}{s_2}$, their areas are in the ratio of $\left(\dfrac{s_1}{s_2}\right)^2 = \dfrac{s_1^2}{s_2^2}$ because areas involve two dimensions.

EXAMPLE 6.9

A farmer has two square gardens. The smaller one has an area of 100 square feet, and one side of the larger garden is twice as long as a side of the smaller garden. What is the area of the larger garden?

SOLUTION 6.9

If the smaller square garden has an area of 100 square feet, then each side must be $\sqrt{100} = 10$ feet. Thus, the larger garden with dimensions twice as long must be 20 feet on a side, and its area must be $(20)^2 = 400$ square feet. Another way to look at this problem is that the ratio of the sides of the larger to smaller garden is given as $\dfrac{2}{1}$, so the areas must be in the ratio of $\left(\dfrac{2}{1}\right)^2 = \dfrac{4}{1}$, which would make the larger garden 400 square feet.

6.7 CIRCLES

6.7.1 Linear Parts of a Circle

The circle is an important shape indeed. A **circle** is defined as all the points at a fixed distance from a certain point called the **center** of the circle. The fixed distance from the center to the circle is called the **radius** of the circle. If we extend the radius across the center to the other side of the circle, we get the **diameter**, which is just twice the radius. A circle is usually named by its center, so this is circle O.

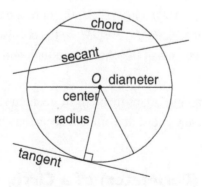

Three other lines in the figure of the circle are the chord, secant, and tangent. These lines can appear anywhere in relation to the circle and can have various lengths (unlike the radius and diameter, which are a specific length for each circle). These lines have important properties in relation to the circle and are defined as:

- **chord**: A line segment whose endpoints are on the circle. The longest chord in a circle is the diameter.

- **secant**: The extension of a chord in both directions. A secant intersects the circle at two points, whereas a chord's endpoints are on the circle.

- **tangent**: A straight line that touches the circle at just one point and all its other points are outside the circle. A radius drawn to the tangent at the point of tangency is perpendicular to the tangent, as shown in the figure.

EXAMPLE 6.10

A triangle is formed by two radii and the chord with endpoints at the points where the radii intersect the circle. If a perpendicular line is drawn from the center of the circle, prove that it bisects the chord.

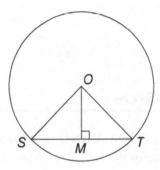

SOLUTION 6.10

Triangle *SOT* is an isosceles triangle because all the radii in a given circle are equal. In right triangles, $\triangle SOM$ and $\triangle TOM$, the radii are the hypotenuses and are equal. Then HL proves that $\triangle SOM \cong \triangle TOM$, so the corresponding sides are equal, and $SM = TM$, or the segments of the chord are equal, and OM bisects the chord.

  Example 6.10 is an important theorem in geometry: The perpendicular line drawn from the center to any chord in a circle bisects the chord.

6.7.2 Circumference (Perimeter) of a Circle

An important value when talking about circles is the special constant represented by the Greek letter pi (π), which is defined as the ratio of C, the **circumference** (perimeter) of the circle, to d, its diameter, or $\pi = \dfrac{C}{d}$. Thus, the circumference of a circle is given by

$$C = \pi d.$$

Since the diameter is twice the radius (r), $d = 2r$, the circumference can also be written as

$$C = 2\pi r.$$

The value of π is the irrational nonrepeating decimal 3.141592654 . . . . (Check that on your calculator by pressing the $\boxed{\pi}$ key and then $\boxed{\text{ENTER}}$.) This ratio is the same for all circles, no matter how large or small they are.

The popular approximation of $\pi = \dfrac{22}{7}$ is not accurate, so don't assume that π is rational because it is frequently expressed as a fraction. $\pi = \dfrac{22}{7} = 3.1428571428571 \ldots$ is close but not exact. Therefore, questions and answers often are given in terms of π, rather than as a decimal.

6.7.3 Area of a Circle

The **area** of a circle is given by

$$A = \pi r^2,$$

and its dimensions are in square units.

EXAMPLE 6.11

For a circle with a diameter of $\dfrac{2}{3\pi}$ units, what is

   a. the circumference

   b. the area

Leave the answers in terms of π.

SOLUTION 6.11

   a. The circumference, $C = \pi d$, so $C = \pi\left(\dfrac{2}{3\pi}\right) = \left(\dfrac{\pi}{1}\right)\left(\dfrac{2}{3\pi}\right)$ units. Cancel the

      π in the numerator and denominator to get $C = \dfrac{2}{3}$ units.

   b. To find the area, we must first find the value of r. Since $d = 2r$, $r =$

      $\dfrac{1}{2}d = \dfrac{1}{2} \times \dfrac{2}{3\pi} = \dfrac{1}{3\pi}$. So the area is $A = \pi r^2 = \pi\left(\dfrac{1}{3\pi}\right)^2 = \left(\dfrac{\pi}{9\pi^2}\right) = \dfrac{1}{9\pi}$

      square units.

Be sure the circumference is always given in linear units and the area is always given in square units.

EXAMPLE 6.12

A circle is drawn inside a larger circle, as shown below. The smaller circle has a diameter of 4 and the larger circle has a diameter of 6. What is the area of the shaded portion?

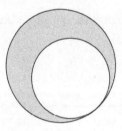

SOLUTION 6.12

The larger circle has a diameter of 6, or a radius of 3, so its area is $\pi r^2 = \pi(3)^2 = 9\pi$. The smaller circle has a diameter of 4, or radius of 2, so its area is $\pi r^2 = \pi(2)^2 = 4\pi$. The shaded portion is the difference between the larger and smaller circle areas, or 5π.

A **semicircle** is a half circle. Its area is exactly one-half of the area of the full circle. Any diameter of a circle cuts it into two equal semicircles. The perimeter of a semicircle, however, is not one half of the circumference of the whole circle, which is seen in the following figure of a semicircle. In this figure, the perimeter is the round part (which is half of the circumference of the whole circle), plus the diameter, which is the straight part of the semicircle.

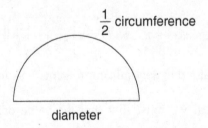

$\frac{1}{2}$ circumference

diameter

6.7.4 Arcs and Sectors

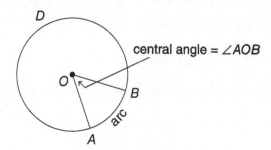

central angle = ∠AOB

The portion of the circumference of a circle between two points is called an **arc**. An angle with its vertex at the center of a circle and two radii as its sides is called a **central angle**. The sum of the central angles in a complete revolution (or circle) is 360°. The pie-shaped area of circle O is called a **sector** of the circle.

Arcs are designated by their endpoints with an arc sign over them; for the figure above, it would be the symbol $\overset{\frown}{AB}$. However, there are actually two arcs between points A and B in the figure, which we can designate as $\overset{\frown}{AB}$ and $\overset{\frown}{ADB}$, which are a **minor arc** (less than 180°) and a **major arc** (greater than 180°), respectively. An intervening point (here, D) avoids ambiguity about which arc is designated.

When not designated as a major arc, remember that "arc" refers to the minor arc.

The measurement of the arc in degrees is the same as the degree measurement of the central angle drawn to it. The length of an arc is simply a fraction of the circumference, with the fraction being equal to $\dfrac{n°}{360°}$, where n is the number of degrees in the arc and 360 is the number of degrees in the whole circle. Therefore, the length of an arc is given by

$$\text{length}_{\text{arc}} = \left(\frac{n°}{360°}\right)(\pi d) = \left(\frac{n°}{360°}\right)(2\pi r)$$

EXAMPLE 6.13

Two 12-inch diameters in a circle meet at right angles. What is the length of the one of the minor arcs formed in this configuration (give the answer in terms of π)?

SOLUTION 6.13

The two perpendicular diameters divide the circle into four equal parts.

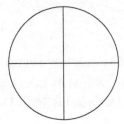

Therefore, each of the equal arcs is one-fourth of the circumference of the circle,

$$\text{or } \left(\frac{1}{4}\right)(\pi d) = \frac{\pi(12)}{4} = 3\pi.$$

The straight sides of a **sector** of a circle are radii, and the curved side is an arc. Since the sum of the central angles in a complete revolution (or circle) is 360°, the area of a sector is found similarly to the length of the arc:

$$A_{\text{sector}} = \left(\frac{n°}{360°}\right)(\pi r^2)$$

 If you think of the hands of a clock to visualize central angles and arcs, be careful. Even though, since a clock shows 12 hours, and the angle between any two numbers on a clock is (360° ÷ 12) = 30°, the angle between the hands of the clock at 10:10 is not equal to 120°. It is less than 120° because the hour hand will have moved beyond the 10, on its way to 11.

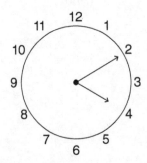

6.7.5 Circle Angles

Whereas the central angle is formed by two radii, the remaining angles within and outside a circle are formed by chords, secants, and tangents. The relations of their measures to their intercepted arcs depend on whether the vertex of the angle is on, within, or outside the circle.

- *Angles with a Vertex on a Circle.* The measure of an angle with its vertex *on* a circle is simply given by (*m* here is shorthand for "the measure of")

$$m(\text{angle}) = \frac{1}{2}m(\text{intercepted arc}).$$

Two cases, one with two chords (on the left) and one with a chord and a tangent (on the right), are shown in the following figures. Note that the angles are indeed half of their intercepted arcs. The endpoints and vertex of an angle formed by two chords all lie on the circle, so it is called an **inscribed angle**.

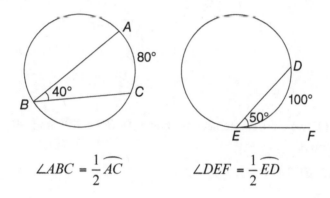

$$\angle ABC = \frac{1}{2}\overset{\frown}{AC} \qquad \angle DEF = \frac{1}{2}\overset{\frown}{ED}$$

EXAMPLE 6.14

What is the size of $\angle CBX$ in the following figure?

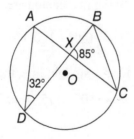

SOLUTION 6.14

Since $\angle ADB = 32°$, as shown, $\angle ACB = 32°$ because both angles intercept $\overset{\frown}{AB}$, and $\angle ACB = \angle XCB$ because they are the same angle. Therefore, in $\triangle BXC$ we know $\angle BXC = 85°$, and $\angle XCB = 32°$. Since the angles of a triangle total $180°$, $\angle CBX + \angle BXC + \angle XCB = 180°$, or $\angle CBX + 85° + 32° = 180°$, and $\angle CBX = 63°$.

- *Angles with a Vertex within a Circle.* An angle whose vertex is *within* a circle is formed by two intersecting chords. Its measure is given by half the *sum* of the intersected arcs, as shown below.

EXAMPLE 6.15

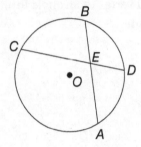

In circle O, two chords intersect as shown. If $\overset{\frown}{BD} = 80°$ and $\overset{\frown}{AC} = 150°$, what is the measure of

    a. $\angle BED$?

    b. $\angle BEC$?

SOLUTION 6.15

The vertices of the four angles formed in this figure are inside the circle, so they each are equal to half the sum of the intercepted arcs. Therefore,

    a. $\angle BED = \dfrac{1}{2}\left(\overset{\frown}{BD} + \overset{\frown}{AC}\right) = \dfrac{1}{2}(80° + 150°) = 115°$.

And since $\angle BED$ and $\angle BEC$ form a straight line, they are supplementary, and

    b. $\angle BEC = 180° - \angle BED = 180° - 115° = 65°$.

- *Angles Outside a Circle*. Angles with a vertex outside a circle intercept two arcs. The measure of any angles with a vertex outside the circle is equal to half the *difference* of these two arcs. For the three cases shown below (left: secant-secant; middle: secant-tangent; right: tangent-tangent), the general formula is

$$m(\text{angle}) = \frac{1}{2}m(\text{larger intercepted arc} - \text{smaller intercepted arc})$$

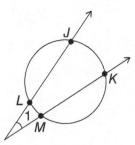 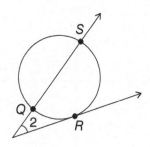 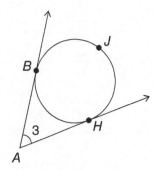

$$\angle 1 = \frac{1}{2}\left(\widehat{JK} - \widehat{LM}\right) \qquad \angle 2 = \frac{1}{2}\left(\widehat{RS} - \widehat{RQ}\right) \qquad \angle 3 = \frac{1}{2}\left(\widehat{HJB} - \widehat{BH}\right)$$

 As you might have guessed from the last figure, the line segments formed by two tangents from the same point outside a circle have the same length, or $AB = AH$. This is an important fact.

6.7.6 Inscribed Polygons

All of the vertices of an **inscribed polygon** are on the circumference of the circle. In other words, every side of the polygon has to be a chord. The polygon doesn't have to be regular. For example, connect any three points on a circle to draw an inscribed triangle. This concept can be extended to as many points on the circle as you wish; the inscribed polygon is regular only if the points are evenly spaced along the circumference of the circle.

If a triangle is drawn inside a semicircle (or inside a circle with the longest side of the triangle being the diameter), it is a right triangle. This fact comes directly from the measure of an angle with its vertex on the circle. The intercepted arc is 180°, so the angle must be 90°.

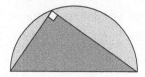

If any quadrilateral is inscribed in a circle, its opposite angles add up to 180° because together the arcs they intercept total the whole circle (360°), and half of 360° is 180°.

EXAMPLE 6.16

How many inscribed polygons are in the following figure of circle O?

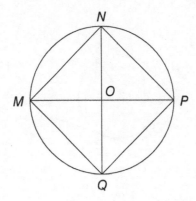

SOLUTION 6.16

Even though there are many polygons inside the circle, only five of them have all of their vertices on the circumference of the circle (and thus are considered inscribed). In addition to the quadrilateral $MNPQ$, four triangles have vertices on the circle: $\triangle MNQ$, $\triangle NPQ$, $\triangle PQM$, and $\triangle MNP$. The triangles that have O as a vertex are not *inscribed* because O is not on the circumference of the circle; they are central angles.

EXAMPLE 6.17

How many right triangles are in circle O from Example 6.16? (They don't have to be inscribed triangles.)

SOLUTION 6.17

There only four right triangles that we are sure of: $\angle MNQ$, $\angle NPQ$, $\angle PQM$, and $\angle QMN$ are right triangles because they are inscribed in a semicircle, or their hypotenuse is a diameter of circle O. The four triangles with O as a vertex may or may not be right triangles if we aren't told that the diameters are perpendicular to each other. Don't assume facts unless you can prove them. In this figure, the angles at O look like right angles, but they could be 89° and 91°.

6.8 COMPOSITE FIGURES

Two-dimensional **composite figures** are shapes composed of different triangles, polygons, and circles. The *perimeter* of a composite figure includes only the exterior sides; the *area* of a composite figure is the sum of all of its parts.

A silo viewed from a distance may look like a rectangle with a semicircle on top of it (left figure) with an area equal to that of the rectangle plus the semicircle. In three dimensions (see Section 6.10), it looks like a cylinder with a hemisphere (half a sphere) on it. The surface area of this composite figure would be calculated by adding the surface area of the hemispherical part (half of the surface area of a sphere, as discussed in Section 6.10.5a) and adding this to the area of the rectangle that comes from the cylinder that makes up the bottom part (like the label on a soup can). The length of this rectangle is the same as the circumference of the spherical part of the figure, as shown in Section 6.10.2a.

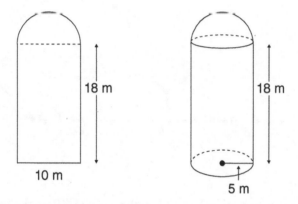

Sometimes composite figures can be viewed as figures with something "taken away" as in the next figure of a two-dimensional mushroom shape. Its area would be the semicircle (half a circle of radius 7 inches) plus the rectangle with dimensions 7 inches for the width and 14 inches for the length, *minus* the areas of the two semicircles. The area of the semicircles is the same as the area of a circle with diameter 7 inches.

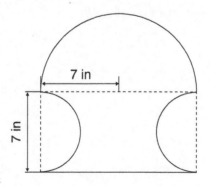

6.9 CONSTRUCTIONS

Constructions of shapes historically were performed with a straightedge, a compass, and a pencil. A straightedge can be a ruler or anything that will allow you to draw a straight line. A compass is a device that draws circles; it also measures equal distances. If the compass is opened a certain width, since all radii of a circle are equal, every arc it draws is the same distance from the point of the compass. A compass is pictured at work in the next figures. Since constructions now are mostly done by computer, we will review only some basic constructions here to show how these tools are used and how the rules of geometry influence the construction.

6.9.1 Bisecting an Angle

To construct the angle bisector of $\angle ABC$, or a ray that divides $\angle ABC$ in half, follow these steps:

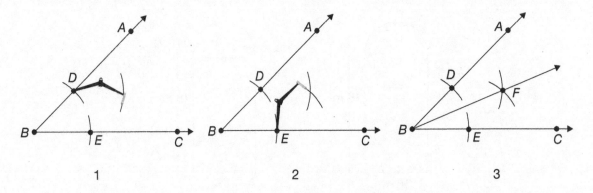

1. Use the compass to mark off equal lengths BD and BE on the rays of the angle.

2. From those two points, D and E, mark off arcs of two circles with the same radius, as shown. Again, the geometric rule here is that the radii of equal circles are equal.

3. Draw line BF from where these two arcs meet at point F to $\angle ABC$.

4. $\angle ABF = \angle CBF$, which follows the definition of **angle bisector**, because all points on BF are equidistant from the rays of $\angle ABC$.

6.9.2 Bisecting a Line Segment

To construct the bisector of a line segment, follow these steps:

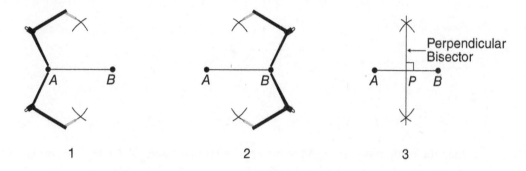

1. Mark the ends of the line segment; here they are *A* and *B*. Then put the point of the compass at the first endpoint and open the compass at a distance that is beyond where you think the middle of the line segment will be. Mark the arcs of the circle the compass would make. You don't need the whole circle, only arcs. Do this above the line and below the line.

2. Keeping the compass opening the same, do this above and below the other endpoint. The arcs will intersect above and below the line segment.

3. Draw a line through these two intersection points.

4. This line is the bisector of line segment *AB*. Not only that, it is the *perpendicular* bisector.

6.9.3 Constructing a Line Perpendicular to a Given Line

The construction of a perpendicular to a line is similar to constructing the perpendicular bisector of a line segment above, except that instead of endpoints of a line segment, the reference points on the line are two points that are equidistant from the point that lies on the perpendicular (*P*).

6.9.3a From a Point above the Line

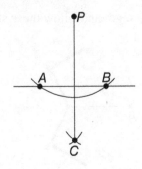

1. Open the compass more than the distance from that point (P) to the line and mark two points on the line (here they are A and B).

2. Use these points on the line as the endpoints and proceed as for the perpendicular bisector of a line segment in the last section, except you need to find only one pair of intersecting arcs (at C) because the point above the line (P) is the other point needed to draw the line.

6.9.3b From a Point on the Line

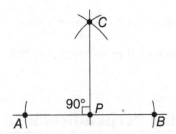

1. Use the point (P here) as the center of a circle and mark the arcs of that circle on the line.

2. Use the points on the line where the arcs intersect it (A and B here) as the endpoints and proceed as for the perpendicular bisector of a line segment in the last section, except you need to find only one pair of intersecting arcs (at C) because the point on the line (P) is the other point needed to draw the line.

6.9.4 Constructing a Line Parallel to a Given Line

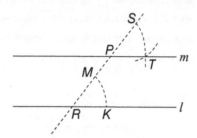

The construction of a line (*m*) parallel to a given line (*l*) and going through a given point (*P* here) uses the fact that when parallel lines are crossed by a transversal, the corresponding angles are equal. In the figure above, start with the bottom line *l* and a point *P* above it to draw a line (*m*) through *P* parallel to a given line (*l*).

1. Draw a transversal that goes through point *P* and intersects the given line at an arbitrary point *R*. This forms ∠*MRK*, and if we can duplicate that angle with *P* as the vertex, we will have equal corresponding angles and therefore parallel lines.

2. Draw an arbitrary arc using *R* as the center and then an arc with the same radius and *P* as its center, which intersects the transversal at *S*.

3. Measure ∠*MRK* by opening the compass the distance from *M* to *K* by putting the point of the compass on *M* and the pencil at *K*. Keep the compass open that exact distance and put the point on *S* and draw an arc that intersects the first arc. Call that point *T*.

4. Draw line *m* through *P* and *T*. Line *m* is parallel to line *l* because corresponding angles ∠*MRK* and ∠*SPT* are equal.

6.10 THREE-DIMENSIONAL FIGURES

Three-dimensional figures have depth in addition to length and width. Three axes for three-dimensional figures reflect these dimensions, even though they are drawn in two dimensions.

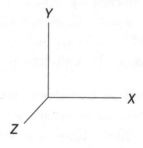

Another way to visualize how the three planes meet is to look at the corner of a room, where the two walls and the floor (or ceiling) form the three planes and the joints are the axes.

A three-dimensional figure that is drawn on a two-dimensional space shows solid lines to indicate edges that you actually see and dashed lines to indicate edges that are obscured from view. **Edges** are the lines where two **faces** (flat surfaces) meet on a three-dimensional figure. **Vertices** are the points where three or more faces meet. On the figure shown below, the arrow indicates which way the figure is facing. It takes a while to get used to this two-dimensional way of looking at three-dimensional figures.

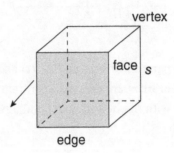

It is important for you to know the vocabulary of three-dimensional figures as well as what the variables in the given formulas mean or the formulas won't be of any use to you when answering questions on the test. This section on three-dimensional figures provides information to help you understand the formulas, but it isn't necessary to memorize them.

The **surface area** of a three-dimensional figure is exactly what it sounds like. It is the total area of all the faces, even those you cannot see in the picture unless it is a specific shape (like a silo that you want to paint, so the bottom isn't considered). For surface area, we need to remember the formulas for the areas of the two-dimensional faces that make up each three-dimensional figure. The surface area of a right rectangular prism (sometimes called a rectangular solid) can be thought of as the area of a shirt box that is covered by wrapping paper with no overlapping. The surface areas would be the sum of the areas of each of the six sides.

Volume is how much space a three-dimensional figure takes up. Basically, for three-dimensional figures that have identical "tops" and "bottoms" (bases), volume is the area of the **base** (bottom or top) multiplied by the height of the figure. Remember, as in two-dimensional figures, that the height is the altitude of the figure and is perpendicular to the base.

Volume is sometimes confused with **capacity**, which is how much a three-dimensional figure can hold. The difference between the two is the thickness of the figure. Think of a storage cube that is 12 inches on a side with 1-inch walls. The volume of the cube is 12 inches on a side, but the capacity is only 10 inches on a side because the walls take up the other 2 inches, one on each side.

The dimensions for each measure are shown in the following table. Often, the answer choices on the test will have the correct number, but different dimensions, so be sure to check both parts of the answer before making your choice. Note that the exponent matches the number of the dimension of the figure.

Unit	Dimension	Examples
Surface area	square units	ft^2, in^2, m^2, cm^2
Volume	cubic units	ft^3, in^3, m^3, cm^3

Three-dimensional figures can be made up of straight lines or curved lines. Those with only straight lines are called polyhedrons, which consist of a collection of polygons joined at their edges (e.g., prisms and pyramids). Those that have curved lines are spheres (balls), cylinders (cans), and cones (think ice cream).

6.10.1 Prisms

One type of three-dimensional figure is known as a **prism**. A prism has two **bases**, which are identical polygons lying in parallel planes. The **bases** can be regular polygons, as pictured below, but they don't have to be regular. In a **right prism**, these bases are directly above (or below) each other; in an **oblique prism**, they are offset from each other.

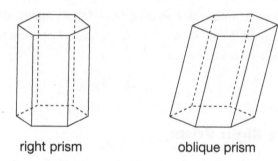

right prism   oblique prism

The lateral (side) **faces** are parallelograms that connect these identical polygons, either perpendicularly (**right prisms**) or tilted at an angle (**oblique prisms**). The faces in a right prism are perpendicular to the bases (which is why "right" is in the name—they meet the base at right angles). They are rectangles (or squares, which are special rectangles), and whenever two faces or bases meet, they form an **edge**. Each set of three edges meets at a point called the **vertex** (plural, vertices). Examples of four **right prisms** are shown below.

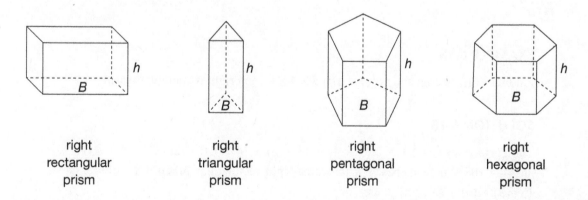

| right rectangular prism | right triangular prism | right pentagonal prism | right hexagonal prism |

The **diagonals of a right prism** are *not* the diagonals of the faces; rather, they are diagonals that run internally from one corner to another opposite corner, as shown below.

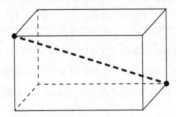

6.10.1a Surface Area of a Right Prism

As stated above, every right prism has one pair of identical faces, which are the polygon bases, and one set of lateral faces that are perpendicular to the bases. The surface area of a right prism is thus the sum of the areas of the two polygon faces and as many rectangles as there are sides in the polygon. The area of each base is usually designated as B and is calculated as shown in the section on two-dimensional figures. The area of each lateral face is the height of the prism (h) times the length of the side of the polygon. Since there are as many of these lateral sides as there are sides of the polygon, when we add up all the sides, we essentially have the perimeter of the base (p) times the height (h). Thus, the surface area becomes

$$SA_{\text{right prism}} = ph + 2B.$$

6.10.1b Volume of a Right Prism

The **volume** of a right prism follows the rule that volume is the area of the base B times the height (h) of the prism. The equation for the area of the base depends on what kind of polygon it is. The volume is thus

$$V_{\text{right prism}} = Bh.$$

The volume of an oblique prism often requires trigonometry and is omitted here.

EXAMPLE 6.18

Find the surface area and volume of a $3 \times 4 \times 6$-inch right rectangular prism.

SOLUTION 6.18

The surface area is $SA = 2[(3 \times 4) + (3 \times 6) + (4 \times 6)] = 2(12 + 18 + 24) = 2(54) = 108$ square inches. For the same right rectangular prism, the volume is $V = (3)(4)(6) = 72$ cubic inches.

6.10.1c Cube

Since a square is a rectangle with equal sides, a **cube**, which has twelve equal edges (designated s), six equal square faces, and eight equal vertices is included in the right prism classification. The surface area of the cube is thus

$$SA_{cube} = 2s^2 + 2s^2 + 2s^2 = 6s^2$$

The volume of a cube comes from the volume of a rectangular solid with $l = w = h = s$. So

$$V_{cube} = s^3$$

EXAMPLE 6.19

Kristen uses a plain wooden cube 18 inches on an edge as a plant stand.

a. She wants to cover it with a patterned adhesive paper, but first she must figure out how much paper she needs to buy. She wants to cover all the sides, including the bottom. How many square feet of paper does she need?

b. If the top of the cube is removable and the thickness of the cube is 1 inch all around, what is the capacity (in cubic inches) of the cube?

SOLUTION 6.19

a. First of all, since the paper is sold in square feet, we should convert the 18 inches into 1.5 feet to make the final calculation easier. Then the square footage Kristen needs is $(1.5)^2 = 2.25$ square feet for each side times the number of sides in a cube (which is 6), or $6(2.25) = 13.5$ square feet of paper.

b. The question asks for cubic inches, so we can leave the dimension of a side in inches. But here we need capacity, which is the "inside" volume. The inside "edge" of the cube is the outside edge minus a 1-inch-thick wall on each side, or $18 - 2(1) = 16$ inches. Then the capacity is given by $V = s^3 = (16)^3 = 4096$ cubic inches.

The capacity of the cube in Example 6.19 is different from its volume ($18^3 = 5832$ cubic inches).

6.10.2 Cylinder

This section discusses only right circular cylinders, which are in the shape of a can. If you take the cylinder apart, you will see that it consists of two round ends plus a rectangle that wraps around the can shape. (Cylinders can also be oblique, in which case the circular ends are not right on top of each other.)

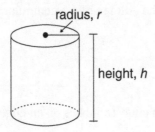

6.10.2a Surface Area of a Cylinder

Hint: Think of a soup can with the label peeled off to see that the ends are two circles, and the label is the area around the cylinder. The figure on the right is a **net**, a two-dimensional shape that is formed by unfolding a three-dimensional figure.

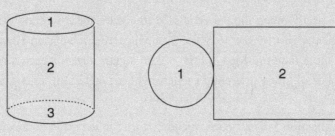

The **surface area** of a cylinder contains the areas of the two circular ends, or $2\pi r^2$, plus the area of the rectangle for the "wrap." One side of this rectangle is the height of the cylinder, h, and the other side is the circumference of the circular end ($2\pi r$), so the area of the rectangle is $2\pi rh$.

NOTE Often a problem will give the diameter of the cylinder, so be sure to change it to the radius, $r = \frac{1}{2}d$.

Therefore,

$$SA_{\text{cylinder}} = 2\pi rh + 2\pi r^2,$$

EXAMPLE 6.20

What is the least amount of paper Lisa needs in full square inches to put a label made from her own design on a can that is 6 inches high and has a diameter of 4 inches?

SOLUTION 6.20

The label on the can is the same as the surface area of the side of a cylinder, which is actually a rectangle with a length that equals the circumference of the can and a width that is the height of the can. The circumference of a circle (in this case, the end of the can) is $C = \pi d = 4\pi$, so the dimensions of the label will be $A_{rectangle} = lw = (4\pi)(6) = 24\pi = 75.398$. Note that the answer is 76 because Lisa needs more than 75 square inches.

6.10.2b Volume of a Cylinder

The **volume** of a cylinder follows the rule that it is the area of the base (πr^2) times the height, h, so

$$V = \pi r^2 h.$$

EXAMPLE 6.21

At 11 a.m., water starts to flow into a cylindrical storage tank that is 6 feet in diameter and 4 feet high. The water is coming into the tank at a rate of 20 cubic feet per hour.

a. Will the tank be above or below halfway full at 2 p.m.?

b. If the water flow into the tank is stopped at noon and a tap is opened at the bottom of the tank that lets water escape at the rate of 10 cubic feet per hour, how long will it take for the tank to empty?

SOLUTION 6.21

a. Above. The full capacity of the storage tank is given by $V = \pi r^2 h = \pi(3^2)(4) = 36\pi \approx 113$ cubic feet. Therefore, halfway full is ≈ 56.5 cubic feet. At 2 p.m., the flow of 20 cubic feet per hour has gone on for 3 hours, so $3(20) = 60$ cubic feet have entered the tank, and the tank is more than half full.

b. 2 hours. The water is escaping at half the rate that it had been entering. At noon, that would had been 1 hour of filling, so it will take 2 hours to empty the tank. No geometric calculation, just basic arithmetic, is necessary for this problem.

6.10.3 Pyramid

A **pyramid** is a three-dimensional figure in which one base is a polygon, the other end is a point, and all the faces are triangles.

In a **right regular pyramid**, the base is a regular polygon, the point is above the center of the polygon, and all of the faces are identical triangles. There is such a thing as a skew pyramid (imagine the point not being directly above the center of the base), but working with it requires trigonometry so we discuss only right regular pyramids here. In the figure below, s is the **slant height**, the distance from the edge of the base to the point, which also happens to be the altitude of the triangle. Since all of the triangles (faces) are congruent, they all have the same slant height.

The slant height s is the height of the triangular side but not the height of the pyramid, which is h.

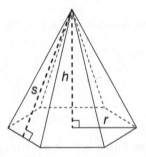

6.10.3a Surface Area of a Pyramid

The **surface area** of a pyramid is the sum of the areas of the base and the n triangles that form the sides, where n is the number of sides of the pyramid base. Obviously, if the base is a square, the sides are four triangles, and if the base is a triangle, three other triangles (not necessarily identical to the base triangle) form the sides.

The area of each triangle is $\frac{1}{2}bs$, where b is a side of the base of the pyramid, and s is the slant height. Since there are n triangles, the sum of the triangle areas is $n\left(\frac{1}{2}bs\right)$, where nb is just the perimeter ($p = nb$) of the pyramid base. So the total area of all the sides is $n\left(\frac{1}{2}bs\right) = \frac{1}{2}ps$. The area of the base, B, is the area of whatever the base polygon is. The final equation of a right regular pyramid is thus

$$SA_{\text{pyramid}} = \frac{1}{2}ps + B.$$

6.10.3b Volume of a Pyramid

 A factor of $\frac{1}{3}$ is used for the volume of all regular solids in which one "base" comes to a point (e.g., pyramid, cone). This $\frac{1}{3}$ factor is because if you filled a pyramid with liquid (turn it upside down) and poured it into a prism with the same base, you would have to do this three times to fill the prism. Hard to believe, but true.

The **volume** of a pyramid, then, instead of being Bh, as volume was for the prism, is now $\frac{1}{3}Bh$, where B is the area of the base and h is the perpendicular height from the base to the point (it is *not* the slant height).

$$V_{\text{pyramid}} = \frac{1}{3}Bh.$$

EXAMPLE 6.22

The approximate measurements of the Great Pyramid of Giza in Egypt are:

Height = 480 feet

Sides = 755 feet at the base

Slant height = 610 feet

a. What is the surface area of the Great Pyramid of Giza in Egypt?

b. How many acres does the pyramid cover? (An acre is equal to 43,560 square feet.) Give the answer rounded to the nearest whole number.

SOLUTION 6.22

a. The surface area of a pyramid is $SA_{\text{pyramid}} = \frac{1}{2}ps + B$, including the base, but since the question asks for the surface area of the pyramid, which doesn't include the base, the equation is just

$$SA_{\text{Great Pyramid}} = \frac{1}{2}ps,$$

where p is the perimeter of the base. Here the base is a square with side equal to 755 feet, so $p = 4(755) = 3020$ feet. The s in the pyramid equation is not a side, but the slant height, 610 feet.

$$SA_{\text{Great Pyramid}} = \frac{1}{2}(3020)(610) = 921{,}100 \text{ square feet}$$

b. Asking how much area the pyramid covers is the same as asking for the area of the base. Since the base is a square, the area is found by squaring one of the sides of the base, which are also the bases of the triangles, 755 feet each. So the area of the base is $(755)^2 = 570,025$ square feet. To find out how big this is in acres, use the proportion $\dfrac{1 \text{ acre}}{43,560 \text{ square feet}} = \dfrac{x \text{ acres}}{570,025 \text{ square feet}}$, which, by cross-multiplication, yields $43,560x = 570,025$, and $x = \dfrac{570,025}{43,560} = 13.09$ acres, which rounds to 13 acres. Impressive!

6.10.4 Cone

A **cone** is a three-dimensional shape that tapers from a base (usually a circle) to a point. Again, there can be skewed cones, but we will restrict our discussion to a **right circular cone**, which is like a cylinder that comes to a point. The formulas for the surface area and volume are similar to those for the pyramid, discussed above. The only difference between the right circular pyramid and cone is that the base is a circle and not a regular polygon.

6.10.4a Surface Area of a Right Circular Cone

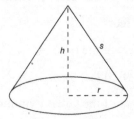

The **surface area** of a cone is the area of the base (circle) and the area of the "wraparound." This last area actually comes from the formula for the pyramid with a little imagination. Imagine that instead of, say, a square as the base of the pyramid, we have a regular polygon of 100 sides. The formula will still be the perimeter of the base times the slant height, right? Now imagine the number of sides on the base increases greatly—the base is coming very close to being a circle with that many sides, and the perimeter is coming very close to being its circumference. So instead of the pyramid's surface area of $\frac{1}{2}ps + B$ that we found for the pyramid in the last section, we substitute the circumference $(2\pi r)$ for the perimeter p. Also, B, the area of the base, now becomes the area of a circle (πr^2). So we get $SA_{\text{cone}} = \frac{1}{2}(2\pi r)s + \pi r^2$, which simplifies to

$$SA_{\text{cone}} = \pi rs + \pi r^2.$$

6.10.4b Volume of a Cone

The **volume** of a cone follows the same reasoning as for the pyramid, except that for the cone, the base is a circle of area πr^2. As mentioned before, the factor $\frac{1}{3}$ appears in the volume formula because the figure comes to a point (because 3 cones = 1 cylinder). And the height is the perpendicular height h from the point to the circular base (not the slant height). So the volume of a cone is given by

$$V_{\text{cone}} = \frac{1}{3}\pi r^2 h.$$

EXAMPLE 6.23

Find the volume of a right circular cone with a base of radius 8 inches and a slant height of 17 inches. Give your answer in terms of π.

SOLUTION 6.23

The given information includes the slant height of the cone, but the formula for a right circular cone uses the altitude, or the perpendicular height from the point to the base. So first find the altitude h by using the Pythagorean formula.

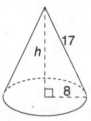

The height h, radius 8, and slant height 17 form a right triangle, as shown. The Pythagorean formula (or just remembering the 8–15–17 Pythagorean triple) yields an altitude of $h = 15$ inches. Therefore,

$$V_{\text{cone}} = \frac{1}{3}\pi r^2 h = \frac{1}{3}\pi(8)^2\left(15\right) = 320\pi \ \text{in}^3$$

6.10.5 Sphere

A **sphere** is a three-dimensional figure in which every point on the surface of the sphere is the same distance, r (the **radius**), from a point called the **center**. The idea is that it is like a three-dimensional circle.

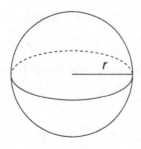

A common example of a sphere is a ball. The reason spheres are so common in nature (a drop of water, for example, or the moon) is that they have the smallest surface area for a given volume. The formulas for the surface area and volume of a sphere have a factor of 4 in them that can be explained only by using calculus (see Chapter 10).

6.10.5a Surface Area of a Sphere

The **surface area** of a sphere is similar to the area of a circle (πr^2) with a factor of 4.

$$SA_{sphere} = 4\pi r^2$$

6.10.5b Volume of a Sphere

Likewise, the formula for the volume of a sphere is similar to the formula for the volume of a cone where the height is the radius r, again with a factor of 4:

$$V_{sphere} = 4\left(\frac{1}{3}\pi r^2\right)r = \frac{4}{3}\pi r^3$$

EXAMPLE 6.24

A sphere is inside a cube so that it touches every side of the cube. If an edge of the cube is 10 inches, what is difference between the volumes of the square and the cube? Round your answer to the nearest hundredth.

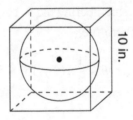

SOLUTION 6.24

The volume of the cube is $V_{cube} = s^3 = 1000$ cubic inches. The volume of the sphere is $V_{sphere} = \frac{4}{3}\pi r^3$, so we need to know the radius of the sphere. We know the diameter of the sphere because it has to be the same as the edge of the cube, or 10 inches. So the volume of the sphere is $V_{sphere} = \frac{4}{3}\pi r^3 = \frac{4}{3}\pi(5)^3 = \frac{500\pi}{3} = 523.5987756$ on the calculator. The difference to the nearest hundredth is therefore $1000 - 523.5987756 = 476.4012244$ cubic inches, which is 476.40 cubic inches when rounded to the nearest hundredth.

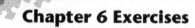

Chapter 6 Exercises

Answers are on the following pages.

1. In scalene triangle ABC, if $\angle A = 65°$ and $\angle B = 40°$, which of the following statements must be true?

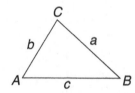

    I.   side c > side a > side b

    II. $\angle C > \angle A > \angle B$

  (A) Only I

  (B) Only II

  (C) Both I and II

  (D) Neither I nor II

2. The three circles pictured below have diameters of 6, 8, and 10 inches. What is the perimeter of the triangle formed by connecting the centers of the circles?

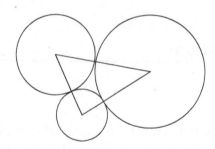

  (A) 12 inches

  (B) 12π inches

  (C) 24 inches

  (D) 48 inches

3. In circle A, what is the measure of $\angle CED$ if $\angle DBC = 35°$?

  (A) 35°

  (B) 55°

  (C) 70°

  (D) 145°

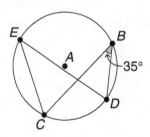

4. What are the values of a and b in degrees in the following figure of two parallel lines cut by a transversal?

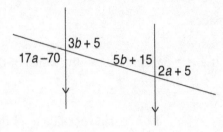

(A) $a = 20$, $b = 27.\overline{2}$

(B) $a = -5$, $b = 5$

(C) $a = 5$, $b = 20$

(D) Cannot solve this problem without more information.

5. The number of degrees between the hands of a clock at 4:20 is

(A) 0

(B) 120

(C) Less than 0

(D) More than 0

Answers and Explanations

1. **(C)**

   Statement I is true because given that $\angle A = 65°$ and $\angle B = 40°$, then $\angle C = 180° - (65° + 40°) = 75°$. Since $\angle C > \angle A > \angle B$, their corresponding sides must have the same relationship, so side $c >$ side $a >$ side b.

2. **(C)**

   The sides of the triangle are made up of the radii of the three circles. The radii are half the diameter, or 3, 4, and 5. The sides of the triangle formed are therefore $3 + 4 = 7$, $3 + 5 = 8$, and $4 + 5 = 9$ inches. Then the perimeter is $7 + 8 + 9 = 24$ inches. Alternatively, since each radius appears twice on the triangle, the perimeter is also just the sum of the diameters.

3. **(A)**

   Both $\angle CED$ and $\angle DBC$ intercept the same arc, $\overset{\frown}{CD}$, so both angles must be equal.

4. (C)

The two angles with the unknown a are supplementary angles, so their sum is 180°:

$$(3b + 5°) + (5b + 15°) = 180°$$
$$8b + 20° = 180°$$
$$b = 20°$$

The two angles with the unknown b are equal angles, so their relationship is:

$$17a - 70° = 2a + 5°$$
$$15a = 75°$$
$$a = 5$$

5. (D)

At 20 minutes past the hour the minute hand is exactly on the 4 but the hour hand has passed the 4. Therefore, the angle between the hands is more than 0 degrees.

Before you begin your review, take this short self-assessment to see how well you know the topics covered in this chapter. Answering all or some correctly will help you identify your strengths so you can focus on those topics where you need the most review. Even if you answer all of the questions correctly, we suggest you still review all the examples in the chapter to ensure you're in good shape to move on. Answers are on the following page.

1. A right circular cone is cut by a plane. If the plane cuts through two oblique sides of the cone at an angle to the base of the cone, what is the form of the intersection?

    (A) A circle

    (B) An ellipse

    (C) A parabola

    (D) A hyperbola

2. Translate the point (–2, 5) up 2 units and to the right 3 units. What are the coordinates of the translated point?

    (A) (0, 8)

    (B) (7, 1)

    (C) (3, –7)

    (D) (1, 7)

3. A rotation of 270° counterclockwise is the same as

    (A) rotating 90° clockwise.

    (B) reflecting across the line $x = y$.

    (C) reflecting across the line $y = x$.

    (D) none of the above.

4. Which of the following "facts" is FALSE?

    (A) The shortest distance between two parallel lines is a perpendicular segment.

    (B) If a line is perpendicular to a line, it is perpendicular to all of the parallels to that line.

    (C) The slopes of two perpendicular lines are reciprocals of each other.

    (D) Parallel lines have the same slope.

5. The coordinates of the midpoint (x, y) of a segment with endpoints (x_1, y_1) and (x_2, y_2) have values that are the averages of the coordinates of the endpoints. This formula is given by

    (A) $(x,y) = \left(\left(\dfrac{x_1 - x_2}{2} \right), \left(\dfrac{y_1 - y_2}{2} \right) \right)$.

    (B) $(x,y) = \left(\left(\dfrac{x_1 + x_2}{2} \right), \left(\dfrac{y_1 + y_2}{2} \right) \right)$.

    (C) $(x,y) = \left(\left(x_1 - x_2 \right), \left(y_1 - y_2 \right) \right)$.

    (D) $(x,y) = \left(\left(x_1 + x_2 \right), \left(y_1 + y_2 \right) \right)$.

1. **(B)**

   The situation described is shown below. The intersection is clearly an ellipse. A plane parallel to the base would make a circle. (Section 7.3)

   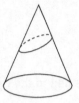

2. **(D).**

   Sketch the point and its translation on a graph. The image point is $(-2 + 3, 5 + 2) = (1, 7)$. (Section 7.5.1)

3. **(A)**

   As the figure on the right shows, rotations by 90° or any multiple of 90° just moves the figure around a point; here it is the origin. The two rotations, 270° counterclockwise and 90° clockwise are identical. (Section 7.5.3)

   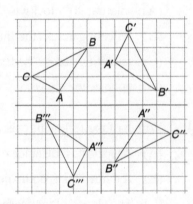

4. **(C)**

   This "rule" is incorrect. It should say: The slopes of two perpendicular lines are *negative* reciprocals of each other. (Section 7.2.5)

5. **(B)**

   The exercise says "the coordinates of the midpoint . . . have values that are the averages of the coordinates of the endpoints." The average of two elements is their sum divided by 2. Answer choice (B) is the only one that shows averages. (Section 7.2.3)

Competency 5: Coordinate Geometry

7.1 THE COORDINATE PLANE

Chapter 3, Section 3.3.2, introduced the algebraic concept of the coordinate system, which involved graphing ordered pairs and lines. In geometry, we use the same grid, called the coordinate plane, with coordinates that tell where points are on this plane, but the graphs are not just straight lines. Coordinate geometry involves distance and midpoint formulas, as well as equations for conic sections, circles, and manipulations of these figures in the plane—all of which are used in the real world.

7.2 DISTANCE AND MIDPOINT FORMULAS

7.2.1 Distance between Two Points

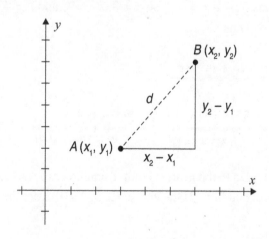

Use the Pythagorean formula to find the **distance between two points** in the coordinate plane. The figure shows two points $A(x_1, y_1)$ and $B(x_2, y_2)$. The distance d between the two points forms the hypotenuse of a right triangle, so the distance formula becomes

$$d^2 = (x_1 - x_2)^2 + (y_1 - y_2)^2$$
$$d = \sqrt{(x_1 - x_2)^2 + (y_1 - y_2)^2}$$

 Distance is always positive, so use only the positive square root of the distance formula.

7.2.2 Distance from a Point to a Line

In geometry, "distance" means the shortest distance, which is the perpendicular distance. **The distance from any point** (x_1, y_1) on the coordinate plane **to a line** $ax + by + c = 0$ is given by the following equation:

$$d = \frac{|ax_1 + by_1 + c|}{\sqrt{a^2 + b^2}}$$

EXAMPLE 7.1

Find the distance from $(3, 4)$ to the line $y = 3x + 4$ to the nearest tenth. Use the distance formula $d = \dfrac{|ax_1 + by_1 + c|}{\sqrt{a^2 + b^2}}$.

SOLUTION 7.1

To find the distance from a point to a line, the line should be in the form $ax + by + c = 0$, so we must change the given equation, $y = 3x + 4$, which is in slope-intercept form, to that form. If we put all of the terms on one side of the equation, it becomes $3x - y + 4 = 0$, so $a = 3$, $b = -1$, and $c = 4$. The point $(3, 4)$ gives $x_1 = 3$, $y_1 = 4$. Thus,

$$d = \frac{|ax_1 + by_1 + c|}{\sqrt{a^2 + b^2}}$$
$$d = \frac{|3(3) + (-1)(4) + 4|}{\sqrt{(3)^2 + (-1)^2}} = \frac{|9 - 4 + 4|}{\sqrt{9 + 1}} = \frac{9}{\sqrt{10}} = 2.8,$$

which is 2.8460 rounded to the nearest tenth. Remember to wait until the final form of the answer before rounding. At the end, enter $9 \div \sqrt{10}$ from the calculator (using the $\boxed{\sqrt{}}$ key).

When rounding to the nearest digit (here, tenths), do the rounding at the end (last step) of the calculation so you don't introduce "rounding errors."

7.2.3 Midpoint of a Line Segment

The formula for the midpoint of a line segment with endpoints (x_1, y_1) and (x_2, y_2) is the point with coordinates that are the average of the coordinates of the endpoints. An **average** is found by adding all the elements and dividing by the number of elements. Here, there are just two "elements"—the x and y values of the two points (x_1, y_1) and (x_2, y_2).

$$\text{Midpoint} = \left(\frac{x_1 + x_2}{2}, \frac{y_1 + y_2}{2} \right)$$

For example, the midpoint of the line segment with endpoints $(2, 6)$ and $(4, 10)$ is calculated as

$$\text{Midpoint} = \left(\frac{x_1 + x_2}{2}, \frac{y_1 + y_2}{2} \right) = \left(\frac{2 + 4}{2}, \frac{6 + 10}{2} \right) = (3, 8)$$

7.2.4 Using Coordinates to Find the Area of a Triangle

By using Cartesian coordinates, we can find the area of any triangle without having to find the altitude to the base if we know the coordinates of each vertex of the triangle. Finding a perpendicular measure isn't always convenient, especially if you're computing the area of a large triangular piece of land.

Heron's formula can be used to find the area of a triangle when you have the measures of the three sides. Heron's formula uses the *semi-perimeter s* (one-half the perimeter) and the measures of the three sides of a triangle (it doesn't have to be a right triangle), a, b, and c:

$$s = \frac{1}{2}(a + b + c),$$
$$A = \sqrt{s(s - a)(s - b)(s - c)}.$$

The measures of the three sides are the distances between two points. Use the distance formula.

EXAMPLE 7.2

Find the area of the triangle below:

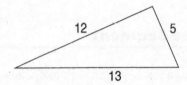

SOLUTION 7.2

Using Heron's formula, we have $S = \dfrac{1}{2}(12 + 5 + 13) = 15$. Then

$$A = \sqrt{s(s-a)(s-b)(s-c)} = \sqrt{15(15-12)(15-5)(15-13)}$$
$$= \sqrt{15(3)(10)(2)} = \sqrt{900} = 30 \text{ square units.}$$

 If you recognized this triangle as a Pythagorean triple with a base of 12 and the perpendicular side 5, the area is $A = \dfrac{1}{2}bh = \dfrac{1}{2}(12)(5) = 30$ square units.

7.2.5 Distance between Parallel Lines

To find the distance between two parallel lines, we combine six facts that we know about points and lines. There is no specific formula, just the steps for these facts. Let's refer to the following figure of two parallel lines (n and m) and a perpendicular line (p) connecting them. What we are seeking is the point of intersection of a line m and a line p that is perpendicular to line n, and then to find a point on line n so we can measure the distance from line n to line m.

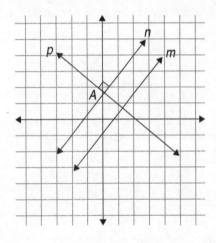

Fact 1: The shortest distance between two parallel lines is a perpendicular segment.

Fact 2: If a line is perpendicular to a line, it is perpendicular to all of the parallels to that line.

Find the equation of line n (if it isn't given) by calculating the slope and y-intercept. The slope is easy enough: Choose two points on line n and calculate slope $= \dfrac{\Delta y}{\Delta x} = \dfrac{y_2 - y_1}{x_2 - x_1}$, which is in fact the slope of both parallel lines, n and m.

Fact 3: The slopes of two perpendicular lines are negative reciprocals of each other.

Determine the equation for perpendicular line p. Its slope is the negative reciprocal of the slope of line n. To find the value of b in the equation of the perpendicular line, $y = mx + b$, substitute values of x and y, an (arbitrary) point on line n through which we will create line p, and solve for b in that equation. Now you have an equation for the perpendicular line.

Fact 4: Parallel lines have the same slope.

Determine the equation of the second parallel line (if it isn't already given). It has the same slope as the first parallel line. Determine the value of y if $x = 0$—that is the y-intercept, so we can write the equation of the second line using the slope-intercept form $y = mx + b$.

Fact 5: Two lines intersect at a point.

To find the x-value of the point of intersection A of the perpendicular line p and line m, write them both in slope-intercept form, set them equal to each other, and solve for x. Substitute this value of x into the equation for the perpendicular p to find the corresponding value of y. This point (x, y) is the point of intersection of the perpendicular line on the line m.

Fact 6: To find the distance between two points, use $d = \sqrt{(x_1 - x_2)^2 + (y_1 - y_2)^2}$.

Use the formula for the distance between the two points of intersection on line p, which lies perpendicular to both parallel lines; this is the distance between the two parallel lines.

EXAMPLE 7.3

What is the distance between $y = x + 1$ and $y = x + 6$? Round the answer to the nearest tenth.

SOLUTION 7.3

In this problem, we are given the equations for both parallel lines, so we are just finding the distance on the perpendicular line from one parallel line to the other. We must find the equation of the perpendicular line through both parallel lines. We know the slope of the perpendicular line right away—it is the negative reciprocal of the slope of either parallel line (their slopes are equal). The equations of the parallel lines give 1 as the slope; therefore, the slope of the perpendicular to these two lines is –1. For line $y = x + 1$, pick an arbitrary value for x, let's say $x = 1$. When $x = 1$, $y = 1 + 1 = 2$. This point $(1, 2)$ on the line $y = x + 1$ will also be on the perpendicular to the line $y = x + 6$. To find the equation of the perpendicular to the first line at $(1, 2)$, the slope of the perpendicular line is –1, and the y-intercept can be found by solving $y = mx + b$ for b by using the point $(1, 2)$. We then have $2 = -1(1) + b$, and therefore $b = 3$, and the equation for the perpendicular line is $y = -x + 3$.

The equation for the second line is given as $y = x + 6$, and the perpendicular will intersect it at the point where the two equations are true, or $x + 6 = -x + 3$, or $2x = -3$, and $x = -\frac{3}{2}$. The y value at that point is $y = \frac{9}{2}$.

The problem then is to find the distance from point $\left(-\frac{3}{2}, \frac{9}{2}\right)$ to the point $(1, 2)$ using the distance equation:

$$d = \sqrt{(x_1 - x_2)^2 + (y_1 - y_2)^2} =$$

$$\sqrt{\left(1 + \frac{3}{2}\right)^2 + \left(2 - \frac{9}{2}\right)^2} = \sqrt{\left(\frac{5}{2}\right)^2 + \left(-\frac{5}{2}\right)^2} = \sqrt{\frac{50}{4}} = \frac{5}{2}\sqrt{2} = 3.5355339,$$

or 3.5 rounded to the nearest tenth.

7.3 CONIC SECTIONS

A **conic section** is the intersection of a plane slicing through a cone, which is how it gets its name. Even though a cone is a three-dimensional figure, when it is intersected by a plane, the resulting intersection is a two-dimensional figure called a conic section. Each of the conics is a set of points (called a **locus**) that obeys some sort of rule or rules. The equations of these conics are **second-degree equations**, which means the highest total power of any term is two. Conic sections include **ellipses**, **parabolas**, and **hyperbolas**, as well as circles, depending on the angle of the slicing plane, as shown in the following figures.

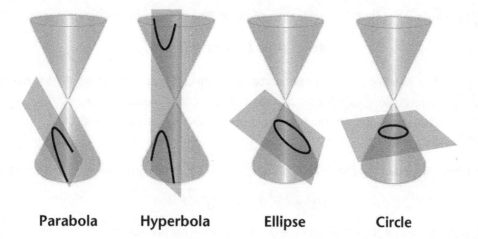

Parabola   **Hyperbola**   **Ellipse**   **Circle**

For the hyperbola, *two* cones are involved. The plane for the other conic sections slice through only one cone.

7.3.1 General Form of Equations for Conic Sections

The **general form** of second-degree equations is $Ax^2 + Bxy + Cy^2 + Dx + Ey + F = 0$, but here we consider only conics with no xy terms, so $B = 0$.

Therefore, the **general equation for conics** is

$$Ax^2 + Cy^2 + Dx + Ey + F = 0$$

From this general equation, we can create specific general equations for the parabola, hyperbola, ellipse, and circle. Given a general equation, we can always figure out what the conic is from the following list and the flow chart that follows it.

For all conic sections, the x-intercepts are found by setting $y = 0$, and the y-intercepts are found by setting $x = 0$.

- **Parabola**. This is the graph of a quadratic equation, which we saw in Chapter 3, Section 3.7. It has no y^2 term. This parabola opens vertically.

$$Ax^2 + Dx + Ey + F = 0$$

For a parabola that opens horizontally—it looks like a vertical parabola lying on its side—the equation would be $Ay^2 + Dx + Ey + F = 0$ with no x^2 term.

- **Hyperbola**. Note that the coefficients of the x^2 and y^2 terms have different signs.

$$Ax^2 - Cy^2 + Dx + Ey + F = 0$$

 The equation $xy =$ constant is actually a special case of a hyperbola that has only an xy term, no x^2 or y^2 terms, and the constant cannot equal 0. Here, we discuss only the general equation of the hyperbola shown above, but you should know that the other one exists.

- **Ellipse**. Note that the coefficients of the x^2 and y^2 terms are different, but have the same sign.

$$Ax^2 + Cy^2 + Dx + Ey + F = 0$$

- **Circle**. Note that the coefficients of the x^2 and y^2 terms are equal.

$$Ax^2 + Cy^2 + Dx + Ey + F = 0, \text{ where } A = C$$

The conics are presented here in this specific order because, given any general form of a conic, we can figure out which one it is by using the following "flow chart" and not have to do any calculations.

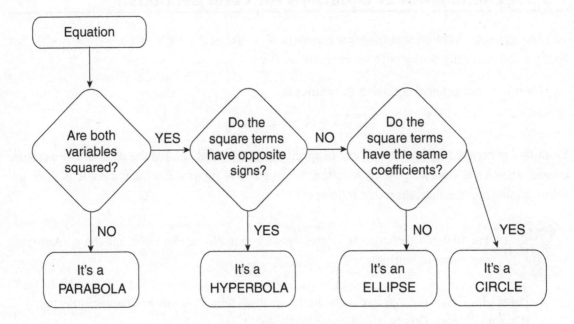

For any conic equation in general form, you have to look **only** at the x^2 and y^2 terms to determine the type of conic.

EXAMPLE 7.4

What conic section does the equation $x^2 + 4y^2 + 8x - 8y + 16 = 0$ represent?

SOLUTION 7.4

Right away you know it isn't a parabola because it has two "square" terms. Now all you have to do is look at the coefficients of x^2 and y^2; +1, and +4—they don't have different signs, so it's not a hyperbola, and they aren't equal, so it can't be a circle—therefore, it must be an ellipse.

Eccentricity is a measure of the curvature of a conic section, we can determine what kind of conic a figure is if all we know is its eccentricity.

- If eccentricity $e = 0$, the figure is a circle.

- If eccentricity $0 < e < 1$, it is an ellipse.

- If eccentricity $e = 1$, it is a parabola.

- If eccentricity $e > 1$, it is a hyperbola.

7.3.2 Standard Form of Equations, Graphs, and Parameters

The values for all of the parameters for a conic section are contained in the **standard form** of the equation. The general form, discussed in Section 7.3.1, can quickly tell the shape of the conic just by looking at the coefficients of the squared terms, but the standard form easily tells the parameters needed to sketch the conic. The two equation forms for a conic are related. In fact, the standard form is found by completing the squares in the general form (see Chapter 3, Section 3.8.1, for the steps used in completing the square).

The following sections describe features of the conic sections, using the standard form of their equations.

7.3.2a Parabola

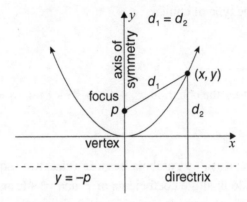

A **parabola**, as we saw in Chapter 3, Section 3.8.2a, is U-shaped. The formal definition of a parabola is the set of all points in a plane equally distant from a fixed line (**directrix**) and a fixed point not on the line (**focus**). The figure above shows a parabola with its vertex at the origin.

The standard form for a parabola is $y = a(x - h)^2 + k$, where $x = h$ is the **axis of symmetry** and the point (h, k) is the **vertex** is the lowest or highest point of the parabola, depending on whether the parabola opens up or down. The sign of a, the coefficient of x^2, tells whether the parabola opens up ($a > 0$) or down ($a < 0$).

The **eccentricity** of a parabola is 1 because the distance from any point on the parabola to the focus equals the distance from that point to the directrix.

 The sign of a, the coefficient of x^2 in either the general or standard form, tells the direction of the parabola. If it is positive, the parabola opens upward; if it is negative, the parabola opens downward.

7.3.2b Hyperbola

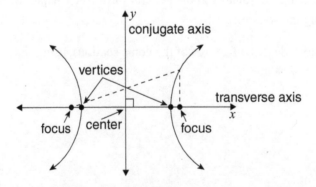

A **hyperbola** looks like two mirror-image parabolas, with each of its "arcs" bound by two slant asymptotes. It is defined as the set of all points in the plane such that the difference of their distances from two fixed points, called **foci**, is a constant. The figure on page 232 shows a hyperbola, horizontally oriented, with its center at the origin.

The standard form of a hyperbola is $\dfrac{(x - h)^2}{a^2} - \dfrac{(y - k)^2}{b^2} = 1$. To find the parameters of the hyperbola, its general equation must be converted to standard form by completing the two squares (one involving the x^2 and x terms, and one involving the y^2 and y terms). Then the center is at (h, k). The orientation is determined by the placement of the a^2 term: if it is below the x^2 term, the axis of the hyperbola is horizontal; if it is below the y^2 term, the axis is vertical.

The **center** of the hyperbola is the point midway between the foci and midway between the vertices. A hyperbola has two perpendicular **lines of symmetry**, the **focal (transverse) axis** and the **conjugate axis**, and two **asymptotes**. The **eccentricity** of a hyperbola is greater than 1.

The larger the eccentricity for a hyperbola, the straighter the curvature.

7.3.2c Ellipse

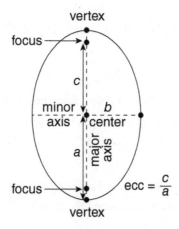

An **ellipse** is the set of all points in a plane such that the sum of the distances from two fixed points (**foci**) is a constant. It has two lines of symmetry, called the **major axis** and the **minor axis**. The major axis is always longer than the minor axis. The ends of the major axis are considered to be the vertices of the ellipse. The center of an ellipse is midway between the foci and midway between each pair of vertices. The figure above shows an ellipse oriented vertically.

The standard form for a vertical ellipse is $\dfrac{(x - h)^2}{b^2} + \dfrac{(y - k)^2}{a^2} = 1$, which is derived from the general form by completing the squares for x as well as y. The point (h, k) is the center of the ellipse. Ellipses are like circles but with major and minor axes, which give them their oval shape. The value of a is half the length of the major axis, and the value of b is half the length of the minor axis. a^2 is always in the denominator of the major axis, and thus $a > b$.

 NOTE The eccentricity of an ellipse $\left(e = \dfrac{c}{a} \right)$ varies from 0 to 1; the closer the eccentricity is to 1, the narrower is the ellipse; the closer the eccentricity is to 0, the closer the ellipse is to a perfect circle.

7.3.2d Circle

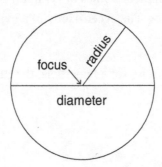

A **circle** is defined as a closed plane curve consisting of all points at a given distance from a point within it called the **center**.

The standard form of the circle is $(x - h)^2 + (y - k)^2 = r^2$. The point (h, k) is the center of the circle and r is the radius, which must always be a positive number. To get the standard form from the general form for a circle, complete the square twice, once for x and once for y. Rewrite any equation for a circle in standard form to find the center and radius readily.

 NOTE The eccentricity of a circle is 0 because the center and focus of the figure are the same point, so the distance between them is 0.

EXAMPLE 7.5

Describe the shape of the graph of the general equation $x^2 + 4x - y - 5 = 0$.

SOLUTION 7.5

First, since this equation has no y^2 term, it is a parabola. To find the standard form, move the y term to one side of the equation and complete the square of $(x^2 + 4x)$. (Take half of the coefficient of x, square it, and add and subtract the result (4) to the equation.) This yields $y = (x^2 + 4x + 4) - 5 - 4$ or $y = (x + 2)^2 - 9$, which is in the form $y = a(x - h)^2 + k$. Thus, the vertex is at $(h, k) = (-2, -9)$, the axis of symmetry is $x = -2$, and the parabola opens upward.

7.3.3 Summary

A summary of the terminology for conic sections is presented in the following table.

Parameter	Circle	Ellipse	Parabola	Hyperbola
center	(h, k)	(h, k)	None	(h, k)
vertex		Endpoints of major axis	Highest or lowest point: (h, k)	Turning point of a branch
focus, directrix, and eccentricity	Point and line from which distances are measured in forming a conic. The ratio $e = \dfrac{\text{focus to conic}}{\text{directrix to conic}}$, called the eccentricity, determines which conic it is.			
	$e = 0$	$0 < e < 1$	$e = 1$	$e > 1$
axis		Major axis is a line segment of an ellipse and passing through the foci; also called the principal axis of symmetry. The semi-major axis is half the major axis. Minor axis: a line segment perpendicular to and bisecting the major axis of an ellipse. The axes terminate on the ellipse at either end.	Axis of symmetry: Line perpendicular to the directrix and passing through the vertex.	Transverse axis: Line through the center and two foci; the axis through the center and perpendicular to the transverse axis is called the conjugate axis.

7.4 REAL-WORLD APPLICATIONS OF CONIC SECTIONS

Conic sections can be seen everywhere—from clock faces to "golden" arches. But sometimes they are not as obvious. For example, although some people may think a rainbow is in the shape of a parabola, in the right circumstances (such as when viewed from above), a rainbow can be seen as a circle. But most times we see only a portion of the circle, which looks like a parabola.

A lot less obvious, and a lot more interesting is a sonic boom, the loud noise that is produced by an aircraft traveling faster than the speed of sound. The sound is the shock wave in the form of a cone, as the sound waves in front of the aircraft intersect sound waves carried by the aircraft if it is going about 700 miles per hour. A double sound can be heard if the aircraft is large enough—one from the nose of the aircraft and one from the tail. Usually the aircraft is so small, relatively speaking, that the two booms are detected by the human ear as one loud bang. A sonic boom could also be caused by a meteor traveling close to Earth.

But what does this have to do with the coordinate plane? One theory is that the cone-shaped shock wave intersects with the ground (a plane—not an airplane, but a geometric plane), and the intersection is two points on the plane (see the figure below). These locations are the sources of sounds at two places, which is heard as two sonic booms. The cone is a series of circles perpendicular to the Earth, and the locations of the two places on the ground form a portion of a hyperbola, which also looks like a parabola.

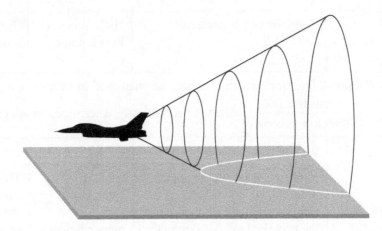

Some more usual real-life applications and occurrences of conic sections are shown in the following sections.

7.4.1 Parabola

Fountains usually arc in the form of a parabola. That is true for the water fountains we drink from as well as fountains in the middle of a lake, as shown here.

The fact that waves bounce perpendicularly off of surfaces makes the parabola useful in the following items: (1) parabolic mirrors converge light beams at the focus of the parabola; (2) parabolic microphones converge sound waves at a focal point; (3) solar ovens using parabolic mirrors converge sunlight for heating; (4) the parabolic lenses of spotlights and car headlights concentrate light beams; and (5) parabolic antennas concentrate radio waves for TV, cell phones, and other devices.

Due to gravity, the trajectories of objects thrown or shot near Earth's surface are in the shape of a parabola. Examples are a baseball hit by a bat, a football kicked for a field goal, and a basketball thrown for a free throw. In fact, to shoot an arrow at a target, you shouldn't just shoot straight at the target because gravity will cause the arrow to fall to the ground short of the target. Instead, shoot up at an angle so the highest point of the parabolic trajectory of the arrow is halfway between yourself and the target, and the arrow will hit the target every time. It does take a lot of practice in all sports to see where that trajectory will hit its highest point (apex) and how hard you have to throw, kick, run, shoot, or pull the bow to reach your target. The path of a bullet also is a parabola, but it is so fast that the apex is way past the target.

Other examples of parabolic trajectories are the path of a rocket or the path of a dolphin dive.

Bridges use the geometry of triangles for strength, as mentioned in Chapter 6, Section 6.4. But bridges also use parabolas, as seen in suspension bridges such as the Golden Gate Bridge (left) or regular arch bridges with support from below (right).

After circles, parabolas are the most common conic sections that we see in everyday life.

7.4.2 Hyperbola

The path some astronomical objects take around the sun is hyperbolic (they do not revolve around the sun over and over, they approach, get close then leave in a hyperbolic path).

Hyperbolas are used in a navigation system known as LORAN (long-range navigation).

Hyperbolic (as well as parabolic) mirrors and lenses are used in systems of telescopes.

Cooling towers of nuclear reactors are in the shape of hyperboloids, which are three-dimensional shapes related to hyperbolas.

A hyperbolic paraboloid is a three-dimensional curve that is a hyperbola in one direction and a parabola in the other. A Pringles potato chip or a Western saddle are examples of hyperbolic paraboloids.

Although not as obvious as parabolas, hyperbolas are evident in everyday life. For example, lamplight often causes a hyperbolic shape on the wall. Note, though, that the shape is a parabola if the light source is a flashlight held against a wall.

7.4.3 Ellipse

One of the most famous examples of ellipses are the orbits of the planets with the sun at one focus. The path of Haley's comet is also an ellipse, but its axes are crosswise to the planets' orbits, which explains why it can be seen at irregular intervals. And, contrary to popular thought, Earth is not a sphere, but something called an oblate spheroid because its equatorial diameter is slightly larger than its polar diameter. Therefore, its cross section from pole to pole is an ellipse with a very small eccentricity rather than a circle.

An interesting feature in architecture, called whispering galleries, is due to sound waves at one focus of an ellipse reflecting off the ceiling and going to the other focus of the ellipse. Many whispering galleries exist around the world; the first was in St. Paul Cathedral in London. The old senate chamber in the U.S. Capitol building was designed as a so-called whispering gallery so that speakers could be heard clearly before electronic amplification was invented. In fact, whispering galleries can be circular or even use two parabolic dishes, but they all must have an ellipsoidal ceiling. Architecture also uses ellipses in arches, which are actually half ellipses.

Although you may not think of coordinate geometry at a football game, often you are sitting in an ellipse (left). Another example of an elliptical arena is the Colosseum in Rome (right), which contains two elliptical formations of arches.

7.4.4 Circle

Examples of circles are all around (no pun intended). Wheels, clocks, camera lenses, pizzas, Ferris wheels, rings, cakes, pies, buttons, gears, and coins are just some of the examples.

As discussed at the beginning of Section 7.4, a rainbow is actually a circle. Its center is the point opposite the sun in the sky.

7.5 TRANSFORMATIONS IN THE COORDINATE PLANE

A geometric **transformation** is a mapping of a figure, called the **preimage** to its corresponding figure, called the **image**. Transformation involves

- *Translation*: moving an object left or right, up or down, but keeping the same orientation

- *Reflection*: flipping the object across either axis

- *Rotation*: turning the object around a point.

These mathematical transformations are useful in graphic arts, architecture, masonry, jewelry design, and many other occupations.

7.5.1 Translation

Translation means moving an object from one place to another. It doesn't change its size or orientation. In other words, the preimage and the image are congruent and have the same orientation.

 Hint: Think of a translation as sliding a penny across a table from one position to another without allowing it to rotate or flip over as you slide it.

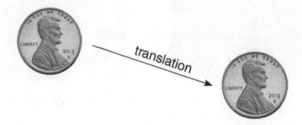

If a translation is vertical, or "up" or "down," the *x*-coordinate stays the same and the *y*-coordinate changes by the amount of the translation (+ for up and – for down). Similarly, if a translation is horizontal, or "left" or "right," the *y*-coordinate stays the same and the *x*-coordinate changes by the amount of the translation (+ for right and – for left). A translation at an angle is done in two steps, horizontal and then vertical (or vice versa).

 Hint: If a translation is in two steps, just do the first one alone, and then the second one starting from the new position.

EXAMPLE 7.6

Point P (5, −3) is plotted on a coordinate grid. If point S is 4 units above point P, what are the coordinates of point S?

SOLUTION 7.6

Here we aren't really physically translating point P, but using translation to figure where point S would be. The translation is up (S is above point P), so we add 4 to the y-coordinate. Point S is aligned in the horizontal direction above point P, and the coordinates of S are (5, 1).

EXAMPLE 7.7

Translate the point (3, −5) down 2 units and to the right 4 units. What are the coordinates of the translated point?

SOLUTION 7.7

Sketch the point and its translation on a graph. The image point is $(3 + 4, -5 - 2) = (7, -7)$.

Translating points isn't very complicated. A little more complicated is translating figures, such as triangles, but you can streamline that translation by looking at the vertices individually instead of thinking about the whole figure, which sometimes is complicating.

EXAMPLE 7.8

Triangle ABC is drawn on the coordinate plane, as shown below. If the triangle were translated to the left 4 units, what would be the new coordinate of point B?

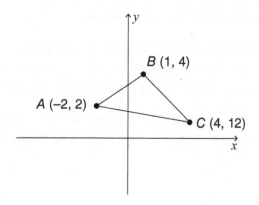

SOLUTION 7.8

This problem is the same as if it had asked, "If the point (1, 4) is translated to the left 4 units, what would be the new coordinates?" Don't let the fact that point B is part of a triangle throw you—it is asking only about point B. We just move 4 units to the left for the new x-coordinate, and the y-coordinate remains the same. Four units left from 1 is –3, so the answer is (–3, 4). For this problem, it really doesn't matter where the rest of the triangle goes. It is asking only about point B.

Another variation of this sort of problem is to be given a choice of four graphed translations. Save time and trouble by first finding only one point, which will probably eliminate one or two answer choices, and then look at the next point—most likely that's all that you would need to do. Only one of the remaining choices will match those two points. The idea is that you don't have to find all the points if you are given a choice of answers in graphed form.

Many test-takers get confused with transformations because they look at the whole picture and it's too many points to keep straight. The tactic should be to streamline the process as much as possible, saving time and frustration. This type of thinking also works for reflections and rotations.

7.5.2 Reflection

A **reflection** over a line is a transformation in which each point on the preimage is mapped to a point that is the same distance from the reflection line as was the preimage point but it is on the opposite side of the line. Reflection is just what it sounds like. If we placed a mirror on the reflection line (usually, the x-axis, the y-axis, or the line $y = x$), we would see where the reflection of a point would go. But that isn't feasible in a test setting, nor is it easy to do anyway. The rule for reflection across an axis is: For a reflection across the x-axis, change the sign of the y-coordinate; for a reflection across the y-axis, change the sign of the x-coordinate.

If a point is reflected across the x-axis, we know we are going up or down, depending on where the original point was. The reflected point must be in the opposite quadrant (up or down), the x value doesn't change, and the new y value is simply the opposite of the old y value.

The usual reflections of a preimage $P(x, y)$ are over the x-axis $\left[P(x, y) \rightarrow P'(x,-y) \right]$; y-axis $\left[P(x, y) \rightarrow P'(-x, y) \right]$; the line $y = x$ $\left[P(x, y) \rightarrow P'(y,x) \right]$; or the line $y = -x$ $\left[P(x, y) \rightarrow P'(-y,-x) \right]$.

EXAMPLE 7.9

Reflect the point (4, –2) across the *x*-axis. What are the new coordinates?

SOLUTION 7.9

Just change the sign of the *y* value: (4, 2).

Again, if the problem presents a triangle and a line of reflection and wants to know how the new triangle will look, the problem will probably present multiple-choice graphs. The same as for translations, break this up into pieces (actually, individual coordinates). Look at one vertex at a time. Make sure the new positions have the same letter, probably with a prime. Eliminate any graphs that don't match up. Probably only two vertices are needed, and maybe not even two. Don't get confused with the sides of the triangle—it's the placement of the vertices that make the difference. Usually, the correct answer choice is obvious early on by elimination.

7.5.3 Rotation

A **rotation** is a transformation that turns an object about a fixed point called the **center of rotation**. Actually, the hardest part of rotation problems is remembering what *clockwise* and *counterclockwise* mean. **Clockwise** means what it sounds like: turning like a clock, from 1 to 2 to 3. The other way is called **counterclockwise**. Chapter 8 shows that trigonometric rotation is usually counterclockwise, but it's a good idea to mention the direction. An **angle of rotation** tells how far to turn; it is the angle formed between the preimage and the image.

Each quadrant is 90 degrees. Rotation is counterclockwise, as can be seen from the numbering of the quadrants (see Section 3.3.2).

- Rotating a figure 90 degrees just means it will go into the next quadrant, for example from Quadrant I to Quadrant II.

- Rotating a figure 180 degrees puts the figure halfway around (clockwise or counterclockwise), for example, from Quadrant I to Quadrant III.

- Rotating a figure 270 degrees goes three-quarters of the way around, for example from Quadrant I to Quadrant IV.

 Hint: Rotating 270 degrees clockwise is the same as rotating 90 degrees counterclockwise (think of a clock face, which will make visualization simpler).

The visualization of a two-blade "fan" shown below (start anywhere and go in any direction) will help to locate a point on a figure that is being rotated. Notice two things: the point closest to the hub (intersection of the axes) remains closest to the hub. It doesn't flip over either vertically or horizontally. Likewise, the point that is farthest from the hub (F) also just rotates as shown and is farthest from the hub in all rotations.

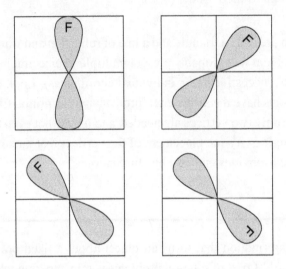

Concentrate on the part of the figure that is in one quadrant, even though the figure itself may cross over into other quadrants. As with the other transformations, look at one point in the figure at a time. The placement of the points (or vertices) is what makes the difference. Usually, the correct answer choice becomes obvious early on by elimination.

EXAMPLE 7.10

What is the orientation of the following figure when it has been rotated 270° clockwise?

SOLUTION 7.10

Imagine the original figure in the first quadrant. Then look at the point of the arrowhead in relation to what would be the hub (lower left corner). Go counterclockwise 90°, which is equivalent to what was asked, 270° clockwise. So the answer comes with the first tumble counterclockwise. This is a rotation by 270° clockwise.

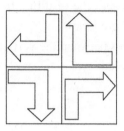

7.5.4 Dilation

A **dilation** is a transformation that reduces or enlarges the size of a figure by a given **scale factor** relative to a fixed point called the **center of dilation**. The preimage and image thus are similar, just different sizes. A dilation by a scale factor a can be thought of as the transformation $\left[P(x, y) \rightarrow P'(ax, ay) \right]$. If a is >1, then the image is an enlargement; if $0 < a < 1$, it is a reduction; and if $a = 1$, there is no change. Dilation is sometimes called a **size transformation**.

 Some people may think that dilation is only an enlargement, like when the pupil of your eye is dilated for a vision exam, but actually *dilation* is a catch-all word meaning to change size (orientation stays the same).

EXAMPLE 7.11

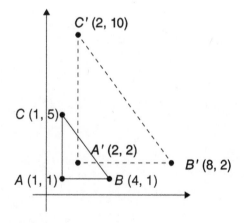

Map the points of triangle *ABC* with vertices at (1, 1), (4, 1), and (1, 5) onto a dilation *A'B'C'* with scale factor 2, translated one unit up and one unit to the right.

SOLUTION 7.11

The mapping of a dilation by a factor of 2 preserves the similarity between the figures—the corresponding angles $(A \rightarrow A', B \rightarrow B', C \rightarrow C')$ are equal, even though their *coordinates* are doubled. The information "translated one unit up and one unit to the right" distinguishes the resulting triangle from the infinite number of other triangles that could be dilations of the original one by fixing one of the resultant vertices. The distances between the vertices, which are the lengths of the sides of the triangles, are doubled.

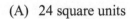

Chapter 7 Exercises

Answers are on the following page.

1. What is the volume of this cube?

    (A) 24 square units

    (B) 64 square units

    (C) 512 cubic inches

    (D) 512 cubic units

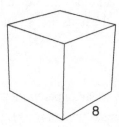

2. What conic section does the equation $x^2 - 4y^2 + 8x - 8y + 16 = 0$ represent?

    (A) Ellipse

    (B) Parabola

    (C) Hyperbola

    (D) Circle

3. If a circle and a line are graphed on the same Cartesian coordinate system, they can intersect in how many points?

    (A) 0

    (B) 1

    (C) 2

    (D) Any of the above.

4. A cone is to a cylinder as

    (A) a pyramid is to a prism.

    (B) a square is to a cube.

    (C) a sphere is to a cone.

    (D) a pyramid is to a cylinder.

5. Sarah and Emily rode their bikes 10 miles east, then 4 miles south, and then 13 miles west. How much farther west were they compared to where they started?

    (A) 13 miles

    (B) 3 miles

    (C) 5 miles

    (D) 27 miles

Answers and Explanations

1. **(D)**

Since this is a cube, all sides are equal to 8 units. The volume is $V = lwh = 8^3 = 512$ cubic units. We aren't told what the units are, so answer choice (C) is wrong.

2. **(C)**

Right away you know it isn't a parabola because it has two "square" terms. Now all you have to do is look at the coefficients of x^2 and y^2; +1, and –4 — they have different signs, so it's a hyperbola.

3. **(D)**

It is possible that the line doesn't intersect the circle at all (picture a line that goes from the third quadrant diagonally to the first quadrant and a circle completely in the fourth quadrant). It is also possible for the line to intersect the circle in only one point, such as the point of tangency of a tangent line. And, of course, a line going through the circle (secant) intersects it in two points.

4. **(A)**

The analogy of a cone to a cylinder is that a cone's volume is one-third that of a cylinder. Likewise, in answer choice (A), a pyramid's volume is one-third that of a prism. Answer choices (B) and (C) involve a combination of three-dimensional and two-dimensional figures, and although answer choice (D) has two three-dimensional figures, they are not related.

5. **(B)**

Be sure you read questions carefully. The question merely asks how much farther west they were, which is the difference between their eastward distance and their westward distance, which is $13 - 10 = 3$. If you misinterpreted the question as asking how far they were from their starting point, the answer is 5 miles.

Before you begin your review, take this short self-assessment to see how well you know the topics covered in this chapter. Answering all or some correctly will help you identify your strengths so you can focus on those topics where you need the most review. Even if you answer all of the questions correctly, we suggest you still review all the examples in the chapter to ensure you're in good shape to move on. Answers are on the following page.

1. Calculate the solution(s) to the equation $\tan^2\theta - \tan\theta = 0$ in the first quadrant.

   (A) $0°$

   (B) $45°$

   (C) $0°$ and $45°$

   (D) The solution isn't in Quadrant I.

2. The notation $\sin^{-1}x$ means

   (A) $\cos x$.

   (B) $\csc x$.

   (C) The angle whose sine is x.

   (D) $\dfrac{1}{\sin x}$.

3. A guy wire for a flagpole makes an angle of $60°$ with the ground. The stake for the guy wire is 12 feet from the flagpole. What is the length of the wire to the nearest foot?

   (A) 21 feet

   (B) 24 feet

   (C) 13 feet

   (D) Cannot tell from the information given.

4. To convert from angle measurement in degrees to radians, multiply by

   (A) 180π.

   (C) $\dfrac{180}{\pi}$.

   (B) 2π.

   (D) $\dfrac{2\pi}{360}$.

5. The general form for the equation of the sine function is $y = A\sin B(x - C) + D$. To change the period of $y = \sin x$, which coefficient or term would be changed?

   (A) A

   (C) C

   (B) B

   (D) D

1.   (C)

   Factor the equation as an algebra equation: $\tan\theta(\tan\theta - 1) = 0$. Set each factor equal to 0 to get $\tan\theta = 0$ and $\tan\theta - 1 = 0$, so $\theta = \arctan 0 = 0°$ and $\theta = \arctan 1 = 45°$. (Section 8.5.4)

2.   (C)

   The notation $\sin^{-1} x$ is the inverse of the sine function, which is the notation for "the angle whose sine is x." (Section 8.4)

3.   (B)

   The guy wire, pole, and the ground form a 30°–60°–90° triangle, in which the side opposite the 30° angle (which is the angle between the pole and the guy wire) is half the hypotenuse (which is the length of the guy wire). Therefore, the guy wire is 2(12) = 24 feet long. Using trigonometry, $\sin 30° = \dfrac{12}{\text{length of guy wire}}$, and since $\sin 30° = \dfrac{1}{2}$, the guy wire must be 24 feet long. (Section 8.3.2)

4.   (D)

   Multiplying by a quantity that equals 1, doesn't change its value. Usually, the conversion multiplication is given by $\dfrac{\pi}{180}$, but that is equivalent to $\dfrac{2\pi}{360}$. (Section 8.2)

5.   (B)

   Inserting a coefficient before the angle measure either stretches the curve out (if $B < 1$) or pulls it tighter (if $B > 1$). The other coefficients change the amplitude (A), cause a phase shift (C), or cause a vertical shift (D). (Section 8.6.1)

CHAPTER 8

Competency 6: Trigonometry

8.1 WHY LEARN TRIGONOMETRY?

Students' questions such as "Why learn algebra?" and "Why learn geometry?" can be answered based on practicality (how to figure out how much change to receive on a purchase; how to estimate distances, etc.). The same type of answer about trigonometry isn't so obvious to some students, however. Nevertheless, trigonometry has relevance in today's world, just as it did centuries ago when astronomers used the principles of trigonometry (although they didn't necessarily have that name for it) for astronomical observations.

Almost every branch of research, development, and manufacture depends on trigonometry in some way, even though it isn't immediately obvious. Examples include the following:

- Modern architecture is highly dependent on trigonometry to calculate angles so that features that are interesting to look at are also structurally sound. In fact, many curved surfaces are made up of thin flat surfaces at small angles to each other that give the appearance of one curved surface.

- The field of medicine uses trigonometry in computer generation of complex imagery such as CAT and MRI scans.

- Interior decorating uses trigonometry to compute aesthetic placements and symmetry.

- Navigation and surveying depend on trigonometry.

- Space travel uses trigonometry to compute launch and reentry trajectories, as well as orbits.

- Navigation of the seas and land surveying are heavily dependent on trigonometry.

- The calculations of sound and light waves in the design of a music venue are trigonometric.

8.2 BASIC TRIGONOMETRIC VOCABULARY

A right triangle is the basis for the definitions of the **trigonometric (trig) functions**. Because all right triangles with the same corresponding angles are similar (see Chapter 6, Section 6.4.2), the ratios between any two sides of all right triangles are the same for a particular angle measurement. In the figure below, we can state these ratios in trigonometric terms for $\angle\theta$, where *opposite* means the side opposite $\angle\theta$, and *adjacent* means the side adjacent to $\angle\theta$ (the other adjacent side being the hypotenuse). The hypotenuse is always opposite the right angle.

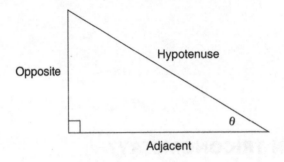

The three basic trigonometric functions are **sine**, **cosine**, and **tangent** (abbreviated as sin, cos, and tan, respectively).

$$\sin\theta = \frac{\text{opposite}}{\text{hypotenuse}}$$

$$\cos\theta = \frac{\text{adjacent}}{\text{hypotenuse}}$$

$$\tan\theta = \frac{\text{opposite}}{\text{adjacent}}$$

The three other trig functions are simply reciprocals of these three, going in the direction from tangent to sine. They are the **cotangent** (cot), **secant** (sec), and **cosecant** (csc).

$$\cot\theta = \frac{1}{\tan\theta} = \frac{\text{adjacent}}{\text{opposite}}$$

$$\sec\theta = \frac{1}{\cos\theta} = \frac{\text{hypotenuse}}{\text{adjacent}}$$

$$\csc\theta = \frac{1}{\sin\theta} = \frac{\text{hypotenuse}}{\text{opposite}}$$

The abbreviation for cosecant cannot be "cos" because that abbreviation is already used for cosine.

Values for only the sine and cosine are needed to get values for the rest of the functions since they are all related to those two functions:

$$\tan\theta = \frac{\sin\theta}{\cos\theta}; \quad \cot\theta = \frac{\cos\theta}{\sin\theta}; \quad \sec\theta = \frac{1}{\cos\theta}; \quad \csc\theta = \frac{1}{\sin\theta}$$

Hint: Keeping the above definitions in mind, most trigonometric relationships can be derived rather than memorized. In other words, you don't have to memorize them because you can figure them out.

Angles are measured in degrees and also in **radians**. The formal definition of a radian is the measure of a central angle that intercepts an arc equal to the radius of the circle. (The name *radian* is a contraction of radius-angle.)

Since the circumference of a circle is $C = 2\pi r$ (see Chapter 6, Section 6.7.2), it makes sense that there are 2π radians in the circumference of a circle. So a circle measures $360° = 2\pi$ radians and therefore

$$1 \text{ radian} = \frac{360°}{2\pi} \approx 57.296°$$

- To convert a degree measurement to radians in terms of π, multiply the degrees by $\frac{2\pi}{360°} = \frac{\pi}{180°}$.

- To convert a radian measurement into degrees, multiply the radians by $\frac{360°}{2\pi} = \frac{180°}{\pi}$ (if there is a π in the radian measurement, it will cancel out).

Hint: If you are looking for degrees, make sure 180° is on top: $\left(\frac{180°}{\pi}\right)$ and multiply by the radian measure. If you are looking for radians, make sure π (radians) is on top: $\left(\frac{\pi}{180°}\right)$ and multiply by the degree measure.

Common conversions between degrees and radians are

Degrees	Radians	Degrees	Radians
0°	0	90°	$\frac{\pi}{2}$
30°	$\frac{\pi}{6}$	180°	π
45°	$\frac{\pi}{4}$	270°	$\frac{\pi}{2}$
60°	$\frac{\pi}{3}$	360°	2π

Radian measure is usually given in terms of π, such as $\frac{\pi}{2}$ for 90°. It is customary to omit the word "radians" if an angle measure is given in terms of π.

Do not think that if you enter $\boxed{\pi}$ $\boxed{\div}$ $\boxed{2}$ on your calculator you will get 90°. What you will get is 1.57 radians, which is a conversion factor from radians to degrees (e.g., $90° = \frac{\pi}{2}$ radians).

8.3 TRIGONOMETRIC FUNCTION VALUES

The trigonometric functions are examples of **periodic functions** because they repeat their output values at regular intervals, or periods. Other examples of periodic functions are sound waves, tides, and heartbeats. One complete repetition of the output values of a periodic function is called a **cycle**, so they are sometimes called **cyclic functions**. The **period** is the horizontal length of one cycle. For sine and cosine functions, the cycle and period can be seen in the rotation of the unit circle (see Section 8.3.1), or $360° = 2\pi$.

8.3.1 Using the Unit Circle

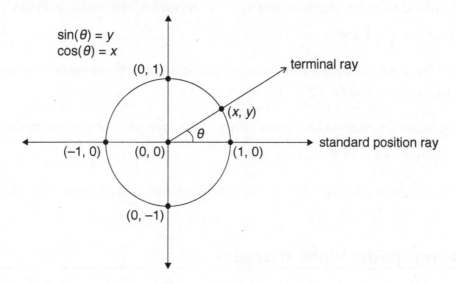

Any angle can be put in standard position in a **unit circle** (a circle with radius = 1) with the vertex at the center (0, 0). The **standard position ray** (one side of the angle) lies along the positive x-axis intersects the circle at (1, 0). The **terminal ray** (the other side of the angle) intersects the circle at some point (x, y). When the angle is graphed in the unit circle, the x-coordinate of the point of intersection of the terminal ray and the circle represents cos θ and the y-coordinate of the point of intersection represents sin θ. The terminal side of the angle is the radius (= 1) to the point (x, y) = (cos θ, sin θ). Measurement is always counterclockwise from the positive x-axis (for positive angles) unless stated otherwise.

An important and useful trigonometric identity comes from the Pythagorean Theorem and the unit circle:

$$x^2 + y^2 = 1,$$

which is the same as $\cos^2 \theta + \sin^2 \theta = 1$ or the more familiar

$$\sin^2 \theta + \cos^2 \theta = 1,$$

known as the **Pythagorean identity**.

The method for finding the sine and cosine of an angle by using the unit circle is outlined below for some common angles. Since (x, y) on the unit circle represents (cos θ, sin θ), this means the point where the terminal ray intersects the unit circle indicates the sine and cosine values of θ (and the other trigonometric functions can be calculated). This method is valid for all angles.

It is helpful to visualize where the terminal ray of an angle intersects the unit circle for the values of sine and cosine of the following important angles:

- The terminal ray of an angle that measures $\frac{\pi}{2}$ radians (or 90°) intersects the unit circle at (0, 1), so $\sin \frac{\pi}{2} = 1$ and $\cos \frac{\pi}{2} = 0$.

- The terminal ray of an angle that measures π radians (or 180°) intersects the unit circle at (–1, 0), so $\sin \pi = 0$ and $\cos \pi = -1$.

- The terminal ray of an angle that measures $\frac{3\pi}{2}$ radians (or 270°) intersects the circle at (0, –1), so $\sin \frac{3\pi}{2} = -1$ and $\cos \frac{3\pi}{2} = 0$.

- The terminal ray of an angle that measures 2π radians (or 360°) intersects the circle at (1, 0), so $\sin 2\pi = 0$ and $\cos 2\pi = 1$.

8.3.2 Using Special Right Triangles

The numerical values for the sine, cosine, and tangent functions are programmed into most calculators, so it isn't necessary to memorize any of their values, but some occur so frequently that you should at least know how to get them from a sketch of the 30°-60°-90° or 45°-45°-90° triangle.

The following table lists the sine, cosine, and tangent of key angles in the first quadrant. The values are readily found by using the definitions of the functions and the facts that in a 30°-60°-90° triangle the side opposite the 30° angle is half the hypotenuse and the ratio of the sides is 1-2-$\sqrt{3}$, and in a 45°-45°-90° triangle the legs are equal and the ratio of the sides is 1-1-$\sqrt{2}$, as was shown in Chapter 6, Section 6.4.2b. If you sketch these two triangles and assign their ratios to their sides, you can figure out most trig questions just from these sketches, which are shown here, where x is the shortest side in each case.

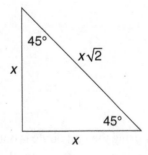
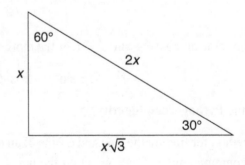

θ, degrees	θ, radians	$\sin\theta = \dfrac{\text{opposite}}{\text{hypotenuse}}$	$\cos\theta = \dfrac{\text{adjacent}}{\text{hypotenuse}}$	$\tan\theta = \dfrac{\sin\theta}{\cos\theta}$
0°	0	0	1	$\dfrac{0}{1} = 0$
30°	$\dfrac{\pi}{6}$	$\dfrac{1}{2}$	$\dfrac{\sqrt{3}}{2}$	$\dfrac{\frac{1}{2}}{\frac{\sqrt{3}}{2}} = \dfrac{1}{\sqrt{3}} = \dfrac{\sqrt{3}}{3}$
45°	$\dfrac{\pi}{4}$	$\dfrac{1}{\sqrt{2}} = \dfrac{\sqrt{2}}{2}$	$\dfrac{1}{\sqrt{2}} = \dfrac{\sqrt{2}}{2}$	$\dfrac{\frac{1}{2}\sqrt{2}}{\frac{1}{2}\sqrt{2}} = 1$
60°	$\dfrac{\pi}{3}$	$\dfrac{\sqrt{3}}{2}$	$\dfrac{1}{2}$	$\dfrac{\frac{\sqrt{3}}{2}}{\frac{1}{2}} = \sqrt{3}$
90°	$\dfrac{\pi}{2}$	1	0	$\dfrac{1}{0}$, undefined

Cofunctions of the functions are named, not surprisingly, with a "co" prefix, so the pairs of cofunctions are sine and cosine, tangent and cotangent, and secant and cosecant. Cofunctions are related in an interesting way: for *complementary* angles, the function and cofunction are equal. This relationship can be seen in the table above for sine and cosine: sin 30° = cos 60°. Likewise, tan 50° = cot 40° and sec 20° = csc 70°. These relationships are evident when looking at a right triangle.

8.3.3 Graphs of the Trig Functions

The following graphs of the six trigonometric functions show their **periodicity** (see Chapter 5, Section 5.3.8). The term $n\pi$ included with each function indicates the periodicity, or the interval for the repeat, as shown in the following graphs of the functions. The periodicity of sine, cosine, secant, and cosecant is 2π, whereas the periodicity of tangent and cotangent is π. The ranges can readily be seen on these graphs. For sine and cosine, the range is $[-1, 1]$, for tangent and cotangent, the range is $(-\infty, \infty)$ and for secant and cosecant it is $(-\infty, -1] \cup [1, \infty)$. The domains for all trigonometric functions is $(-\infty, \infty)$ except for the asymptotes for the tangent and secant $\left(y = \dfrac{\pi}{2} + n\pi\right)$ and the asymptotes for the cotangent and cosecant $\left(y = n\pi\right)$.

Hint: The asymptotes for the tangent and secant functions are the values for which $\cos\theta = 0$ since the cosine is in the denominator of these two functions. Likewise, the asymptotes for cotangent and cosecant are the values for which $\sin\theta = 0$ since sine is in the denominator of these two functions.

$y = \sin x$

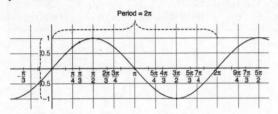

$y = \csc x$

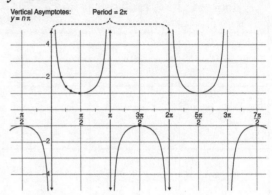

$y = \cos x$

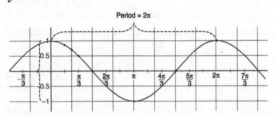

$y = \sec x$

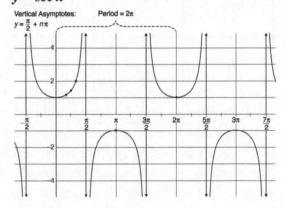

$y = \tan x$

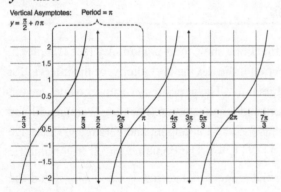

$y = \cot x$

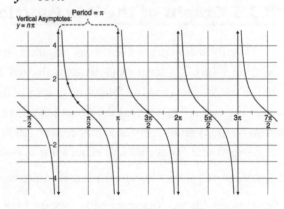

The graphs across from each other are reciprocals.

8.4 INVERSE TRIGONOMETRIC FUNCTIONS

Inverse trigonometric functions are the reverse of trigonometric functions. The inverse in trigonometry is found by reversing the x and y such that the function $y = \arcsin(x)$ is defined to indicate that $\sin(y) = x$. In words, "y is the angle whose sine is x"; thus, "the sine of y is x."

The notation for the **inverse** sine function is $\sin^{-1} x$ or $\arcsin x$, read as "the angle whose sine is." The other trig functions with a -1 exponent also mean "the angle whose [function] is."

 The notation $\sin^{-1}$ does not mean $\dfrac{1}{\sin}$; it means "arcsin" or "the angle whose sign is." The meaning of the -1 exponent in trigonometry is not the same as it was in algebra. (In fact, $\dfrac{1}{\sin\theta} = \csc\theta$.)

Only **one-to-one functions** can have inverses, by definition (see Chapter 5, Section 5.4). To consider the inverse of a trigonometric function, restrict the domain of the function to a section of the graph that is one-to-one. Any of the graphs of the functions turned around one-quarter will reveal their restrictions (where the vertical line test for the inverse would fail). Check these restrictions out with the sine curve.

EXAMPLE 8.1

A ski resort has installed a zip line. The zip line is 1750 feet long and allows its rider to descend a vertical distance of 450 feet. What is the angle of depression to the nearest degree? (The angle of depression is the angle between the horizontal and the zip line, as shown in the figure below.)

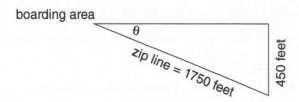

SOLUTION 8.1

From the figure, it is clear that $\sin\theta = \dfrac{\text{opp}}{\text{hyp}} = \dfrac{450}{1750} = \dfrac{9}{35}$. So the problem is to find $\arcsin\dfrac{9}{35} \approx 15°$. Remember when using the calculator, that arcsin is the same as $\sin^{-1}$.

Be sure that the calculator is in degree mode, since this problem asks for degrees. Use the [DRG] key and the arrows to choose degrees (DEG). Be sure to press [ENTER] so the calculator is in degree mode. To find arcsin $\frac{9}{35}$, enter the calculation [2nd] [SIN] [9] [÷] [35] [)] [=] to get the answer, 14.9, which is 15 rounded to the nearest degree. Note that [2nd] [SIN] gives $\sin^{-1}$ with an opening parenthesis, so you have to enter only the closing parenthesis.

Don't waste time finding the decimal equivalent of $\frac{9}{35}$ in Solution 8.1 and then using that answer when entering $\sin^{-1}$ for two reasons: (1) the calculator accepts fractions for inverse trig functions (and most everything else as long as you remember to include it in parentheses); and (2) finding the decimal equivalent of a fraction and rounding it in the middle of a calculation can introduce rounding errors in the result.

8.5 SPECIAL CASES

8.5.1 Reference Angles

Every angle whose measure is greater than 90° or less than 0° has a corresponding **reference angle**, which is the acute angle formed by the terminal side of the given angle and the negative or positive x-axis. This reference angle can be used to calculate the absolute trigonometric values for the given angle, and then, depending on the quadrant of the terminal side of the original angle and the trigonometric function, positive or negative values can be applied.

Always start in Quadrant I and remember that each quadrant is 90° or $\frac{\pi}{2}$ radians. Once you have the approximate position of the given angle, let's call it θ, its quadrant determines how you proceed.

- For Quadrant II, the reference angle is the difference $180° - \theta$.

- For Quadrant III, the reference angle is the difference $\theta - 180°$.

- For Quadrant IV, the reference angle is the difference $360° - \theta$.

The simple sketches below show how to find the reference angle by using these rules. It may be easier to remember the sketches than to try to memorize the rules.

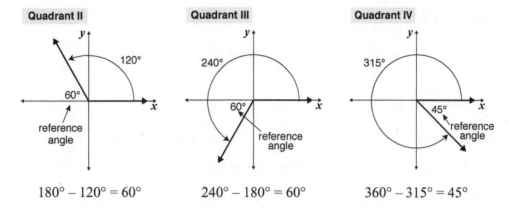

$$180° - 120° = 60° \qquad 240° - 180° = 60° \qquad 360° - 315° = 45°$$

The x (cos θ) and y (sin θ) values are positive or negative depending on the quadrant. All trigonometric functions in Quadrant I are positive. The following table shows the signs of the trig functions in the four quadrants, but they can be figured out readily by determining the signs of x and y in each quadrant, remembering that $x = \cos\theta$ and $y = \sin\theta$. The relationships of the other four functions with relation to sin θ and cos θ can be deduced from what you know about sin θ and cos θ in each quadrant. These are summarized in the following table. Don't just memorize it—instead see how you can figure them out knowing just the signs of sine and cosine in each quadrant.

Reciprocal functions	Quadrant containing terminal side			
	I	II	III	IV
Sine and Cosecant	+	+	−	−
Cosine and Secant	+	−	−	+
Tangent and Cotangent	+	−	+	−

Hint: Use the mnemonic ASTC (All Students Talk Constantly) to remember which function (and its reciprocal) are positive in which quadrant. (The others are negative.)

A (all functions) are positive in Quadrant I, and going counterclockwise,
S (sin and csc) are positive in Quadrant II,
T (tan and cot) are positive in Quadrant III, and
C (cosine and secant) are positive in Quadrant IV.

EXAMPLE 8.2

If $\tan\theta = -\dfrac{5}{12}$ and $\dfrac{3\pi}{2} < \theta < 2\pi$, evaluate $\sin\theta$.

SOLUTION 8.2

The restriction on θ in the problem $\left(\dfrac{3\pi}{2} < \theta < 2\pi\right)$ puts it in Quadrant IV, where $\tan\theta$ is negative. Sketch the reference angle in the fourth quadrant with the information that $\tan\theta = -\dfrac{5}{12}$:

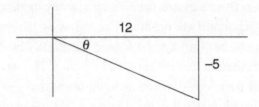

Find the hypotenuse and use that information to write $\sin\theta$. The Pythagorean formula gives the hypotenuse as $\sqrt{12^2 + 5^2} = \sqrt{169} = 13$; the hypotenuse, because it is a length, is always the positive square root. This triangle is a 5-12-13 Pythagorean triple. So $\sin\theta = \dfrac{\text{opp}}{\text{hyp}} = -\dfrac{5}{13}$.

NOTE Lengths are always positive, so if a calculation finds a length as a square root, such as $\sqrt{169}$, use only the positive root.

EXAMPLE 8.3

An airborne kite 80 feet high is staked to the ground by a string that forms a 50° angle with the ground. How long is this string to the nearest tenth of a foot?

SOLUTION 8.3

Sketch the information.

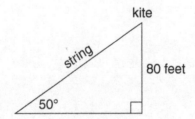

The only trigonometric function that relates an angle (50° here) to the side opposite it and the hypotenuse is sin. So $\sin 50° = \dfrac{80}{x}$, where x is the length of the string.

Then use the calculator to get $x = \dfrac{80}{\sin 50°} = 104.4325831 \approx 104.4$ feet.

Do not find sin 50° and divide that value into 80 in Example 8.3. Just enter the fraction $\dfrac{80}{\sin 50°}$ into the calculator as follows (make sure you are in DEG mode:

$\boxed{80}$ $\boxed{\div}$ $\boxed{\sin}$ $\boxed{50}$ $\boxed{)}$ $\boxed{=}$, remembering that the $\boxed{\sin}$ key yields "sin (".

8.5.2 Angles Greater Than 360° (2π radians)

One full rotation of the unit circle is 360° or 2π radians. Since trig functions are cyclic, the trig functions for any angle are repeated in every rotation.

Change a given angle greater than 360° to an angle in the interval [0, 360°] (or [0, 2π]) by repeatedly *subtracting* 360° (or 2π) from the angle measurement until the difference is ≤ 360° (or ≤ 2π), which is an angle coterminal with the given angle. **Coterminal** angles are two angles that share the same terminal ray. Coterminal angles differ by 360° or 2π radians. The given angle will have the same trigonometric values as this coterminal angle equivalent. If this angle is not in Quadrant I, figure out the reference angle as shown in Section 8.5.1.

This procedure is mostly unnecessary since most calculators are programmed to give the sine, cosine, and tangent of any angle, large or small, positive or negative.

EXAMPLE 8.4

What is sin 750°?

SOLUTION 8.4

Subtract 360° from 750°. The result is 390°, so repeat the subtraction: 390° − 360° = 30°. Since 30° is in the first quadrant, the trig functions of 750° are the same as those for 30°, so $\sin 750° = \dfrac{1}{2}$.

8.5.3 Negative Angles

Change a **negative angle** to an angle in the interval [0, 360°] (or [0, 2π]) by repeatedly *adding* 360° (or 2π) to the angle measurement until the difference is positive. That positive number is the coterminal angle for the given angle. Therefore, –70° is coterminal with 290°; 45° is coterminal with 405°, 765°, and –315°, among others; and π radians is coterminal with 3π radians, 5π radians, and $-\pi$ radians, among others.

The given angle will have the same trigonometric values as its coterminal angle. If the coterminal angle is not in Quadrant I, figure out the reference angle as shown in Section 8.5.1.

Sometimes it is easier to just sketch the negative angle—but remember in the sketch to start at the positive x-axis and go clockwise to show a negative angle. All operations (such as adding 360°) are still done counterclockwise.

EXAMPLE 8.5

Find $\cos(-330°)$.

SOLUTION 8.5

Adding 360° to –330° yields 30°, so $\cos(-330°) = \cos(30°) = \dfrac{\sqrt{3}}{2}$.

 $\cos(-330)°$ is not the same as $-\cos(330°)$, which is $-\dfrac{\sqrt{3}}{2}$.

8.5.4 Using Algebra with Trig Functions

Trig functions (together with their angles) are treated the same as variables in an algebraic equation. As a start to doing algebra with trig functions, use your knowledge of the following:

1. The fundamental Pythagorean identity from the unit circle is $\sin^2 a + \cos^2 a = 1$.

2. The relationships (definitions) of the trig functions can be written in terms of $\sin \theta$ and $\cos \theta$: $\tan \theta = \dfrac{\sin \theta}{\cos \theta}$, $\cot \theta = \dfrac{\cos \theta}{\sin \theta}$, $\sec \theta = \dfrac{1}{\cos \theta}$, and $\csc \theta = \dfrac{1}{\sin \theta}$.

3. Basic algebra and recognizing that $\sin \theta$ and $\cos \theta$ (as well as the other trig functions) take the place of the variables used in algebra.

For example,

$$\sin \theta + 3 \sin \theta = 4 \sin \theta$$

$$\cos^2 \theta = \cos \theta \times \cos \theta$$

are treated identically to

$$s + 3s = 4s$$

$$c^2 = c \times c$$

NOTE

$\sin A + \sin 3A \neq \sin 4A$ because the angles are different, even though they are written in terms of the same angle ($A \neq 3A \neq 4A$).

EXAMPLE 8.6

In right triangle ABC with right angle C, $c = 25.0$, and $A = 40°$. Find the other angle and the other two sides to the nearest tenth.

SOLUTION 8.6

* First, sketch the triangle.

* To find $\angle B$, use the fact that the two acute angles in a right triangle are complementary. So $\angle A + \angle B = 90°$. Since $\angle A = 40°$, $\angle B = 50°$.

* To find a, use $\sin A = \dfrac{a}{c}$, or $\sin 40° = \dfrac{a}{25}$. With the given values and using the calculator for the sines of the angles, $a = 25(\sin 40°) = 16.07$, or $a = 16.1$, rounded to the nearest tenth.

* To find b, use $\sin B = \dfrac{b}{c}$. Then $\sin 50° = \dfrac{b}{25}$ or $b = 25(\sin 50°) = 19.15$, or $b = 19.2$, rounded to the nearest tenth.

Thus, $\angle B = 50°$; $a = 16.1$, and $b = 19.2$.

EXAMPLE 8.7

A guy wire reaches from the top of a pole to a stake in the ground, 10 feet from the foot of the pole. The wire makes an angle of $65°$ with the ground. Find the length of the wire rounded to the nearest foot.

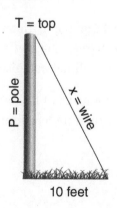

T = top

P = pole

x = wire

10 feet

SOLUTION 8.7

The function to use here is cosine 65° because the values that are needed to find x are given. The equation is $\cos 65° = \dfrac{10}{x}$. Thus, $x = \dfrac{10}{\cos 65°} = 23.662$ feet, which is rounded to 24 feet.

The height of the pole doesn't have to be known to solve Example 8.7 because once we know one acute angle of a right triangle, we need to know only one side to solve the triangle, and we know that one leg is 10. We could then find the height of the pole by using the Pythagorean Theorem.

EXAMPLE 8.8

Simplify $\dfrac{\sec x}{\cot x + \tan x}$ to a single trigonometric function by using the relations among the functions.

SOLUTION 8.8

First, rewrite the three trigonometric functions in terms of sine and cosine only:
$\dfrac{\sec x}{\cot x + \tan x} = \dfrac{\frac{1}{\cos x}}{\frac{\cos x}{\sin x} + \frac{\sin x}{\cos x}}$. Then multiply the fraction through by $(\sin x \cos x)$, the LCD (lowest common denominator) of all of the fractions, to get

$$\frac{\sin x \cos x \left(\frac{1}{\cos x}\right)}{\sin x \cos x \left(\frac{\cos x}{\sin x} + \frac{\sin x}{\cos x}\right)} = \frac{\sin x}{\cos^2 x + \sin^2 x} = \frac{\sin x}{1} = \sin x.$$

8.6 TRANSFORMATIONS OF TRIGONOMETRIC FUNCTIONS

Trigonometric function graphs follow the same basic transformation rules as transformations in the coordinate plane (see Chapter 7, Section 7.5): shifting up, down, left, right; reflection about the axes; expanding and contracting.

The one graph that is indispensable for graphing trigonometric functions is the sine curve. You can see that the sine function starts at (0, 0) (meaning sin 0 = 0), and that it has a period of 2π. Those facts are all you need, and everything else will fall into place.

Trigonometric functions can be transformed, just like other functions. We will use the sine curve for the following discussion, but the same rules for transformations apply to the other functions.

The period of tangent and cotangent is π, not 2π, so adjust the changes to the period (horizontal dilation and phase shift) accordingly.

8.6.1 Transformations of the Sine Function

The general form for the equation of the sine function is

$$y = A\sin B(x - C) + D,$$

where the values for A, B, C, and D change the basic $y = \sin x$ curve in some way.

Let's see how each of the general form variables affect the basic $y = \sin x$ curve.

- A changes the **amplitude**, which is a kind of vertical dilation. The amplitude of a periodic function is the absolute value of one-half the difference between the highest and lowest y values. Instead of the graph of the sine function having an amplitude of 1 (meaning its maximum is +1 and its minimum is −1), if the amplitude is changed, the graph will "bounce" between $+A$ and $−A$. If no other changes are made, changing the amplitude has the effect of changing the steepness of the curve because now it has to go A units in the same horizontal distance. The larger the value of $|A|$, is, the steeper the curve, and the closer A is to 0, the flatter the curve, as seen in the next figure, where the bold curve is $y = \sin x$, the thinner curve is $y = 2 \sin x$, and the dashed line is $y = \left(\dfrac{1}{2}\right)\sin x$. If A is negative, the curve would also flip over the horizontal axis.

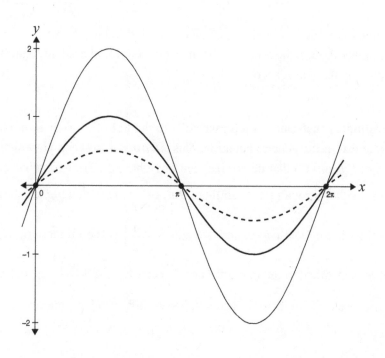

- **B** affects the **period** of the curve, but the change actually is the reciprocal of the horizontal dilation. The period of $\sin x$, instead of being 2π or $360°$, will now be $\dfrac{2\pi}{B}$ or $\dfrac{360°}{B}$, as shown in the next figure, where the bold curve is $y = \sin x$, the thinner curve is $y = \sin 2x$, and the dashed line is $y = \sin\left(\dfrac{1}{2}x\right)$. If B is less than 1 (in other words, a proper fraction or its decimal equivalent), it has the effect of stretching the graph out, and if it is greater than 1, it has the effect of pulling the graph tighter. To visualize the effect of B, consider that for $B > 1$, the period is $\dfrac{1}{B}$ times what it was without this horizontal dilation. In other words, B tells how many complete cycles the curve will make in the space that originally had only one.

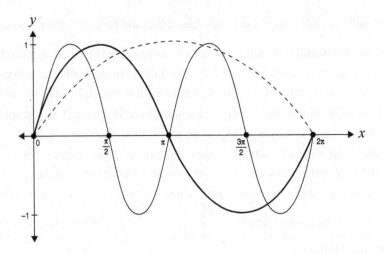

 Hint: For an easy way to visualize a change in period (B) for the sine function, renumber the x-axis so $x = 2\pi$ becomes the new value Bx, and renumber the other values on the x-axis accordingly.

- **C** is a **horizontal translation**, or a **phase shift** to the left ($C < 0$) or right ($C > 0$) with no dilation. Note that in the general equation, C is *subtracted*, so keep your signs straight—it is the value of C (not $-C$) that determines left or right shift. Trigonometric cofunctions are related to each other through phase shifts of $90°$, or $\dfrac{\pi}{2}$. For example, as shown in the next figure, $y = \sin x$ is the bold curve, and $y = \sin\left(x + \dfrac{\pi}{2}\right)$ is the thinner curve. Note that the thinner curve is identical to the curve for $\cos x$ because $\sin\left(x + \dfrac{\pi}{2}\right) = \cos x$, and the shift is to the left because $C = -\dfrac{\pi}{2}$ here. In general, phase shifts can have any value.

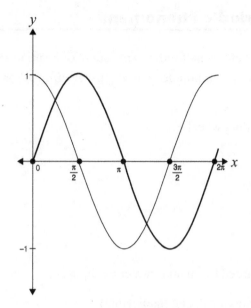

- **D** is a **vertical shift**, up (if $D > 0$) or down (if $D < 0$). The whole graph, is raised or low-ered. In other words, this is a vertical translation with no dilation. The midline of the graph, which is the horizontal line about which the graph of a periodic function oscillates, becomes $y_{new} = y_{old} + D$. For example, the midline of the sine or cosine graphs would change from $y = 0$ to $y = D$. In the figure below, $D = 2$ and the sine curve oscillates around the line $y = 2$.

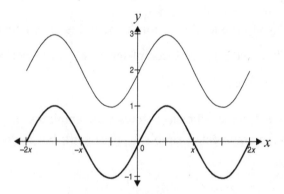

 Hint: For an easy way to remember the direction of a horizontal shift, use a standard sine curve and determine by how many units (0, 0) has moved to the right or left. For an easy way to visualize vertical shift, just renumber the y-axis so the line $y = 0$ becomes $y = D$ and renumber the other values on the y-axis accordingly.

8.6.2 Real-World Periodic Phenomena

Most real-world periodic phenomena follow a sine curve or a variation of it. The equations for these phenomena would involve its amplitude, period, phase shift, and/or vertical shift. Examples of such phenomena are

- A fixed position on a rolling wheel

- Animal populations

- The "bounce" of a spring

- Sunspot cycles

- Tides

- Tsunami (tidal waves caused by an underwater earthquake)

- Biorhythms (physical, emotional, and intellectual)

EXAMPLE 8.9

What is the period of $y = 5 \sin\left(\dfrac{x}{3} + \pi\right)$?

SOLUTION 8.9

The only number you have to look at for the period is the coefficient of x, which is $\dfrac{1}{3}$. This means that the sine curve completes only $\dfrac{1}{3}$ of its period in 2π, and the whole period is therefore $3(2\pi) = 6\pi$.

In Example 8.9, the coefficient 5 adjusts the amplitude from 1 to 5 units, and the π added to the argument is simply a phase shift; but neither of these changes the period.

8.7 USING TRIG TO FIND THE AREA OF A TRIANGLE

In Chapter 6, Section 6.4.4, we found the areas of several triangles. The basic formula for the area of a triangle is

$$A = \frac{1}{2}bh,$$

where b is the base of the triangle and h is the perpendicular distance from the base to the opposite vertex. For right triangles, the two legs can be considered as the base and the height, so the area is simply half the product of the lengths of the two legs.

For triangles that aren't right triangles, Heron's formula (see Chapter 7, Section 7.2.4) works if we know three sides. Or we can graph the triangle if we know enough about the vertices and find the area that way.

But what if none of these methods works? What if, for example, all we know are two sides and the angle between them? Or all we know are two angles and the side between them? Can we get enough information about an acute or obtuse triangle to find the area or the missing side(s) or angle(s)?

The answer is yes, by using trigonometry.

8.7.1 SAS—Area of a Triangle

To find the area of a triangle if all we know are two sides and the included angle, we use the basic equation, $A = \frac{1}{2}bh$, and a sketch of the triangle to guide our solution. Let's say we know sides a and b and the included angle C. First, draw the height, h, to side b (shown by a dashed line).

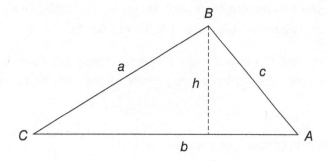

By using trigonometry, and looking at only the left triangle formed by h, we see that $\sin C = \frac{h}{a}$, or $h = a \sin C$. So for the area of the whole triangle $\left(\text{Area} = \frac{1}{2}(\text{base}) \times (\text{height}) \right)$, we have

$$\text{Area} = \frac{1}{2}bh = \frac{1}{2}b(a \sin C) = \frac{1}{2}ab \sin C .$$

This formula for finding the area of any triangle when you know only two sides and the included angle is sometimes called the ***a-b-C* formula**. However, since the assignment of letters was arbitrary, it is also true that Area $= \frac{1}{2}bc \sin A$ and Area $= \frac{1}{2}ca \sin B$. Just be sure that the angle you are using is the one *between* the two sides.

EXAMPLE 8.10

In triangle ABC, $a = 9$, $b = 8$, and $\sin C = \dfrac{5}{12}$. What is the area of triangle ABC?

SOLUTION 8.10

$$\text{Area} = \frac{1}{2}ab\sin C = \frac{1}{2}(9)(8)\left(\frac{5}{12}\right) = 15$$

8.7.2 SAS—Law of Cosines

We can use the Pythagorean Theorem ($c^2 = a^2 + b^2$) to find the third side of a right triangle. But what if we want to find the third side of a triangle that isn't a right triangle? The law of cosines makes that calculation fairly simple. All you need to know are the lengths of the other two sides and the angle between them, just as for the area formula in Section 8.7.1. It is important that the angle between the sides is the known angle because otherwise those two sides could be two sides of an infinite number of triangles, depending on how close or far apart they are. By specifying the exact angle between these two sides, there is only one triangle possible. That's why SAS works for proving two triangles are congruent (see Chapter 6, Section 6.4.5).

The formula for the **law of cosines** looks like the Pythagorean Theorem with the last term considered as a kind of "correction" term to compensate for the fact that this isn't a right triangle.

$$c^2 = a^2 + b^2 - 2ab\cos C$$

The assignment of letters is arbitrary, so it is also true that

$$a^2 = b^2 + c^2 - 2bc\cos A$$
$$b^2 = a^2 + c^2 - 2ac\cos B$$

Again, just be sure that the angle you are using is the one between the two sides.

8.7.3 ASA—Law of Sines

If we know two angles of any triangle, we can compute the remaining angle by simply subtracting their sum from 180°, the total number of degrees in a triangle. Knowing the three angles in a triangle, though, doesn't tell us the size of the triangle. There are infinitely many similar triangles with any particular configuration of angles. However, if we know just one side, the size of the triangle is locked in—there is only one triangle that has those three angles and that side. That's why SAS works for proving two triangles congruent (see Chapter 6, Section 6.4.5). Of course, which side is known is important.

Knowing which angle is opposite the known side, we can use the **law of sines** to find the other two sides. This is because the ratios of the sides of a triangle and their opposite angles are constant in any triangle. The law of sines states this relationship as:

$$\frac{\sin A}{a} = \frac{\sin B}{b} = \frac{\sin C}{c}$$

Thus, if you know the three angles (even if you are given only two of them, you can find the third) and only one side, you can find the other two sides by successive use of the law of sines. And then you have the complete triangle.

EXAMPLE 8.11

Two transversals on parallel line segments cross with the following configuration. How long is the upper (shorter) parallel segment to the nearest whole number?

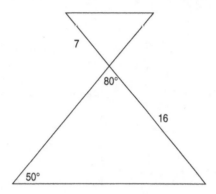

SOLUTION 8.11

Use the fact that the horizontal lines are parallel to determine the angle opposite the side of length 7. It is an alternate interior angle to the one marked 50° so it is also 50°, and it is opposite the side of length 7. The top angle in the cross is a vertical angle to the one marked 80°, so it is also 80°, and it is opposite to the side we want to find. So the law of sines gives:

$$\frac{\sin 50°}{7} = \frac{\sin 80°}{x} \text{ or } x = \frac{7\sin 80°}{\sin 50°} = 8.999026536 \approx 9.$$

Note once again that rounding should wait until the last step. Use the calculator.

Chapter 8 Exercises

Answers are on the following page.

1. Find acute angle x when $4 \cos^2 x = 1$.

   (A) $30°$

   (B) $60°$

   (C) $90°$

   (D) $120°$

2. Multiply: $\dfrac{1 + \sin A}{\sin A} \cdot \dfrac{\sin^2 A}{1 - \sin^2 A} =$

   (A) 1

   (B) $\dfrac{\sin A}{1 - \sin A}$

   (C) $\sin A$

   (D) $\dfrac{\sin^2 A}{1 - \sin A}$

3. If $\sin A = \dfrac{4}{7}$, what function of A is equal to $\dfrac{7}{4}$?

   (A) $\sec A$

   (B) $\csc A$

   (C) $\cos A$

   (D) cannot tell from the information given

4. As an acute angle $\angle A$ increases, which of the following functions decreases?

   (A) sine

   (B) cosine

   (C) tangent

   (D) secant

5. What is the phase shift of $y = 2 \sin(x + 3\pi) + 4$?

    (A) 2

    (B) 3π

    (C) -3π

    (D) 4

Answers and Explanations

1. **(B)**

    Treat $\cos x$ as a variable, so $4\cos^2 x = 1$ is the same as $\cos^2 x = \frac{1}{4}$. Take the square roots of both sides of that equation to get $\cos x = \pm\frac{1}{2}$. The problem asks for an acute angle, so $x = 60°$.

2. **(B)**

    Treat $\sin A$ as you would a variable and do the algebra. For simplicity, we can use the substitution $y = \sin A$. Then the original problem is $\frac{1+y}{y} \cdot \frac{y^2}{1-y^2} = \frac{(1+y)y^2}{y(1+y)(1-y)}$. With cancellations, this becomes $\frac{y}{1-y} = \frac{\sin A}{1-\sin A}$.

3. **(B)**

    Since $\frac{7}{4}$ is the reciprocal of $\frac{4}{7}$, the requested function of angle A must be the reciprocal of sin A, or csc A.

4. **(B)**

    As an acute angle increases, the functions sine, tangent, and secant increase, and their cofunctions, cosine, cotangent, and cosecant decrease. The angle is in the first quadrant.

5. **(C)**

    In the general form of the sine function, $y = A\sin B(x - C) + D$, C represents the phase shift. In this case, the value of C would equal -3π because $-C = -(-3\pi) = 3\pi$, which is the positive value shown in the equation.

Before you begin your review, take this short self-assessment to see how well you know the topics covered in this chapter. Answering all or some correctly will help you identify your strengths so you can focus on those topics where you need the most review. Even if you answer all of the questions correctly, we suggest you still review all the examples in the chapter to ensure you're in good shape to move on. Answers are on the following page.

1. The median of 8 data points

    (A) must be one of the data points.

    (B) cannot be found because there is no number that has as many points below it as above it.

    (C) equals the mean of the 8 data points.

    (D) None of the above.

2. What type of graph should be used to show the correlation between how long customers have to wait on the phone versus the number of personnel in the customer service department?

    (A) Pie chart

    (B) Bar graph

    (C) Dot plot

    (D) Scatter plot

3. In a group of 25 students, 12 were studying French, 15 were studying German, and 8 were studying neither. What is the universal set?

    (A) 35 students

    (B) 27 students

    (C) 25 students

    (D) 18 students

4. A golfer has four different golf shirts and three different pairs of golf pants. How many outfits are possible?

    (A) 3

    (B) 4

    (C) 7

    (D) 12

5. A homeowners' association elected 5 board members. The board members then chose a president and treasurer. To find out how many choices were possible, we would use

    (A) a tree diagram.

    (B) permutations.

    (C) combinations.

    (D) factorials.

1. (D)

The median of an even number of data points is the average of the middle two data points when they are put in numerical order. Therefore, it need not be one of the data points. The median and mean need not be the same, and often aren't. For example, for the data set 1, 2, 3, 4, 9, 11 has a median of $\frac{3+4}{2} = 3.5$ and a mean of $\frac{1+2+3+4+9+11}{6} = \frac{30}{6} = 5$. (Section 9.1.2b)

2. (D)

The first two answer choices are for categorical data, so they wouldn't be used for quantitative data. A dot plot is used for one set of data, whereas the scatter plot determines the association (or correlation) between two variable quantities. (Section 9.1.5a)

3. (C)

The universe is given in the first sentence. Since the numbers total more than 25, some students must be studying both languages, but that doesn't change the universe, which is the total number of students. (Section 9.2.7)

4. (D)

There are 4(3) = 12 different outfits possible. (Section 9.2.2)

5. (B)

Order is important, so we use a permutation. (Section 9.2.4)

Competency 7: Statistics and Probability

9.1 STATISTICS

Statistics is the study of data. In general, this involves four steps:

- collecting data

- analyzing data

- presenting data

- interpreting data

Statistics presents data on elections as well as on money, age, and brand names, among myriad other subjects. It can involve a small amount of data, such as determining the average number of children per hour who visited Santa in the past several years at a particular store to determine whether and when to employ a Santa next year. And it can involve a large amount of data when the possibilities are humongous. For example, what if we wanted to represent responses on hours of sleep per day from everyone in the United States? The answer lies in inferential statistics, as shown in the following sections in this chapter.

Inferential statistics presents data from a representative sample taken from a specific population and states the probability of a statement about the whole population based on the sample results being representative of that whole population. (*Population* here means the population of interest, even though here the statistical population is actually the population of the whole United States.)

9.1.1 Collecting Data

How we pick the sample from the population is most important. To be valid, the sample must be representative of the population of interest and unbiased. As a simple example, if we wanted to gather information on egg sizes from chicken farms in New Jersey, the population would be all the chicken farms in New Jersey. The sample therefore would not include chicken farms in any other state. It would not include farms in New Jersey that didn't have egg-producing chickens. It would include only egg-producing chicken farms in New Jersey, which would take care of the representative part of sampling.

In addition, the sample would not include farms in just one county in New Jersey because that would introduce a bias. Suppose the farms in the southern part of the state used a breed of chicken that produced larger eggs than the breed used in the northern part of the state? Suppose the water in the western part of the state was remarkably different from that in the eastern part, and that contributed to the size of eggs produced? To be unbiased, the sample must be drawn from the whole population with every member of the population having an equal chance of being picked for the sample. Random sampling—for example, every tenth name on a relevant list from the entire population—is one way to take bias out of a sample.

You could question why we don't just use every member of the population in the first place. If we are talking about a small population, it is possible to do that, but for a large population, the costs and time involved in querying every member quickly become prohibitive. If the constraints on statistics (such as representative and unbiased samples) are strictly followed, the results from a sample are an accurate estimate of the whole population.

It is important, however, that the sample be large enough to be truly representative of the whole population. If a machine can package 5-ounce bags of potato chips at the rate of 100 per minute, and the foreman of the factory wants to be sure, allowing slight variation, that the bags contain close to 5 ounces of chips, a sample of 3 bags won't give as much assurance as a sample of, say, 100 bags taken at random throughout the production day.

The four basic methods of data collection are census, sample survey, experiment, and observational study.

- A **census** is a study that observes, or attempts to observe, every individual in a population. The **population** is the collection of all individuals under consideration in the study. The U.S. census is an example.

- A **sample survey** is a study that collects information from a representative sample of a population to determine one or more characteristics of that population. A **sample** is a selected subset of a population from which data are gathered. The sample needs to be unbiased and large enough to be representative, such as randomly selecting a small number of students to determine statistics on course load for the entire student body.

- An **experiment** is a study in which the researcher deliberately influences individuals by imposing conditions and then determining the individuals' responses to those conditions. An example is a pharmaceutical study of the effectiveness of a new drug by comparing a group that takes the drug versus a group that takes a placebo, with the participants not knowing which group they are in.

- An **observational study** attempts to determine relationships between variables, but the researcher imposes no conditions such as was done in an experiment. Surveys are a form of observational study.

Suppose we want to know how satisfied customers are with a new checkout procedure in a supermarket. Let's look at four groups to see which would be the best sample to use for such a survey.

1. Choose every 50th name in the phone directory for the city in which the supermarket is located. This sampling method is wrong on several counts. It is biased toward only people who have telephones and are listed in the phone directory, so it excludes a whole lot of people who no longer have landlines or choose not to be listed in the phone directory. In addition, it includes many more people than those who shop at that particular store.

2. Go door-to-door in the neighborhood within five blocks of the supermarket. This method is biased and not inclusive because not everyone who lives within five blocks of the store is necessarily a customer, and such a sample excludes all the people who are customers but live farther away.

3. Wait in the parking lot and ask every customer who returns a cart in a given period of time. This method excludes customers who didn't drive to the store (and likely includes only the considerate ones who returned their carts).

4. Choose every 20th customer leaving the store throughout a day. This method is the best, especially if the day is chosen at random, because it is representative of the population—people who actually shop at that supermarket and use the checkout. The choice of every 20th customer makes the sample random, and the choice to do the sampling throughout the day doesn't incidentally exclude any part of the population. For example, possible biases due to time of day include senior citizens who are less likely to shop late at night, and certainly people who have a daytime job and probably don't shop during the hours of 8 a.m. to 5 p.m.

9.1.2 Analyzing Data

Once the data are collected, they must be analyzed so the results can be interpreted statistically. For **raw data** (the actual data points that are collected), we must first determine whether they are **categorical** (answers are categories, such as yes/no—sometimes called **qualitative**), or **quantitative** (answers are numbers—therefore, these are sometimes called **numerical**).

9.1.2a Categorical Data

Categorical data are best represented pictorially, such as on a pie chart or bar chart (see Section 9.1.3) or variations of them. Descriptive comparisons can be made among categories, but there can be no "average" as such. For example, if the categories are Democrat, Republican, and Other, what is the average political party? There is no meaningful answer to that question—what we can see, however, is which category had the most respondents.

The categories in this type of data can also be ordered choices, such as "poor," "fair," "average," "good," "excellent," but the idea is still the same—the data are categories, not numerical values. We can see the tally of each category, but not the average.

Categories may include numbers, but that doesn't make the data numerical. It is the data, not how they are sorted, that determines whether a data set is numerical or categorical. If we don't have the individual data points but have only the categories into which they fall, the data are categorical.

9.1.2b Quantitative Data

Quantitative data can be analyzed by standard statistical methods. Three measures, the mean, median, and mode, give a sense of **central tendency**, or how the group of data typically look, whether the data points represent age, height, hours, or another numerical value.

- The **mean**, also called the **average**, is the most familiar measure of central tendency. It is calculated by totaling all the data points and dividing by the number of points. For example, a student who scored 45, 65, 80, and 90 on four tests would have an average of $\frac{45 + 65 + 80 + 90}{4} = 70$ on the four tests. The good grades on the last two tests are offset by the poor performance on the first two tests. Notice that the mean doesn't have to be a member of the data set. It is just the average so that the differences of the data points from it cancel each other out, giving it the quality of being representative of the whole data set. In this case, the four differences from 70 are 25, 5, –10, and –20, which total 0.

The mean is the average of the data, computed by totaling all the data and dividing by the number of data points.

$$\text{Mean} = \frac{\text{total of data points}}{\text{total number of data points}}$$

- The **median** is the middle data point. To find the median, the data must be arranged in order. It makes no difference if it is lowest to highest or highest to lowest. The exact middle point, which has as many data points above it as below it, is the median. For a data set with an odd number of points, it is easy to count over to find the median. For an even number of data points, two points are in the middle; the median is the average of these two points. For example, for the data set 1, 2, 4, 5, 6, 9, 10, the median is 5, with three data points above it and three below it. If the data set didn't have the 10, the median would be the average of the two middle points, 4 and 5, and it would be 4.5. The median need not be a member of the data set if the number of data points is even. The mean and median are often close, but they don't have to be equal. Notice that the mean of the 7-number set is not 5 but

$$\frac{1+2+4+5+6+9+10}{7} \approx 5.3.$$

- The **mode** is the data point with the highest frequency. This has meaning if the data points repeat, such as in 3, 4, 5, 5, 5, 6, 7, 7, 8, 9, 9, 9, 9. The mode here is 9, with a frequency of 4 (the frequency of 5 is 3, and the frequency of 7 is 2). This value (remember to use the value, not its frequency) is *always* a member of the data set. It is less precise in describing the data set, as we can see in this data set, where 9 is not very representative of the rest of the numbers.

It is possible to have no mode (all numbers have the same frequency) or more than one mode (two or more numbers have the same highest frequency).

Another measure of quantitative data is called the **range**, which is simply the highest value minus the lowest value. The range gives information on the spread of the data. For example, for the data set {2, 2, 15, 16, 45}, the range is 45 – 2 = 43. This measure isn't a measure of central tendency, since it doesn't tell us anything about the data values, not even what the highest and lowest points are. It just tells how spread out they are.

Usually, the mean is used as the measure of central tendency for quantitative data, and it works fine unless the data are skewed. **Skew** means one or a few high (or low) points pull the mean too far in one direction or the other. To illustrate how skew affects data, consider the salaries of nine bank employees, *in thousands of dollars*:

25   25   27   28   30   35   35   40   200

Let's look at the mode: there are two, $25,000 and $35,000, and both are fairly representative of most of the salaries. How about the median? It is $30,000, also fairly representative of the salaries. However, the mean (average) is $49,444, which is far from being representative of the salaries of the employees because included in the data set is the $200,000 salary of the CEO of the bank. If the CEO's salary is excluded from the data set, the mode doesn't change and the median changes only slightly (to $29,000), but the mean now becomes a more representative $30,625.

If the data points are in the thousands, drop the 000 and work with the less cumbersome numbers, but remember to (1) state that the numbers are "in thousands" or (2) multiply the result (e.g., mean, median, or mode) by 1,000.

EXAMPLE 9.1

A children's baseball team played a 14-game season. The number of runs scored in each game, respectively, is shown below:

Runs scored:

6   2   0   17   4   5   3   8   1   13   4   7   2   4

What was the average number of runs scored per game in the season, rounded to the nearest whole number?

SOLUTION 9.1

Add the 14 numbers and divide by 14 to get the average = 5.42857 (use the calculator), which rounds to 5 runs per game.

EXAMPLE 9.2

The freshman class at a local college is required to take a test in their first week of class. Anyone who fails the test must take a remedial course to continue taking classes in the school. Four versions of the same test were given, with the following numbers of students passing and failing:

Version of Test	Pass	Fail
A	200	50
B	225	25
C	210	40
D	220	30

What kind of data are presented in this table?

SOLUTION 9.2

Categorical, or qualitative. They involve two categories, "pass" and "fail." The numbers are just the number of data points, not the data.

EXAMPLE 9.3

This question is similar to Example 9.2, except that it includes the criteria for pass/fail, which is a score of 70. The table becomes:

Version of Test	≥ 70 points	< 70 points
A	200	50
B	225	25
C	210	40
D	220	30

What kind of data are presented in this table?

SOLUTION 9.3

Categorical, or qualitative. The data still involve two categories. Even though these categories have numbers in them (≥ 70 points and < 70 points), they are still categories, just different ways of stating "pass" and "fail."

EXAMPLE 9.4

The freshmen at a local college are required to take a test in their first week of class. The scores of 20 students taking a particular test are:

45, 95, 69, 99, 86, 71, 68, 79, 69, 68, 87, 94, 85, 68, 91, 83, 88, 87, 88, 99

These data represent what kind of data?

SOLUTION 9.4

Quantitative. These are quantitative, or numerical, data. Of course, we can categorize these into scores that are 70 and above (pass), and below 70 (fail), as we did for Examples 9.2 and 9.3, but now that we have the individual scores, we can say a lot more about the data by presenting and analyzing the data points as shown in Section 9.1.3c and following sections.

Notice that of the scores that indicate "failing," only one (45) is far from passing, but five of them, the 68s and 69s, are close to passing scores. That could be useful information for the college, but it isn't shown when the data are just put into categories. For example, what if, instead of scores of 68 and 69, they were 38 and 39. Then the college should consider that the test is perhaps biased or that their admission standards should be revised.

9.1.3 Presenting Data

9.1.3a Categorical Data

Table. The table for categorical data points usually consists of two columns, and it may be sufficient for most data sets. The left column lists the categories and the right column lists the number of responses for that category or the percentage of all responses for that category.

Bar Graph. A **bar graph** is another technique to present data in a visual form. A bar graph may be either vertical (the usual presentation, shown on the left) or horizontal (shown on the right).

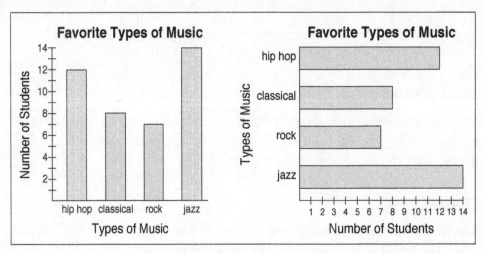

Bar graphs have an axis (called a **scale**) and a series of labeled horizontal or vertical bars resting on the axis. The greater the length or height of the bar, the greater is its value, whether numerical or by frequency. The widths of the bars should be consistent. Each bar represents a different category and is labeled as such.

Vertical bar graphs are useful for depicting time series data (years, minutes, hours or months), as shown in the graph in Example 9.5

EXAMPLE 9.5

The following chart shows attendance totals at a park for the years 2014 to 2018.

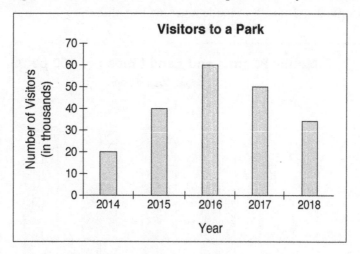

What is the maximum annual attendance, and in which year?

SOLUTION 9.5

The legend on the vertical axis indicates that the numbers shown are in thousands, and the graph clearly shows the maximum number of visitors was 60,000 people in 2016.

A double (or group) vertical bar graph is another effective means of comparing sets of data about the same places or items by giving two or more pieces of information for each item on the *x*-axis. The double vertical bar graph shown in Example 9.6 compares two series of data: land lines and mobile phones for various countries. Notice that the identities of the groupings (here, type of phone) must appear somewhere on the graph. This is called the **legend** for the graph.

EXAMPLE 9.6

According to the following bar graph, for which country are the number of phones per 100 people the closest for mobile and land use phones?

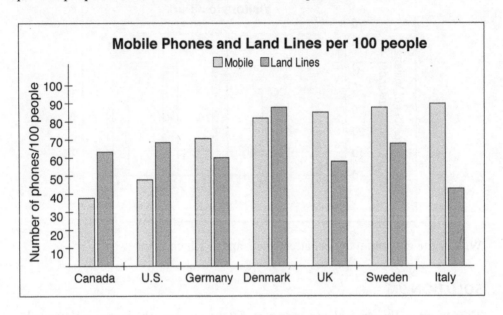

Mobile Phones and Land Lines per 100 people

□ Mobile ■ Land Lines

SOLUTION 9.6

The number of phones (given per 100 people, as indicated on the left axis) are closest in the country for which the difference between the two bars is least. That is true for Denmark.

The graph in Example 9.6 clearly shows the numbers for the two types of phones are closest for Denmark. However, to compare differences in group bar graphs, what we should compare are the percentage differences. For example, for the U.S. and UK numbers in that graph, looking only at the difference (and not whether it is a gain or loss), it is difficult to say which country has a greater change.

Pie chart. Sometimes called **circle graphs**, **pie charts** are constructed from percentages, even though they may report actual numbers. As the name implies, these graphs are in the form of a circle in which the size of each "wedge" indicates the percentage for that category. Graphs are usually parts of a circle, but other innovative presentations also exist. For example, to show the favorite kind of pie in a bakery, the visual can use a picture of an actual pie for the circle.

In a pie chart, the percentages must add up to 100%. This means a pie chart is not appropriate for a survey in which people are asked to "select all that apply" from the choices, since multiple answers to a question will make the total more than 100%. For example, if a survey asks what type of vacation people prefer, person A may choose mountains, beaches, and international; person B may choose only mountains; and person C may choose mountains and cities. The tally for this would be as follows:

Mountains	3
Beaches	1
International	1
Cities	1

This tally implies that there were six inputs, and half of them chose the mountains, when in fact there were three inputs, and they all chose the mountains.

 Multiple-response data cannot be shown on a pie chart.

A search of the Internet came up with the following somewhat humorous (but probably true) pie chart.

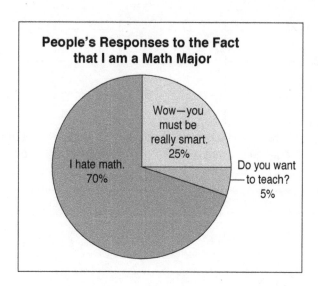

9.1.3b Sample Categorical Presentations

An example of a table shows the education levels of the chief executive officers (CEOs) of the 500 top U.S. companies. Note that this table shows numbers of CEOs as well as percentages. Usually only one or the other measurement is shown, but if you know the total number of respondents, either column can be calculated from the other.

Education Level	Number of CEOs	Percentages
No college	15	3%
Bachelor's degree	165	33%
MBA	190	38%
Law degree	50	10%
Other higher education degree	80	16%

In the above table, the total number of CEOs is 15 + 165 + 190 + 50 + 80 = 500, and the percentages are found by dividing each data point by this total. The total of all percentages must equal 100%. The bar graph for these data is shown below.

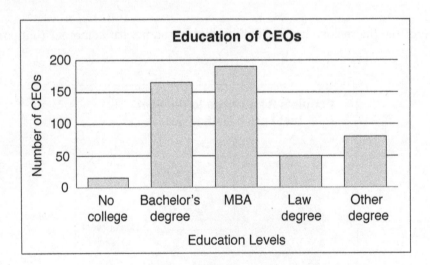

The pie chart of the education levels of the CEOs, showing both actual numbers and percentages, is as shown below.

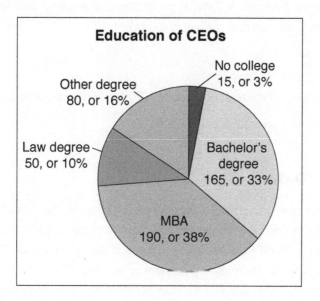

Education of CEOs

EXAMPLE 9.7

From the following pie chart, what is the missing numerical value (for Other) if the total number of students is 500?

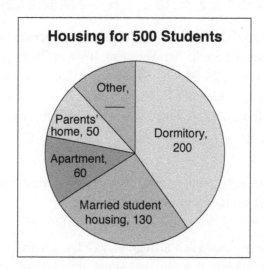

Housing for 500 Students

SOLUTION 9.7

The total of all of the sectors must equal 500, so $200 + 130 + 60 + 50 + x = 500$, or $440 + x = 500$; thus, $x = 60$.

EXAMPLE 9.8

For the data given in Example 9.7, what percentage of students live in college housing (dormitories and married student housing)?

SOLUTION 9.8

The number of students who live in dormitories (200) and married student housing (130) totals 330, so the percentage is $\frac{330}{500} = 66\%$.

9.1.3c Quantitative Data

The choice of how to present quantitative data depends partly on the size of the data set. For example, if there are just a few (perhaps fewer than 12) numerical data points, each individual data point can be presented clearly. But if there are many numerical data points, it is best to group them. If we were to start with a table for individual data points, let's say 20 points, that could get very unwieldy. But even though we may group data for ease of handling them, these are still quantitative data because they deal with numerical data.

For example, consider the following data points showing years of experience of 20 teachers in a particular school:

$$2, 2, 5, 11, 9, 7, 3, 2, 34, 18, 2, 4, 16, 14, 27, 12, 17, 21, 8, 15$$

A table of these values would be 17 lines long (the value 2 appears four times), but it wouldn't give us much more information than the list. However, if we group the data in intervals, let's say, 1–5, 6–10, 11–15, 16–20, 21–25, 26–30, and 31–35 years, the table would be only 7 lines long, which is much more readable, although it is still not ideal. A better choice for readability in this case would be a histogram. If the data are not all whole numbers, the interval could be, for example, 1–5.99, 6–10.99, 11–15.99, etc.

When grouping data into intervals, each grouping must have the same span, even if some have no data points associated with them.

Quantitative data can be presented in a histogram, as a line graph, in a stem-and-leaf plot, on a dot plot, as a pictograph, or as a box-and-whiskers plot. Each of these is described below.

Histogram. A **histogram** looks like a bar chart, but it has one important difference. It is continuous because each equal interval is numerical and there are no gaps in values between the bars. All of the bars touch each other. The histogram for the data on the years of teacher experience above, grouped in five-year intervals, is shown next. This readily shows that the majority of the teachers at that school have 15 or fewer years of experience.

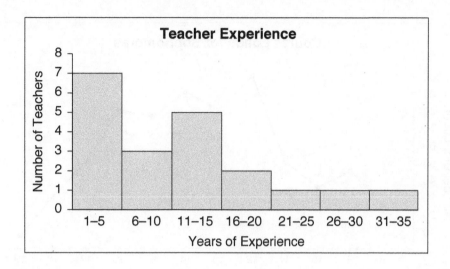

EXAMPLE 9.9

Based on the histogram shown below, how many sophomores had a course load of more than 16 credits?

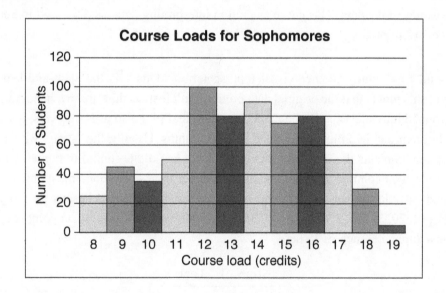

SOLUTION 9.9

More than 16 credits means 17, 18, and 19, credits, but not 16. Add up the number of students in each of these groups: $50 + 30 + 5 = 85$.

Line graph. This same group of data on sophomore course load can also be shown in a **line graph**. The straight line graph shown next was obtained by joining the midpoints of each column for the grouped data for course loads for sophomores from Example 9.9. This plot gives an idea of the data distribution.

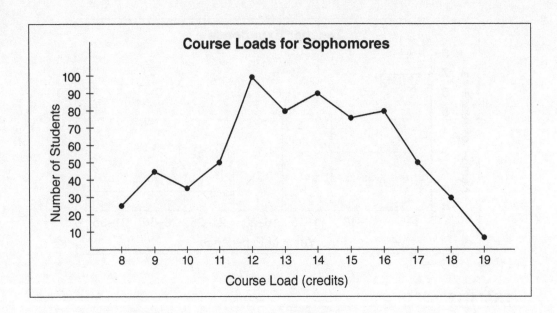

For very large numbers of data or small intervals, this line can be smoothed out to a frequency curve, in which the vertical axis can be frequency or percentage of the total and the horizontal axis shows the values of the data. This curve can aid in interpreting data, as discussed in Section 9.1.4 on normal distributions.

Stem-and-Leaf Plot. Another visual representation of data is the stem-and-leaf plot. The advantage of this plot is that the original data points aren't lost, as they are in a histogram when the data are grouped into intervals, although the stem-and-leaf plot also uses intervals, just in a different way. The stem-and-leaf plot is presented in two columns. Usually, the "stem," which appears in the left column, contains the data values except for the last digits (units) in numerical order. The "leaves," in the right column, show all the unit values for their corresponding stems. For example, the stem-and-leaf plot for the annual number of snowy days in Massachusetts for ten years, with data points {12, 20, 33, 43, 37, 14, 38, 46, 38, 27} is shown below. Each data point is represented, even if it is a duplicate, such as 38 here.

Stem	Leaf
1	2 4
2	0 7
3	3 7 8 8
4	3 6

Even though this doesn't look so impressive because it has only 10 data points, it is an easy way to plot data points (you just need a pencil and paper, and not even a ruler or graph paper) and can provide a quick assessment of the data—here, that there were more days of snow in the 33- to 38-inch range. If you look at a stem-and-leaf plot sideways, you will see that it resembles a histogram—that isn't a coincidence. However, if these data were plotted on a histogram with the intervals 10–19, 20–29, 30–39, 40–49, you couldn't see on a histogram that the snowfalls in the 30s were mostly on the high side.

Dot plots. Another way to present data is by using **dot plots**, which is like tallying, as shown below. These data points are from the histogram on Teacher Experience shown earlier. A tally for the data is shown on the left of the dot plot. Note that the dot plot is like a tally viewed from the side.

Years of Experience

1–5	✝✝✝ //
6–10	///
11–15	✝✝✝
16–20	//
21–25	/
26–30	/
31–35	/

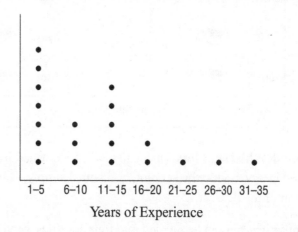

Years of Experience

The mean and median can be calculated from a dot plot that has quantitative data, and the mode can be seen right away (the interval 1–5 years of experience). If, instead of the intervals in the dot plot above, we used the middle of each interval as the value (so we have the years labeled as 3, 8, 13, 18, 23, 28, and 33 years), we would use **weighted means** to calculate the mean of the data. To find the weighted means, we multiply each data point (here they are the midpoints of the intervals) by the frequency of the interval, sum them, and then divide by the total number of data points. The calculation shows that 11.5 is an estimation of the average number of years of experience.

$$\text{mean} = \frac{3(7) + 8(3) + 13(5) + 18(2) + 23(1) + 28(1) + 33(1)}{20} = \frac{230}{20} = 11.5$$

Pictographs. An eye-catching way to display data is the use of pictographs. These are related to dot plots, but use icons instead of dots; in addition, each icon can represent multiples of the data. In the example shown below, note that each ice cream sandwich icon represents not one, but 100 ice cream sandwiches, and the half sandwiches represent 50 ice cream sandwiches.

Cafeteria Ice Cream Sales			
Sept.	🥪🥪🥪	Feb.	🥪
Oct.	🥪🥪	Mar.	🥪🥪
Nov.	🥪🥪	Apr.	🥪🥪
Dec.	🥪	May	🥪🥪🥪
Jan.	🥪	June	🥪🥪🥪🥪
🥪 = 100 Ice Cream Sandwiches			

Box-and-Whiskers Plots. Data can also be identified by quartiles in a five-number summary and plotted in a box-and-whisker plot, also called simply a **box plot**, which will show the statistical distribution of the data set.

Quantitative data can be divided into four quartiles, each of which has an equal number of data points. Therefore, each quartile contains 25% of the data. The five-number summary consists of the lowest value; the first quartile (Q_1); the second quartile (Q_2), which is also the median of the data; the third quartile (Q_3); and the highest value. Q_1 is the median between the lowest value and Q_2, and Q_3 is the median of the data between Q_2 and the highest value.

Therefore, to find the quartiles and plot the box-and-whiskers, all you need to do is put the data into lowest-to-highest order and count to find the median of all the data (Q_2); then count to find the median of the data points before Q_2, which is Q_1; and then count to find the median of the data points after Q_2, which is Q_3. Then draw the plot as follows. Draw a horizontal line on which you mark the five numbers (including the lowest value and highest value of the data). For evenly distributed data, this will look like the figure below. You can see how the box-and-whisker plot got its name.

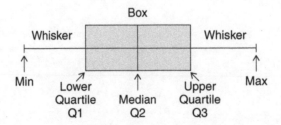

Half the data will be within the box, with one-quarter outside and to the left of the box and one-quarter outside and to the right of the box. But not all data sets are that even. Box-and-whisker plots for data that are skewed, which means more data on the high end or more data on the low end, will show up looking like the plots shown below, where the top plot is for data skewed left and the bottom plot is for data skewed right.

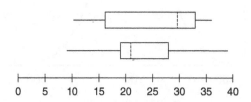

EXAMPLE 9.10

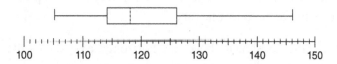

The boxplot above represents the weights of freshmen boys trying out for the soccer team.

If 50 boys tried out, how many weighed more than or equal to 118 pounds?

SOLUTION 9.10

The median is the middle line in a box plot, or 118. Half of the data are above the median and half are below. So at least half of the 50 boys weighed more than or equal to 118. The answer cannot be more precise because we don't know whether there are some values of 118 between 114 and 118.

9.1.4 Interpreting Data: Normal Distributions

For numerical data, the **frequency curve** is a smoothed-out line that more or less connects all points. An ideal frequency curve, called a **bell-shaped curve** for obvious reasons, is the **normal curve**, or **normal distribution curve.**

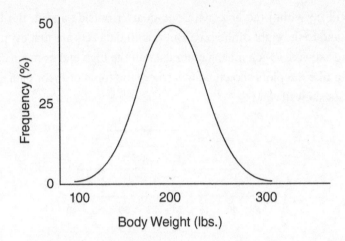

Some examples of a **normal distribution** are (a) the heights of all adult women, (b) the weights of all adult men, (c) the highest daily temperatures in a given city over a period of time, and (d) the diameters of cylinders manufactured in a factory.

In the bell-shaped curve, as shown above, the horizontal axis shows the data (often but not necessarily in intervals), with the center point being the mean (μ) of the data. The vertical axis is the frequency of the data points, with the maximum corresponding to the mean. The normal curve forms the basis of statistics; how actual data points vary from it allows statisticians to make their analyses.

An example of a situation that would have a normal curve is the result of several tosses of a fair coin, where the horizontal axis would be the number of heads. (The term "fair coin" simply means it is equally weighted, so there is no bias for heads or tails.) The vertical axis would be the frequency of getting a specific number of heads in a number of trials.

Let's say we flip a coin 32 times, and write down the possible number of heads (0 through 32) on the horizontal axis and the frequency of each number on the vertical axis. If we then repeat the experiment 1,000 times, a graph of the number of 32-flip sets that resulted in a given number of heads would look very much like a bell-shaped curve. The high point would be for exactly 16 heads.

Most of the data appears near the middle of a bell curve (see Section 9.1.4c), and the farther from the middle a data point is, the less likely it is to have happened by chance. That is what statistics is all about—finding **significant** results, or results not attributable to chance. Basically, if a verifiable data point (one not due to error) is very far from the mean of the data, which is the middle of the bell curve, then the likelihood that it occurred due to chance are very slim, so that data point must be due to something, or in statistics-speak, it must be "significant."

As a practical example, DNA sampling uses statistics by comparing certain parameters to what would be expected in a random sample of the population. When the conclusion in court is that there is a 1 in 400 million chance that the DNA found at a crime scene isn't that of the defendant, it means that the DNA match for that defendant is so extremely far from the middle of the bell curve determined by statistical analysis that it cannot be due to chance, and the conclusion is that the defendant was at the crime scene.

9.1.4a Properties of the Normal Curve

When graphed, a group of data that is normally distributed will resemble a symmetric histogram. The perfect normal curve has these general properties:

- The mean and median are equal.

- The curve is symmetric about the mean.

- The y-coordinate of the mean is the maximum point on the curve.

- The curve never touches the x-axis and all y-values are positive.

- The curve is continuous and assumes all values of x.

9.1.4b Variance and Standard Deviation

To measure how spread the data are and to assess whether any data point is significant, we calculate the variance and standard deviation (the square root of the variance). The standard deviation measures the significance of a data point, and tells whether this significance is strong, moderate, or weak. Often the strength of significance depends on how many data points were used to determine significance. Statistical significance plays the primary role in statistics, as is shown in the rest of this section.

This becomes evident when we look at the formula for **variance**, which tells how much variability exists in a distribution. Without going into the derivation of the formula, it is enough to know that variance, designated as σ^2, is the average of the squared differences between the data values and the mean. The square of the differences is used rather than the differences themselves. The variance, although it is a measure of the variability of the data distribution, is not as important in statistical analysis as is its square root, called the **standard deviation**, σ, which can be thought of as the typical distance of each data point from the mean.

The question arises as to why we have to square the differences in the variance and then have to take the square root to find the standard deviation, which tells how spread out the data points are. The answer is simple: If we just summed the differences of the data points from the mean, by the very definition of the mean, the sum would always be 0. Not any information about the spread there. We sum the squares of the differences and then take the square root to get a value that has meaning.

For example, the mean of $\{1, 2, 3, 4, 5\}$ is 3. The sum of the distances from the mean are $(1-3) + (2-3) + (3-3) + (4-3) + (5-3) = (-2) + (-1) + 0 + 1 + 2 = 0$, and when divided by 5 it is still 0, and the standard deviation is $\sqrt{0} = 0$. The sum of the *squares* of the distances from the mean are $(1-3)^2 + (2-3)^2 + (3-3)^2 + (4-3)^2 + (5-3)^2 = (-2)^2 + (-1)^2 + 0^2 + 1^2 + 2^2 = 10$, which when divided by 5 is 2, and $\sqrt{2} = 1.414$. Sure enough, for our sample of five numbers, the average distance from the mean is $\dfrac{2+1+0+1+2}{5} = 1.2$, a better indicator than 0.

9.1.4c Normal Distribution Percentages

So how do we use standard deviation—what does it mean? Let's look at the normal distribution, the force behind statistics, to see how standard deviation plays an important role. A standard deviation is a measure of how spread out the data are. The percentages of the areas under the normal curve between the mean and plus or minus 1, 2, or 3 standard deviations are important for solving normal distribution problems.

- Approximately 68.2% of the data are within one standard deviation of the mean.

- Approximately 95.4% of the data are within two standard deviations of the mean.

- Approximately 99.7% of the data are within three standard deviations of the mean.

 The tenths place of these percentages may vary slightly in statistics books due to rounding. In the classroom, use the values in your text.

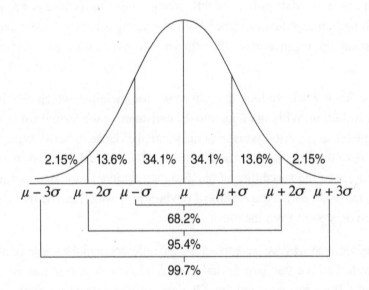

The cumulative frequency for any data point you choose is the total of the frequencies less than or equal to that data point. For example the cumulative frequency for $\mu + \sigma$ is, according to the normal curve, 2.15% + 13.6% + 34.1% + 34.1% = 83.95%, which states that 83.95% of the data fall below or at $\mu + \sigma$.

EXAMPLE 9.11

What is the average monthly rainfall and standard deviation in inches in Cotswolds, England, if we use the following data from one year to come to a general statement? (The variance in the data is 0.084 inches.)

Monthly Rainfall (inches)

January	February	March	April	May	June
2.3	1.9	2.1	1.8	2.2	2.2
July	August	September	October	November	December
2.0	2.8	2.2	2.1	2.5	2.6

SOLUTION 9.11

The mean (average) is found by $\mu = \dfrac{\text{sum of data points}}{\text{total number of data points}} = \dfrac{26.7}{12} = 2.225$.
To compute the standard deviation, take the square root of the variance $\sigma = \sqrt{0.084} = 0.290$. Therefore, the mean is 2.225 inches and the standard deviation is 0.290 inches.

We can state a conclusion that the monthly mean rainfall in Cotswolds is 2.225 inches, and it varies by about ±0.290 inches 68.2% of the time. Said another way, about 68.2% of the time, the monthly rainfall in Cotswolds is between 1.935 and 2.515 inches. Similarly, the data show that about 95.4% of the time, the monthly rainfall in Cotswolds is 1.645 to 2.805 inches, and about 99.7% of the time, the monthly rainfall in Cotswolds is 1.355 to 3.095 inches. These last calculations were for two standard deviations and three standard deviations from the mean.

To give a simple idea of what this means, let's say the analysis from Example 9.11 was taken from data over a 10-year period (to give the results more validity). Suppose it rained a monthly average of 3.05 inches the following year. Based on these calculations, would that be a significant rainfall (meaning *statistically* significant, since we can assume it might have been emotionally significant to some people in Cotswolds)? If we decided that anything within 3 standard deviations of the mean is not significant (in other words, it can be expected 99.7% of the time), then no, it is not statistically significant. What if it rained a monthly average of only 1 inch the year after that—is that statistically significant? Yes, in this case it is because that is outside of −3 standard deviations, which suggests that so little rain is probably not due to chance and may be due to another reason, such as global warming, which is a common explanation for a lot of weather anomalies.

9.1.4d Z-Scores: Standard Normal Distribution

A **standard normal distribution** is a special case of the normal distribution above, in which the mean is normalized to 0, one standard deviation is 1, and the area under the whole curve above the *x*-axis is 1. This is just a neater way to write the normal distribution, and it is easier to calculate and understand. Compare the curve on the left with the actual numbers to the curve on the right with the standardized numbers for the data from Example 9.11.

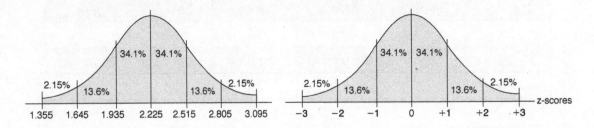

The values of *x* of a normal distribution (the curve on the left, 1.355, 1.645, etc.) are called **raw scores**. For a *standard* normal distribution, the independent values become **z-scores**, or **standard scores**. Z-scores are used to determine how many standard deviations from the mean a data value lies. Just as *x*-scores can assume any value, *z*-scores can also assume any value. A negative *z*-score indicates how many standard deviations below the mean, and a *z*-score of 0 indicates a raw score that is equal to the mean.

Raw scores (*x*-scores) are converted to *z*-scores by the simple formula

$$z = \frac{x - \mu}{\sigma}$$

 The formula $z = \frac{x - \mu}{\sigma}$ applies to *any* distribution of data, not just those that belong to a normal distribution.

The next figure shows the same bell curve, but with *z*-scores and percentiles. Since *z*-scores are normalized, each *z*-score is associated with a percentage of the area under the curve above (or below) the mean (rounded to the nearest tenth in the figure). Therefore, the *z*-score of 1 is still associated with 34.1% of the data above the mean, which is equivalent to an 84.1 percentile because, due to the symmetry of the curve, *z* = 0 to the left "end" of the curve is 50% of the area, and that is added to the 34.1% for *z* = 1. Similarly, *z* = 2 means (34.1 + 13.6) = 47.7% of the data above the mean, or the 97.7 percentile of the whole data set.

 There is no true end to the graph because it goes on to infinity in either direction. The area from the mean to either end is treated as 50%, however.

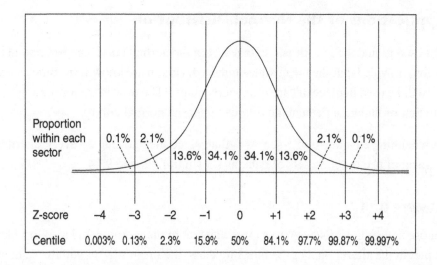

Due to the symmetry of the curve, the area between $z = 0$ and a given positive z value is equivalent to the area between $z = 0$ and the corresponding negative z value. That is, the area between $z = 0$ and $z = 1.5$ is the same as the area between $z = 0$ and $z = -1.5$. A z-score of 0 means 50% of the data are below and 50% of the data are above that point. In other words, $z = 0$ at the median (as well as the mean) in a true normal curve.

EXAMPLE 9.12

What is the area between $z = 0$ and $z = 1$?

SOLUTION 9.12

From the graph of the standardized normal distribution, this area is 34.1%.

EXAMPLE 9.13

What percentage of the data are below $z = -1$?

SOLUTION 9.13

There are two ways to look at this problem. The more accurate way to calculate this is to compute the area to the right of $z = -1$ and subtract it from 100%. Use the fact that everything from z to either end of the curve is 50% of the area, so the answer is $1 - (.50 + 34.1) = 15.9\%$, the correct answer. Using the other solution, add $13.6\% + 2.1\% + 0.1\% = 15.8\%$. However, beyond the z-scores of ± 3 is a tiny percentage of data that isn't being counted. Of course, the percentile at the bottom of the curve, if given, is an instantaneous answer.

9.1.4e Applications of the Normal Distribution

The steps used to find the area or percentages from the normal curve can be applied to any normal distribution, provided that the mean and standard deviation are known. In some cases, the word "probability" will be used in place of "area" or "percentage." The procedure for finding a probability is identical to that of finding a percentage or area under the normal curve.

The overwhelming advantage of z-scores is that, since they normalize every distribution, they allow comparison of two different sets of data, as shown in Example 9.14.

EXAMPLE 9.14

Suppose a math test was given to a class that met in the morning and also to a class that met in the afternoon. For the morning class, the mean was 84 and the standard deviation was 3.4. For the afternoon class, the mean was 82 and the standard deviation was 3.6. A student in each class scored a 90. Which student had the higher score relative to the class?

SOLUTION 9.14

z-scores allow us to compare the results between these two classes. For the morning class, a raw score of 90 corresponds to a z-score of $z = \dfrac{90 - 84}{3.4} = \dfrac{6}{3.4} \approx 1.76$.

For the afternoon class, a raw score of 90 has a z-score of $z = \dfrac{90 - 82}{3.6} = \dfrac{8}{3.6} \approx 2.22$. Thus, the grade of 90 corresponds to a higher z-score in the afternoon class than in the morning class, indicating a *relatively* better score for the afternoon class, even though both raw scores were 90.

EXAMPLE 9.15

A watch company makes watches with a mean lifetime of 38 months, and a standard deviation of 5 months. What percentage of this company's watches is expected to last longer than 4 years?

SOLUTION 9.15

Before starting this solution, recognize that the question is asking about 48 months. Then recognize that 48 months is the mean (38) plus two standard deviations (2 × 5). So this example translates to "What is the percentage of a normal curve above 2 standard deviations?" The percentage below 2 standard deviations is 50 + (34.1 + 13.6) = 97.7%, so the percentage above 2 standard deviations is 100 − 97.7 = 2.3%. (Note that this differs from the percentage of 2.15% shown on the graph of the standard normal distribution because 2.15%

is the percentage between 2 and 3 standard deviations not including the small percentage above 3 standard deviations.)

EXAMPLE 9.16

The mean score of the first two tests in a math class is 80, and the standard deviation is 10.5. Assume a normal distribution and that the score on a third test will have the same distribution. What is the probability that the mean score for the third test will be higher than 59 (passing)?

SOLUTION 9.16

First, compute the z-score for the passing grade of 59: $z = \dfrac{x - \mu}{\sigma} = \dfrac{59 - 80}{10.5} = -2$.
So a score of 59 is 2 standard deviations below the mean, and the requested probability includes the scores from 59 to 80 plus the scores greater than 80. The scores from 59 to 80 (from $z = -2$) have a probability of 47.7%. To that we have to add the probability of getting above 80 (the mean), which is 50%. Therefore, the requested probability is 47.7% + 50% = 97.7%.

9.1.5 Comparing Data Sets: Correlations

The **correlation** of two or more variables is an indication of the extent to which the variables fluctuate together. The values of one variable are plotted against the values of the other variable, similar to (x, y) values on a Cartesian coordinate system. Correlation is the measure of the corresponding mathematical relationship between the two sets of data. The discussion and examples in the next sections consider **bivariate data**, which refers to the fact that there are two variables.

9.1.5a Scatter Plots

To determine whether there is a **correlation** (or association) between two variable quantities, we use **scatter plots**. Scatter plots use Cartesian coordinates and plot the pairs of points, where the horizontal axis represents the independent variable and the vertical axis represents the dependent variable. By using a scatter plot, we may determine the best linear relationship between two given quantities if in fact a relationship exists. Be sure to be consistent in which variable you consider to be dependent and which independent for all points.

9.1.5b Correlation Coefficient

Correlation between the variables is measured by a **correlation coefficient**, usually designated as r, which works quite well if the relationship between the variables is somewhat linear. The value of r varies between +1 and –1.

- A positive correlation indicates the extent to which variables increase or decrease in parallel. A value of $r = 1$ indicates a perfect fit (a line with a positive slope).

- A negative correlation indicates the extent to which one variable increases as the other decreases. A value of $r = -1$ indicates a perfect fit but in a reverse pattern (a line with a negative slope).

- A correlation of 0 indicates that there is no relationship between the variables.

- The closer the correlation coefficient is to ± 1, the stronger the correlation.

Examples of scatter plots of the three types of correlation are shown below with their correlation coefficients, r, which measure the strength of the association between the variables.

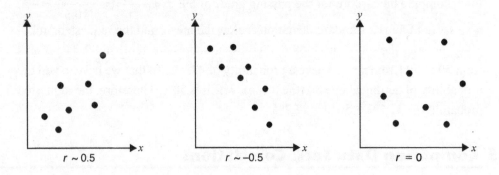

9.1.5c Linear Regression

Determining **linear regression** consists of finding the best-fitting straight line through the data points in a scatter plot. The line that approximates the correlation relationship is called the **regression line** or **line of best fit**. Do the data points line up exactly in a straight line? Usually not, but the distances of the data points above the regression line are offset by the distances of the data points below the line.

If two variables are perfectly correlated (meaning a definite cause-and-effect relationship exists), the plot is a straight line. The more the line deviates from a straight line, the less the two variables are correlated. A common example of very good correlation is hours of study time and grades—as the hours of study time increase, so do grades, as shown in the next figure.

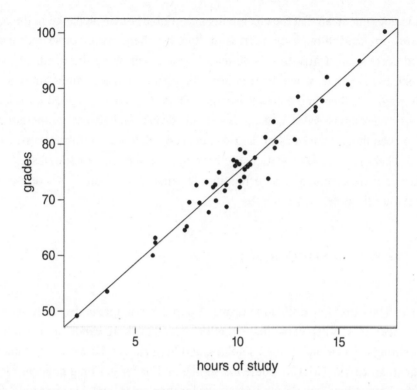

For linear regression, be sure the relationship can be approximated by a straight line. Linear regression is often inappropriately used to model nonlinear relationships, such as when one of the variables is squared. Sometimes, the "best fit" is in the form of a curve, such as for an exponential function, a quadratic equation, or even a circle—these may show up with a 0 correlation coefficient if they are tested by using *linear* regression criteria.

 The value of the correlation coefficient does not show how steep the regression line is. It shows only how good the correlation is and whether it is positive or negative. Linear regression is used to predict trends.

Many organizations use statistical analysis to interpret data and to predict future **trends**. Trend estimation is used to make and justify statements about the data; it is a statistical technique that helps to describe and analyze data. A trend can be seen in the regression line, or line of best fit, of the data. A trend is more likely the closer the correlation coefficient is to ±1.

If one of the variables in the data is time, trend analysis can be used to predict future events, known as trend estimation. **Extrapolation** is estimation of a value outside of the known data based on extending the data by continuing the regression line at the same slope. **Interpolation** is like extrapolation but, as the name implies, it involves figuring values *within* the data set by using the regression line.

Correlation does not mean that the change in one variable *causes* a change in the other variable. The two can be correlated through the regression line, but there can be other reasons for the data to have a good correlation. **Causation** is defined as one event being the result of the occurrence of another event. For example, when the weather gets warmer in the summer, more sunglasses and more ice cream are sold than in the cooler weather. There is probably a good correlation between temperature rise and sunglass sales, and another good correlation between temperature rise and ice cream sales, so even though the sales of the two items correlate, the common cause is temperature not each other. There is no causal relationship between the purchase of sunglasses and ice cream sales, even though there seems to be a correlation. In other words, sunglasses do not make people crave ice cream, nor the other way around.

 Correlation is NOT Causation.

Causation can be extremely difficult to prove. A popular example is the relation between smoking and lung cancer. It is indisputable that smoking *can* cause lung cancer and that historical data have shown a strong correlation between smoking and lung cancer. However, is smoking the cause of lung cancer in all cases? No. Can someone smoke and never get lung cancer? Of course. Can someone smoke but get lung cancer for a reason other than smoking? Also possible. So the causal relationship between the two is not 100 percent, which would imply that every single person who smoked even just one cigarette would get lung cancer.

Some Internet viral facts are humorous because they state a true and strong "correlation" between totally disparate events, implying that there is a cause and effect. One, for example, is the near perfect 99.79% correlation between U.S. spending on science, space, and technology versus the number of suicides by hanging, strangulation, and suffocation. Thousands of these absurd correlations exist—even though they are statistically correlated, it is just due to chance and there is no causal relationship. When finding correlations, engage your brain.

9.1.5d Two-Way Frequency Tables

Similar to the one-way tables, which are familiar (for example, the tables in this chapter (see Section 9.1.3b) used to construct a bar graph and pie charts), are **two-way frequency tables**. These tables represent the possible relationships between *two* sets of categorical data whose values have been paired in some way. They are also called **contingency tables**.

Two-way tables visually represent the possible relationships between two sets of categorical data. Let's look at the simple two-way table shown below, in which the two sets of data are the ages of students (indicated by their grade in school) and whether they eat or skip breakfast.

	Eat breakfast	Skip breakfast	Totals
Middle school students	50	32	82
High school students	42	48	90
Totals	92	80	172

The categories are labeled along the top of the table (whether a student eats breakfast) and the left side (the school class of the student), with the counts appearing in the interior cells of the table. From these data, we can fill out the totals for the rows, columns, and the whole table. For example, we see that there were 172 students in the data set. We can also state that 32 of the middle school students skip breakfast and 42 of the high school students eat breakfast.

In a two-way table, the total of the rows equals the total of the columns.

The numbers in the table are frequency counts, but we cannot make any *relative* comparisons because we would have to compare their relative frequencies to see whether there really is a difference. **Relative frequencies** compare the frequencies *in relation to* the rest of the data (thus the term "relative" frequencies).

Even though this table contains numbers, it is still a categorical table because the numbers are just how many of each category, or a **frequency count**, like a tally. Remember that for categorical data, there is no average, and that is true here.

The data presented as relative frequencies make comparisons easier. A similar two-way table converts each count to a **relative frequency**, which is the ratio of the value of the count to the value of the total count. Frequencies that appear within the table are called **joint frequencies**, and those in the margins are called **marginal frequencies**. The frequencies are stated in fractions, in decimals rounded to the nearest hundredth, or in percentages.

We can construct a table that gives relative frequencies based on the total (here, 172) or conditional frequencies, which are ratios of a joint relative frequency and the related marginal frequency. The choice depends on which question we want to answer. Let's look at each situation.

This first table is based on the total number of students, 172, and that proportion tells how the data compare to the total number of inputs.

	Eat breakfast	Skip breakfast	Totals
Middle school students	$\frac{50}{172} = .29$	$\frac{32}{172} = .19$	$\frac{82}{172} = .48$
High school students	$\frac{42}{172} = .24$	$\frac{48}{172} = .28$	$\frac{90}{172} = .52$
Totals	$\frac{92}{172} = .53$	$\frac{80}{172} = .47$	1.00

From this table, we can answer questions such as how the proportion of middle school students who eat breakfast compares with high school students who skip breakfast. Our answer would be that they are comparable, with a slightly higher percentage in the first category (29% versus 28%). We can also, from the marginal frequencies, tell what percentage of students in the group were middle school students (48%) by following the middle school row to its total. Likewise, we see that 53% of the students in the group eat breakfast.

If instead, however, we wanted to compare *within* a category, we would construct the relative frequency table differently, so the emphasis is on that particular category. Each entry in the table is relative to the total for that category, not the grand total of 172. Consider the frequencies by student class, from which we can answer questions comparing the percentage of *middle school students* who eat breakfast versus those who skip breakfast. Since we are considering the proportion just among middle school students, each original joint frequency is divided by the total of the middle school students, as seen in the table below. The difference is that 22% (or 61% – 39%) more of the middle school students eat breakfast than skip it. We would do likewise for the second row if high school students was the group of interest.

	Eat breakfast	Skip breakfast	Totals
Middle school students	$\frac{50}{82} = .61$	$\frac{32}{82} = .39$	1.00
High school students	$\frac{42}{90} = .47$	$\frac{48}{90} = .53$	1.00
Totals	$\frac{92}{172} = .53$	$\frac{80}{172} = .47$	1.00

In relative frequency problems, concentrate only on the row or column that is "given" in the wording. In the preceding paragraph, the words "comparing the percentage of *middle school students* who eat breakfast versus those who skip breakfast" are essentially saying, "*given* that a student is a middle school student, compare the percentage who eat breakfast versus skip it."

If we were interested in comparing students who eat breakfast, we would construct a relative frequency table by column, as shown below. Then we could compare whether high school students were more likely than middle school students to skip breakfast, and we would see that the difference is 20% (60% − 40%) or 20% more high school students skip breakfast compared to middle school students. Here, the question can be construed as asking "*given* that the student skips breakfast, what is the difference between high school and middle school students?"

	Eat breakfast	Skip breakfast	Totals
Middle school students	$\frac{50}{92} = .54$	$\frac{32}{80} = .40$	$\frac{82}{172} = .48$
High school students	$\frac{42}{92} = .46$	$\frac{48}{80} = .60$	$\frac{90}{172} = .52$
Totals	1.00	1.00	1.00

EXAMPLE 9.17

The following frequency table counts show how many of a group of 34 high school students work at an after-school job and how many have a car. What is the relative frequency of those students who work and have a car to those who have a car?

	Have a Car	Do Not Have a Car
Work	12	4
Do Not Work	8	10

SOLUTION 9.17

The question is the same as asking, "Given that the student has a car, what is the relative frequency (probability) that the student also works?" That means the conditional relative frequency is the ratio of the number of students who have both a car and a job to the number of students who have a car, or $\frac{12}{12 + 8} = \frac{12}{20} = .60$.

9.2 PROBABILITY

9.2.1 Basics

Probability is simply the chance that something will occur. The probability of something happening is calculated as

$$\text{Pr(something happening)} = \frac{\text{number of ways something can happen}}{\text{total number of ways something can and cannot happen}}.$$

Probability is therefore a fraction (or its equivalent ratio or percentage) between 0 and 1.

At one end, a probability of 0 means that something cannot happen. Period. Since in this case, the number of ways something can happen is 0, we don't even have to worry about the number of ways it can and cannot happen (the denominator, which is also called the **sample space**) because 0 divided by anything (except another 0) is 0. An example is pigs flying. Pigs cannot fly (at least not on their own), so the probability of a pig flying is 0.

At the other end, a probability of 1 means that something always happens. It cannot "not happen" so we have the same number at the top and bottom of the fraction, and it equals 1. Do you have to know how many ways something can happen if it always happens? No, what you have to know is that it cannot *not* happen, so the probability is 1, or 100% certain. A simple example is the probability that your birthday will be on the month and day you were born. It's a sure thing—there is no wiggle room. The probability is 1.

All other types of probability always fall between 0 and 1. There are no negative probabilities. Here and in the rest of the discussion on probability, we are talking about **theoretical probability**, or the number of ways that an event can occur divided by the total number of possible outcomes. This is somewhat different from empirical, or experimental, probability, which is probability determined by experiment or observation.

Since the probability of something not happening plus the probability of it happening equals 100%, we can say Pr(something not happening) = 1 – Pr(something happening) or,

$$\text{Pr(not A)} = 1 - P(A),$$

in which Pr(not A) and Pr(A) are **complementary events**. Complementary events are events that are the subject of the annoying answer to the question "Will such and such happen?" Answer: "Either it will or it won't." The "such and such" can be any event that has only two outcomes, both of which cannot happen at the same time (mutually exclusive, see Section 9.2.5c), such as rolling a 5 on a die (singular of dice).

Let's look at some examples and follow them to their logical conclusions. We will introduce more complicated situations as we go, but the idea is the same for all. Notice in these examples that everything must be fair. **Fair** means that a coin must not be weighted to favor one side, or a die also must not be weighted to favor a particular top number. Therefore, the probability of tossing heads on one flip of a fair coin is $\frac{1}{2}$, and the probability of tossing any particular number on a fair die is $\frac{1}{6}$.

EXAMPLE 9.18

What is the probability of tossing a number less than 7 on the toss of a die?

SOLUTION 9.18

The numbers on a die are 1 through 6, so you always will toss a number less than 7. $Pr(<7) = 1$.

9.2.2 Fundamental Counting Principle

Probability and statistics have a lot to do with counting, and thus with the **counting principle**, which states:

> If there are m ways to do one thing, and n ways to do another,
> then there are $m \times n$ ways of doing both.

The counting principle works with any number of inputs.

For example, if there are 2 ways for one activity to happen and 3 ways for a second activity to happen, then there are $2 \times 3 = 6$ ways for both to happen. A tree diagram shows how this works. **Tree diagrams** show all the possible outcomes of an event as branches.

As an example, suppose a soft-serve shop has two ice cream flavors and three toppings. How many choices are there? The tree diagram shows there are 6.

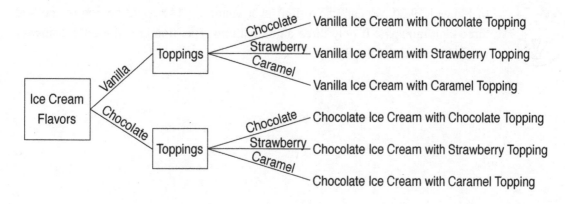

Even though a tree diagram for the following scenario would be too big to show here, the principle is the same: If a restaurant offers 3 types of meat, 2 types of potato, 4 types of vegetable, and 5 different desserts, how many choices does a customer have, picking only one from each category? The answer is $3 \times 2 \times 4 \times 5 = 120$ choices. Notice that if, in addition, one of the choices was to not have a vegetable or dessert, we would have to add 1 (none) to each of those choices, and the customer would then have $3 \times 2 \times 5 \times 6 = 180$ choices.

If the choices were random, the probability that someone picked a specific type of meat, potato, vegetable, and dessert (assuming "no thank you" isn't allowed). That would be $1 \times 1 \times 1 \times 1 = 1$ choices out of 120, $\dfrac{1}{120}$ or .0083.

EXAMPLE 9.19

A pizza shop sells small, medium, and large pizzas. Each pizza can be ordered in thin or thick crust. And each pizza has a choice of five toppings—extra cheese, pepperoni, sausage, mushrooms, or anchovies. If a one-topping pizza is ordered, how many different pizzas choices are there?

SOLUTION 9.19

There are $3(2)(5) = 30$ different pizzas possible.

EXAMPLE 9.20

A certain lottery has only three-digit numbers, 100 to 999. How many number choices are there?

SOLUTION 9.20

There are 9 possible first digits (1–9, since if 0 were allowed in the first position, it would be a two-digit number), 10 possible second digits, and 10 possible third digits. So there are $9(10)(10) = 900$ different valid three-digit numbers.

In Example 9.20, we can use a digit over again, so 444 could be one of the 900 three-digit numbers. If only three digits with no repetition are allowed, the answer would be calculated $9 \times 9 \times 8 = 648$.

9.2.3 Factorials

Similarly, using the counting principle, we can determine, for example, how many ways five people can line up: $5 \times 4 \times 3 \times 2 \times 1$. A special symbol for this calculation is !, called **factorial**. So n factorial is written as $n! = n \times (n-1) \times (n-2) \times ... \times 3 \times 2 \times 1$, or the product of n and every number 1 less than n all the way down to 1. Five people can line up in $5! = 120$ ways because the first person has a choice of 5 places, the next has a choice of only 4, the next only 3, then 2, and the last one has only 1 choice because every other slot is taken.

0! is defined as 1, or $0! = 1$.

EXAMPLE 9.21

Evaluate $\dfrac{n!}{(n+2)!}$.

SOLUTION 9.21

$$\frac{n \times (n-1) \times (n-2) \times ... \times 2 \times 1}{(n+2) \times (n+1) \times n \times (n-1) \times (n-2) \times ... \times 2 \times 1} = \frac{1}{(n+2) \times (n+1)}.$$ Note that all the terms $n \times (n-1) \times ... \times 2 \times 1$ in the numerator and denominator cancel each other out. This will be useful in the next section on permutations and combinations.

9.2.4 Permutations and Combinations

Factorials are handy when choosing r objects out of n objects, either when order makes a difference (called a **permutation** and denoted $_nP_r = \dfrac{n!}{(n-r)!}$) or when order doesn't make a difference (called a **combination** and denoted $_nC_r = \dfrac{n!}{r!(n-r)!}$).

On the calculator, press PRB to select choices for permutations, $_nP_r$; combinations, $_nC_r$, or factorial, !.

The mechanics of working with these formulas is important. Fortunately, many factors cancel each other out in permutations and combinations, so the arithmetic is usually simple. For example,

$$_{12}P_2 = \frac{12!}{10!} = \frac{12 \times 11 \times \cancel{10} \times \cancel{9} \times \cancel{8} \times \cancel{7} \times \cancel{6} \times \cancel{5} \times \cancel{4} \times \cancel{3} \times \cancel{2} \times \cancel{1}}{\cancel{10} \times \cancel{9} \times \cancel{8} \times \cancel{7} \times \cancel{6} \times \cancel{5} \times \cancel{4} \times \cancel{3} \times \cancel{2} \times \cancel{1}} = 12 \times 11 = 132.$$

 On the calculator, enter the following: $\boxed{1}\boxed{2}\boxed{\text{PRB}}$ then choose $\boxed{_nP_r}\boxed{\text{ENTER}}\boxed{2}\boxed{=}$.

Likewise,

$$_{12}C_2 = \frac{12!}{2!10!} = \frac{12 \times 11 \times \cancel{10} \times \cancel{9} \times \cancel{8} \times \cancel{7} \times \cancel{6} \times \cancel{5} \times \cancel{4} \times \cancel{3} \times \cancel{2} \times \cancel{1}}{2 \times 1 \times \cancel{10} \times \cancel{9} \times \cancel{8} \times \cancel{7} \times \cancel{6} \times \cancel{5} \times \cancel{4} \times \cancel{3} \times \cancel{2} \times \cancel{1}} = \frac{12 \times 11}{2 \times 1} = 66.$$

 On the calculator, enter the following: $\boxed{1}\boxed{2}\boxed{\text{PRB}}$ then choose $\boxed{_nC_r}\boxed{\text{ENTER}}\boxed{2}\boxed{=}$.

Permutations and combinations are always whole numbers, which means every number in the denominator always cancels out with something in the numerator. Let's try a few of these calculations.

EXAMPLE 9.22

Find the value of $\frac{10!}{8!}$.

SOLUTION 9.22

$$\frac{10!}{8!} = \frac{10 \times 9 \times \cancel{8} \times \cancel{7} \times \cancel{\ldots} \times \cancel{2} \times \cancel{1}}{\cancel{8} \times \cancel{7} \times \cancel{\ldots} \times \cancel{2} \times \cancel{1}} = 10 \times 9 = 90.$$

 On the calculator, enter the following: $\boxed{1}\boxed{0}\boxed{\text{PRB}}$ then choose $\boxed{!}\boxed{\text{ENTER}}\boxed{\div}\boxed{8}\boxed{\text{PRB}}$ then choose $\boxed{!}\boxed{\text{ENTER}}\boxed{=}$. Note that $\boxed{\text{ENTER}}$ and $\boxed{=}$ are the same key.

Permutations are used when order makes a difference. The equation for a permutation of n things taken r at a time is $_nP_r = \dfrac{n!}{(n-r)!}$, which always reduces down to only the first $(n-r)$ factors of $n!$. Thus, as Example 9.22 showed, $\dfrac{10!}{8!} = 10 \times 9 = 90$. Since $(n-r) = 2$, only the first two factors of $n!$ are multiplied.

Recognize that $_nP_r = \dfrac{n!}{(n-r)!}$ reduces down to only the first $(n-r)$ factors of $n!$, so when $(n-r)$ equals 1, 2, or 3, just multiply the first one, two, or three (respectively) factors of $n!$; for larger differences, use the calculator.

Combinations are used when order doesn't make a difference. The equation for a combination of n things taken r at a time is $_nC_r = \dfrac{n!}{r!(n-r)!}$, which always reduces down to only the first $(n-r)$ factors of $n!$ divided by $r!$. Recognize that $_nC_r = \dfrac{n!}{r!(n-r)!}$ reduces down to only the first $(n-r)$ (or r, whichever is less) factors of $n!$ divided by $(n-r)!$ (or $r!$, whichever is less). Then, since combinations are always integers, the factors in the denominator will cancel out the factors in the numerator.

EXAMPLE 9.23

Find the value of $_8C_3$.

SOLUTION 9.23

$_8C_3 = \dfrac{8!}{3!5!} = \dfrac{8 \times 7 \times \cancel{6} \times \cancel{5} \times \cancel{4} \times \cancel{3} \times \cancel{2} \times \cancel{1}}{\cancel{3} \times \cancel{2} \times 1 \times \cancel{5} \times \cancel{4} \times \cancel{3} \times \cancel{2} \times \cancel{1}}$. Since all of these numbers are multiplied, we can do a lot of cancellations, and the problem reduces to $\dfrac{8!}{3!5!} = 8 \times 7 = 56$.

 For $_8C_3$ on the calculator, enter the following: $\boxed{8}$ $\boxed{\text{PRB}}$ then choose $\boxed{!}$ $\boxed{\text{ENTER}}$ $\boxed{3}$ $\boxed{=}$. The answer is 56.

EXAMPLE 9.24

An office has 16 workers. The boss decides to choose a manager and then an assistant from that group. This can be done in $_{16}P_2 = \dfrac{16!}{(16-2)!}$ ways. What is the value of $_{16}P_2$?

SOLUTION 9.24

This is a permutation of 16 things choosing 2 because order is important. John as the manager and Jane as the assistant is different from Jane as the manager and John as the assistant. $_{16}P_2 = \dfrac{16!}{(16-2)!} = \dfrac{16!}{14!} = 16(15) = 240$.

A simple way to remember whether a problem should use permutations or combinations is that order makes a difference in a combination lock (9-2-3 will open the lock, whereas 3-9-2 will not) and that the combination formula is *NOT* the one that needs order. Why they call the one that needs order a *permutation* instead of a combination (like the lock) is a puzzle.

9.2.5 Special Events

9.2.5a Compound Events

What if we are considering something that has more than one part, for example, two parts that we'll call A and B. What is the probability that A *or* B will occur? Or what is the probability that A *and* B will occur? The following general rules will help:

Addition Rule of Probability "or" means add

Multiplication Rule of Probability "and" means multiply

To remember that "and" means *multiply*, think of a jar of only yellow marbles. Of course, the probability of picking a yellow marble from the jar is 1 since they all are yellow. The probability of picking two yellow marbles is likewise 1. But if we used addition for "and," we would have gotten Pr(yellow and yellow) = 1 + 1 = 2, which is impossible since all probabilities are between 0 and 1. So "and" uses multiplication, and Pr(yellow *and* yellow) = 1 × 1 = 1.

EXAMPLE 9.25

What is the probability of tossing a number greater than 4 on a die?

SOLUTION 9.25

A number greater than 4 would be a 5 or a 6, which means 2 of the possible tosses, so $\Pr(5 \text{ or } 6) = \frac{2}{6} = \frac{1}{3}$. Another way to think of this problem is $\Pr(5 \text{ or } 6) = \Pr(5) + \Pr(6) = \frac{1}{6} + \frac{1}{6} = \frac{2}{6} = \frac{1}{3}$.

This is all well and good because we are talking about one toss of one die at one time. What if we now talk about tossing two dice, or even one die twice? We must decide whether the problems involving more than one event are **independent** (the outcome of one doesn't influence the outcome of the other), **mutually exclusive** (both outcomes cannot happen at the same time), or **overlapping** (there are outcomes in common). They are treated differently, as shown next.

9.2.5b Independent Events

Any string of events that each don't influence the others are called independent events. These types of events don't have any effect on the probability of any other event. For example, if you throw two dice, what shows up on die 1 is independent of what shows up on die 2.

EXAMPLE 9.26

What is the probability of getting two 1's on two tosses of one die or on one toss of two dice (called "snake eyes")?

SOLUTION 9.26

This is an "and" situation, so we multiply the probabilities: $\Pr(1 \text{ and } 1) = \Pr(1) \times \Pr(1) = \frac{1}{6} \times \frac{1}{6} = \frac{1}{36}$. The probability of either case is the same.

 Several tosses of a fair coin or one toss of several fair coins give the same result.

EXAMPLE 9.27

The probability of rain on each of the next three days is shown in the following table.

Day	Tuesday	Wednesday	Thursday
Probability of Rain	30%	45%	50%

Based on the table, assuming the probability of rain each day is independent, what is the probability (in percent) that it will rain all three days?

SOLUTION 9.27

We assume that these are independent events, so the probability of rain on any day is independent of the probability of rain the day before or after. Then the probability that it will rain all three days is the product of the three probabilities, or $.30 \times .45 \times .50 = .0675 = 6.75\%$.

The probability of tossing a fair coin four times and getting four heads is an "and" situation, so the probability of getting a head (H), and another H, and another H, and another H is $\Pr(HHHH) = \Pr(H) \times \Pr(H) \times \Pr(H) \times \Pr(H) = \frac{1}{2} \times \frac{1}{2} \times \frac{1}{2} \times \frac{1}{2} = \frac{1}{16}$. This calculation would be the same, whether it is four successive tosses of the same coin, or a toss of four coins, the probability of landing heads or tails doesn't have any effect on the probability of any other coin or other toss.

EXAMPLE 9.28

If you tossed a fair coin seven times and it came up heads each time, what is the probability of the eighth toss being a head?

SOLUTION 9.28

Each toss is independent of the other tosses, so the probability is $\frac{1}{2}$.

Even though the probability of a heads on the eighth toss is $\frac{1}{2}$ (as shown in Example 9.28), the probability of the exact string of eight heads, $\Pr(HHHHHHHH) = \left(\frac{1}{2}\right)^8 = \frac{1^8}{2} = \frac{1}{256}$, or 1 in 256.

EXAMPLE 9.29

What is the probability of tossing snake eyes (two 1's) on each of four successive tosses of two dice?

SOLUTION 9.29

The probability of one toss of snake eyes is $\frac{1}{36}$ (see Example 9.26). If we rolled snake eyes once, does it influence the next toss? No, they are totally independent events. So the probability here is an "and" situation: Pr(snake eyes on first toss *and* snake eyes on second toss *and* snake eyes on third toss *and* snake eyes on fourth toss) $= \left(\frac{1}{36}\right) \times \left(\frac{1}{36}\right) \times \left(\frac{1}{36}\right) \times \left(\frac{1}{36}\right) = \left(\frac{1}{36}\right)^4$, which is the same as 1 in 36^4 or 1 in 1,679,616.

Now let's look at a combination "or" and "and" situation. Notice that each independent situation presented so far has just involved logic and multiplication or division. So does a combination, but it needs some more thinking.

For example, to find the probability of getting a *total* of 4 with a toss of two dice needs more thought. We have to first figure out how many ways we can get a total of 4 with two dice. There are three ways: (1, 3), (3, 1), and (2, 2). The probability for a total of 4 on two dice is

$$\text{Pr}(1 \text{ and } 3 \textit{ or } 3 \text{ and } 1 \textit{ or } 2 \text{ and } 2) = \text{Pr}(1 \text{ and } 3) + \text{Pr}(3 \text{ and } 1) + \text{Pr}(2 \text{ and } 2) =$$
$$[\text{Pr}(1) \times \text{Pr}(3)] + [\text{Pr}(3) \times \text{Pr}(1)] + [\text{Pr}(2) \times \text{Pr}(2)] = \frac{1}{36} + \frac{1}{36} + \frac{1}{36} = \frac{3}{36} = \frac{1}{12}.$$

The challenge in this example was figuring out all of the parts, but they are the same as the calculations in all of the preceding independent examples.

The reason we didn't count another (2, 2) as a possibility is that (2, 2) is the same whether the first or second die comes up a 2. To see how (2, 2) counts as only one possibility, whereas the combination of 1 and 3 counts as two possibilities, look at the following chart of the 36 tosses of two dice, where the horizontal column is the first die and the vertical column is the second die.

	1	2	3	4	5	6
1	(1, 1)	(1, 2)	(1, 3)	(1, 4)	(1, 5)	(1, 6)
2	(2, 1)	(2, 2)	(2, 3)	(2, 4)	(2, 5)	(2, 6)
3	(3, 1)	(3, 2)	(3, 3)	(3, 4)	(3, 5)	(3, 6)
4	(4, 1)	(4, 2)	(4, 3)	(4, 4)	(4, 5)	(4, 6)
5	(5, 1)	(5, 2)	(5, 3)	(5, 4)	(5, 5)	(5, 6)
6	(6, 1)	(6, 2)	(6, 3)	(6, 4)	(6, 5)	(6, 6)

All of the double tosses (1, 1), (2, 2), and so on appear only once (the main diagonal), whereas (3, 1) is considered a different toss from (1, 3).

 There are 36 possibilities on a toss of two dice: 6 possible numbers on the second die (or second toss of a single die) for each of the 6 numbers on the first die (or second toss of the same die).

Now let's consider a favorite scenario in probability problems on most tests: selecting socks in a drawer. This involves two assumptions. First, the socks are chosen randomly without looking. (Besides, if the person selecting the socks looks, then the probability would be 100% that the socks selected are the ones that are wanted.) Second, the socks are in color-matched pairs, not just tossed into the drawer when they come from the dryer, which is usually the case.

EXAMPLE 9.30

Jim has 9 pairs of socks in a drawer, 2 tan, 3 brown, and 4 black, and he selects a pair without looking.

    a. What is the probability that Jim picks a pair of brown socks?

    b. What is the probability that Jim picks a pair of brown or tan socks?

    c. What is the probability that Jim doesn't pick a pair of black socks?

SOLUTION 9.30

    a. Jim has 9 pairs of socks and 3 are brown, so the probability of picking a brown pair is $\frac{3}{9} = \frac{1}{3}$.

    b. This is Pr(brown or tan) = Pr(brown) + Pr(tan) = $\frac{2}{9} + \frac{3}{9} = \frac{5}{9}$.

    c. This question asks for the probability of something *not* happening. The "something" is choosing a pair of black socks. So Pr(not black) = $1 - \text{Pr(black)} = 1 - \frac{4}{9} = \frac{5}{9}$.

The answer to the probability of picking brown or tan socks is the same as the probability of not picking a black pair, which makes sense. If Jim doesn't pick black socks, he must pick brown or tan socks.

9.2.5c Mutually Exclusive Events

Mutually exclusive events are not the same as the independent events discussed so far. Whereas independent events don't influence each other and therefore can both occur at the same time with some probability, mutually exclusive events cannot both occur at the same time. The probability of both occurring is 0. The "or" type of probability of mutually exclusive events can be calculated, but the "and" type of probability for mutually exclusive events is always 0.

As an example, let's say we have a special type of die. In addition to having the usual six numbers, the even numbers are red and the odd numbers are blue. The probability of tossing the die and getting a red number *or* a 5 is $\frac{2}{3}$. This is an "or" situation, so the probabilities of each are added:

$$\text{Pr(red or 5)} = \text{Pr(red)} + \text{Pr(5)} = \frac{1}{2} + \frac{1}{6} = \frac{3}{6} + \frac{1}{6} = \frac{4}{6} = \frac{2}{3}.$$

The probability of tossing the die and getting a red number *and* a 5, however, is 0. It is impossible to get both a red side and a 5 since the 5 is only blue. So Pr(red and 5) = 0.

Hint: The distinction between mutually exclusive and independent events is sometimes difficult to grasp. It is a little easier if you realize that the distinction involves "and" situations, since for mutually exclusive events, "and" *cannot happen*, whereas for independent events, "and" is possible.

9.2.5d Non–Mutually Exclusive, or Overlapping, Events

Overlapping events have outcomes in common, or one or more outcomes occur at the same time. An example is the probability of rolling an odd number or a number greater than 4 in a roll of a die. These events overlap because it is possible for both to occur at the same time, such as rolling a 5. Let's look at these events individually to see how they differ from mutually exclusive events.

- The probability of rolling a number greater than 4 is $\Pr(5 \text{ or } 6) = \dfrac{2}{6} = \dfrac{1}{3}$.

- The probability of rolling an odd number is $\Pr(1 \text{ or } 3 \text{ or } 5) = \dfrac{3}{6} = \dfrac{1}{2}$.

If these events were mutually exclusive, the "or" rule gives

$$\Pr(\text{number is} > 4 \text{ or odd}) = \frac{1}{3} + \frac{1}{2} = \frac{5}{6}.$$

But we know that the complementary event in this scenario is

$$\Pr(\text{number is} \leq 4 \text{ or even}) = \Pr(2 \text{ or } 4) = \frac{2}{6} = \frac{1}{3}.$$

Certainly $\dfrac{5}{6} + \dfrac{1}{3} \neq 1$. What happened is that we included the 5 in the first probability ($5 > 4$) and then we included it again in the second probability (5 is an odd number). How this translates into probability is that with an "or" situation, if any of the events overlap, we must be careful not to count the overlap twice, so we have to subtract the probability of the "double" situation, $\Pr(5) = \dfrac{1}{6}$. Therefore,

$$\Pr(\text{number is} > 4 \text{ or odd}) = \frac{1}{3} + \frac{1}{2} - \frac{1}{6} = \frac{4}{6} = \frac{2}{3}$$

EXAMPLE 9.31

The number of boys and girls at a school is the same, and the eighth-graders are one-third of the student population of 600. What is the formula for the probability that a student chosen at random is in the eighth-grade or is a girl?

SOLUTION 9.31

Pr(8th grade or girl) = Pr(8th grade) + Pr(girl) – Pr(8th-grade girl) = $\frac{1}{3} + \frac{1}{2} - \frac{\text{number of 8th-grade girls}}{600}$. Be careful here and don't assume the number of 8th grade girls is 100. The number of girls and boys *in the school* is the same, but not necessarily in the eighth grade.

Formally, the **addition rule for probability** of overlapping cases is given by

$$\text{Pr (A or B)} = \text{Pr(A)} + \text{Pr(B)} - \text{Pr(A and B)}.$$

In fact, this calculation works for all cases, but if the two situations are mutually exclusive, meaning they do not overlap, the Pr(A and B) part equals 0.

9.2.6 Conditional Probability

Conditional probability is the probability of an event happening dependent on another event already occurring. This ratchets up the probability a little more, but the logic is similar. The symbol for conditional probability is Pr(A|B), read as "the probability of A occurring when B has already occurred" or "the probability of A given B." This is obviously a dependent type of probability.

A popular form of conditional probability involves whether there is **replacement**. As an example, let's say we have a jar that contains 20 marbles: 3 red, 4 yellow, 6 green, and 7 blue. Further, suppose we randomly pick one or more marbles from the jar (meaning we don't look). The probability of picking a yellow marble from the jar, putting it back in the jar, and then picking a blue marble is the same as the standard independent event probability.

$$\text{Pr(yellow and blue, with replacement)} = \text{Pr(yellow)} \times \text{Pr(blue)} = \frac{4}{20} \times \frac{7}{20} = \frac{28}{400} = \frac{7}{100}.$$

The probability of picking a yellow marble from the jar, but this time not replacing it before picking a blue marble is another matter. This scenario is different because in the second pick, there aren't 20 marbles anymore. The yellow one is missing. The method is similar—only the numbers change.

$$\text{Pr(yellow and blue, without replacement)} = \text{Pr(yellow)} \times \text{Pr(blue)} = \frac{4}{20} \times \frac{7}{19} = \frac{28}{380} = \frac{1}{95}.$$

The difference between these two situations is the replacement of the first marble. With replacement, the two picks are independent. But without replacement, the probability of picking a blue marble on the second pick depends on the fact that once the yellow marble was taken out, there was a greater chance of picking a blue marble.

EXAMPLE 9.32

Jerrod turns up the top card of a deck of playing cards and it is an ace.

    a. What is the probability that Jerrod would pick the ace in the first place?

    b. On a second pick, what is the probability that Jerrod picks another ace?

SOLUTION 9.32

    a. $\frac{1}{13}$. There are four aces in a deck of 52 cards, so the probability is $\frac{4}{52} = \frac{1}{13}$.

    b. $\frac{1}{17}$. For the second pick, without replacement, there are only three aces and only 51 cards, so the probability is $\frac{3}{51} = \frac{1}{17}$.

EXAMPLE 9.33

What is the probability of choosing a "1" from a standard deck of cards when aces don't count as 1's?

SOLUTION 9.33

There are no 1's in a deck of cards if aces don't count as 1's, so the probability is 0.

The following table summarizes how to find probabilities.

Summary of Probability Types

Description	Example	Formula	Type of Probability
One event	Flip of a fair coin	$\Pr(A) = \dfrac{\text{number of ways A can happen}}{\text{number of ways A can and cannot happen}}$	Simple probability
Event A or event B	Tossing a 5 or 6 on a die	$\Pr(A \text{ or } B) = \Pr(A) + \Pr(B)$	Mutually exclusive
Event A and event B	Getting THHT in 4 tosses of a coin (or a toss of 4 distinct coins)	$\Pr(T \text{ and } H \text{ and } H \text{ and } T)$ $= \Pr(T) \times \Pr(H) \times \Pr(H) \times \Pr(T)$ where T = tails and H = heads	Independent events
Events (A and B) or (C and D)	Getting a total of 4 with a toss of 2 dice	$\Pr(A \text{ and } B \text{ } or \text{ } C \text{ and } D)$ $= \Pr(A \text{ and } B) + \Pr(C \text{ and } D)$ $= [\Pr(A) \times \Pr(B)] + [\Pr(C) \times \Pr(D)]$	Independent events
Pr(not A)	Probability of event A not happening	$\Pr(\text{not } A) = 1 - \Pr(A)$	Complementary events
Pr(A and not A at same time)	Probability of a 2 and an odd number in 1 pick	$\Pr(A \text{ and not } A \text{ at same time}) = 0$	Mutually exclusive
Pr(A and B) in two events with replacement	Picking a blue marble and then a yellow marble	$\Pr(A \text{ and } B) = \Pr(A) \times \Pr(B)$	Independent events
Pr(A and B) in two events, with no replacement	Picking a blue marble and then a yellow marble	$\Pr(A \text{ and } B) = \Pr(A) \times \Pr(B|A)$, where the denominator for event B depends on event A	Dependent events
Pr(A or B) with Pr(A and B) ≠ 0	Dealing with overlapping events	$\Pr(A \text{ or } B) = \Pr(A) + \Pr(B) - \Pr(A \text{ and } B)$	Non–mutually exclusive events

9.2.7 Venn Diagrams

Situations that involve events that overlap are often shown by using **Venn diagrams.** All the space within the borders of a **Venn diagram** represents the **universe**, U, which simply means the population of interest. In the space within the borders are two or more circles, each representing a specific part of the universe. For mutually exclusive events, the circles don't intersect, but consider here cases in which they do intersect.

The Venn diagram below consists of two overlapping circles, one labeled A and one labeled B. The intersection of the two circles is labeled A & B. Each section of the Venn diagram represents the items that belong to A, to B, or to both. The items can be anything that sometimes "overlaps."

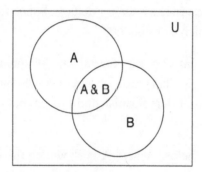

EXAMPLE 9.34

In a class of 30 students, 20 students have a dog or a cat. Thirteen have a dog, and 10 have a cat. If a student is chosen at random from the class, what is the probability that the student has a dog or cat?

SOLUTION 9.34

This problem can be answered right away by reading just the first sentence, it is $\frac{20}{30} = \frac{2}{3}$. But if that clue wasn't caught and we don't take into consideration that some students might have both pets, we might incorrectly calculate Pr(dog or cat) = Pr(dog) + Pr(cat) = $\frac{13}{30} + \frac{10}{30} = \frac{23}{30}$. But 3 of the students must have both pets, and the correct calculation is:

$$Pr \text{ (dog or cat)} = Pr(\text{dog}) + Pr(\text{cat}) - Pr(\text{dog and cat}) = \frac{13}{30} + \frac{10}{30} - \frac{3}{30} = \frac{20}{30} = \frac{2}{3}$$

The Venn diagram for this situation is

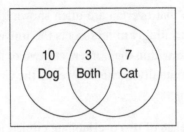

In this Venn diagram, we can see that 13 students do have dogs (the whole left circle for dogs and both) and 10 students do have cats (the whole right circle for cats and both). But we have counted the students who have both pets twice, once for dogs and once for cats. We have to subtract one of the duplicate "both" cases, which is 3 students.

Now let's consider two different scenarios for students' language classes. Suppose students at School A can study only one foreign language, so students who have Spanish classes cannot also have French classes. School B also offers Spanish and French, but allows students to take two languages at the same time.

In the Venn diagrams shown below, School A is shown on the left, with all the students at the school being the universe. There is no overlap between the circles because no student is in both Spanish and French class. School B is shown on the right, with the universe again being all the students in the school. The two circles represent students who are taking at least one language. The portion shared by the two circles represents those students who are taking both Spanish and French. The space outside of the circles in both diagrams represents all the students who aren't taking Spanish or French at all.

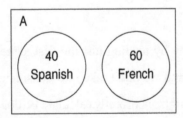 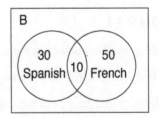

This diagram also allows us to figure out how many students in each school are taking at least one language. For school A, it is easy to see that $40 + 60 = 100$ students take one language, French or Spanish. In this case, the "or" question is simply the sum of the students in each language class. For school B, however, the Venn diagram shows that only 90 students take French or Spanish. Ten of these students take both languages. We cannot count those students twice in the total, which is 30 Spanish only + 50 French only + 10 both Spanish and French = 90. If we had just totaled the students in Spanish class (30 + 10) and the students in French class (50 + 10), we would have gotten 40 + 60 = 100, which is incorrect. We cannot count students who take both classes twice, so we must subtract the extra 10 for those who take both classes.

9.2.8 Expected Value

Expected value deals with the different outcomes associated with a specific event. It provides a method of determining the potential value or the likelihood of each particular outcome of that event. In short, expected value is the average of all possible outcomes, adjusted (or "weighted") for the likelihood that each outcome will occur.

A lottery is an excellent example of the usefulness of expected value. Suppose you are thinking of buying a $10 ticket to a fundraising lottery in which the grand prize is $20,000. If you bought the only ticket, your chance of winning is 100%; otherwise, your chance of winning depends on how many people buy tickets. If the number of tickets is limited to 10,000, then your chance of winning becomes 1 in 10,000, or $\frac{1}{10,000}$ = .0001. The expected *value* of winning $20,000 would then be $\frac{1}{10,000}$ × $20,000 = $2. What does this mean? It means on average, you would win $2, but remember that the ticket cost you $10, so your expected value is down to –$8, or a loss of $8.

Expected value usually involves more than one outcome, however, and its value is what you should expect, *on average*. Let's consider a second scenario in which the lottery has not only one $20,000 prize, with an expected value of $2, but also 20 prizes of $500 each with an expected value of $\frac{20}{10,000}$ × $500 = $1. (This is the *value* you could expect, not a probability of 1, which would have meant you always win.) To complete the scenario, we must also include the expected value of losing, which is –$10, reflecting the $10 that you paid out. If we add up the values of all the possible outcomes, you will realize that your expected value is $2 + $1 + (–$10) = –$7. The chance of winning either of the top prizes is very, very small, and in fact your expected value is to lose $7.00, or for every $10 ticket sold, the ticket holder is losing about $7.00 on average.

In plain terms, the formula for expected value (*EV*) is

$$EV = \Pr(A) \times (\text{value of A}) + \Pr(B) \times (\text{value of B}) + \ldots + \Pr(n) \times (\text{value of } n) - (\text{cost of event}).$$

If *EV* is positive, that means on average you will win *something*; if it is negative, on average you will lose *something*. Is it evident, then, that if the *EV* equals zero, on average you will just break even, and so will the organization that sponsored the lottery.

EXAMPLE 9.35

A local club plans to invest $10,000 to host an outdoor concert. They expect to sell tickets worth $25,000. But the forecast for the day of concert is 20% for severe thunderstorms, in which case the club will have to refund the money collected and in addition lose all the money it invested. Is this a good investment? (Note that in reality, the concert would probably go on anyway or be postponed, so there wouldn't be a refund, but let's look at this specific scenario and assume that if the concert was canceled the club would still have its expenses.)

SOLUTION 9.35

In this scenario, the club has an expected value of

$$\text{(income without rain)} + \text{(income with rain)} - \text{(investment), or}$$

$$EV = \left(\frac{8}{10} \times (+\$25,000)\right) + \left(\frac{2}{10} \times 0\right) - \$10,000 = \$20,000 + 0 - \$10,000 = \$10,000$$

The expected value is that they will double the $10,000 they invested, so it's a good investment indeed.

In Example 9.35, if there were no thunderstorms forecast, the equation would have been $EV = \left(\frac{10}{10} \times (+\$25,000)\right) - \$10,000 = \$25,000 - \$10,000 = \$15,000$.

Chapter 9 Exercises

Answers are on the following page.

1. Which of the following is NOT a measure of central tendency?

    (A) Mean

    (B) Median

    (C) Mode

    (D) Range

2. Which of the following is inappropriate for showing the relationship between the birthweights of babies and how long they stay in the neonatal intensive care unit (NICU)?

    (A) Correlation coefficient

    (B) Bar graph

    (C) Regression line

    (D) All of the above are appropriate.

3. If a sandwich menu offers 6 types of meat, 4 types of cheese, and 2 types of bread (rye or white), what is the probability that someone chooses a sandwich on rye bread?

    (A) $\dfrac{1}{2}$

    (B) $\dfrac{1}{4}$

    (C) $\dfrac{1}{6}$

    (D) $\dfrac{1}{48}$

4. An ice cream shop offers 20 flavors. Derek purchases a dish of 3 different flavors. To figure how many choices Derek has, the easiest method is to use

    (A) a tree diagram.

    (B) permutations.

    (C) combinations.

    (D) factorials.

5. What type of probability is choosing a card that is NOT an ace from a deck of cards on two successive picks without replacement?

(A) Independent

(B) Dependent

(C) Overlapping

(D) Impossible

Answers and Explanations

1. (D)

The range tells how spread out the data are (highest minus smallest) but nothing about what value is close to the center of the data. The mean, median, and mode are values that represent the "typical" data point in a distribution, so they measure central tendency.

2. (B)

A bar graph is used for categorical, not quantitative data. The other three answer choices measure the extent to which variables fluctuate together.

3. (A)

The total number of choices are $6 \times 4 \times 2 = 48$. The number of choices of a sandwich on rye would be $6 \times 4 \times 1 = 24$. So the probability is 24 out of 48, $\frac{1}{2}$, or .50. This solution is much simpler if only the bread choices are considered, since that is all that is asked. There are two bread choices, and rye is one of them: 1 out of 2, $\frac{1}{2}$.

4. (C)

This is a combination because order is not important. A dish of chocolate, vanilla, and strawberry is the same as a dish of strawberry, vanilla, and chocolate. Although a tree diagram will work, it ends up with 1140 choices, so it isn't as easy as figuring the combination, especially when using the calculator.

5. (B)

This is dependent because the probability of the second pick is affected by the absence of the card of the first pick.

Before you begin your review, take this short self-assessment to see how well you know the topics covered in this chapter. Answering all or some correctly will help you identify your strengths so you can focus on those topics where you need the most review. Even if you answer all of the questions correctly, we suggest you still review all the examples in the chapter to ensure you're in good shape to move on. Answers are on the following page.

1. If $y = \dfrac{1}{\sqrt[3]{t}}$, which of the following expressions is equivalent to $\dfrac{dy}{dt}$?

   (A) $\dfrac{1}{3}t^{-\frac{4}{3}}$

   (B) $t^{-\frac{1}{3}}$

   (C) $-\dfrac{1}{3}t^{-\frac{4}{3}}$

   (D) $-\dfrac{1}{3}t^{\frac{4}{3}}$

2. Let $s = t^3 - 6t^2$ be the position function of a particle, where t is in seconds and s is in feet. What is the particle's velocity at 1 second?

   (A) -6 ft/sec

   (B) 9 ft/sec

   (C) -9 ft/sec

   (D) -9 ft/sec^2

3. Is the piecewise function $g(x) = \begin{cases} 3x - x^2, & x < -1 \\ 6x + 2, & x > -1 \end{cases}$ continuous at $x = -1$?

   (A) Yes, since $\lim\limits_{x \to 1^+} g(x) = \lim\limits_{x \to 1^-} g(x)$.

   (B) Yes, since $g(-1) = -4$ for both functions.

   (C) No, since $g(-1)$ doesn't exist.

   (D) Yes, since we can replace $<$ with $\leq$ or $>$ with $\geq$ in the original equation.

4. What is the solid formed by a right triangle, with its base on the x-axis and height on the y-axis, rotating around the y-axis?

   (A) A cylinder

   (B) A cone

   (C) A pyramid

   (D) A prism

5. If the first derivative of a function equals zero at a point a, what can this mean about the graph of $f(x)$ at a?

   (A) The graph is increasing at $f(a)$.

   (B) The graph is decreasing at $f(a)$.

   (C) There is a critical point at $f(a)$.

   (D) Depends on the value of the second derivative.

1. (C)

Rewrite $y = \dfrac{1}{\sqrt[3]{t}} = t^{-\frac{1}{3}}$ to be able to use the power rule. Then $y' = -\dfrac{1}{3}t^{-\frac{1}{3}-1} = -\dfrac{1}{3}t^{-\frac{4}{3}}$. Answer choices (A) and (D) are missing minus signs. Answer choice (B) is equivalent to the given (undifferentiated) expression. (Section 10.2.4)

2. (C)

For $s = t^3 - 6t^2$, $v(t) = \dfrac{ds}{dt} = 3t^2 - 12t$. At $t = 1$, $v(t) = -9$ ft/sec, which means the particle is moving in the opposite direction (negative velocity, with "opposite" not necessarily meaning down—it could be a car backing up). (Section 10.3.4a)

3. (C)

For a function to be continuous at a point, the limits from the left and right must be equal (they are), and the point must be in the domain of the functions (it isn't). Although changing one of the inequality signs to include equality would make a continuous function, it would be a different function than $g(x)$. (Section 10.2.7)

4. (B)

When the base of the triangle is rotated around the y-axis, it sweeps out a circle with the base as a radius. The top of the triangle rotates in place, since it just a point. The rest of the triangle sweeps out a cone-shaped solid. (Section 10.4.5b)

5. (C)

If $f'(a) = 0$, either the slope of the graph is changing sign at a, so a is a critical point, or the tangent line may be parallel to the x-axis. (Section 10.3.1)

10.1 LIMITS

10.1.1 Definitions and Notations for Limits

Limits are fundamental to understanding calculus. A limit is the y-value that a function is closing in on as it approaches a certain x-value. The function doesn't have to actually equal the limit, but it clearly must *intend* to do so. The notation for limits is $\lim_{x \to c} f(x)$, which is read as "the limit of $f(x)$ as x approaches c." In this two-sided limit, x approaches c from either side (each is a one-sided limit). If x is approaching c from the left (or negative side), c is usually denoted as c^-, and if x is approaching c from the right (or positive side), c is usually denoted as c^+. For a two-sided limit to exist the function must approach the same value from both sides. The one-sided limits may sometimes exist and have different values from either side of c, but if so, the two-sided limit does not exist. The notation $\lim_{x \to \infty}$ means x is getting infinitely large; likewise, $\lim_{x \to -\infty}$ means x is getting more and more negative.

Limits involve asymptotes. **Asymptotes** are lines that a curve gets closer and closer to. On the graph of a curve that has an asymptote (a graph may have more than one), the asymptote is not part of the curve but it may be drawn in as a dashed line to show that the curve is getting closer and closer to that particular line. Asymptotes can be vertical, horizontal, or oblique (called a slant asymptote). Although a curve never crosses a vertical asymptote, it may cross a horizontal or oblique asymptote at a point away from the limit. An example is $y = \dfrac{x}{x^2 + 2}$, for which the x-axis is a horizontal asymptote $x \to \pm\infty$, but the curve crosses the x-axis at $(0, 0)$.

The graphs of the trigonometric functions shown in Chapter 8, Section 8.3.3, show that of the six basic functions, only sine and cosine don't have asymptotes. The other functions, defined with denominators (either sine or cosine) that can equal 0, are all asymptotic when either sine or cosine equals 0 because division by 0 is not possible. For example, $\lim\limits_{x \to \frac{\pi}{2}^-} \tan x = \pm\infty$.

In limit notation,

- If $\lim\limits_{x \to c} f(x) = \infty$, or $\lim\limits_{x \to c} f(x) = -\infty$, and $\lim\limits_{x^+ \to c} f(x) = +\infty$, c is a vertical asymptote of $f(x)$.

- If $\lim\limits_{x \to \infty} f(x) = c$ or $\lim\limits_{x \to -\infty} f(x) = c$, then $y = c$ is a horizontal asymptote of $f(x)$.

- If the degree of the denominator of a rational function $f(x)$ is greater than the degree of the numerator, the function has a horizontal asymptote at $y = 0$, and $\lim\limits_{x \to \infty} f(x) = 0$.

- If the highest powers in the numerator and denominator of a rational function are the same, their coefficients become the limit as $x \to \pm\infty$. So for $f(x) = \dfrac{3x^2 - x + 4}{5x^2 + 2x - 3}$, $\lim\limits_{x \to \infty} f(x) = \dfrac{3}{5}$ and $\lim\limits_{x \to -\infty} f(x) = \dfrac{3}{5}$.

- If the limit of a rational function is $\lim\limits_{x \to n} f(x) = \infty$ or $-\infty$, there is a vertical asymptote where the denominator equals 0. But check to see whether the numerator also equals 0 at this point because if so it's a hole, not an asymptote. In both cases, the limit still exists.

An asymptote is a limit that a function approaches and never reaches. That is, if a function $f(x)$ for which $\lim\limits_{x \to \infty} f(x) = c$ will never reach c, $f(x) = c$ is an asymptote.

EXAMPLE 10.1

Find the horizontal asymptote for $f(x) = \dfrac{x^3 + 2}{x^2 + 4}$.

SOLUTION 10.1

Since the degree of the numerator is greater than the degree of the denominator, there is no horizontal asymptote. (However, if the denominator is divided into the numerator [using long division] there is a slant asymptote of $y = x$.)

EXAMPLE 10.2

Find $\lim\limits_{x \to \infty} \dfrac{c}{x^2}$.

SOLUTION 10.2

The degree of the denominator (2) is greater than the degree of the numerator, which is 0 (since $c = c \cdot 1 = cx^0$). Therefore, $\lim\limits_{x \to \infty} \dfrac{c}{x^2} = 0$.

If for any function $f(x)$ these limits aren't equal, $\lim\limits_{x \to c^+} f(x) \neq \lim\limits_{x \to c^-} f(x)$,

- there is an asymptote or a discontinuity on the graph of $f(x)$ at $x = c$.

- the limit of $f(x)$ at c, $\lim\limits_{x \to c} f(x)$, does not exist,

- the graph of $f(x)$ is not continuous at c.

Two special limits that are important to know are

- $\lim\limits_{x \to 0} \left(\dfrac{\sin x}{x} \right) = 1$, which means, for example, that $\lim\limits_{x \to 0} \left(\dfrac{\sin 5x}{5x} \right) = 1$.

- $\lim\limits_{x \to 0} \left(\dfrac{\cos x - 1}{x} \right) = 0$, which means, for example, that $\lim\limits_{x \to 0} \left(\dfrac{\cos x - 1}{x} \right) = 0$.

EXAMPLE 10.3

Given the special limit $\lim\limits_{x \to 0} \dfrac{\sin 5x}{5x} - 1$, find the value of $\lim\limits_{x \to 0} \dfrac{\sin 5x}{x}$.

SOLUTION 10.3

We want the denominator to be the same as the argument of the sine function, so multiply the limit by $\dfrac{5}{5}$ to get $\lim\limits_{x \to 0} \dfrac{\sin 5x}{x} = \lim\limits_{x \to 0} \left(\dfrac{5}{5} \right) \left(\dfrac{\sin 5x}{x} \right) = \lim\limits_{x \to 0} \dfrac{5 \sin 5x}{5x} =$ $\lim\limits_{x \to 0} \dfrac{\sin 5x}{5x} = 5(1) = 5$.

 Just as in algebra, multiplying the numerator and denominator by the same quantity (in Example 10.3, multiplying by $\dfrac{5}{5}$) doesn't change the value, but may be necessary and it sure can make the math easier.

10.1.2 Continuity

If a function is *everywhere* continuous, there are no holes, asymptotes, or breaks in the graph of $f(x)$. However, part of a function can be called continuous even if the graph isn't everywhere continuous.

A function is continuous at a point $x = c$ if $\lim\limits_{x \to c} f(x) = f(c)$; $\lim\limits_{x \to c} f(x)$ exists; and $f(c)$ exists. If any of these requirements is unfulfilled, $f(x)$ is discontinuous at $x = c$.

(**Hint:**) A graph is continuous if you can draw it without lifting your pencil from the paper.

10.1.3 Operations on Limits

- The limit of a sum equals the sum of the individual limits. $\lim_{x \to c}\left[f(x) + g(x)\right] = \lim_{x \to c} f(x) + \lim_{x \to c} g(x)$.

  This fact is true for the other basic operations.

- The limit of a difference equals the difference of the individual limits.

- The limit of a product is equal to the product of the individual limits.

- The limit of a quotient is equal to the quotient of the individual limits unless the denominator equals zero.

- $\lim_{x \to c} k f(x) = k \lim_{x \to c} f(x)$.

10.1.4 Methods for Finding Limits

10.1.4a Substitution

To find the limit by **substitution**, just plug in the limit for the unknown. This works only if the function is continuous in the vicinity of the limit. In simpler terms, $\lim_{x \to c} f(x) = f(c)$ for any c on the continuous curve between two other points, a and b. So substitution works for all continuous functions, but it fails for some values if the function is not continuous in the interval of interest. This also means that if a portion of a discontinuous function is continuous, let's say between a and b, $\lim_{x \to c} f(x) = f(c)$ for any c on the continuous part of the curve between a and b.

> **EXAMPLE 10.4**
>
> Evaluate $\lim_{x \to 3}(x^2 - 2x + 3)$.

SOLUTION 10.4

Since $x^2 - 2x + 3$ is a continuous function, $\lim_{x \to 3}(x^2 - 2x + 3) = 3^2 - 2(3) + 3 = 9 - 6 + 3 = 6$.

EXAMPLE 10.5

Evaluate $\lim\limits_{x \to 6} \dfrac{2x}{x-6}$.

SOLUTION 10.5

$\lim\limits_{x \to 6} \dfrac{2x}{x-6}$ does not exist because at the limit, the denominator $x - 6 = 6 - 6 = 0$, and division by 0 is undefined. Therefore, there is a vertical asymptote in the graph at $x = 6$.

EXAMPLE 10.6

Evaluate $\lim\limits_{x \to -1} 3^x$.

SOLUTION 10.6

Substitute $x = -1$ into the expression to get: $\lim\limits_{x \to -1} 3^x = 3^{-1} = \dfrac{1}{3}$.

10.1.4b Factoring

If substitution doesn't work right away in finding the limit, try **factoring**. If the function is a fraction, eliminate any factors that make the denominator equal to zero because the function will be discontinuous at that point, even though the limit may still exist.

EXAMPLE 10.7

Evaluate $\lim\limits_{x \to 4} \dfrac{x^2 + 2x - 24}{x - 4}$.

SOLUTION 10.7

The original function, with $x - 4$ in the denominator, has a hole at $x = 4$. But if we factor the function $\lim\limits_{x \to 4} \dfrac{x^2 + 2x - 24}{x - 4} = \lim\limits_{x \to 4} \dfrac{(x - 4)(x + 6)}{(x - 4)} = \lim\limits_{x \to 4} \dfrac{x + 6}{1} = 10$, the graph is the same as $f(x) = x + 6$ except for the hole at $(4, 10)$. However, the limit at $x = 4$ exists because the limit of the function *approaches* 10 from either side of 4.

Remember that for the limit to exist, the function doesn't have to actually equal the limit, it just must clearly "intend" to do so.

Hint: If the function is a quadratic divided by a binomial, try factoring the quadratic by using the opposite of F-O-I-L with the binomial as one factor. It will usually work.

Sometimes, the limit will result in $\frac{0}{0}$, which is called **indeterminate**, such as happens with direct substitution into $\lim_{x \to -2} \frac{3x^2 - 3x - 18}{x + 2}$. But $\lim_{x \to -2} \frac{3x^2 - 3x - 18}{x + 2}$ can be factored. $\lim_{x \to -2} \frac{3x^2 - 3x - 18}{x + 2} =$

$\lim_{x \to -2} \frac{\cancel{(x + 2)}(3x - 9)}{\cancel{(x + 2)}} = \lim_{x \to -2}(3x - 9) = -15$. So the limit exists, even though the graph has a hole at

$x = 2$ (because both the numerator and denominator of the original expression are 0).

EXAMPLE 10.8

Evaluate $\lim_{x \to 2} \frac{4x^2 - 5x - 6}{x - 2}$.

SOLUTION 10.8

Since the function is a fraction, try to factor the numerator to reduce the fraction. It is a good idea, if the numerator isn't readily factored, to try the denominator as one of the factors. Sure enough, we find that $4x^2 - 5x - 6 = (x - 2)(4x + 3)$ by either the opposite of F-O-I-L or by division (long or synthetic) of the numerator by the

denominator. Therefore, $\lim_{x \to 2} \frac{4x^2 - 5x - 6}{x - 2} = \lim_{x \to 2} \frac{\cancel{(x - 2)}(4x + 3)}{\cancel{(x - 2)}}$ to get the equiv-

alent limit of $\lim_{x \to 2}(4x + 3) = 4(2) + 3 = 11$. So $\lim_{x \to 2} \frac{4x^2 - 5x - 6}{x - 2} = 11$.

NOTE The *limit* exists even though the function is discontinuous at $x = 2$. (See the preceding Note.)

10.1.4c Conjugate Method

Often, if the function contains a radical and nothing else works readily, you can use the **conjugate method** with radicals. For example, for $\lim_{x \to 4} \frac{x - 4}{\sqrt{x} - 2}$, just substituting $x = 4$ right away gives the indeterminate answer $\frac{0}{0}$. The conjugate method says to multiply the numerator and denominator of a radical fraction by the conjugate of the radical. Remember that **conjugate** just means changing the sign in the middle of the two terms. Thus, the conjugate of $\sqrt{x} - 2$ is $\sqrt{x} + 2$.

 $(\sqrt{x} - 2)(\sqrt{x} + 2) = x - 4$, because it is the difference of two squares, just like $(a + b)(a - b) = a^2 - b^2$.

EXAMPLE 10.9

Find $\lim\limits_{x \to 4} \dfrac{x - 4}{\sqrt{x} - 2}$.

SOLUTION 10.9

4. $\lim\limits_{x \to 4} \dfrac{x - 4}{\sqrt{x} - 2} = \lim\limits_{x \to 4} \dfrac{x - 4}{\sqrt{x} - 2} \cdot \dfrac{\sqrt{x} + 2}{\sqrt{x} + 2} = \lim\limits_{x \to 4} \dfrac{(x - 4)(\sqrt{x} + 2)}{(x - 4)} = \lim\limits_{x \to 4}(\sqrt{x} + 2) =$

$\sqrt{4} + 2 = 4$. Therefore, $\lim\limits_{x \to 4} \dfrac{x - 4}{\sqrt{4} - 2} = 4$.

10.2 DERIVATIVES AND DIFFERENTIATION

One of the defining characteristics of the graph of a linear equation is its **slope** $= \dfrac{\text{change in } y}{\text{change in } x}$ (see Chapter 3, Section 3.3.1b), which is easy to see if $f(x)$ is a line. If $f(x)$ is a curve, however, that slope changes as x changes. A **tangent line to a curve** is a line that touches the curve at one point, similar to the tangent to a circle (see Chapter 6, Section 6.7.1). At the tangent point, the curve and the tangent line have the same slope. The figure below shows tangent lines to various points on a curve.

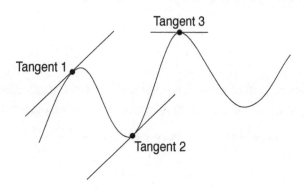

10.2.1 Average Rate of Change

Because the slope keeps changing for a nonlinear function, there isn't just one slope for the whole graph. However, the **average rate of change** will give information about the slope over an interval of the curve. The method to find the average rate of change between two points on the curve is to find the slope between the two points, $\dfrac{\Delta f(x)}{\Delta x}$ or $\dfrac{\Delta y}{\Delta x}$, where Δ means "change." In other words, the slope between two points approximates the average of all the rates of change between the designated two points on the curve. It isn't the *actual* rate of change at a point, but as long as the curve is continuous (has no holes), the average rate of change is a good approximation.

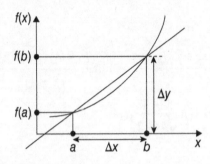

EXAMPLE 10.10

What is the average rate of change of $x^2 - 6x - 7 = 0$ on the interval between $x = 2$ and $x = 3$?

SOLUTION 10.10

We know the change in x is $2 - 3 = -1$, but we have to calculate the change of y in that interval. At $x = 2$, $y = (2)^2 - 6(2) - 7 = -15$, and at $x = 3$, $y = (3)^2 - 6(3) - 7 = -16$.

Therefore, the average rate of change between $x = 2$ and $x = 3$ is $\dfrac{(-15) - (-16)}{2 - 3} = \dfrac{1}{-1} = -1$.

Hint: It makes no difference which point goes first in the calculation as long as the x and y values of the first point are in corresponding places. In Example 10.10, the calculation could also have been written as $\dfrac{(-16) - (-15)}{3 - 2} = \dfrac{-1}{1} = -1$.

10.2.2 Mean Value Theorem

Related to the idea of the average rate of change is the **Mean Value Theorem**. Using a continuous function $f(x)$ on a closed interval $[a, b]$, this theorem states:

There is at least one value c, between a and b in the open interval (a, b) for which the instantaneous rate of change (slope of the tangent line) equals the average rate of change of $f(x)$ over the closed interval $[a, b]$.

To understand what this theorem means, see the figure shown below. The average rate of change between two points, a and b, on a continuous curve equals the slope of at least one point (here, c) in the interval $[a, b]$. As the distance between the points a and b gets smaller and smaller, the average rate of change approaches the slope at c.

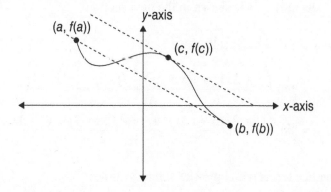

 For most functions, to find the rate of change at a specific point on a curve, choose two x values, one close to and below and the other close to and above the point in question, calculate the value of y at each of those points and then use the method above between these two points to approximate the slope at the point in question.

10.2.3 Limit Definition of Derivatives

The average rate of change method works if an approximation is all that is needed, but to get a precise value for the slope at any point on a curve, we need the concept of the **limit definition of derivatives**, which give the **instantaneous rate of change**. The limit definition of derivatives essentially says to use the basic idea behind the average rate of change, but to make the interval $\Delta f(x)$ around the point in question small—infinitesimally small—in fact, to make the distance between $f(x + \Delta x)$ and $f(x)$ approach zero.

Derivatives are limits of the difference quotient, $\dfrac{\Delta f(x)}{\Delta x}$. The most common formula for calculating the **first derivative** $f'(x)$ of a function $f(x)$ is

$$f'(x) = \lim_{\Delta x \to 0} \frac{\Delta f(x)}{\Delta x} = \lim_{\Delta x \to 0} \frac{f(x + \Delta x) - f(x)}{\Delta x}.$$

The three common ways in which derivatives are indicated are $f'(x)$, y', and $\dfrac{dy}{dx}$.

The derivative $f'(x)$ can evaluate the slope at any point along the curve. For example, to find the slope of the curve $f(x) = x^2 + 4x - 7$ at the point $x = 2$, we first use the above equation literally, but for illustration purposes only because there is an easier "shortcut" that doesn't involve going through this lengthy calculation, as is shown in the next section.

$$
\begin{aligned}
f'(x) &= \lim_{\Delta x \to 0} \frac{f(x + \Delta x) - f(x)}{\Delta x} \\
&= \lim_{\Delta x \to 0} \frac{[(x + \Delta x)^2 + 4(x + \Delta x) - 7] - (x^2 + 4x - 7)}{\Delta x} \\
&= \lim_{\Delta x \to 0} \frac{[x^2 + 2x\Delta x + (\Delta x)^2 + 4x + 4\Delta x - 7] - x^2 - 4x + 7}{\Delta x}
\end{aligned}
$$

which, after canceling like terms with opposite signs, becomes

$$
\begin{aligned}
f'(x) &= \lim_{\Delta x \to 0} \frac{2x\Delta x + (\Delta x)^2 + 4\Delta x}{\Delta x} \\
&= \lim_{\Delta x \to 0} 2x + \Delta x + 4 \\
&= 2x + 4.
\end{aligned}
$$

Then we can say that at the point $x = 2$, the derivative, or the slope of the curve, is 8, or

$$f'(2) = 2(2) + 4 = 8$$

The time spent in this lengthy calculation is eliminated by the use of the power rule, as shown in the next section.

10.2.4 Power Rule

Differentiation, or the method to find the derivative, of $f(x) = x^2 + 4x - 7$ shown in the last section is not overly complicated, but imagine if the curve were $g(x) = 3x^4 - 2x^3 + x^2 - 6$. Wow!! That would take a lot of time, even just to expand $3(x + \Delta x)^4$, let alone all the other terms. Fortunately, the **power rule** is a shortcut for differentiating functions that involves only simple powers of the variable given in the form ax^n. The power rule is stated as:

$$f'(ax^n) = \frac{d}{dx}(ax^n) = (n \cdot a)x^{n-1}.$$

In words, the **power rule** says that the first derivative $f(x)$ is found as follows.

For every term in $f(x)$, multiply the coefficient by the exponent
and then subtract 1 from the existing exponent on the variable.

Even though that doesn't look so simple, it really is. First, you must realize that $\frac{d}{dx}f(x)$ is just another way to write $\frac{df(x)}{dx}$ — they both mean the derivative of $f(x)$ with respect to x.

Therefore, $\frac{d}{dx}(2x^3) = (3 \cdot 2)x^{3-1} = 6x^2$. Likewise, $\frac{d}{dx}(5x^4 - 2x^2 + 6x - 7) = 20x^3 - 4x + 6$.
Note two important things in this last differentiation:

- The differentiation of an "x" term results in just the coefficient of x because when you subtract 1 from the exponent of $x = x^1$ you get $x^0 = 1$

- Constant terms just drop out because the x term for a constant is x^0 and zero times anything is zero.

So now let's go back to the equation that we differentiated the "hard" way in Section 10.2.3: $f(x) = x^2 + 4x - 7$. Right away we can say that $\frac{d}{dx}(x^2 + 4x - 7) = 2x + 4$.

The power rule also works for negative exponents and radicals. If $f(x)$ has the variable in the denominator, rewrite it with a negative exponent to do the differentiation quickly. If $f(x)$ contains a radical, replace it by its equivalent fractional exponent.

EXAMPLE 10.11

Use the power rule to differentiate $s = \dfrac{6}{\sqrt{t}}$ with respect to t.

SOLUTION 10.11

First, we rewrite $\dfrac{6}{\sqrt{t}}$ as $6t^{-\frac{1}{2}}$ so we can use the power rule. Then $\dfrac{d}{dt}\left(6t^{-\frac{1}{2}}\right) = -\dfrac{1}{2}(6)t^{(-\frac{1}{2}-1)} = -3t^{-\frac{3}{2}}$. (The step in the middle of that calculation can easily be done mentally.)

In the calculation for Example 10.11, s took the place of the usual y and t took the place of the usual x since the names of variables are arbitrary.

EXAMPLE 10.12

Use the power rule to differentiate $y = \sqrt[3]{x^2}$ with respect to x.

SOLUTION 10.12

First, rewrite the variable in exponent notation (see Chapter 2, Section 2.7) to use the power rule: $y = x^{\frac{2}{3}}$. Then $\dfrac{dy}{dx} = \dfrac{2}{3}x^{\frac{2}{3}-1} = \dfrac{2}{3}x^{-\frac{1}{3}} = \dfrac{2}{3x^{\frac{1}{3}}}$ or $\dfrac{2}{3\sqrt[3]{x}}$.

10.2.5 Product and Quotient Rules

Not all functions are plain polynomials, though. To take the derivatives of functions that are products or quotients of functions, we must use the following specific rules.

- Derivative of a product of functions: $\left(f(x)g(x)\right)' = f'(x)g(x) + f(x)g'(x)$

In other words, multiply the derivative of the first function by the second function, and then add the derivative of the second function multiplied by the first function.

Hint: You should know the derivative of a product. The following derivative of a quotient looks harder to remember, but see the Note below.

- Derivative of a quotient of functions: $\left(\dfrac{f(x)}{g(x)}\right)' = \dfrac{f'(x)(g(x) - f(x)g'(x)}{\left(g(x)\right)^2}$, if $g(x) \neq 0$.

The numerator of the quotient rule is the same as the derivative of a product with the plus sign replaced by a minus sign, and the denominator is just the original denominator squared.

EXAMPLE 10.13

If $y = (x^2 - 2x + 9)(6x + 3)$, what is $\dfrac{dy}{dx}$ at $x = 2$?

SOLUTION 10.13

Here, and in most functions that are of the form (polynomial) $\times$ (polynomial), we can just multiply them out and use the power rule, or we can use the formula for the derivative of a product of functions. Either way, we end up with the same polynomial.

- Using the power rule: Use the distributive law to multiply:

$$y = (x^2 - 2x + 9)(6x + 3)$$
$$= 6x^3 + 3x^2 - 12x^2 - 6x + 54x + 27$$
$$= 6x^3 - 9x^2 + 48x + 27, \text{ so}$$

$$\frac{dy}{dx} = (3)(6)x^2 - (2)(9)x + 48$$
$$= 18x^2 - 18x + 48.$$

Then at $x = 2$, $\frac{dy}{dx} = (18)(2^2) - (18)(2) + 48 = 84$.

- Using the derivative of a product, let $f(x) = x^2 - 2x + 9$ so $f' = 2x - 2$ and $g(x) = 6x + 3$ so $g'(x) = 6$. Therefore,

$$\left(f(x)g(x)\right)' = f'(x)g(x) + f(x)g'(x)$$
$$= (2x - 2)(6x + 3) + (x^2 - 2x + 9)(6)$$
$$= 12x^2 - 6x - 6 + 6x^2 - 12x + 54$$
$$= 18x^2 - 18x + 48.$$

Again, at $x = 2$, $\left(f(x)g(x)\right)' = (18)(2^2) - (18)(2) + 48 = 84$.

The choice of which method to use depends on the complexity of the problem.

EXAMPLE 10.14

Use the quotient rule to differentiate $s = \dfrac{6}{\sqrt{t}}$ with respect to t.

SOLUTION 10.14

For this problem, let $f(t) = 6$, $f'(t) = 0$, $g(t) = t^{\frac{1}{2}}$, $g'(t) = \dfrac{1}{2}t^{-\frac{1}{2}}$, so the quotient

rule gives us $s'(t) = \dfrac{0(t^{\frac{1}{2}}) - 6\left(\frac{1}{2}t^{-\frac{1}{2}}\right)}{(t^{\frac{1}{2}})^2} = -3\dfrac{t^{-\frac{1}{2}}}{t} = -3t^{-\frac{3}{2}}$.

Example 10.14 is the same problem as in Example 10.11, proving that sometimes differentiating quotients can be done more easily with negative exponents and the power rule.

10.2.6 The Chain Rule

The chain rule is used for differentiating composite functions, such as $f(g(x))$. Both $f(x)$ and $g(x)$ must be differentiable to use the chain rule. The chain rule is

$$\left(f(g(x))\right)' = f'\left(g(x)\right)g'(x).$$

EXAMPLE 10.15

Use the chain rule to differentiate $y = (3x - 2)^2$.

SOLUTION 10.15

In this problem, use $f(g(x))$ with $g(x) = 3x - 2$ and $f(x) = x^2$. Then $g'(x) = 3$ and $f'(x) = 2x$. Plug these values into the chain rule formula to get

$$\frac{d}{dx}(3x - 2)^2 = 2\left(g(x)\right) \cdot g'(x) = 2(3x - 2) \cdot 3 = (6x - 4) \cdot 3 = 18x - 12.$$

If we were to just use algebra on the original function in Example 10.15, we would get $(3x - 2)^2 = 9x^2 - 12x + 4$, which differentiates as $\frac{d}{dx}(9x^2 - 12x + 4) = 18x - 12$. This method seems perhaps easier than the chain rule here, but it wouldn't be easier if the original function was $f(x) = (2x^3 + 4x^2 - 3x + 5)^4$.

Hint: The most difficult part of the chain rule is deciding what to call $f(x)$ and $g(x)$. Usually, the $f(x)$ part is something raised to a power, and the $g(x)$ part is that "something." Using this hint for Example 10.15, we can see right away that $f(x) = x^2$ and $g(x) = 3x - 2$.

10.2.7 Derivatives of Trigonometric and Logarithmic Functions

In addition to the power rules and other rules for differentiation of functions, the derivatives of the basic trigonometric and logarithmic functions are useful. The following table shows the rules you are expected to know.

Function	Derivative
$f(x) = \sin x$	$f'(x) = \cos x$
$f(x) = \cos x$	$f'(x) = -\sin x$
$f(x) = e^x$	$f'(x) = e^x$
$f(x) = a^x$	$f'(x) = (\ln a)a^x$
$f(x) = \ln x$	$f'(x) = \dfrac{1}{x}$
$f(x) = \log_a x$	$f'(x) = \dfrac{1}{x(\ln a)}$

The derivatives of other trigonometric functions can be found from those for sine and cosine by using trig identities and the quotient rule.

EXAMPLE 10.16

If $y = \dfrac{1}{\ln x}$, what is $\dfrac{dy}{dx}$?

SOLUTION 10.16

Use the quotient rule for derivatives, with $f(x) = 1$, $g(x) = \ln x$, $f'(x) = 0$, $g'(x) = \dfrac{1}{x}$.

Then $\dfrac{dy}{dx} = \dfrac{\ln x \cdot (0) - 1 \cdot \dfrac{1}{x}}{\left(\ln x\right)^2} = -\dfrac{1}{x\left(\ln x\right)^2}$.

Often, using the chain rule and power rule is easier than using the quotient rule.

10.2.8 Differentiability

Since derivatives are slopes, **differentiability** implies a smooth curve so the slope at that point exists. The slope at either side of that point must be the same, which is another way of saying the derivative at that point as approached from the left and from the right are the same. If this isn't true, the function is not differentiable at that point.

If a function is differentiable at a point, it is **continuous** there as well. Keep in mind here that we are talking about a specific region of a function, such as the region in the vicinity of point *a*. We aren't talking about the entire function because we frankly don't care what happens outside of the region right around point *a*.

Let's review here the definition of **continuity**: A function $f(x)$ is continuous at point *a* if $\lim_{x \to a} f(x)$ exists (which means it exists from the left and from the right) and is equal to $f(a)$. The simple way to think of continuity is that if you were to trace the graph of a continuous function, you would never have to lift your pencil. It is easy to see that all smooth functions (no gaps, no asymptotes, no cusps) are continuous. But what about those exceptions? Obviously, a gap or an asymptote would cause you to lift your pencil, so the function is discontinuous at that point. A corner or cusp, on the other hand, can be traced without lifting your pencil, so the function is continuous at a corner or cusp. But they are sharp points in the graph, and the function is not differentiable at that point, which can be seen in the graphs of functions with a cusp and a corner shown below.

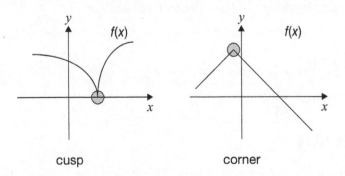

cusp   corner

The important conclusion here is that

- all differentiable functions are continuous,

but

- not all continuous functions are differentiable.

10.3 FIRST AND SECOND DERIVATIVES

The derivatives discussed in all of Section 10.2 are **first derivatives** (thus, only one "prime" in $f'(x)$). What about a **second derivative**? Of course there is a second derivative, and it is denoted as $f''(x)$. It is obtained by taking the derivative of the first derivative. Therefore, the derivatives of $f(x) = 3x^2 + 2x + 1$ are $f'(x) = 6x + 2$ and $f''(x) = 6$. But what do these derivatives mean?

10.3.1 First Derivative

We saw that for any function, the first derivative gives us the instantaneous rate of change of the function, which is the slope of the tangent line to any point on the graph of the function, or essentially the slope of the function at a specific point.

The first derivative tells whether the graph of $f(x)$ is increasing at a point and by how much. In summary,

- If $f'(a) > 0$, the graph is increasing at $x = a$.

- If $f'(a) < 0$, the graph is decreasing at $x = a$.

- If $f'(a) = 0$, the graph is parallel to the x-axis (a horizontal tangent) at a or the slope of the graph is changing sign at a. The second derivative (see Section 10.3.2) explains what the change in sign indicates.

- If $f'(a)$ is undefined (e.g., the denominator is 0), either the graph has a critical point or there is a vertical asymptote at $x = a$.

Critical points are places where the graph of the function changes direction smoothly and an extremum (a maximum or a minimum) could possibly occur, as shown, in the figure below.

A **point of inflection** is a point at which the concavity of the graph changes from positive to negative or negative to positive, as shown at the origin in the figure below. Another way to look at it is as the point where a curve changes from concave up to concave down, or vice versa.

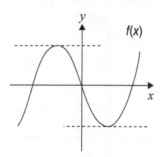

10.3.2 Second Derivative

The second derivative, denoted by $f''(x)$ or $\dfrac{d^2}{dx^2}f(x)$, then, should give us the slope of the slope. Right? Technically, that is true; the slope of the slope tells the shape of the curve, whether it is curving upward or curving downward. In other words, the first derivative tells us whether the function is increasing or decreasing, and the second derivative tells us whether the slope is increasing or decreasing, which tells whether the shape of the curve at that point is concave up (like a parabola open upward) or concave down (like a parabola open downward), or maybe (if $f''(a) = 0$), the graph has a point of inflection.

To summarize:

- If $f''(x) > 0$ at $x = a$, then $f(x)$ is concave up at $x = a$. If, in addition, $f'(a) = 0$, then $f(a)$ is a local minimum value.

- If $f''(x) < 0$ at $x = a$, then $f(x)$ is concave down at $x = a$. If, in addition, $f'(a) = 0$, then $f(a)$ is a local maximum value.

- If $f''(x) = 0$ at $x = a$, then we possibly have a point of inflection of $f(x)$ at a (see previous figure).

Let's consider $f(x) = 3x$, which is simply the graph of a line with a slope of 3. We find that $f'(x) = 3$, which just confirms that the instantaneous rate of change at any point is 3. Now let's look at $f''(x) = 0$, which means that there is no change in the first derivative. This is no surprise because the slope of any line is constant; a line is neither concave up nor concave down.

As an example, let's look at $g(x) = x^2 - x$. If we want to determine the values of x for which the tangent line has a positive slope, we only need to solve $g'(x) = 2x - 1 > 0$. This leads to $x > \dfrac{1}{2}$, which means that the tangent line has a positive slope for all x values greater than $\dfrac{1}{2}$. With a similar argument, we can show that the tangent line has a negative slope for $x < \dfrac{1}{2}$. Also, since $g'\left(\dfrac{1}{2}\right) = 2\left(\dfrac{1}{2}\right) - 1 = 0$, we know that a critical point exists for $x = \dfrac{1}{2}$, as seen in the following graph.

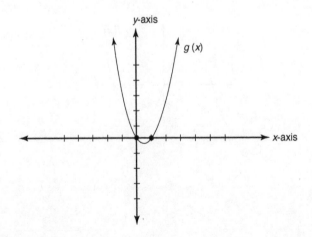

This graph immediately tells us that if we were to choose a point whose x value is less than $\frac{1}{2}$, the slope of the tangent line would be negative. By choosing a value of x greater than $\frac{1}{2}$, the tangent line has a positive slope.

To understand the second derivative of $g(x) = x^2 - x$, $g''(x)$, let's consider any two values of x. For $x = -3$, $g'(x) = 2x - 1$, so $g'(-3) = (2)(-3) - 1 = -7$; for $x = 0$, $g'(0) = -1$. Bearing in mind that the second derivative measures the change in the first derivative, we can see that $g'(0)$ is actually greater than $g'(-3)$. So, as x increases by three units, from -3 to 0, $g'(x)$ increases six units, from -7 to -1. This implies that for $x = -3$, $g'(x)$ is actually increasing. In fact, since $g'(x) = 2x - 1$, it follows that $g''(x) = 2$. This statement tells us that for $g(x) = x^2 - x$, the second derivative is always the positive number 2, so the curve is concave up throughout.

EXAMPLE 10.17

If $f(x) = 2x^3 + x^2 - 4x + 2$, find $f'(x)$ and $f''(x)$.

SOLUTION 10.17

Using the power rule, we get

$$f(x) = 2x^3 + x^2 - 4x + 2$$

$$f'(x) = 6x^2 + 2x - 4$$

$$f''(x) = 12x + 2$$

10.3.3 Graphing the Derivative Function

The graph of $f'(x)$ provides information about the original function $f(x)$. Consider the following two basic facts about the first derivative of a function $f(x)$:

1. The value of $f'(x)$ at $x = a$, $f'(a)$, is the slope of the tangent to the graph of the function at point a.

2. $f'(x)$ is also a function of x, which means the slope at a point on the graph isn't a constant, but depends on the x-coordinate of that point.

Example 10.18 shows how to sketch the graph of $f'(x)$ from the graph of $f(x)$.

EXAMPLE 10.18

Sketch the graph of $f'(x)$ between $x = 0$ and $x = 3.5$, given the following graph of $f(x)$.

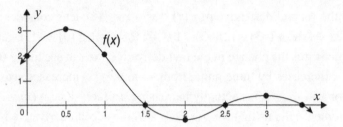

SOLUTION 10.18

Let's get as much information about $f'(x)$ as we can from the slope of $f(x)$. We set up a table to keep track of the information. We are interested here in the intervals where the slope changes direction.

$f(x)$	Interval	$f'(x)$
increasing	$x = [0, 0.5)$	positive
maximum	$x = 0.5$	0
decreasing	$x = (0.5, 2)$	negative
minimum	$x = 2$	0
increasing	$x = (2, 3)$	positive
maximum	$x = 3$	0
decreasing	$x = (3, 3.5]$	negative

So a rough sketch of $f'(x)$ will have the following summary: The slope is positive from $x = 0$ to 0.5, equal to 0 at $x = 0.5$, negative from $x = 0.5$ to 2, equal to 0 at $x = 2$, positive from $x = 2$ to 3, equal to 0 at $x = 3$, and negative from $x = 3$ to 3.5. In any graph of $f''(x)$, or $f'(x)$ (slope) versus x, positive or negative mean above or below the x-axis respectively. Since we don't have the actual function for $f(x)$, we can just give an educated guess of what the values of the slope $f'(x)$ can be from the graph of $f(x)$. We know that the graph of $f'(x)$ changes direction somewhere in the intervals between $x = 0$ and $x = 0.5$, between $x = 0.5$ and $x = 2$, and between $x \doteq 2$ and $x = 3$. A first sketch of $f''(x)$ would look like the following graph. The actual "turning points" for this graph would be found at the points for which the second derivative $f''(x) = 0$, or at $x = 0.5$, $x = 2$ and $x = 3$, which indicate where the slope $f'(x)$ changes direction. The graph between these points is accurate only in shape—actual values cannot be determined unless the actual function $f(x)$ is known.

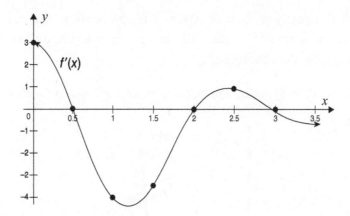

 The inflection points in the graph of $f(x)$ correspond where the graph of $f'(x)$ changes direction (and thus the concavity of $f(x)$ changes), at approximately $x = 1.25$ and $x = 2.5$.

10.3.4 Using Derivatives

10.3.4a Position, Velocity, and Acceleration

On a position-time graph (also called a displacement-time graph):

- Positive slope implies motion in the positive direction.

- Negative slope implies motion in the negative direction.

- Zero slope implies a state of rest.

- Average velocity over an interval is the slope of the straight line connecting two points of the position-time curve.

- Instantaneous velocity is the slope of the line tangent to the position-time curve at any point.

- Acceleration is the slope of the velocity-time curve.

Let's look at an equation for the **position** of a particle as a function of time,

$$s(t) = t^3 - 8t^2 + 10t.$$

The equation for the **velocity** is given by the first derivative of the position function:

$$v(t) = s'(t) = 3t^2 - 16t + 10$$

and the equation for **acceleration** is given by the second derivative of the position function:

$$a(t) = v'(t) = s''(t) = 6t - 16.$$

Speed is velocity without direction. The speedometer in a car shows speed, not velocity, as it says "50 mph," but not "50 mph northward." Here the sign of the velocity indicates its direction.

The graphs of these three equations are shown for a particular position function *s*.

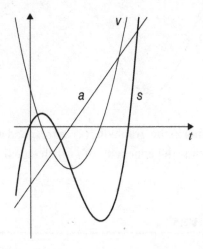

Let's assume the position is in centimeters (cm) and time is in seconds (sec). Note that we are looking at a small part of a large graph and calling our starting point $t = 0$ sec. At $t = 0$ sec (along the vertical axis), the position of the particle is $s(0) = 0$ cm, the velocity of the particle is $(v) = 10$ cm/sec, and the acceleration of the particle is $(a) = -16$ cm/sec^2.

Note the following attributes of these curves:

- *Position function* (thick solid curve): The curve for the position function crosses the *x*-axis at three points, which is to be expected since the highest power in the equation is t^3. The graph of $s(t)$ goes to $-\infty$ and ∞ as $t \to -\infty$ and ∞, respectively. If $s(t)$ is positive, the particle is situated on the side that is toward the direction that is designated as positive; here, of course, that is anything above the horizontal (*t*)-axis. Negative values of $s(t)$ indicate the particle is positioned on the opposite side of the origin point, $s = 0$.

 In dealing with position, it is important to make a distinction between displacement (which is the difference in positions) and distance. This is easily visualized by this simple scenario: Let's say you leave your house to go to the gym, which is 2 miles away, and then you return home. When you return home, what distance did you travel? Easy, 4 miles. But what is your displacement compared to when you started? Also easy, 0 miles.

- *Velocity function* (thin solid curve): This curve is a parabola. In the part of the graph we are concerned with ($t \geq 0$), the particle is already slowing down and eventually it will reach a minimum negative velocity at its vertex, at about $t = -2.7$ sec and then speed up again. A positive velocity indicates the particle is traveling in the positive direction and a negative velocity indicates that the particle is traveling in the opposite direction. Note that when the velocity is zero, the position curve changes direction.

 Although velocity is a parabola and acceleration is a line in this situation, that is not always the case for other situations.

- *Acceleration function* (straight line): For this example, the acceleration is a straight line, which means the velocity changes with time at a constant rate. When acceleration is zero, the velocity changes direction. The positive slope of the acceleration line indicates that acceleration is increasing with time.

 Positive acceleration is called acceleration, and "negative acceleration" is actually called deceleration, such as happens when you put your foot on a brake. Positive acceleration increases velocity; deceleration decreases velocity.

In general, we can imply the following information when looking at a **position-time graph** (without velocity or acceleration graphed):

- If the position function is a straight line, the velocity is constant (neither increasing nor decreasing) and the acceleration is zero. This makes sense because a straight line has a constant slope, and if the velocity is constant, there is no acceleration to change it.

- If the position function is a portion of a parabola, then the velocity is a straight line whose slope tells whether the velocity is constantly increasing (positive slope) or decreasing (negative slope). A velocity with a constant slope implies constant acceleration.

- If the position function is a curved line other than a parabola, the velocity will change direction, which implies varying acceleration.

EXAMPLE 10.19

If a position function is given as $s(t) = 4t^2 - 3t + 5$, what are the position, velocity, and acceleration at time $t = 2$ seconds?

SOLUTION 10.19

To find the answer for position, just plug $t = 2$ into the position equation:

$$s(2) = 4(2)^2 - 3(2) + 5 = 16 - 6 + 5 = 15.$$

To find the velocity, differentiate the position function and plug $t = 2$ into the resulting velocity equation:

$$v(t) = s'(t) = 8t - 3 \text{ so } v(2) = 8(2) - 3 = 16 - 3 = 13.$$

To find the acceleration, take the second derivative of the position function or the first derivative of the velocity function and plug $t = 2$ into the resulting acceleration equation:

$$a(t) = v'(t) = 8$$

 The acceleration in Example 10.19 is constant, as it is for any parabolic position function.

No matter what the equation for the distance traveled, the velocity and acceleration at any time t can be calculated from the first and second derivatives of the displacement equation. Given an equation of $s = t^3 + 2t + 6$, we know the equation for the velocity at any time t is $v = \dfrac{ds}{dt} = 3t^2 + 2$, and the acceleration at any time t is $a = \dfrac{dv}{dt} = 6t$.

 An acceleration of zero means the velocity doesn't change and there is no force on the zero accelerating body.

10.3.4b Optimization

Optimization focuses on maximizing or minimizing a particular quantity. Since this relates to maxima and minima, we use the first derivative of the appropriate function. Write the equation of interest as a function of one variable by using the given information, take the first derivative, and find the critical points by setting the first derivative equal to zero. Then take the second derivative (derivative of the first derivative), and if it is positive, the curve is concave up (basically ∪) so the point is a minimum; if it is negative, the curve is concave down (basically ∩) so the point is a maximum. Be sure the point found is feasible, or makes sense given any other information in the problem.

EXAMPLE 10.21

Find the smallest possible sum of the squares of two numbers if their product is –9.

SOLUTION 10.21

The given information is that we want the smallest value of $(x^2 + y^2)$ when we know that $xy = -9$. Solve this last equation for y and substitute it into the first equation to get a function of one variable: Then take the first derivative of that function: $y = \dfrac{-9}{x}$. Substituting $y = \dfrac{-9}{x}$ or $y = -9x^{-1}$, into $(x^2 + y^2)$ gives

$$S = x^2 + \left(-9x^{-1}\right)^2 = x^2 + 81x^{-2}$$

$$S' = 2x - 162x^{-3}$$

Now set $S' = 0$ to get $2x = 162x^{-3}$. Multiply both sides by x^3 to clear the fraction and solve for x:

$$2x^4 = 162$$
$$x^4 = 81$$
$$x = \pm 3$$

Once we know that $x = 3$, we substitute $x = 3$ into the second derivative of S to check whether it is a maximum or minimum. Since $S' = 2x + 162x^{-3}$, the second derivative is $S'' = 2 - 3(162x^{-4})$, which is always positive, so the graph is concave up, and $x = 3$ is a minimum. The other number is $3y = -9$, $y = -3$. The answer to the problem is $3^2 + (-3)^2 = 9 + 9 = 18$.

 The calculations for Example 10.21 are lengthy, so you probably won't get a question that asks you to get the answer; however, you may need to pick a correct answer from four choices. You can do this by simply checking that the product of the numbers is –9 and their sum is a minimum (of the choices).

10.3.4c Related Rates

As a general rule, **related rates** mean if z is related to y and y is related to x, then z is related to x by using the following first derivatives (a variation of the chain rule, see Section 10.2.5).

$$\frac{dz}{dx} = \left(\frac{dz}{dy}\right)\left(\frac{dy}{dx}\right)$$

In this sort of problem, the rate of change of one variable is given and you need to find the rate of change of another variable at a certain point in time. Before you start a related rate problem, determine which information is general and which is particular to the problem. **General information** is information that is always true and is usually contained in the text of the problem, and **particular information** is true only at the instant of the problem, usually contained in the final question. Particular information must be set aside and not be used until the very last step of solving the problem.

A frequent mistake is to use the particular information too early, which invariably leads to incorrect answers. Wait until the last step of the problem (Step 5 below) to insert this information.

Use the following steps in related rate problems. The solution to Example 10.22 follows these steps.

Step 1. Identify the known rate of change and the desired rate of change given in the problem.

Step 2. Use known values to relate the variable with the known rate of change to the variable with the unknown rate of change.

Step 3. Differentiate both sides of the equation with respect to time to find a relationship between their rates of change (i.e., their derivatives).

Step 4. Use known geometric formulas or whatever pertains to the problem, and then use the chain rule, since we are taking derivatives with respect to t.

Step 5. Plug in the particular information to solve for the desired rate.

EXAMPLE 10.22

The radius of a spherical balloon is increasing at a rate of 4 inches per minute. At what rate is the volume increasing when the radius is equal to 12 inches?

SOLUTION 10.22

The general information is that the radius is growing at the rate of 4 inches per minute, or $\dfrac{dr}{dt} = \dfrac{4}{1}$. The particular information is "when the radius is equal to 12 inches," or $r = 12$.

1. The known rate is $\dfrac{dr}{dt}$, and we want to find $\dfrac{dV}{dt}$, the rate of change of the volume.

2. The chain rule for this problem is $\dfrac{dV}{dt} = \left(\dfrac{dV}{dr}\right)\left(\dfrac{dr}{dt}\right)$.

3. Since this is a sphere, $V = \frac{4}{3}\pi r^3$ (see Chapter 6, Section 6.10.5b).

4. Thus $\frac{dV}{dr} = 4\pi r^2$.

5. This is when we use the particular information, that the radius is equal to 12 inches.

$$\frac{dV}{dt} = \left(\frac{dV}{dr}\right)\left(\frac{dr}{dt}\right) = \left(4\pi r^2\right)\left(\frac{4}{1}\right) = \left(4\pi(12)^2\right)(4) = 2304\pi$$

So when the radius of the balloon is 12 inches, the volume is increasing at a rate of 2304π cubic inches per second.

10.4 INTEGRALS

An **antiderivative**, as the name implies, is a general function $F(x)$ of $f(x)$ if $F' = f(x)$. Determining an antiderivative (or **integral**, which is the more popular name for antiderivative) is the reverse process of finding a derivative. In fact, integration and differentiation are inverse operations. The symbol for an integral is $\int dx$, where the usual letter x can be replaced by any other letter, depending on the function. For example, if $s = f(t) = 16t^2 + 3t - 10$, the integral would be written as $\int f(t)\,dt$. It is important that the part of the function in question be continuous (no holes, asymptotes, or breaks).

10.4.1 Fundamental Theorem of Calculus

The Fundamental Theorem of Calculus has two parts that are interrelated and come from the fact that the antiderivative of a function is the reverse of the derivative of a function, as the name implies. We will use the more common term "integral" for "antiderivative" here. Integrals can be either **indefinite**, which means they are a family of functions giving indefinite solutions (which have a constant added to them, as we will see), or **definite**, which produce definite solutions with finite numbers, emphasizing the fact that definite integrals are used to measure the signed area under a curve.

10.4.1a First Fundamental Theorem of Calculus

The **first fundamental theorem of calculus** deals with the derivative of an antiderivative. It states that one of the indefinite integrals F of some function f may be obtained as the integral of f with a variable bound of integration. The function f must be a continuous function in a closed interval $[a, b]$. Symbolically, for all x in that interval,

$$F(x) = \int_a^x f(t)\,dt \text{ and } F'(x) = f(x).$$

10.4.1b Indefinite Integrals

Just as there are rules for differentiating functions, there are rules for integrating functions as well. Luckily, the work to find certain functions, given the derivatives, has been done by mathematicians and is available for everyone's use in tables of integrals. The table on the next page shows both derivatives and integrals for various functions, where k is a constant, e is the constant related to the natural logarithm ln, and n is an exponent. Notice that the results of integration all have a "$+C$" following them. This is because they are indefinite integrals, which can vary by a constant C.

The constant C must be used in each of these indefinite integrals. For example, if $f'(x) = 6x$, which of the following functions could be $f(x)$? $f(x) = 3x^2$, $f(x) = 3x^2 - 10$, or $f(x) = 3x^2 + 4$? The answer is it could be any of the three choices because if we take the first derivative of any of them, we get $f'(x) = 6x$. So there are an infinite number of functions for which $f'(x) = 6x$, and they each differ from the others by the constant term. This constant is known as the **constant of integration**.

Likewise, when we find the integral $\int 6x\,dx$, we are looking for a function for which $f'(x) = 6x$. For an integral of this type, we use the integration rule $\int kx^n\,dx = \dfrac{k}{n+1}x^{n+1} + C$ (from the table on the next page) with $k = 6$ and $n = 1$, so $\int 6x\,dx = \dfrac{6}{1+1}x^{1+1}$ plus a constant, or $\int 6x\,dx = 3x^2 + C$. The value of C may be determined by the context of the problem if additional information is provided.

The notation for the derivative $\dfrac{d}{dx}f(x) = f'(x)$ is an inverse of the notation $\int f'(x)\,dx = f(x) + C$, so every differentiation formula has an inverse integration formula. Finding the antiderivative is the same as asking, "Given the derivative of a function, what is the function?" Or said another way, "If we take the derivative of an antiderivative of a function, we get the function back again," or

$$\frac{d}{dx}\left[\int f(x)\,dx\right] = f(x).$$

Differentiation and Integration Rules for Various Functions

Rule	Function, $f(x)$	Differentiation of the Function f', or $\dfrac{d}{dx}f(x)$	Integration of the Function $\int f(x)\,dx$
1	kx	$\dfrac{d}{dx}kx = k$	$\int kx\,dx = \dfrac{k}{n+1}x^2 + C$
2	kx^n	$\dfrac{d}{dx}kx^n = knx^{n-1}$, provided that $n \neq 0$	$\int kx^n\,dx = \dfrac{k}{n+1}x^{n+1} + C$, provided that $n \neq -1$
3	ke^x	$\dfrac{d}{dx}ke^x = ke^x$	$\int ke^x\,dx = ke^x + C$
4	$\left[f(x) \pm g(x)\right]$	$\dfrac{d}{dx}f(x) \pm \dfrac{d}{dx}g(x)$	$\int f(x)\,dx \pm \int g(x)\,dx + C$
5	$\sin x$	$\dfrac{d}{dx}\sin x = \cos x$	$\int \sin x\,dx = -\cos x + C$
6	$\cos x$	$\dfrac{d}{dx}\cos x = -\sin x$	$\int \cos x\,dx = \sin x + C$
7	a^x	$\dfrac{d}{dx}a^x = a^x \ln a$	$\int a^x\,dx = \dfrac{a^x}{\ln a} + C$
8	$\ln(x)$	$\dfrac{d}{dx}\ln x = \dfrac{1}{x}$, $x > 0$	$\int \ln(x)\,dx = x\ln x + C$
9	kx^{-1}	$\dfrac{d}{dx}kx^{-1} = -kx^{-2} = -\dfrac{k}{x^2}$	$k\int \dfrac{1}{x}\,dx = k\ln\left|x\right| + C$

NOTE

All derivatives of trigonometric cofunctions, as shown in the table above, are negative (e.g., $\dfrac{d}{dx}\cos x = -\sin x$) and all integrals of trigonometric non-cofunctions are negative (e.g., $\int \sin x\,dx = -\cos x + C$).

The use of the differentiation and integration table is illustrated by Example 10.23.

EXAMPLE 10.23

What is $\int \left(8^x + \frac{3}{4} x^4 \right) dx$?

SOLUTION 10.23

Using Rule 4, we simply add the values for $\int 8^x dx = \dfrac{8^x}{\ln x}$ (Rule 7) and

$\int \dfrac{3}{4} x^4\, dx = \dfrac{\frac{3}{4}}{5} x^5$ (Rule 2), we have $\int \left(8^x + \dfrac{3}{4} x^4 \right) dx = \dfrac{8^x}{\ln 8} + \dfrac{3}{20} x^5 + C$.

10.4.1c Second Fundamental Theorem of Calculus

The second fundamental theory of calculus builds on the first. It states that if $f(x)$ is continuous on an interval, so $F'(x) = f(x)$ for all x in the interval, then

$$\int_a^b f(x)\, dx = F(b) - F(a)$$

where a and b are two points in the continuous interval. This is a definite integral, so its value doesn't have the variable C because the C for each point that showed up in the first fundamental theorem of calculus cancel each other out.

The evaluation of the definite integral is the same as for indefinite integrals, and when the subtracting is done, the C values disappear.

10.4.1d Definite Integrals

The first two of the following properties of definite integrals come from the corresponding properties for indefinite integrals. Functions f and g are continuous on $[a, b]$, point c is any point within $[a, b]$, and k is a constant. Properties 3, 4, and 5 come from the Fundamental Theorem of Calculus.

1. The definite integral of a function multiplied by a constant equals the constant multiplied by the definite integral of the function:

$$\int_a^b kf(x)\, dx = k \int_a^b f(x)\, dx$$

2. The definite integral of the sum or difference of functions equals the sum or difference of the definite integrals of the functions:

$$\int_a^b [f(x) \pm g(x)]\, dx = \int_a^b f(x)\, dx \pm \int_a^b g(x)\, dx$$

3. The definite integral in the interval $[a, a]$ is zero because there is no change in x:

$$\int_a^a f(x)\, dx = 0$$

4. The definite integral between two points has the opposite sign if the two points are reversed:

$$\int_a^b f(x)\, dx = -\int_b^a f(x) \text{ because } [F(b) - F(a)] = -[F(a) - F(b)]$$

5. The definite integral between two points on an interval $[a, b]$ can be calculated as the sum of the definite integrals on the intervals $[a, c]$ and $[c, b]$, provided $a < c < b$:

$$\int_a^b f(x)\, dx = \int_a^c f(x)\, dx + \int_c^b f(x)\, dx$$

10.4.2 Integration by Parts

An additional property is **integration by parts**, the antiderivative of the product rule for differentiation $\left(f(x)g(x)\right)' = f'(x)g(x) + f(x)g'(x)$, generally written using the notation for functions $u = f(x)$ and $v = g(x)$. The product rule for differentiation can be rewritten with u and v as

$$(uv)' = u'v + uv' = uv' + u'v.$$

Integration by parts is a technique for expressing an integral in the form $\int d(uv)$ in terms of a known integral $\int v\, du$ by expanding the differential of a product of functions $d(uv)$. Integration by parts starts with a rewrite of the product rule above as

$$d(uv) = udv + vdu.$$

Integrating both sides, and remembering that $\int d(uv) = uv$,

$$\int d(uv) = uv = \int u\, dv + \int v\, du,$$

which can be rearranged to give the rule for integration by parts:

$$\int u\, dv = uv - \int v\, du.$$

But we are still left with figuring out what type of integral has "parts" and how to determine which part is u and which part is dv. Generally, the integral has to have two functions multiplied together and the variable of integration has to be the variable in each function.

EXAMPLE 10.24

Find $\int x \cos x \, dx$.

SOLUTION 10.24

Use integration by parts with $u = x$ and $dv = \cos x\,dx$. Now determine what du, the derivative of u, is, which is dx. Next, find what v is by integrating dv. Here, $v = \int dv = \int \cos x \, dx = \sin x$. Finally, substitute these equivalents, $u(=x)$, $v(=\sin x)$, and $du (= dx)$, into the formula for integration by parts:

$$\int u \, dv = uv - \int v \, du = \int x \cos x \, dx = x \sin x - \int \sin x \, dx = x \sin x + \cos x + C.$$

The most difficult part of integration by parts is determining what u and dv should be. The rest, after a bit of simple integration, is substitution into the formula for integration by parts.

 Integration by parts does not always succeed because some choices of u may lead to more complicated integrals than the original. If u and v aren't simple functions, don't use integration by parts. Generally, u should be a function that gets simpler when differentiated and v should be a function that is easy to integrate.

10.4.3 Area Under a Curve

The second fundamental theorem of calculus allows us to evaluate definite integrals, such as the signed area under a curve or the volume of a three-dimensional figure, through the following method:

- Determine the antiderivative of the integrand.

- Evaluate the antiderivative at the upper limit.

- Evaluate the antiderivative at the lower limit.

- Subtract the value at the lower limit from the value at the upper limit.

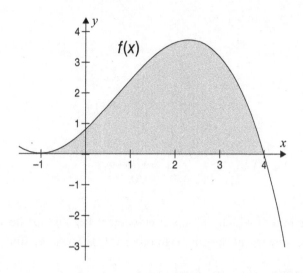

10.4.3a Basis for Finding Area Under a Curve

Finding the area under a curve involves, among other methods, **Riemann sums**. This method, presented here for information purposes, divides the space (area under a curve) into rectangles, finds the area of each rectangle by multiplying the value of width of each rectangle, Δx, by the height of the rectangle (using the value of x at the left side of Δx), and adding up all those rectangular areas. This method, which results in a rough estimate of the area under the curve, is sometimes referred to as an **accumulation**, and looks like the figure below.

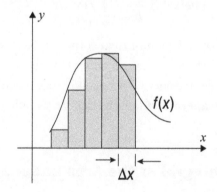

The accuracy of this accumulation could be improved by making the widths smaller, similar to what we did with derivatives when we calculated the limit as $\Delta x \to 0$. As the slices of area get smaller, the area gets closer to the true area, as shown by the figure that follows.

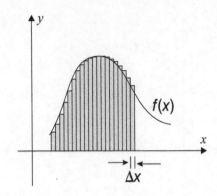

Integration is a method of adding these slices together because as the slices get narrower, the area approaches the true area under the curve. In other words, dx is the limit of each $\Delta x \to 0$.

The **mean value theorem for integration** states:

For any continuous function $f(x)$ over the interval $[a, b]$,

there exists a c, $a \leq c \leq b$, for which $\displaystyle\int_a^b f(x)\, dx = f(c)(b - a)$.

This guarantees that there will be a value $x = c$ between a and b such that the signed area of the rectangle from a to b with height c equals the signed area between $f(x)$ and the x-axis between a and b.

As a consequence of the mean value theorem, we can say the average, or mean, value of an integral of a function in a closed interval is $\displaystyle\frac{1}{b - a}\int_a^b f(x)\, dx$.

Riemann sums use the height to the left or right corner of these rectangle slices. The **midpoint rule** uses height to the midpoint of each rectangle rather than the left or right corner when measuring the area of the rectangles under the curve. The result is very much the same, especially as $\Delta x \to 0$. Another method, called the **trapezoid rule**, uses trapezoids rather than rectangles, but the idea is the same.

10.4.3b The Definite Integral as the Area under a Curve

The definition of a **definite integral** says that it represents the signed area between a curve and the x-axis between an upper and lower limit. A simple example of this fact for a "curve" that is actually a straight line is shown in the next example.

EXAMPLE 10.25

Find the area under line $y = 2x$ between $x = 1$ and $x = 3$.

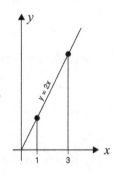

SOLUTION 10.25

The definite integral for this problem is $\int_1^3 2x\,dx$. The area is found by evaluating $\int_1^3 2x\,dx = x^2$, at $x = 3$ and at $x = 1$ and subtracting: $F(3) = 3^2 = 9$, and $F(1) = 1^2 = 1$, so

$$\int_1^3 2x\,dx = x^2 \bigg|_1^3 = 9 - 1 = 8.$$

Note that the answer is the same as the geometric solution for a trapezoid:
$A = \dfrac{1}{2}(2 + 6) \times 2 = 8$.

 The notation $F(x)\bigg|_a^b$ is shorthand that indicates evaluating $F(x)$ at the endpoints a and b.

EXAMPLE 10.26

Find the area between $y = \sin x$, the x-axis, $x = \dfrac{\pi}{2}$, and $x = 2\pi$.

SOLUTION 10.26

Sketch the associated diagram as shown below.

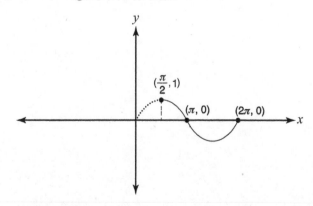

Evaluate the areas above the axis and below the axis separately. Since we are evaluating the areas, and areas are positive, we are evaluating the absolute values and adding them.

$$\text{Area} = \left| \int_{\frac{\pi}{2}}^{\pi} \sin x \, dx \right| + \left| \int_{\pi}^{2\pi} \sin x \, dx \right| = \left| \cos \pi - \cos \frac{\pi}{2} \right| + \left| \cos 2\pi - \cos \pi \right|$$

$$= \left| -1 - 0 \right| + \left| 1 - (-1) \right| = 1 + 2 = 3.$$

Finding the area is different from finding the "value" of a definite integral. The value of the definite integral of a function that crosses the x-axis is the net value of the areas above and below the x-axis, where a minus sign for the area just tells us that the area is below the x-axis.

For example, for $\int_{\frac{\pi}{2}}^{2\pi} \sin x \, dx$ although the actual geometric area is 3 (see Example 10.26), the

value of the definite integral is

$$\text{Value} = \int_{\frac{\pi}{2}}^{2\pi} \sin x \, dx = -\cos x \bigg|_{\frac{\pi}{2}}^{2\pi} = -\cos 2\pi - \left(-\cos \frac{\pi}{2} \right) = 0 - 1 = -1.$$

The minus sign in the value of the integral tells us that there is more area below the x-axis than above it.

EXAMPLE 10.27

Find the area of the cosine curve between $\frac{\pi}{2}$ and π.

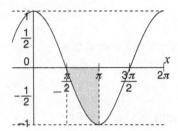

SOLUTION 10.27

The definite integral for this area is

$$A = \int_{\frac{\pi}{2}}^{\pi} \cos(x)\,dx = \sin x \Big|_{\frac{\pi}{2}}^{\pi} = \sin\pi - \sin\frac{\pi}{2} = 0 - 1 = -1.$$

The value of the definite integral is −1, but the area is actually $|-1| = 1$ square unit.

In summary, the value of the definite integral is positive if the curve is above the x-axis (for positive values of $f(x)$, or y), and the value of the definite integral is negative if the curve is below the x-axis (for negative values of $f(x)$, or y). The value(s) of x at which the function $f(x) = 0$ determines the value(s) at which $f(x)$ changes sign. Then add the absolute values of the definite integrals for each part of the curve, the part above plus the part below the x-axis.

 Draw a sketch of the curve for the required range of x-values to see how many separate calculations will be needed. Then calculate the area between the curve and the x-axis, by calculating the parts of the curve above the axis separately from the parts of the curve below the axis. The integral for any part of a curve below the x-axis will be negative.

In summary, to find the area between a function and the x-axis between two points, follow these steps:

1. Make a sketch of the function between the two points, which is very helpful.

2. Find the zeros of the function (where $f(x) = 0$) to see where the area changes from positive to negative or vice versa.

3. Calculate the value of the integral between two points by breaking the curve into parts above and below the x-axis and summing the absolute values of their areas.

EXAMPLE 10.28

Find the value of the integral of $f(x) = -x^2 + 4$ from $x = -5$ to $x = +2$.

SOLUTION 10.28

First, sketch the function. Set the function equal to 0 to find where the function crosses the x-axis: $-x^2 + 4 = 0$, so $x = \pm 2$. The critical values of the function are the points where the first derivative (or slope) equals 0, or $-2x = 0$, which occurs at $x = 0$. The value of y at that point is (putting $x = 0$), $f(0) = -(0)^2 + 4 = 4$. The sketch of the function is shown below.

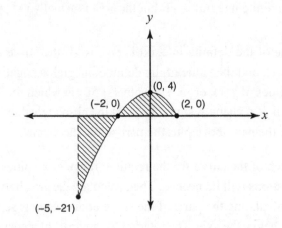

This sketch shows two areas: the area between $x = -5$ and $x = -2$, and the area between $x = -2$ and $x = +2$. According to the fifth property of definite integrals (see Section 10.4.1d), which says $\left| \int_a^b f(x)\,dx \right| = \left| \int_a^c f(x)\,dx \right| + \left| \int_c^b f(x)\,dx \right|$, we have

$$\left| \int_{-5}^2 (-x^2 + 4)\,dx \right| = \left| \int_{-5}^{-2} (-x^2 + 4)\,dx \right| + \left| \int_{-2}^2 (-x^2 + 4)\,dx \right| = \left| -\frac{1}{3}x^3 + 4x \right|_{-5}^{-2} + \left| -\frac{1}{3}x^3 + 4x \right|_{-2}^2$$

$$= \left| \left(\frac{8}{3} - 8 \right) - \left(\frac{125}{3} - 20 \right) \right| + \left| \left(-\frac{8}{3} + 8 \right) - \left(\frac{8}{3} - 8 \right) \right| = \left| -\frac{117}{3} + 12 \right| + \left| -\frac{16}{3} + 16 \right|$$

$$= \left| -27 \right| + \left| \frac{32}{3} \right| = 27 + \frac{32}{3} = \frac{113}{3}$$

So the combined area of the function $f(x) = -x^2 + 4$ between $x = -5$ and $x = +2$ is $\frac{113}{3} = 37\frac{2}{3}$.

Note, however, that the *value* of the definite integral is

$$\int_{-5}^2 (-x^2 + 4)\,dx = \int_{-5}^{-2} (-x^2 + 4)\,dx + \int_{-2}^2 (-x^2 + 4)\,dx = \left[-\frac{1}{3}x^3 + 4x \right]_{-5}^{-2} + \left[-\frac{1}{3}x^3 + 4x \right]_{-2}^2$$

$$= \left[\left(\frac{8}{3} - 8 \right) - \left(\frac{125}{3} - 20 \right) \right] + \left[\left(-\frac{8}{3} + 8 \right) - \left(\frac{8}{3} - 8 \right) \right] = -\frac{81}{3} + \frac{32}{3} = -\frac{49}{3} = -16\frac{1}{3}$$

The area between two curves $f(x)$ and $g(x)$ bounded by points $x = a$ and $x = b$ is simply the difference in the area between the upper curve and the x-axis, or $\int_a^b f(x)\,dx$, and the lower curve and the x-axis, $\int_a^b g(x)\,dx$. Therefore, the area between the curves is given by $\int_a^b |f(x) - g(x)|\,dx$. It helps to sketch the two curves to determine what the bounds should be. Note that if the curves intersect at an intermediate point c, the bounds for the area to the left of the point of intersection would be between points a and c, and that for the area to the right of the point of intersection would be between points c and b, and these two areas would be added.

10.4.4 Position, Velocity, and Acceleration

Earlier we showed that the equation for position as a function of time is $s(t)$, the equation for the velocity is the first derivative, $v(t) = s'(t)$, and the equation for acceleration is the second derivative, $a(t) = s''(t)$. Acceleration is therefore also the first derivative of velocity, $a(t) = v'(t)$. Now let's look at this scenario from the viewpoint of integration.

Let's look at the position formula $s(t) = 2t^3 - 6t^2 + 6t$. Every point on the graph of this function gives a position at a particular time. We can differentiate to get velocity and acceleration, but if all we are given is acceleration, can we get velocity? Yes, we can use the antiderivative, or integral, and work the other way around: The integral of the acceleration function gives the velocity function, and the integral of the velocity function gives the position function.

EXAMPLE 10.29

A police officer arrives on the scene of a one-vehicle auto accident. The only information that she has is the 200-foot skid marks on the road before the car hit the barricade. Weather doesn't seem to be a factor. Can she figure out how fast the car was going before the driver hit the brakes, using the police department's standard breaking deceleration of -16 ft/sec^2? If so, what was it?

SOLUTION 10.29

Let's let the time be $t = 0$ at the time of braking, and $t = n$ seconds at the point of impact. We know that the velocity $v(n) = 0$ at the point of impact because the car certainly was stopped, and we know that the distance $s(n) = 200$ feet. Now, working backward from the acceleration of -16, we can write the velocity function as the antiderivative of acceleration, and we use the indefinite integral because we don't know what n, the time of impact, is yet.

$$v(t) = \int a(t)\,dt = \int (-16\,dt) = -16t + C$$

There were two forces on the car at the moment of impact: the velocity due to the deceleration of the brakes and the velocity due to the forward motion of the car, so C is a constant due to the speed of the car.

Now, let's write the position function as the antiderivative of the velocity,

$$s(t) = \int v(t)\,dt = \int(-16t + C)\,dt = -\frac{16t^2}{2} + Ct + D = -8t^2 + Ct + D.$$

At this point, we have two constants of integration, C from the velocity integration and D from the position integration. However, our starting point has $s(0) = 0$ at $t(0) = 0$, so we can substitute those values into the equation for position, and we have $s(0) = -8(0)^2 + C(0) + D$, which gives us $D = 0$.

Now let's evaluate the functions at the point of impact, $t = n$. We know that $v(n) = 0$, so let's substitute these values into $v(t) = -16t + C$ to get

$$v(n) = -16n + C = 0, \text{ or } C = 16n.$$

Likewise, using $s(t) = -8t^2 + Ct$ at $t = n$, $s(n) = 200$, we get

$$s(n) = -8n^2 + (16n)n = 200, \text{ or}$$
$$-8n^2 + 16n^2 = 8n^2 = 200$$
$$n^2 = 25$$
$$n = 5.$$

So it took 5 seconds for the car to stop, and since $C = 16n$, the car was traveling at 80 mph at $t = 0$.

Police departments have a simple table that uses the industry standard of −16 ft/sec as deceleration due to braking to tell car speed versus skid mark length. Therefore, police officers don't have to use a calculator to find whether the driver was speeding.

10.4.5 Using Integrals for Volume

10.4.5a Cross-Section Method

One of the methods of using integrals to find volume simply extends the method of using integrals to find area by adding a third dimension (depth). This can be done by using a cross-section along one of the axes (usually the z-axis) or by rotating the area around the x-axis or y-axis. So we are extending the accumulation process to three dimensions.

This approach involves combining areas of small widths Δx over the interval of interest, similar to Riemann sums for area (Section 10.4.3a). As $\Delta x \to 0$ the sum of all these areas approaches the area under a smooth curve.

Finding the volume between two surfaces of areas $A(x)$ and $B(x)$ is analogous to finding the area between two curves. In general, it involves an integral of the form $V = \int_{c}^{d} |A(x) - B(x)|\, dx$ or a double integral, which is beyond the scope of the FTCE test and thus this book.

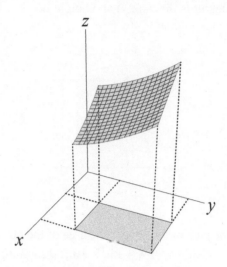

10.4.5b Volumes of Solids of Revolution

Other methods to find volume involve revolving an area about a line, which can be an axis or, in fact, any straight line in the x-y plane. Since volume is basically the area of the base times the height, we can approximate the volume of the solid by adding the small volumes of disks that are the products of each small slice times the circular area bounded by the curve of the solid at that point, with $A = \pi r^2$, and r determined by the figure.

 If the area is revolved around a horizontal line, the integral will use dx, the limits of integration are x values, and all variables are changed to x; if the revolution is around a vertical line, the integral will use dy, the limits of integration are y values, and all variables are changed to y.

Let's look at an example to show how this works.

EXAMPLE 10.30

What is the volume of the figure produced by revolving the region in the first quadrant bounded by $x = 0$, $x = 4$, $y = 0$, and $y = 6$ about the y-axis of a rectangular region?

SOLUTION 10.30

The area of the rectangle of width 4 and height 6 is 24 square units. If we will rotate this rectangle around the y-axis, the resulting volume is a right circular cylinder of radius 4 (because the center is the y-axis) and height 6.

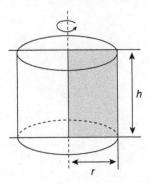

By integration, since the area of the base is the area of the circle formed by the revolution of the rectangle of side 4, or $A = \pi r^2 = 16\pi$, the equation for the volume is:

$$V = \int_0^6 16\pi \, dy = 16\pi y \Big|_0^6 = 16\pi(6) - 16\pi(0) = 96\pi.$$

Let's compare the volume by integration to the volume using the equation for the volume of a right rectangular cylinder given in Chapter 6, Section 6.10.2b, as $V = \pi r^2 h = \pi(4)^2(6) = 96\pi$. True, in this case, the volume found by the formula is easier, but not all shapes are as regular as a rectangle. Or even a triangle. For example, the rotation around the y-axis of a right triangle with one leg along the y-axis forms a cone.

Chapter 10 Exercises

Answers are on the following page.

1. Evaluate $\lim\limits_{x \to 4}\left(\dfrac{2x^2 + 7x + 6}{x + 2} + \dfrac{2x + 7}{x - 2}\right)$.

   (A) $16\dfrac{1}{2}$

   (B) $18\dfrac{1}{2}$

   (C) 11

   (D) $\dfrac{15}{2}$

2. Let $s = t^3 - 6t^2$ be the position function of a particle, where t is in seconds and s is in feet. What is the particle's acceleration at 1 second?

   (A) -9 ft/sec^2

   (B) 9 ft/sec^2

   (C) 6 ft/sec^2

   (D) -6 ft/sec^2

3. Find the average value of $f(x) = x^2$ between $x = 0$ and $x = 4$, by using the formula

   $\dfrac{1}{b - a}\displaystyle\int_a^b f(x)\,dx$.

   (A) 4

   (B) $\dfrac{8}{3}$

   (C) 16

   (D) $\dfrac{16}{3}$

4. Use the power rule, $f'(ax^n) = (n \cdot a)x^{n-1}$, to differentiate $g(x) = ax^{a+2}$, where a is a real number.

   (A) ax^{a+1}

   (B) $(a^2 + 2a)x^{a+1}$

   (C) $(a - 1)x^{a+2}$

   (D) $(a^2 + 2a)x^{a+2}$

5. Integrate the expression $\int (5 - \sin x)\,dx$.

    (A) $5x + \cos x + C$

    (B) $5x - \cos x + C$

    (C) $\cos 5x + C$

    (D) $5\cos x + C$

Answers and Explanations

1. **(B)**

    Resist the urge to combine the two fractions $\left(\dfrac{2x^2 + 7x + 6}{x + 2} + \dfrac{2x + 7}{x - 2} \right)$ into one with a common denominator of $(x - 4)$, which would give a 0 denominator at the limit of 4. Since one of the fractions has a quadratic, perhaps it can be factored to simplify the problem. The quadratic is divisible by $(x + 2)$—no surprise here—so the equation is simplified to $\lim\limits_{x \to 4} \left(\dfrac{(2x + 3)(x + 2)}{(x + 2)} + \dfrac{2x + 7}{x - 2} \right) = \lim\limits_{x \to 4}(2x + 3) + \lim\limits_{x \to 4}\left(\dfrac{2x + 7}{x - 2} \right) = 11 + \dfrac{15}{2} = 18\dfrac{1}{2}$.

2. **(D)**

    Acceleration is the second derivative. For $s = t^3 - 6t^2$, $v(t) = \dfrac{ds}{dt} = 3t^2 - 12t$ and $a(t) = \dfrac{dv}{dt} = 6t - 12$. At $t = 1$, $v(t) = -9$ ft/sec and $a(t) = -6$ ft/sec^2.

3. **(D)**

    Here $a = 0$ and $b = 4$, and thus $\dfrac{1}{b - a} \int\limits_a^b f(x)\,dx = \dfrac{1}{4 - 0} \int\limits_0^4 x^2\,dx$, which has the value $\dfrac{1}{4 - 0} \left(\dfrac{1}{3} \right) x^3 \Big|_0^4 = \dfrac{1}{4(3)}(64 - 0) = \dfrac{16}{3}$.

4. **(B)**

    Using the power rule, $g'(x) = a(a + 2)(x^{a+2-1}) = \left(a^2 + 2a \right)x^{a+1}$.

5. **(A)**

    The given integral can be written as the difference of two integrals, or $\int 5\,dx - \int \sin x\,dx = 5x - (-\cos x) + C = 5x + \cos x + C$.

Before you begin your review, take this short self-assessment to see how well you know the topics covered in this chapter. Answering all or some correctly will help you identify your strengths so you can focus on those topics where you need the most review. Even if you answer all of the questions correctly, we suggest you still review all the examples in the chapter to ensure you're in good shape to move on. Answers are on the following page.

1. Which of the following is a counterexample to the statement, "The set of irrational numbers is closed under all operations"?

   (A) $(2 + \sqrt{3}) + (2 - \sqrt{3}) = 4$

   (B) $(2 + \sqrt{3})(2 - \sqrt{3}) = 1$

   (C) $(2 + \sqrt{3}) - (2 - \sqrt{3}) = 0$

   (D) All of the above.

2. A teenager is going out for the evening, and he promises his mother that when he comes home he will turn off the porchlight. The mother infers from his promise that if the porchlight is off, then he is home. The teenager comes home at 3 a.m., expecting to see his worried mother or angry father, but the light is already off, so he just goes to bed, happy that he didn't get caught coming home late. This scenario is an example of

   (A) A valid argument   (C) A true premise

   (B) An invalid argument   (D) A true conclusion

3. Which of the following is proven to be true?

   (A) a conjecture

   (B) a theorem

   (C) an argument

   (D) a conditional statement

4. Which of the following is a conditional statement?

   (A) If P, then Q.   (C) P implies Q.

   (B) $P \rightarrow Q$.   (D) All of the above.

5. Validity and invalidity apply only to

   (A) inductive arguments.

   (B) deductive arguments.

   (C) fallacies.

   (D) none of the above.

1. **(D)**

   All of the above operations show that irrational numbers can result in a rational number. The best answer is that all of them are counterexamples. Be sure to read all of the answer choices because of the four possible answers, (D) is the relevant one. (Section 11.2)

2. **(B)**

   The argument is invalid for two reasons: (1) The mother misinterpreted her son's promise as a conditional statement. (2) The truth of the premise of that conditional argument does not guarantee the truth of its conclusion. This doesn't allow for any contingencies, such as the bulb burned out or someone inside the house turned the porchlight off at bedtime. (Section 11.2.1)

3. **(B)**

   If a statement (which can be but doesn't have to be conditional) or a conjecture is proven to be true, it becomes a theorem. Without that proof, it cannot be called a theorem. An argument has a premise (or premises) and a conclusion, but neither is necessarily proven to be true. (Section 11.2.1)

4. **(D)**

   They are all versions of conditional statements. (Section 11.3)

5. **(B)**

   Validity refers only to arguments. In a deductive argument, the premises claim to give conclusive grounds for the truth of the conclusion. In inductive reasoning, the premises do not guarantee the conclusion. (Section 11.2.1)

CHAPTER 11

Competency 9: Mathematical Reasoning

11.1 INTRODUCTION

Reasoning, whether mathematical or not, has a lot to do with what "sounds right." Often, instincts tell us that something is incorrect, even if we cannot state what led us to that conclusion. Reasoning involves logic, which Merriam-Webster defines as "a proper or reasonable way of thinking about or understanding something."

The human brain uses logic (correctly or incorrectly) from an early age, such as when a 2-year-old thinks an avocado is a dinosaur egg because of its shape, to riddles, to—you guessed it—mathematics.

A classic riddle involves a father and son who are in an auto accident. Two ambulances take them to two different hospitals. The son is seriously injured and is taken to surgery, but the surgeon sees him and says, "I can't do the surgery on him because he is my son." Assuming this is hospital protocol and the two are indeed blood relations, how is this possible? The simple answer is that the surgeon is his mother.

The rest of this chapter addresses logic in thought processes, especially in a mathematical setting.

11.2 ARGUMENTS

Simply put, **logic** is the study of argument. In logic, an **argument** is an example of reasoning in which one or more statements are offered as **support** for a **conjecture**, which is consistent with known data, but has neither been verified nor shown to be false. (A conjecture is really just an "educated guess"). The argument can take the form of justification, grounds, reasons, evidence, or counterexamples, as we saw in previous chapters. The statement being supported is the **conclusion** of the argument, and the statements that support the conclusion are the **premises** of the argument.

Mathematics, and geometry in particular, offers many different conjectures. A conjecture arises when a pattern holds true for many cases but isn't proven. An excellent example is that the sum of the measures of the angles in a triangle equals 180°. Conjectures must be proved for the mathematical observation to be fully accepted. When a conjecture is rigorously proved, it becomes a **theorem**.

The ancient Babylonians applied the geometry known today as the Pythagorean theorem (see Section 6.4.2a) without proving it. Pythagoras (c. 570–495 BCE), was the first to record its proof, so the theorem bears his name.

Many conjectures in math are proposed as math puzzles. In fact, a search of the Internet lists hundreds of mathematical conjectures, such as "There are an infinite number of twin primes." **Twin primes** is the term used for two prime numbers that are adjacent in a list of primes (examples are 3 and 5, 5 and 7, 41 and 43). Since there are an infinite number of numbers, are there an infinite number of primes? Will there ever be a twin prime theorem? Problems such as this pique students' interest.

Another interesting case of a conjecture is the four-color map, which states that no more than four different colors are sufficient to color the countries of the world on a map in such a way that no two adjacent countries have the same color. This was first proposed as a conjecture in 1852, and could not be disproven, although many people tried to find a counterexample. Finally, it was proven mathematically 124 years later (in 1976) with the use of high-speed computers and is now known as the four-color map *theorem*. Try it on a map of the states of the United States.

The method of proof of the four-color theorem can be called "brute force," usable when there are only a finite number of cases that could lead to counterexamples. In this approach, all possible cases are considered and shown not to give counterexamples. This requires, as a practical matter, the use of a computer algorithm to check all the cases.

Conjectures that turn out to be useful for many reasons (not the least of which is that it sometimes pops up on a test such as the FTCE), are those that have to do with divisibility. It is well known that all even numbers are divisible by 2; all numbers that end in 5 are divisible by 5, and all numbers that end in 0 are divisible by 10. The chart is constructed as conditional (if-then) statements (Section 11.3, Conditional Statements), with an example number given in the last column.

Divisibility Rules

If:	Then the number is divisible by:	Example
The last digit of the number is even (0, 2, 4, 6, 8)	2	98,765,432: 2 is even
The sum of the digits in the number is divisible by 3	3	456,302,178: the individual digits total 36, which is divisible by 3
The last two digits in the number is divisible by 4	4	287,547,345,716: the last two digits are 16, which is divisible by 4
The last digit of the number is 0 or 5	5	194,673,920,495: the last digit is 5
The number is even *and* divisible by 3	6	456,302,178: it is even *and* divisible by 3 (see above)
When you take away the last digit, double it, and then subtract it from the remaining number the result is divisible by 7	7	4,571: double the 1, and subtract 457 − 2 = 455, which is divisible by 7.*
The last three digits of the number is divisible by 8	8	24,681,357,640: the last three digits are 640, which is divisible by 8
The sum of the digits of the number is divisible by 9	9	436,815: the sum of the individual digits is 27, which is divisible by 9
The last digit of the number is 0	10	1,234,567,890: the last digit is 0
When you take away the last digit and then subtract it from the resulting number, the result is divisible by11	11	6,402: subtract 2 from 640 to get 638.*
The number is divisible by both 3 *and* 4	12	8,189,808: the digits add to 42, so it is divisible by 3, and the last two digits are divisible by 4.

* The rules for 7 and 11 may have to be repeated if the original number is large.

EXAMPLE 11.1

Is 1,178,066,952 divisible by 8?

SOLUTION 11.1

Yes. The last three digits, 952, are divisible by 8, so the whole long number is also. The question doesn't ask what the quotient is, so don't waste time getting it.

Hint: It's probably a good idea to know some of these divisibility rules, but certainly division by 7 or 11 may be determined more quickly by using the calculator if the number is long. The advantage of the table is, as shown in Example 11.1, that if you don't recognize that 952 is divisible by 8, it is easier to enter $952 \div 8$ on the calculator (and less prone to error) than entering a whole 10-digit number and dividing by 8.

11.2.1 Truth and Validity

Two aspects need be considered in assessing an argument: the **truth** of the premises and the **validity** of the reasoning from the premises to the conclusion.

An argument is considered valid for several somewhat equivalent reasons:

- The truth of its premises guarantees the truth of its conclusion.

- The conclusion would necessarily be true if it is assumed that all the premises were true.

- It is impossible for the conclusion to be false and all the premises true at the same time.

- The conclusion can be deduced from the premises in accordance with certain valid rules.

If an argument is not valid, it is **invalid**.

The first fundamental principle of logic is the independence of truth and validity:

Truth pertains only to *statements*; validity pertains only to *arguments*.

A further distinction is that validity pertains to reasoning, not propositions, whereas truth pertains to propositions, not reasoning.

11.3 CONDITIONAL STATEMENTS

A **conditional statement** relates to an "if-then" statement: "if P then Q," or in logic symbols, "$P \rightarrow Q$" or "P implies Q." An "if-then" statement is also known as an **implication**, and is *true* for all instances except when P is *true* and Q is *false*. To understand this logic, consider the following statement: "If you wash the car [P], then I'll give you five dollars [Q]."

- Suppose you wash the car (P is *true*) and I give you five dollars (Q is *true*). Since I kept my promise, the implication is *true*.

- Suppose you wash the car (P is *true*) but I don't give you five dollars (Q is *false*). Since I didn't keep my promise, the implication is *false*.

- Suppose you don't wash the car (*P* is *false*). Then whether I give you five dollars because I am just nice (*Q* is *true*) or I don't give you five dollars because I want to teach you a lesson (*Q* is *false*), I haven't broken my promise. So the implication can't be false, and the implication must be *true*.

In logic, the word "or" means either or both conditions are possible.

11.3.1 Inverses, Converses, Contrapositives

Inverses, **converses**, and **contrapositives** exist for conditional $P \rightarrow Q$ (if-then) statements, which consist of two parts: the hypothesis (*P*, the "if" clause) and the conclusion (*Q*, the "then" clause). In the following list, read "~" as "not."

- The **inverse** of $P \rightarrow Q$ is $\sim P \rightarrow \sim Q$.

- The **converse** of $P \rightarrow Q$ is $Q \rightarrow P$.

- The **contrapositive** of $P \rightarrow Q$ is $\sim Q \rightarrow \sim P$. It is the combination of the inverse and the converse.

The following table summarizes these statements

Statement	If *P*, then *Q*.
Converse	If *Q*, then *P*.
Inverse	If not *P*, then not *Q*.
Contrapositive	If not *Q*, then not *P*.

If the conditional statement is true, then the contrapositive is also logically true. If the converse is true, then the inverse is also logically true. But if the statement is false, there is no rule for the truth of the other related statements. Let's look at a couple of typical conditional statements and examine the truth of the related statements.

EXAMPLE 11.2

If it is raining, then the sky is cloudy. Assuming this statement is true, write the converse, inverse, and contrapositive, and tell whether these statements are true or false.

SOLUTION 11.2

- Converse: If the sky is cloudy, it is raining (false).

- Inverse: If it is not raining, the sky is not cloudy (false).

- Contrapositive: If the sky is not cloudy, then it is not raining (true).

EXAMPLE 11.3

If a quadrilateral is a square, then the diagonals are equal. Assuming this statement is true, write the converse, inverse, and contrapositive, and tell whether these statements are true or false.

SOLUTION 11.3

- Converse: If the diagonals of a quadrilateral are equal, it is a square (false; it could be a rectangle).

- Inverse: If a quadrilateral is not a square, then the diagonals are not equal. (false; it could be a rectangle).

- If the diagonals of a quadrilateral are not equal, it is not a square (true).

11.4 MATHEMATICAL REASONING

11.4.1 Direct and Indirect Reasoning

Direct reasoning is used almost all the time when problem solving. It is used to reach a valid conclusion from $P \rightarrow Q$ statements. The rule of direct reasoning states that if $P \rightarrow Q$ is true, and if P is true, then we conclude Q is true. For example, referring to Example 11.2, P is the statement "it is raining" and Q is the statement "the sky is cloudy." Assuming P is really true (it is raining), by the rule of direct reasoning, Q must be true, and the sky must be cloudy.

Sometimes math problems are not easily solved by using direct reasoning; then we must use **indirect reasoning**. The rule of indirect reasoning states that if $P \rightarrow Q$ is true, and if Q is false, then P cannot be true. An indirect proof relies on a contradiction (such as something that doesn't make sense or breaks a rule) to prove a given conjecture. It assumes the conclusion is not true, and then finds a contradiction, proving that the conjecture must be true. Indirect reasoning involves the following steps:

- First, assume the opposite of the conclusion, or assume that the conclusion is false.

- Try to prove that assumption directly until there is a contradiction.

- If there is a contradiction, then the assumption that the opposite of the hypothesis is true, is false. (In other words, the opposite of the hypothesis must be false.)

- State that, by contradiction, the original conjecture must be true.

For example, if the conjecture is "If it is raining, then the sky is cloudy" is true, and if the sky is not cloudy, is it true that, "If it is raining, then the sky is not cloudy"? The idea of this rule is that if P always makes Q happen, and if Q does not happen but P still happens, there is a contradiction. Therefore, the original statement is true. (In other words, it cannot rain without a cloud in the sky.)

EXAMPLE 11.4

Prove the following conjecture is true by the indirect method: Every prime number greater than 2 is an odd number.

SOLUTION 11.4

To prove "every prime number greater than 2 is an odd number," assume the opposite of the conclusion, so choose any non-odd (even) number, let's say 6. For a number to be prime, it must be divisible only by 1 and itself. But 6 is an even number, and in fact every number greater than 2 is an even number, and being an even number it is divisible by 2 so it isn't prime. This is true for all even numbers except 2. Thus, there is no contradiction, and the original statement must be true.

The number 2 is the only even prime number.

11.4.2 Deductive and Inductive Reasoning

Arguments can be either deductive or inductive.

- In a **deductive** argument, the premises claim to give conclusive grounds for the truth of the conclusion, or the premises claim to necessarily support the conclusion. The categories of validity and invalidity apply only to deductive arguments. An argument is valid if whenever the premises are true, it is impossible for the conclusion to be false. The conclusion of a valid deduction never contains more information than was contained in the premises.

- An **inductive** argument claims that its premises support but do not guarantee the conclusion. Inductive arguments are strong or weak. In a strong inductive argument, if all of the premises are true, the truth of the conclusion is merely probable and its falsehood is merely improbable; inductions are always uncertain to some degree. The conclusion of an induction always contains more information than was contained in the premises.

An example of a typical deductive argument would have the premises

(1) all A's are B's, and

(2) all B's are C's,

which support the conclusion that

(3) all A's are C's.

If (1) and (2) are true, then it must be the case that (3) is also true.

An example of a typical inductive argument would have as its premises:

(1) I have seen a hundred tigers, and

(2) they have all been orange.

If (1) and (2) are true, then *inductively* the conclusion is

(3) all tigers are orange.

Here, if (1) and (2) are true, the conclusion (3) is merely probable. One counterargument (e.g., white tigers) can prove the conclusion false.

 The difference between deduction and induction is not the difference between good and bad reasoning, but between two ways to support the truth of conclusions.

A **fallacy** is a bad method of argument, whether deductive or inductive, meaning one of the following may have occurred:

- One or more of the premises may be false (or irrelevant).

- The reasoning from the premises may be invalid.

- The language expressing the premises may be ambiguous or vague.

The term "fallacy" is usually used for faults in arguments that nevertheless are persuasive.

An example of a fallacy is

(1) I saw a black cat and

(2) ten minutes later, I crashed my car.

Premises (1) and (2) are true, but the conclusion

(3) therefore, black cats are bad luck

is a fallacy because the reasoning from the premises is invalid.

11.5 MATHEMATICAL INDUCTION

Mathematical Induction is a special form of direct proof. It is used mostly in algebra and usually for natural numbers. It involves only two steps: (1) show that it is true for the first case; (2) assume that if the conjecture is true for the kth case, it is also true for the $(k + 1)$th case. Then induction shows it is true for all cases.

This is best shown by example.

EXAMPLE 11.5

Prove by mathematical induction that for any natural number n, the sum of the first n numbers is:

$$1 + 2 + 3 + ... + n = \frac{n(n + 1)}{2}$$

SOLUTION 11.5

Step 1: This is true for $n = 1$: $1 = \dfrac{1(1 + 1)}{2} = 1$.

Step 2: Assume it is true for any natural number $n = k$ and show that it is also true for $n = k + 1$.

For k: $1 + 2 + 3 + ... + k = \dfrac{k(k + 1)}{2} = \dfrac{k^2 + k}{2} = \dfrac{k^2}{2} + \dfrac{k}{2}$

For $k + 1$: $1 + 2 + 3 + ... + k + (k + 1) = \dfrac{(k + 1)(k + 2)}{2} = \dfrac{k^2 + 3k + 2}{2}$

But since we assumed $1 + 2 + 3 + ... + k = \dfrac{k(k + 1)}{2} = \dfrac{k^2 + k}{2}$ is true, when we add $(k + 1)$ to the left side of that equation, we should be able to just add $(k + 1)$ to the right side of that equation. Checking whether this is true,

$$1 + 2 + 3 + ... + k + (k + 1) = \frac{k^2 + k}{2} + (k + 1) = \frac{k^2 + k + 2(k + 1)}{2} = \frac{k^2 + 3k + 2}{2}.$$

It checks, so we have proved that assuming the equation for k, it also works for $k + 1$, so it is true for all n.

Chapter 11 Exercises

Answers are on the following page.

1. Which of the following statements is NOT true?

   (A) A number is divisible by 2 if it is even.

   (B) A number is divisible by 3, no matter how long it is, if the last two digits are divisible by 3.

   (C) A number is divisible by 4, no matter how long it is, if the last two digits are divisible by 4.

   (D) A number is divisible by 5, no matter how long it is, if it ends in 5 or 0.

2. Which of the following arguments is invalid?

   (A) If a city is in New Jersey, then it is in the United States. Trenton is a city in New Jersey. Thus, Trenton is in the United States.

   (B) All squares are rectangles. All rectangles are parallelograms. Therefore, all squares are parallelograms.

   (C) All cities in the United States are led by mayors. New York has a mayor. Hence, New York is in the United States.

   (D) None of the above.

3. Which of the following is the converse of the statement, "If two lines intersected by a transversal are parallel, the corresponding angles formed by the lines and transversal are equal"?

   (A) If the corresponding angles formed by two lines intersected by a transversal are equal, the lines are parallel.

   (B) If the corresponding angles formed by two lines intersected by a transversal are unequal, the lines are not parallel.

   (C) If two lines intersected by a transversal are not parallel, the corresponding angles formed by the lines and transversal are unequal.

   (D) All of the above.

4. Which of the following is a counterexample to the conjecture that for all real numbers n, $n^2 \geq n$?

   (A) All negative n

   (B) $0 < n < 1$

   (C) $n = n^2$

   (D) The conjecture is true, so there are no counterexamples.

5. State a counterexample to the statement "The difference of two odd numbers is always even."

(A) The sum of two odd numbers is always even.

(B) The difference of two even numbers is always even.

(C) The difference of two even numbers is always odd.

(D) There is no counterexample to the statement because it is always true.

Answers and Explanations

1. **(B)**

Answer choices (A) and (D) are giveaways. They are always true. If you didn't already know about answer choices (B) and (C), you can determine whether they are false by finding a counterexample. As an example, for (B) suppose the last two digits are 12 — is 512 divisible by 3? No, so statement (B) is false. Try the same for (C) only to discover that you cannot think of a counterexample, so it must be is true.

2. **(C)**

Although the conclusion in choice (C) is true, the argument is invalid because the conclusion does not follow from the premises. Choice (A) is an example of direct reasoning that is valid because there is a direct link from the premises to the conclusion. Choice (B) uses deductive reasoning in which the premises are true and it is impossible for the conclusion to be false.

3. **(A)**

If the corresponding angles formed by two lines intersected by a transversal are equal, the lines are parallel. Although answer choices (A) through (C) are all true, only (A) is the converse. Answer choice (B) is the contrapositive of the original statement, and (C) is the inverse of it.

4. **(B)**

The inequality $0 < n < 1$ indicates all positive fractions less than 1; any one of them is a counterexample. For example, if $n = \dfrac{1}{2}$, $n^2 = \dfrac{1}{4}$, and $n^2 < n$. Answer choice (A) is always true because any square of a negative number is positive, and all positives are greater than any negatives. Answer choice (C) is a subset of the conjecture, not a counterexample. It takes only one counterexample to prove a conjecture false.

5. **(D)**

There is no counterexample to the statement because it is always true.

Before you begin your review, take this short self-assessment to see how well you know the topics covered in this chapter. Answering all or some correctly will help you identify your strengths so you can focus on those topics where you need the most review. Even if you answer all of the questions correctly, we suggest you still review all the examples in the chapter to ensure you're in good shape to move on. Answers are on the following page.

1. Mathematics is a means of communication with its own grammar. When teaching students to "decode" word problems, the teacher should emphasize that the unknown, such as _____, is the subject of the problem sentence.

   (A) x

   (B) what

   (C) how many

   (D) all of the above

2. Which of the following is the best concise definition of a square?

   (A) A square is a quadrilateral with four right angles.

   (B) A square is a quadrilateral with congruent sides and four right angles.

   (C) A square is a quadrilateral with four right angles, with opposite sides parallel and equal, and with equal diagonals.

   (D) A square is a quadrilateral with congruent sides.

3. Addressing the most likely errors at the time of instruction of a new concept

   I. is a good idea to ward off student errors.

   II. could confuse the lesson and may actually reinforce the errors rather than the intended concepts.

   III. should be postponed until the teacher can assess any misconceptions in students' understanding of the lesson.

   (A) II and III

   (B) I and III

   (C) I and II

   (D) I, II, and III

4. Adolescent brains begin to think more logically and formally. Which of the following abilities is already developed before years 12–18?

   (A) Processing many points of view

   (B) Abstract thinking

   (C) Concrete thinking

   (D) Logical thinking

5. Teachers frequently ask students to recognize and express math in four different ways: symbolically, numerically, graphically, and _____

   (A) verbally.

   (B) in an explanation.

   (C) as a real-world scenario.

   (D) All of the above.

1. (D)

    The answer to a word problem is the value of the unknown, which is the subject of the problem question and can take the form of a variable or words that are translated into variables.

2. (B)

    A concise definition pinpoints the square precisely without going into excessive description, such as in answer choice (C), which has too much information. Answer choices (A) and (D), although true *descriptions* of a square, are not unique to a square because they are also true for a rectangle and a rhombus, respectively.

3. (A)

    Statement I is incorrect because of statement II. Therefore, any choice that includes statement I is incorrect because statement I is incompatible with statements II and III.

4. (C)

    Prior to age 12, students have been developing the ability to think in concrete ways. Theories of cognitive development recognize that not until about age 12 do students develop complex thinking processes, such as reasoning, abstract thinking, and logic.

5. (A)

    Answer choices (B) and (C) are only parts of the first representation, verbal.

CHAPTER 12

Competency 10: Instruction and Assessment

12.1 COGNITIVE DEVELOPMENT

Many theories of cognitive development recognize that the thinking processes of students aged 12 to 18 are more complex than when they were younger. Prior to age 12, students have been developing the ability to think in concrete ways. But with adolescence, starting at age 12, students begin to think more logically and formally. This is a period of cognitive growth, and an opportunity for teachers to make more of a mark on the futures of their students.

With the adolescent brain development comes the ability for these students to think more abstractly to reason, process many points of view, recognize possibilities, and form new ideas. These students manifest these new developments in their thought processes by forming their own opinions, analyzing, and questioning—all of which present new and challenging opportunities for teachers.

It is often said of younger schoolchildren and pre-schoolers that they are like "sponges"—wanting to learn everything about their immediate environments. How often do very young children seem to repeat one word: "Why?" Adolescents have this same "why" mentality, but in their case it is because they want to be able to develop thought processes, to compare different points of view, to debate, to challenge, and to develop more complex thinking.

Students in grades 6 through 12 look to their teachers for guidance. Teachers have the ability to make a difference in how their students handle their newfound cognitive skills and possibly how they handle their lives.

12.2 SEQUENCING LESSONS

The Concrete-Representational-Abstract (CRA) instructional model is a three-step approach to **sequencing lessons**. It first seeks to develop conceptual understanding before introducing the mathematical procedure, and it is particularly helpful for struggling learners.

The CRA instructional model can be used to teach virtually any mathematical concept. It is also a natural way to differentiate learning, as it appeals to multiple intelligence levels and varying interests. Some students may progress through the sequence quickly, choosing to utilize the abstract representation exclusively, but other students may continue to use either the concrete or representational model as a tool to support their learning until they are more comfortable with the abstract concept.

12.2.1 Concrete Stage

A concrete introduction to a concept allows students to physically represent mathematics with objects, which are most often referred to as **manipulatives**. Pre-adolescent students are familiar with concrete learning, so this is a good place to start with new math concepts.

Many different types of manipulatives are available, from strips of paper (algebra tiles) to multicolored cubes. Even common household items such as paper plates can be used to physically represent mathematics. For example, when introducing two-step equations, a teacher may use small paper plates and counters to represent the equation $4x + 3 = 15$. The variable x is represented by a plate. Since the coefficient is 4, each student would need 4 plates. The counters represent the constant 3 and the sum 15. The students would then model the equation using the plates and counters. Addition and equals symbols could be written on slips of paper and then placed appropriately.

Once the equation is represented, the class would go through the steps for solving a two-step equation. First, to isolate the variable—to subtract 3 from both sides of the equation—the students would remove 3 counters from both sides of the equation. Then to divide both sides by 4, the 4 plates would be divided into 4 groups of 1 plate, and the 12 counters would be divided by dealing out to 4 groups, with each group having 3 counters. Finally, the 1 plate, which represents the variable x, is equal to one group of 3 counters, so $x = 3$.

12.2.2 Representational Stage

Once students are comfortable with a concrete example, teachers can lead them to illustrate the same concept with a drawing or **visual representation**. To visually represent the equation $4x + 3 = 15$, students would draw x four times followed by an addition symbol, three red dots, an equal sign, and 15 red dots. Again, as a group, they would go through the steps to isolate the variable x. To subtract 3 from each side, the students would simply draw a line through 3 of the red dots on each side of the equation. Then, the students would divide each side by 4 by drawing four circles. On the left side of the equation, each circle would contain an x, and on the right side of the equation, each circle would contain 3 red dots. One x equals three dots, or $x = 3$.

12.2.3 Abstract Stage

As students are developing conceptual understanding by way of concrete and representational examples, teachers should simultaneously provide the abstract representation, which is $4x + 3 = 15$, using the appropriate numbers, symbols, and notation. This allows the students to make the connection among the three representations. Of course, some students may be able to skip the first two stages and go right to the abstract stage.

12.2.4 Resources

Myriad resources that can be used effectively with the CRA instructional model are available to teachers. As already noted, manipulatives can range from objects specifically designed to teach mathematics, such as algebra tiles, to a simple deck of playing cards. A wide assortment of virtual tools are available on the Internet.

The incorporation of technology can be highly engaging for students and can provide immediate and more precise representation of more complex concepts. For example, online geometry tools can be used to represent transformations in a plane. Students are able to see how the orientation of the sides and angles of a polygon change as it is rotated around a point, usually the origin (see Chapter 7, Section 7.5.3). Doing this by hand would be arduous and time-consuming. Similarly, computer algebra systems can demonstrate how the Riemann sum approximation of an integral becomes more accurate as the number of rectangles increases (see Chapter 10, Section 10.4.3a). These programs and others are valuable tools in the representational stage of the CRA sequence because they give students a visual model that can be manipulated easily.

12.3 MULTIPLE REPRESENTATIONS IN MATHEMATICS

A key component of instruction is to help students to think flexibly about mathematics. Conceptual understanding and procedural competence are both vital for students to interpret and represent mathematical concepts in multiple ways. Teachers frequently ask students to recognize and express math in four different ways: symbolic, numerical, graphical, and verbal.

Math most often is associated with its *symbolic* representation, using numbers, letters, symbols, and mathematical notation. However, it can also be represented *numerically*—in tables and charts; *graphically*—in a diagram, graph or picture; and *verbally*—in an explanation of a real-world scenario.

The table below demonstrates the four different mathematical ways to represent a basic price (c) per hour (h) relationship, such as calculating the cost of parking.

Symbolic	Numerical		Graphical	Verbal
$3h = c$	h	c		Event parking costs $3 per hour.
	1	3		
	2	6		
	3	9		
	4	12		
	5	15		

A student should be able to recognize the price per hour relationship looking at any *one* of these representations. Additionally, if given one—for example, the graphical representation—a student also should be able to provide each of the other three representations.

This flexibility in thinking demonstrates solid conceptual understanding, and it helps students connect math with real-world experiences.

12.4 PROBLEM-SOLVING SKILLS

Flexibility in thinking is also a key component in the development of sound problem-solving skills. Coaching students to become problem-solvers involves four main steps: (1) making sense of the problem, (2) choosing a strategy to solve the problem, (3) implementing the strategy, and (4) checking to ensure the accuracy of the solution.

When a problem is introduced, teachers should coach students to look for the important information. Teachers should pose questions such as "What is the problem asking?," "What information is essential to solving this problem?," and "Is there any information included in the problem that is irrelevant?" The answers to these questions can be highlighted, underlined, or crossed out to help students break down the problem into manageable pieces of information. Students can also be encouraged to restate the problem in their own words.

In the problem below, the essential information is in an *italic* font. The irrelevant information has been crossed out, and the solutions that must be found are in a **bold** font.

Jane needs to buy fertilizer for her yard. She is trying to decide how much fertilizer she will need. *The bag says it will cover an area of 300 square feet.* Jane's rec-

tangular yard is 30 feet by 11 feet, but she has flower beds in all four corners. ~~Jane has 96 tulips to plant in the flower beds.~~ Each bed is in the shape of *an isosceles triangle with a side length of 5 feet.* **How many square feet of lawn does Jane have? Will one bag of fertilizer be enough?**

Once the students understand the problem and what it is asking, they should choose a strategy to solve the problem. This is where flexibility in thinking becomes advantageous. Often, many different strategies can be successfully applied. Teachers have an opportunity to foster creative thinking by supporting students who suggest different approaches to the same problem.

12.4.1 Strategies for Problem Solving

Strategies for problem solving include:

- draw a picture

- make an estimate

- create a chart

- use guess-and-check

- work backwards

- break the problem into several small problems

- make an organized list

- look for a pattern

- use a formula

- test for reasonableness

In the given example, several strategies can be combined to find the solutions.

12.4.1a Draw a Picture

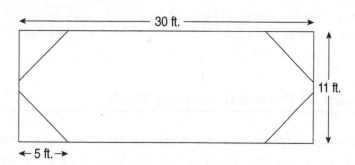

12.4.1b Make an Estimate

To find the area of a rectangle, the student needs to multiply the length times the width. By mentally rounding numbers as a quick estimate, the student can determine that the area of the entire yard (including the beds) would be approximately 300 square feet. By looking at the picture, the student might make an estimate that the four beds have a combined area of about 50 square feet. Subtracting 50 from 300, the student would estimate that the area of the yard that needs to be fertilized is somewhere between 250 and 300 square feet. (This range is a guide for reasonableness of the final answer.)

12.4.1c Use a Formula

$$\text{Area of a rectangle} = \text{length} \times \text{width}$$
$$A = 30 \times 11 = 330 \text{ square feet}$$
$$\text{Area of a triangle} = \left(\frac{1}{2}\right) \text{base} \times \text{height}$$
$$A = \left(\frac{1}{2}\right)(5) \times 5 = 12.5 \text{ square feet}$$

There are four triangular beds in the yard, so the combined flower beds have an area of $4 \times 1.25 = 50$ square feet. The area of the yard minus the area of the flower beds determines the square feet of the part of the lawn that is to be fertilized.

$$330 - 50 = 280 \text{ square feet}$$

12.4.1d Test for Reasonableness

Given that the estimated area to be fertilized was between 250 and 300 square feet, the solution of 280 square feet is reasonable.

Once students have utilized their chosen strategies to find a reasonable solution, they should be reminded to go back to the original problem and ensure their solution actually answers the question. In this case, the question has two parts: (1) How many square feet of lawn does Jane have? (280 square feet), and (2) Will one bag of fertilizer be enough? (Yes. Since one bag of fertilizer will cover 300 square feet, and Jane's lawn is only 280 square feet, one bag of fertilizer will be sufficient.)

12.4.2 Summary of Problem-Solving Skills

Students will approach problems differently. Some students may be able to work with a mental image, making a drawing unnecessary. When teachers encourage students to think creatively and offer them opportunities to share how they approached a particular problem, the entire class benefits. For instance, in a discussion of how the above problem was solved, a student might volunteer how he or she chose to compose the four triangles into one rectangle to increase efficiency. Students who hadn't even considered this are given a new perspective. In this way, students learn from one another.

Problem-solving in the classroom offers students insight into how math can be applied in the real world. It makes math relevant, but it can also be very intimidating for some students. Learning effective problem-solving strategies is like putting essential tools in your toolbox. It makes the work easier.

Guess-and-check can be useful if there are a small number of possible solutions or if solutions can be easily tested. To emphasize the usefulness of this approach (and its limitations) the teacher should ask students to show the work for each guess and subsequent check.

Frequent discussions about various problem-solving strategies will help students find the most efficient strategy for specific types of problems. Thinking aloud is invaluable when teaching problem-solving. As a teacher articulates the steps needed to break down a problem, students are learning to create an internal dialogue that they can then use as they approach problems independently. The teacher should model reflective questioning, as well. For example, "Why did I choose this particular strategy?" or "Is there a more efficient strategy?"

The last of the strategies, testing for reasonableness, is as important as any of the other strategies but is often overlooked. If the answer doesn't make sense, the student should check the calculations all the way through—this doesn't mean redoing the problem, but rather making sure the result of each step makes sense. In math, one of the most important questions for students to ask themselves is, "Does this solution make sense?"

12.5 CONCEPTUAL MISUNDERSTANDING

During instruction, it is critical for teachers to identify student misconceptions about the mathematical content being taught. Conceptual misunderstanding can lead to repeated procedural errors. Simply re-teaching the procedure is unlikely to clear up the confusion.

Minor mistakes early in problem-solving can take on lives of their own. Examples of common mistakes made early in the problem-solving process include setting up a proportion with one of the ratios upside down, answering a question in radians when it should be in degrees, finding a probability that is greater than 1 (rather than ranging from 0 to 1), dividing by 0 and getting an answer of 0, and not identifying the correct side (or angle) in a triangle. Rather than pointing out the mistake to the student, the teacher should prompt students to recognize their own mistakes—because an effective tool is learning from one's own mistakes.

As an example, if students confuse the x- and y-coordinates in an ordered pair, they will have difficulty accurately plotting them on a coordinate plane. By swapping the x- and y-coordinates, students will consistently plot the point in the wrong quadrant. To help students correctly identify the coordinates, teachers may point out that x comes before y in the alphabet, just as the x-coordinate comes before the y-coordinate in an ordered pair. However, the error may originate from confusion about the features of a coordinate plane. Students may not realize that the x-axis runs horizontally and the y-axis runs vertically, another alphabetic analogy. To take this alphabet analogy one step further, in a function $y = f(x)$, the domain refers to x values and the range refers to y values.

12.5.1 Correction Strategies

An important way that teachers can ascertain the root of misconceptions is through dialogue. It is important for students not only to model their work, but also as they do so to be encouraged to explain the steps they are taking. Teachers should prompt students' thinking by asking "why" questions.

Another way to reveal conceptual misunderstanding is to deconstruct incorrect solutions to a problem. When analyzing a solved problem, students first should be encouraged to test the solution to see that it is reasonable. A student who recognizes that the solution does not make sense is more invested in determining what the error is and how the error was made. Through guided discussion, teachers can help students identify common errors. Teachers and students should both use mathematical vocabulary as they break down the procedure.

For example, when teaching the distributive property, a teacher might ask whether the value of the expression $3(x + 12)$ is 27 when $x = 5$. The students should first be encouraged to consider whether 27 is a *reasonable* value. A teacher might have the students turn and talk in pairs about why 27 is or is not reasonable. Some students may volunteer that 3 multiplied by 12 equals 36, which is a product larger than 27. Others may say that the sum of 12 and 5 (the two addends in parentheses) is larger than 12, so 27 is not a reasonable solution. Still other students may simply substitute 5 for x and evaluate the expression, finding the correct solution of 51. Once students can agree that the value of 27 does not make sense, they will begin to look critically at the procedure to determine how the error was made.

Incorrect Procedure	Correct Procedure
$3(x + 12)$	$3(x + 12)$
$3x + 12$	$3(x) + (3)(12)$
$3(5) + 12$	$(3)(5) + (3)(12)$
$15 + 12 = 27$	$15 + 36 = 51$

While reviewing this problem, a teacher might ask the students why the correct procedure did not use order of operations. Students may volunteer that order of operations requires that the operation inside the parenthesis be completed first, but because one of the addends inside the parenthesis is a variable, this is not possible. The teacher might prompt the students to suggest that this is when the distributive property should be used, which would lead to a discussion of how to "distribute" the factor of 3 to the two terms inside the parentheses. At this point, students would recognize that in the incorrect procedure the 3 was distributed to only the first term in the parentheses. Students should compare the correct procedure with the incorrect procedure.

Through this guided discussion, students are able to construct their own understanding and identify their own misconceptions about the distributive property. This strategy can easily be used when reviewing assigned work. It ultimately makes math practice more meaningful to students.

12.6 FORMS OF ASSESSMENT

A comprehensive assessment program consists of diagnostic, formative, and summative assessments. Traditionally, assessments were designed to determine a student's mastery of certain content or to compare a student's own progress to the progress of peers. Increasingly, teachers are using assessment to guide instruction and meet the needs of diverse student populations.

12.6.1 Diagnostic Assessments

Diagnostic assessments are used to determine a student's background knowledge, skill level, and conceptual understanding. Many math skills build on existing knowledge, so it is pertinent for teachers to determine a student's competence with those prerequisite skills *before* beginning a new unit of study. This awareness will help teachers to design lessons and curriculum to meet student needs. Diagnostic assessment may mean revisiting a subject. It also may indicate that some students have achieved mastery in certain concepts and skills; these students might need enrichment opportunities or perhaps to move to more advanced concepts. By targeting instruction to meet the students where they are, a teacher can use time and resources more efficiently.

A diagnostic assessment may reveal to a teacher that the entire class needs to review a particular skill before moving forward with new material. For example, before beginning a unit on solving multistep equations and inequalities, a teacher may need to ensure that students recall how to simplify algebraic expressions and solve one-step equations and inequalities.

Diagnostic assessments can be formally structured—such as a traditional pretest—or they might be more informal in style. An example of an informal diagnostic assessment would be to ask students to create a *mind map*. The teacher would divide the class into small groups and give each group a large piece of paper. The content to be covered would be written in the center of the paper. Students would be asked to write or draw anything and everything they know about that particular topic. This type of preassessment engages all types of learning, including kinesthetic and visual. It allows all students to participate and everyone to synergize their thinking to make even more connections than each would do individually. After students are given ample time to create their maps, each group shares its map with the class, and the teacher guides the conversation by asking open-ended questions, further enabling students to share and expand their thinking.

12.6.2 Formative Assessments

Whereas diagnostic assessments are administered at the beginning of a new unit of study, **formative assessments** are generally given *during* a unit of study. They help inform the teacher how well the students are grasping a concept as it is presented. Teachers use student feedback to adjust their instruction. As with diagnostic assessment, the purpose of formative assessment is to help teachers design targeted instruction to meet each individual student's needs.

Formative assessments are almost always informal and seldom account for a grade or substantial point values. Formative assessments such as exit tickets and observation during think-pair-share activities can also reveal conceptual misunderstanding. Examples of formative assessments are listed in the table below.

Formative Assessment	Description
Entrance/Exit Tickets	A short written response to a question as the students enter or leave the classroom.
Think-Pair-Share	In response to a question, students are asked to think quietly for a moment, pair up with another student to discuss the question briefly, and then share their thinking with the entire class.
Thumbs-up/Thumbs-down	Students give a quick thumbs-up or thumbs-down to indicate their level of understanding for a particular concept.
Rate Your Mastery	Students are asked to rate themselves from 1 to 4 on a particular concept. If students hold up 1 finger, it indicates they have no understanding; a show of 2 fingers indicates they could do the work with support; 3 fingers indicates that they could do the work independently; and 4 fingers indicates that they could teach the concept to another student.
Identify the Error	Students are asked to look at solved problems critically to determine the accuracy of the solution, as well as the procedural or conceptual reasons for any error.
Show Down	Every student responds to the same question on a small whiteboard. The teacher stands at the front of the room and at the same time, students hold up their boards to show their solutions.

The most common method of formative assessment is questioning and observation. Creating a culture in which students feel safe to take risks and share their thinking allows the teacher to engage students in rich conversation and to ask open-ended questions. These conversations can give teachers deep insight into a student's conceptual understanding. This immediate feedback helps a teacher to provide remediation for students who are struggling with a concept, or enrichment for those who have already reached mastery.

12.6.3 Summative Assessments

Summative assessments are given at the end of a unit, a semester, or the year. They are typically formal in style and are an important measure for determining growth, achievement, and mastery. As such, the assessment is usually tied to a grade or proficiency rating. Examples of summative assessments include standardized tests, district benchmark assessments, classroom end-of-unit tests, and semester exams.

Even though summative assessments are formal in nature and high stakes in terms of point value, they do not have to be structured as a test or exam. Often students are able to demonstrate mastery in other formats that are more engaging and more tailored to a student's particular strengths.

For example, students could present a **portfolio** with examples of work and **journal** entries collected during the unit, written explanations of the concepts that were covered, and an analysis and reflection of what they learned through the course of the unit.

Another type of summative assessment would be a **performance task**, which requires students to *apply* the skills and concepts they have learned to a task that mimics a real-world situation. This application draws on higher-order analytical skills and gives teachers a broader understanding of the student's grasp of the content.

Performance assessments can be project oriented or paper-and-pencil tasks; they can be done individually or in small groups. This flexibility in style and grouping is one way a teacher can differentiate the assessment. Regardless of the format, students must utilize problem-solving skills to determine the most efficient and most effective procedure to complete the task. Often, students will need to apply multiple mathematical procedures during a performance assessment. In addition, students are required to explain their thinking process in writing.

The comprehensive nature of a performance task allows teachers to assess both procedural and conceptual understanding. To provide students with meaningful feedback in both these areas, teachers often will grade a performance assessment with a **rubric**. The rubric, which is generally shared with the student prior to assigning the task, might have scoring areas for procedural accuracy; the clarity, completeness, and neatness of calculations; and the conceptual understanding demonstrated in the written explanations. If students worked in small groups, the rubric might also have a scoring section for collaboration. In addition, students often are asked to create a model, draw a diagram, or create a chart as part of their solution process. In this event, the rubric would include a scoring section for this aspect of the project as well.

Chapter 12 Exercises

Answers are on the following page.

1. To teach the students about the formula for the number of diagonals in a polygon, a teacher asks the students to draw several polygons and their diagonals. What question(s) could the teacher ask to help students make a reasonable conjecture about the relationship between the number of sides (n) and number of diagonals (d) in a polygon $\left(d = \frac{(n-3)}{2} \right)$?

    I.   What is the relationship between the number of sides and the number of vertices?

    II. How many diagonals can be drawn from one vertex?

    III. If you draw diagonals from every vertex, are some of them the same diagonal?

    IV. How can you account for the fact that each diagonal is drawn twice?

    (A) I and III only.

    (B) I, II, and III only.

    (C) All questions I–IV.

    (D) All questions in the order shown in I–IV.

2. To help students develop the skill of recognizing the reasonableness of a problem solution, the teacher should

    (A) ask the students to defend their work as they go along, either to themselves or to others.

    (B) stop a student's work when the teacher sees that it will result in an unreasonable solution.

    (C) make changes to a student's process when it is obvious to the teacher that it is wrong.

    (D) present several alternative paths to a correct solution while the student is working.

3. Which of the following is NOT an example of informal assessment?

    (A) Observation

    (B) Questioning

    (C) Standardized testing

    (D) Written feedback on practice assignments

4. Journals have the advantage of

    (A) offering a medium for students to self-assess what they have learned.

    (B) encouraging students to understand the reasoning behind mathematical processes.

    (C) providing students an opportunity to build conceptual understanding.

    (D) All of the above.

5. The Concrete-Representational-Abstract (CRA) instructional model is a three-step approach to sequencing lessons. Which of the following is NOT part of the CRA model?

(A) Manipulatives

(B) Visuals

(C) Symbolic representation

(D) Fact-checking

Answers and Explanations

1. (D)

To guide the students to the correct answer, all four questions should be asked in the precise order shown because each question depends on the answer to the preceding question.

2. (A)

The operative phrase here is to help "students develop the skill of recognizing reasonableness" in their work. The best way to do this is to have the students self-check their work for reasonableness as they go along, not to interrupt the students' thought processes when they are first learning a skill. Direction and correction of the student may put them on the correct path, but self-assessment will help students to develop the skill of recognizing reasonableness on their own. Of course, direction and correction have their place when the students ask for help, but students should develop the skill to recognize reasonableness before they ask for assistance.

3. (C)

Standardized testing is a hallmark of formal assessment. Informal assessments provide teachers and students with immediate, nonthreatening feedback, which includes observation, questioning, and written notes.

4. (D)

All of the answer choices show the advantages of journaling as a valuable tool for enhancing mathematical communication.

5. (D)

Answer choices (A), (B), and (C) are all manifestations of the Concrete-Representational-Abstract (CRA) approach. Answer choice (D) is not necessarily a part of the CRA model.

FTCE Mathematics 6–12
Practice Tests

FTCE Mathematics 6–12
Practice Test 1

FTCE Mathematics 6–12
Practice Test 1 Answer Sheet

1. Ⓐ Ⓑ Ⓒ Ⓓ   26. Ⓐ Ⓑ Ⓒ Ⓓ   51. Ⓐ Ⓑ Ⓒ Ⓓ

2. Ⓐ Ⓑ Ⓒ Ⓓ   27. Ⓐ Ⓑ Ⓒ Ⓓ   52. Ⓐ Ⓑ Ⓒ Ⓓ

3. Ⓐ Ⓑ Ⓒ Ⓓ   28. Ⓐ Ⓑ Ⓒ Ⓓ   53. Ⓐ Ⓑ Ⓒ Ⓓ

4. Ⓐ Ⓑ Ⓒ Ⓓ   29. Ⓐ Ⓑ Ⓒ Ⓓ   54. Ⓐ Ⓑ Ⓒ Ⓓ

5. Ⓐ Ⓑ Ⓒ Ⓓ   30. Ⓐ Ⓑ Ⓒ Ⓓ   55. Ⓐ Ⓑ Ⓒ Ⓓ

6. Ⓐ Ⓑ Ⓒ Ⓓ   31. Ⓐ Ⓑ Ⓒ Ⓓ   56. Ⓐ Ⓑ Ⓒ Ⓓ

7. Ⓐ Ⓑ Ⓒ Ⓓ   32. Ⓐ Ⓑ Ⓒ Ⓓ   57. Ⓐ Ⓑ Ⓒ Ⓓ

8. Ⓐ Ⓑ Ⓒ Ⓓ   33. Ⓐ Ⓑ Ⓒ Ⓓ   58. Ⓐ Ⓑ Ⓒ Ⓓ

9. Ⓐ Ⓑ Ⓒ Ⓓ   34. Ⓐ Ⓑ Ⓒ Ⓓ   59. Ⓐ Ⓑ Ⓒ Ⓓ

10. Ⓐ Ⓑ Ⓒ Ⓓ   35. Ⓐ Ⓑ Ⓒ Ⓓ   60. Ⓐ Ⓑ Ⓒ Ⓓ

11. Ⓐ Ⓑ Ⓒ Ⓓ   36. Ⓐ Ⓑ Ⓒ Ⓓ   61. Ⓐ Ⓑ Ⓒ Ⓓ

12. Ⓐ Ⓑ Ⓒ Ⓓ   37. Ⓐ Ⓑ Ⓒ Ⓓ   62. Ⓐ Ⓑ Ⓒ Ⓓ

13. Ⓐ Ⓑ Ⓒ Ⓓ   38. Ⓐ Ⓑ Ⓒ Ⓓ   63. Ⓐ Ⓑ Ⓒ Ⓓ

14. Ⓐ Ⓑ Ⓒ Ⓓ   39. Ⓐ Ⓑ Ⓒ Ⓓ   64. Ⓐ Ⓑ Ⓒ Ⓓ

15. Ⓐ Ⓑ Ⓒ Ⓓ   40. Ⓐ Ⓑ Ⓒ Ⓓ   65. Ⓐ Ⓑ Ⓒ Ⓓ

16. Ⓐ Ⓑ Ⓒ Ⓓ   41. Ⓐ Ⓑ Ⓒ Ⓓ   66. Ⓐ Ⓑ Ⓒ Ⓓ

17. Ⓐ Ⓑ Ⓒ Ⓓ   42. Ⓐ Ⓑ Ⓒ Ⓓ   67. Ⓐ Ⓑ Ⓒ Ⓓ

18. Ⓐ Ⓑ Ⓒ Ⓓ   43. Ⓐ Ⓑ Ⓒ Ⓓ   68. Ⓐ Ⓑ Ⓒ Ⓓ

19. Ⓐ Ⓑ Ⓒ Ⓓ   44. Ⓐ Ⓑ Ⓒ Ⓓ   69. Ⓐ Ⓑ Ⓒ Ⓓ

20. Ⓐ Ⓑ Ⓒ Ⓓ   45. Ⓐ Ⓑ Ⓒ Ⓓ   70. Ⓐ Ⓑ Ⓒ Ⓓ

21. Ⓐ Ⓑ Ⓒ Ⓓ   46. Ⓐ Ⓑ Ⓒ Ⓓ   71. Ⓐ Ⓑ Ⓒ Ⓓ

22. Ⓐ Ⓑ Ⓒ Ⓓ   47. Ⓐ Ⓑ Ⓒ Ⓓ   72. Ⓐ Ⓑ Ⓒ Ⓓ

23. Ⓐ Ⓑ Ⓒ Ⓓ   48. Ⓐ Ⓑ Ⓒ Ⓓ   73. Ⓐ Ⓑ Ⓒ Ⓓ

24. Ⓐ Ⓑ Ⓒ Ⓓ   49. Ⓐ Ⓑ Ⓒ Ⓓ   74. Ⓐ Ⓑ Ⓒ Ⓓ

25. Ⓐ Ⓑ Ⓒ Ⓓ   50. Ⓐ Ⓑ Ⓒ Ⓓ   75. Ⓐ Ⓑ Ⓒ Ⓓ

FTCE Mathematics 6–12 Practice Test 1

TIME: 150 minutes (2 hours and 30 minutes)
75 questions

> **Directions: Read each item and select the best response.**

1. In the binary number system, what is the sum of 111 and 10?

   (A) 1101

   (B) 111

   (C) 1001

   (D) 9

2. Which of the following numbers is NOT irrational?

   (A) π

   (B) $\dfrac{\sqrt{10}}{2}$

   (C) $\sqrt{10}$

   (D) $\dfrac{\sqrt{8}}{\sqrt{2}}$

3. $45 \times 60 \times 3 \times (-479) = ?$

   (A) $-3,879,905$

   (B) $-3,879,900$

   (C) $3,879,900$

   (D) $3,879,905$

4. Which of these statements is true?

   (A) Every integer is a whole number.

   (B) Every rational number is a whole number.

   (C) Every counting number is a rational number.

   (D) Every whole number is a positive integer.

5. If s and t are real numbers, then

   (A) $s > t$ or $t > s$.

   (B) $s > t$ or $t < s$.

   (C) $s > t$ or $t \le s$.

   (D) $s > t$ or $t \ge s$.

6. Which of the following are the solutions for $2x^2 - 5x = 0$?

   (A) $x = \dfrac{1}{2}, -3$

   (B) $x = -\dfrac{1}{2}, 3$

   (C) $x = \dfrac{1}{2}, 3$

   (D) $x = -\dfrac{1}{2}, -3$

7. Mira pays $15 for a book that has been marked down 25%. What was the original cost of the book?

   (A) $3.75

   (B) $11.25

   (C) $20.00

   (D) $60.00

8. Solve for x: $3|2x - 1| - 4 > 11$.

   (A) $x < -2$ or $x > 3$

   (B) $x > -2$ or $x > 3$

   (C) $x > -2$ or $x < 3$

   (D) $x < -2$ or $x < -8$

9. If Jack pours three six-ounce glasses $\frac{5}{6}$ full of milk from a full quart carton, how much milk is left in the carton? (1 quart = 32 ounces)

   (A) 110 ounces

   (B) 113 ounces

   (C) 14 ounces

   (D) 17 ounces

10. How many hours will it take an airplane to travel 900 miles north if its airspeed is 315 miles per hour but it is facing a wind blowing south at 15.1 miles per hour? (Round your answer to the nearest hundredth of an hour.)

   (A) 2.86

   (B) 2.72

   (C) 3.01

   (D) 3.00

11. Solve for x in the following equation:
$$\left[3^2 + 2(48) + 7\right]x = 0.$$

   (A) 112

   (B) −112

   (C) 1

   (D) 0

12. Which of the following terms cannot be combined with $2ax^3y$ into a single term, where a is a constant?

   (A) $3x^3y$

   (B) $5a^2x^3y$

   (C) $2ax^3y^2$

   (D) $-2x^3y$

13. Given the formula $F = \frac{9}{5}C + 32$, which converts a temperature in Celsius (C) to Fahrenheit, what is the temperature in Fahrenheit for a Celsius temperature of 40 below 0?

   (A) 129.6°F

   (B) 104°F

   (C) −14.4°F

   (D) −40°F

14. Which of the following numbers is irrational?

   (A) $\sqrt[3]{-5}$

   (B) $\sqrt[4]{\frac{81}{16}}$

   (C) $\sqrt[5]{-32}$

   (D) $\sqrt{49}$

15. Which of the following values are solutions to the following system of equations?

$$x + y = 3$$
$$5x + 8y = 21$$

(A) $x = -1, y = -2$

(B) $x = -1, y = 2$

(C) $x = 1, y = -2$

(D) $x = 1, y = 2$

16. Express the equation $5^{-2} = \dfrac{1}{25}$ as a logarithm.

(A) $\log_5\left(\dfrac{1}{25}\right) = -2$

(B) $\log_{-2}\left(\dfrac{1}{25}\right) = 5$

(C) $\log\left(\dfrac{1}{25}\right) = -2$

(D) $\log_5\left(\dfrac{1}{25}\right) = 2$

17. How many real and complex roots can $x^5 + x^4 - 6x^3 + 5x^2 + 5x - 6 = 0$ possibly have?

(A) 6 real roots

(B) 3 real roots and 2 complex roots

(C) 4 real roots and 1 complex root

(D) 2 real roots and 3 complex roots

18. $(x - 6)$ is a factor of $2x^3 + 4x^2 - 82x - 84 = 0$. The remaining quadratic has

(A) two negative integral roots.

(B) negative complex roots.

(C) negative irrational roots.

(D) both positive and negative roots.

19. Solve for x: $\sqrt{x + 2} = x - 4$.

(A) -2

(B) 2

(C) 2, 7

(D) 7

20. What is the value of $(7 + 2i)(7 - 2i)$?

(A) 45

(B) 47

(C) 51

(D) 53

21. The characteristic of log .001 is

(A) 10^{-3}.

(B) -1.

(C) -3.

(D) 3.

22. If one of the roots is 0, the value of c in the equation $ax^2 + bx + c = 0$ is

(A) 0.

(B) a.

(C) b.

(D) Can be anything.

23. Which value cannot be a number in a geometric series?

(A) 0.5

(B) -1

(C) 0

(D) a fraction

24. A handyman's fee is based on the length of time, as follows:

- Up to 1 hour costs $50.

- From 1 to 2 hours costs $80 total, or an additional $30.

- Over 2 hours costs $80 plus $20 per 15-minute interval above 2 hours.

The piecewise function for this fee schedule with t given in hours is

$$f(t) = \begin{cases} \$50 & \text{if } t \le 1 \\ \$80 & \text{if } 1 < t \le 2 \\ \$80(t-1) & \text{if } t > 2 \end{cases}$$

If the handyman works for 90 minutes, what is the fee?

(A) $75

(B) $80

(C) $100

(D) $130

25. If $f(x) = x^2 + 4x - 2$, $f(-2) =$

(A) 10

(B) 2

(C) −6

(D) −14

26. The area of a rectangle is $A = lw$, where l is the length and w is the width, and the perimeter of a rectangle is $P = 2l + 2w$. Express the area of the rectangle as a function of the width if $P = 24$ inches.

(A) $f(w) = 12w - w^2$

(B) $f(w) = w(12 - w)$

(C) $f(w) = -w^2 + 12w$

(D) All of the above.

27. For distances of more than 1 mile, find the cost C as a function of distance x of riding x miles in a cab if the rate is $4.00 for the first mile or less and $1.50 for each additional quarter mile.

(A) $C = f(x) = \$4 + 4(x - 1)(\$1.50)$

(B) $C = f(x) = \$4 + 4x(\$1.50)$

(C) $C = f(x) = \$4 + 4(x + 1)(\$1.50)$

(D) $C = f(x) = \$4 + \dfrac{1}{4}(x - 1)(\$1.50)$

28. A periodic function $f(x)$ has which of the following properties?

(A) $f(x) = f(x + n)$

(B) Examples include sound waves, tides, and the basic trigonometric functions.

(C) Can look like

(D) All of the above.

29. Which of the following is NOT true for the graph of any polynomial function?

(A) It is continuous.

(B) It is smooth (e.g., no cusps).

(C) All roots cross the x-axis.

(D) The y-intercept is the constant term.

30. If you know the lengths of two sides of a triangle and an acute angle that isn't between the two given sides, can you find the length of the third side?

(A) Yes, if it is a right triangle.

(B) Yes, if the given angle is a base angle of an isosceles triangle.

(C) Yes, if the given angle is the vertex angle of an isosceles triangle.

(D) All of the above.

31. Triangle *ABC* is inscribed in a circle, whose diameter is *AB*. If $\angle A = 40°$, what is the measure of arc *AC*?

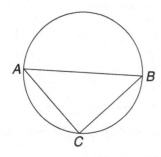

(A) 20°

(B) 40°

(C) 100°

(D) 260°

32. In scalene $\triangle ABC$, $AB = 6$, $AC = 10$, and *h* is the height to side *BC*. If this is all you know, which of the following statements is true about finding the area of $\triangle ABC$?

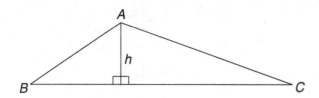

(A) To find the area, you also need the measure of $\angle C$.

(B) To find the area, you also need the measure of *BC*.

(C) You can find the area by using Heron's formula.

(D) You can find the area because the altitude forms similar triangles with a ratio of $AB : AC$.

33. Complete the proof below by choosing a reason for Statement 4.

Prove: The area of the kite *ABCD* with sides *a* and *b* and with diagonals d_1 and d_2 as shown below is $\dfrac{d_1 d_2}{2}$.

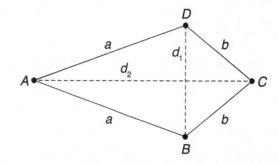

Statement	Reason
1. In kite *ABCD*, $d_1 \perp d_2$.	1. The diagonals of a kite are perpendicular to each other.
2. $AC = AC$, $a = a$, $b = b$	2. Identity
3. Area of $\triangle ADC = \dfrac{1}{2}\left(\dfrac{1}{2}d_1\right)d_2$	3. The area of a triangle is $A = \dfrac{1}{2}bh$
4. $\triangle ADC \cong \triangle ABC$	4. ?
5. Area(kite *ABCD*) = Area($\triangle ADC$) + Area($\triangle ABC$)	5. The whole is equal to the sum of its parts.
6. Area(kite *ABCD*) = $2\left(\dfrac{1}{2}\left(\dfrac{1}{2}d_1\right)d_2\right) = \dfrac{1}{2}d_1 d_2$	6. Substitution

The missing reason is best stated as:

(A) SAS.

(B) AAS.

(C) SSS.

(D) None of the above.

34. What kind of triangle is formed by two radii and the chord with endpoints at the points where the radii intersect the circle?

(A) Equilateral

(B) Isosceles

(C) Scalene

(D) Right

35. How many degrees are there in ∠*GKH* on the following figure?

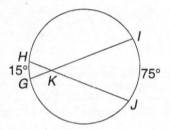

(A) 15°

(B) 30°

(C) 45°

(D) 75°

36. Lines *j* and *k* are parallel. Lines *m* and *n* are also parallel. Angle 10 is not equal to which of the following angles?

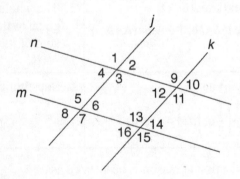

(A) ∠12

(B) ∠3

(C) ∠16

(D) ∠8

37. You ask your students to fold a rectangular sheet of paper in half lengthwise and to cut the resulting folded paper diagonally in half as shown.

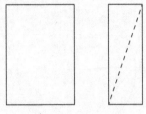

When they unfold paper, the resulting figure is a(n)

(A) isosceles triangle.

(B) equilateral triangle.

(C) scalene triangle.

(D) small rectangle.

38. In the figure below, which pairs of angles are alternate interior angles with respect to the transversal?

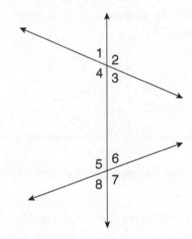

(A) ∠4 and ∠8

(B) ∠3 and ∠5

(C) ∠1 and ∠7

(D) ∠6 and ∠2

39. Three angles in a triangle are in the ratio 2 : 3 : 4. What is the smallest angle?

    (A) 40°

    (B) 20°

    (C) 60°

    (D) 80°

40. Fill in the blank: If a quadrilateral is inscribed in a circle, the opposite angles _____ add up to 180°.

    (A) always

    (B) sometimes

    (C) never

    (D) Can't tell.

41. You ask the class to construct a rhombus with one side 4 inches long and two consecutive angles of 45° and 135°. Which of the statements below is true?

    (A) All of the given information is necessary.

    (B) Both angles don't have to be given.

    (C) You have to know the length of an adjacent side.

    (D) You have to know the measure of the opposite angles.

42. Which of these solid figures is symmetrical with respect to a plane?

    (A) Sphere

    (B) Cube

    (C) Right circular cone

    (D) All of the above.

43. The dimensions in feet of a rectangular box are in an arithmetic progression with a common difference of 2 feet. If its volume is 48 cubic feet, what is the smallest dimension of the box?

    (A) 4

    (B) 2

    (C) 1

    (D) Cannot determine with the information given.

44. Find the area of a triangle with sides 7, 24, and 25 inches. (Heron's formula is $A = \sqrt{s(s-a)(s-b)(s-c)}$, where s is half the perimeter of the triangle.)

    (A) 28

    (B) 56

    (C) 84

    (D) Need to know one of the angles.

45. The general form of second-degree equations is $Ax^2 + Bxy + Cy^2 + Dx + Ey + F = 0$. Which term is omitted for conics?

    (A) Ax^2

    (B) Bxy

    (C) Cy^2

    (D) F

46. Find the angle θ that satisfies the equation $3(\sin\theta + 1) = \sin\theta + 4$ on the interval $[0°, 90°]$.

    (A) 0°

    (B) 30°

    (C) 45°

    (D) 60°

47. How does the graph of $y = \sin 2x + \pi$ differ from the $y = \sin x$ graph?

    (A) The period of the graph is doubled and the graph is shifted π units to the right.

    (B) The period of the graph is halved and the graph is shifted π units to the right.

    (C) The period of the graph is halved and the graph is shifted up by π units.

    (D) The period of the graph is doubled and the graph is shifted up by π units.

48. $\angle A$ and $\angle B$ are both acute angles, and $\angle B = \angle A + 30°$. If $\tan A = \cot B$, how many degrees are in $\angle A$?

    (A) 30°

    (B) 60°

    (C) 15°

    (D) Cannot tell from information given.

49. Find the numerical value of $\sin^2 x + \cos^2 x$ when $x = 30°$.

    (A) $\left(\dfrac{1}{2}\right)^2$

    (B) $\left(\dfrac{1}{2}\sqrt{3}\right)^2$

    (C) $\left(\dfrac{1}{2} + \dfrac{1}{2}\sqrt{3}\right)^2$

    (D) 1

50. If $\tan A = \dfrac{12}{5}$, find $\cot A$.

    (A) $\dfrac{12}{13}$

    (B) $\dfrac{5}{12}$

    (C) $\dfrac{5}{13}$

    (D) $\dfrac{12}{5}$

51. The perfect normal curve has all of these general properties EXCEPT:

    (A) the mean and median are equal.

    (B) the curve is symmetric about the mean.

    (C) the curve touches the x-axis above and below $\mu \pm 3\sigma$ and all y-values are positive.

    (D) the curve is continuous and assumes all values of x.

52. What is the median of the following dot plot?

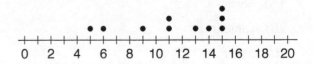

    (A) 12

    (B) 13

    (C) 14

    (D) 15

53. A sample of U.S. adults was asked how many days per week each read a daily newspaper (defined as reading at least one article besides sports or the comics). What is the average number of days per week these adults read the newspaper, rounded to the nearest whole number? The data are:

$$
\begin{array}{ccccccccc}
5 & 3 & 0 & 7 & 4 & 0 & 7 & 6 & 1 \\
0 & 1 & 3 & 2 & 3 & 2 & 0 & 5 &
\end{array}
$$

    (A) 2.88

    (B) 3

    (C) 3.5

    (D) 4

54. On a standardized normal curve, what percentage of the area under the curve is between $z = -1$ and $z = 1$?

   (A) 1.0%

   (B) 34.1%

   (C) 50.0%

   (D) 68.2%

55. Eighteen books are purchased at an average cost of $40 each, and 54 other books are purchased at an average cost of $50 each. What is the average cost of all the books?

   (A) $45.00

   (B) $47.50

   (C) $63.33

   (D) $190.00

56. Which of the following dot plots does NOT have a single mode?

   (A)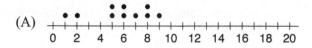

   (B)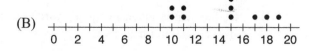

   (C)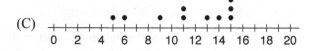

   (D)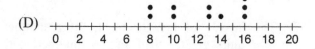

57. What is the probability of tossing a 1 or a 2 or a 3 or a 4 or a 5 or a 6 on a die?

   (A) $\dfrac{1}{6}$

   (B) $\left(\dfrac{1}{6}\right)^6$

   (C) 1

   (D) 6

58. If $f(x)$ and $g(x)$ are continuous functions for all real numbers and some of their values are defined by the following table, evaluate $\lim\limits_{x \to -1}\left(f(x) + 2g(x)\right)$.

x	$f(x)$	$g(x)$
-1	5	-7
0	-3	1
1	-1	3
2	0	-4

   (A) -2

   (B) -3

   (C) -9

   (D) 19

59. Given a position function of a particle, what does it mean when the velocity and acceleration are both negative (meaning in the opposite direction, or backward)?

   (A) The particle is moving forward and speeding up.

   (B) The particle is moving forward and slowing down.

   (C) The particle is moving backward and slowing down.

   (D) The particle is moving backward and speeding up.

60. Given the special limit $\lim\limits_{x \to 0}\left(\dfrac{\cos x - 1}{x}\right) = 0$, find the value of $\lim\limits_{x \to 0}\dfrac{\cos 3x - 1}{x}$.

    (A) 0

    (B) 3

    (C) $3x$

    (D) 1

61. What is the velocity of a particle whose position function is $s(t) = 2t^3 - 12t^2 + 20t$ when the acceleration is zero?

    (A) 0

    (B) 14

    (C) 20

    (D) negative

62. Log tan $x =$

    (A) $\dfrac{\log \sin x}{\log \cos x}$

    (B) $\log \sin x - \log \cos x$

    (C) $\log \cos x - \log \sin x$

    (D) $\dfrac{\log \cos x}{\log \sin x}$

63. What is the value of $\lim\limits_{x \to -\infty}\dfrac{7x^2 + 3}{5x^5 + x^3 + 7}$?

    (A) $-\infty$

    (B) $\dfrac{7}{5}$

    (C) 0

    (D) $\dfrac{3}{7}$

64. If $y = x^4 + 5x^3 + 8$, what is the value of $y'' = \dfrac{d^2 y}{dx^2}$ at $x = -2$?

    (A) -12

    (B) 32

    (C) 38

    (D) 38^2

65. Determine whether this argument is valid: All cities in the United States are led by mayors. Chicago has a mayor. Hence, Chicago is in the United States.

    (A) Yes, the conclusion is true.

    (B) Yes, the premises are true.

    (C) No, the conclusion does not follow from the premises.

    (D) No, the premises do not follow from the conclusion.

66. A rectangular lot contains 200 square yards. To determine how much it will cost to fence the lot at $25 a foot including labor, do we have enough information?

    (A) Yes, the size and cost are given.

    (B) No, the size is given in square yards but the cost is given in linear feet.

    (C) No, many rectangles of different sizes can have an area of 200 square yards.

    (D) No, it is not stated whether the cost includes material.

67. The inverse of the statement, "If a number n is d units greater than another number r, then $n = d + r$," is:

    (A) If a number n is not d units greater than another number r, then $n \neq d + r$.

    (B) If $n = d + r$, then n is d units greater than another number r.

    (C) If $n \neq d + r$, then n is d units less than another number r.

    (D) If a number n is d units greater than another number r, then $n = d + r$.

68. To help the class understand negative numbers, ask the class to give examples of how negative numbers are encountered in the real world. To prompt the discussion, which of the following models will most likely elicit class responses?

    (A) An outdoor thermometer

    (B) Loss and gain of yardage in a football game

    (C) Sea levels

    (D) All of the above.

69. An excellent means for a teacher to determine whether the concepts developed have been understood is oral exercises because

    (A) they hold the students' interest.

    (B) the teacher can use a wrong answer as a basis for clarification of a concept.

    (C) the students who don't get the concept will be engaged.

    (D) the teacher can learn the students' names.

70. The purpose of word problems is to

    (A) illustrate applications of the principles taught in a lesson.

    (B) show students that applications go hand-in-hand with mathematical theory.

    (C) point out real-world situations that can be solved mathematically.

    (D) All of the above.

71. Review of material is sometimes easier for mathematics than for other subjects because

    (A) math concepts build on prior knowledge more than concepts from humanities.

    (B) review by using drills helps the students to remember concepts.

    (C) review is helpful on a "bad" day because the students don't have to learn something new.

    (D) it makes the students feel smart.

72. Which of the following statements applies to manipulatives for math?

    (A) They are hands-on only in the classroom.

    (B) They should be restricted to remedial classes only.

    (C) They are best restricted to primary school students.

    (D) They can demonstrate or model abstract concepts.

73. If a student is making a lot of erasures when doing a geometric construction with a compass and straightedge, a possible reason could be that

    (A) the student started to do the work before understanding the instructions.

    (B) the hinge on the compass is either too loose or too tight.

    (C) the student is erasing the construction lines, which shouldn't be done.

    (D) (A) and/or (B) and/or (C) is true.

74. Examples of manipulatives that are NOT appropriate at the 6–12 level are a/an

    (A) Decahedral (10-sided) Dice.

    (B) abacus.

    (C) geometry template.

    (D) deck of playing cards.

75. Making connections within the structure of mathematics requires the ability to

    (A) communicate mathematics ideas clearly.

    (B) understand mathematics at a high level.

    (C) recite properties, rules, and theorems of mathematics.

    (D) understand math topics at the most basic level.

FTCE Mathematics 6–12
Practice Test 1 Answer Key

1.	(C)	26.	(D)	51.	(C)
2.	(D)	27.	(A)	52.	(A)
3.	(B)	28.	(D)	53.	(B)
4.	(C)	29.	(C)	54.	(D)
5.	(D)	30.	(D)	55.	(B)
6.	(B)	31.	(C)	56.	(A)
7.	(C)	32.	(B)	57.	(C)
8.	(A)	33.	(C)	58.	(C)
9.	(D)	34.	(B)	59.	(D)
10.	(C)	35.	(C)	60.	(A)
11.	(D)	36.	(B)	61.	(B)
12.	(C)	37.	(A)	62.	(B)
13.	(D)	38.	(B)	63.	(C)
14.	(A)	39.	(A)	64.	(A)
15.	(D)	40.	(D)	65.	(C)
16.	(A)	41.	(B)	66.	(C)
17.	(B)	42.	(D)	67.	(A)
18.	(A)	43.	(B)	68.	(D)
19.	(D)	44.	(C)	69.	(B)
20.	(D)	45.	(B)	70.	(D)
21.	(C)	46.	(B)	71.	(A)
22.	(A)	47.	(C)	72.	(D)
23.	(C)	48.	(A)	73.	(D)
24.	(B)	49.	(D)	74.	(B)
25.	(C)	50.	(B)	75.	(D)

PRACTICE TEST 1: ANSWERS AND EXPLANATIONS

1.   (C)

Follow the rule that we add from the right, and if the sum exceeds the base limit (1 in the binary, or base 2, system), we "carry" 1 to the place to the left. So

$$
\begin{array}{r}
1\ 1\ 1 \\
+\ 1\ 0 \\
\hline
1\ 0\ 0\ 1
\end{array}
$$

Here, the $1 + 0$ in the 2^0 column becomes a $\underline{1}$, then the 2^1 column has $1 + 1$, so its total is $\underline{0}$ with 1 carried over to the 2^2 column, which is then $1 + 1$, so its total is 0 with a 1 carried over to the 2^3 column. The correct answer is 1001, which equals 9 in the decimal system, but the question asks for binary system.

2.   (D)

"Not irrational" means "rational," which means the number can be expressed as an integer divided by a nonzero integer (a fraction). Answer choices (A) and (C) are clearly irrational. Although answer choice (B) is a fraction, the numerator is not an integer. Answer choice (D) is a bit of a trick, until you recognize that $\dfrac{\sqrt{8}}{\sqrt{2}} = \sqrt{\dfrac{8}{2}} = \sqrt{4} = 2$, which indeed is a rational number.

3.   (B)

Shame on you if you used your calculator and then wasted time matching it to one of the choices. Just looking at the factors, the answer must be even since there is one even number in the multiplication, and the answer must be negative because there is only one negative factor. Answer choice (B) is the only number that has both of these restrictions. Of course you could just use your calculator and match the answer to one of the choices, but that takes more time than using your knowledge of basic math.

4.   (C)

Rational numbers are numbers that can be expressed as fractions, and all whole numbers can be expressed as fractions with a denominator of 1. The other statements are false because counting numbers are $\{1, 2, 3, \ldots\}$; whole numbers are counting numbers plus 0; and integers are whole numbers plus their negatives. Answer choice (D) is false because 0 is not considered to be a positive integer.

5.   (D)

Answer choice (D) translates to the fact that s is either greater than or less than or equal to t, which is true for real numbers. Answer choice (A) doesn't include the case where $s = t$. Answer choices (B) and (C) don't allow for the case that $s < t$.

6.   (B)

You don't have to solve this problem to choose the correct answer. The fact that the sign of c is negative says that the roots must be of different signs, which eliminates answer choices (C) and (D). To check whether it is (A) or (B), substitute $x = 3$ into the equation to see if it works. Pick $x = 3$ instead of $x = -3$ because it is easier and faster to not have to bother with negatives. It works, so the correct answer is (B).

7.   (C)

This is a variation of the usual $\dfrac{\text{decrease}}{\text{original}} =$ percentage way of doing percentage decreases because we are asked to find the original price, given the percentage. But before you try to use algebra to solve this problem (which will work, as shown below), look at the answers. Answer choices (A) and (B) should be eliminated right away because they are less than the sale price, and common sense should tell you that $60 is way too much, so the answer must be (C) $20, but check it out to see that it is right. Twenty-five percent of $20 is $5, and $20 – $5 = $15.00.

For the algebra (although doing this problem by elimination is the way to go): Set up the equation, using x for the unknown original price: $\dfrac{\text{decrease}}{\text{original}} = \dfrac{x - \$15}{x} = 25\% = .25$. Then, by algebra, $x - \$15 = .25x$, which gives us $3x = \$60$, or $x = \$20$. Another way to think of this problem is that since the book was marked down by 25%, Mika paid 75% of the original price, so the equation is $.75x = \$15$, or $x = \dfrac{\$15}{.75} = \$20$.

8. (A)

Absolute value means the positive value of whatever is within the absolute value signs, so when an absolute value equation or inequality is evaluated, both the positive and negative values must be considered. This is an inequality, so if any operations include multiplication or division by a negative, the inequality sign has to be switched. The steps to solve this problem are as follows:

Put the inequality on one side by adding 4 and dividing by 3 on both sides of $3|2x - 1| - 4 > 11$, to get $|2x - 1| > 5$. Then solve the two cases within the absolute value sign, one for positive and one for negative.

$2x - 1 > 5$ then add 1 to each side	$-(2x - 1) > 5$ then remove parentheses to get
$2x > 6$ then divide by 2	$-2x + 1 > 5$ then subtract 1 from each side
$x > 3$	$-2x > 4$ then divide by -2 (remember to switch $>$ sign)
	$x < -2$

The answer is thus $x < -2$ or $x > 3$.

9. (D)

Answer choices (A) and (B) are based on a gallon, not a quart. Also, each glass is holding only $\dfrac{5}{6} \times 6 = 5$ ounces of milk, and there are three glasses. The calculation is $32 - 3(5) = 17$ ounces left.

10. (C)

Since the wind is directly opposite the direction of the airplane's path, the resultant airspeed is cut to $(315 - 15.1) = 299.5$. To travel 900 miles at 299.5 miles per hour takes 3.005 hours, which is 3.01 hours rounded to the nearest hundredth of an hour.

11. (D)

If a product equals zero, at least one of the factors must equal zero. Since the quantity in brackets is clearly not 0, x must equal 0.

12. (C)

For terms to be combined, they must be like terms, which means they differ only in their numerical coefficients. Their unknowns, including their powers, must match. For the given expression, $2ax^3y$, that means only terms that contain x^3y and no other variables or different powers of the given variables.

13. (D)

Use the given conversion formula, $F = \dfrac{9}{5}C + 32$, for $C = -40°$. Then $F = \dfrac{9}{5}(-40) + 32 = -72 + 32 = -40$. A key part of this solution is recognizing that "Celsius temperature of 40 below 0" translates into $-40°C$. Note that $-40°F = -40°C$, the only point at which the two scales have the same numerical value.

14. (A)

The next three answer choices are rational for the following reasons: (B) $\sqrt[4]{\frac{81}{16}} = \frac{3}{2}$; (C) $\sqrt[5]{-32} = -2$; (D) $\sqrt{49} = 7$.

15. (D)

The term "system of equations" means the equations have the same solution. You don't have to check every pair of values to answer this question. Only answer choice (D) holds for the first equation, $x + y = 3$, and a check shows that it also holds for the second equation.

16. (A)

Use the definition $y = \log_b x$ if and only if $b^y = x$. So just determine what x, y, and b are from the given equation: $x = \frac{1}{25}$, $y = -2$, and $b = 5$. Thus, $\log_5\left(\frac{1}{25}\right) = -2$.

17. (B)

The polynomial is of degree 5, so it cannot have more than 5 roots. Complex roots always come in pairs, so there cannot be an odd number of complex roots. The question does not ask what the roots actually are.

18. (A)

If $(x - 6)$ is a factor, then $x = 6$ is a root. To find the remaining quadratic, divide the given third-degree polynomial by the given root (synthetic division works well here).

$$
\begin{array}{r|rrrr}
6 & 2 & 4 & -82 & -84 \\
  & \downarrow & 12 & 96 & 84 \\
\hline
  & 2 & 16 & 14 & 0
\end{array}
$$

(Since the remainder is 0, 6 is indeed a root.) The remaining polynomial is found from the quotient to be $(2x^2 + 16x + 14) = (2x + 2)(x + 7)$, which indicates two

negative roots, eliminating answer choice (D). The quadratic is of the form $ax^2 + bx + c$, for which the discriminant is positive (so no complex roots) and a perfect square (so rational roots), $\sqrt{b^2 - 4ac} = \sqrt{(16)^2 - 4(2)(14)} = \sqrt{256 - 112} = \sqrt{144} = 12$ so the roots are negative integers. Answer choice (A) is correct.

19. (D)

This equation is simple enough that you should just plug the numbers into the original equation to determine the correct answer choice. Answer choice (A) yields $0 = -6$, and answer choice (B) yields $2 = -2$, so they are both eliminated, as is answer choice (C) because it includes $x = 2$. Check answer choice (D) to be sure: $3 = 3$, so it is correct. On a question containing a radical equation and some answer choices, it is less time-consuming to just check each answer choice—remember that more than one choice may be correct, especially if an answer choice is "all of the above," or as in this case, some choices might be only partial answers.

20. (D)

The answer is the difference of two squares since this is the product of a complex term and its complex conjugate. The square of 7^2 is 49, and $(2i)^2 = (4)(-1) = -4$. Therefore, the answer is $(7 + 2i)(7 - 2i) = 7^2 - (2i)^2 = 49 - (-4) = 49 + 4 = 53$.

21. (C)

The characteristic is the number in the log before the decimal point. Rewrite log .001 as log 10^{-3}, so log .001 $= -3$, with characteristic -3.

22. (A)

Substitute the value 0 of the root into the quadratic equation $ax^2 + bx + c = 0$ to get $c = 0$. This is true no matter what the values of a and b are.

23. (C)

A geometric series is defined by ratios between elements. Therefore, 0 cannot be a number in a geometric series because we cannot divide by 0.

24. (B)

Since 90 minutes is more than 1 hour and less than 2 hours $1 < t \leq 2$, it is $80.

25. (C)

$f(-2)$ represents the value of $f(x)$ when x is replaced by -2. So $f(-2) = (-2)^2 + 4(-2) - 2 = -6$.

26. (D)

$24 = 2l + 2w$, or $12 = l + w$, or $l = 12 - w$. Substitute this into the area formula: $A = lw = (12 - w)w = 12w - w^2$, which is the equivalent to answer choices (B) and (C).

27. (A)

There are several ways to find the correct answer, but in a multiple-choice test, it is often best to find the correct answer by elimination. Think of a scenario for which the answer is obvious, such as going 2 miles, which should cost $4.00 for the first mile plus $6.00 for the second mile (four quarter miles), or $4.00 + 4($1.50) = $10.00. Check each answer choice, remembering that x is the total number of miles, or $x = 2$. Only answer choice (A) gives the correct fare.

28. (D)

All answer choices pertain to period functions: (A) is a typical definition of a periodic function with period n, (B) lists common functions with periodic repeats, and (C) has a periodic repeat (even though it is not continuous—see the periodic tangent function, for example).

29. (C)

Answer choice (C) isn't true for imaginary roots; all *real* roots cross the x-axis. Answer choices (A), (B), and (D) are true. The graphs of all polynomial functions are smooth and continuous with no "corners" or cusps, and the y-intercept occurs when $x = 0$, so it is the value of the constant term.

30. (D)

Given two sides of a triangle and the included angle, there is only one triangle that can be drawn because length of the third side (connecting the end points of the given sides) cannot change. In answer choices (A), (B), and (C), the included angle isn't given, but it can be found easily, since the total number of degrees in a triangle is 180°. If the triangle is a right triangle, the second acute angle is complementary to the given acute angle; if the triangle is an isosceles triangle, the base angles are equal, so the third angle can be found by subtracting their sum from 180°; or, in an isosceles triangle, the base angles can be found by subtracting the given vertex angle from 180° and taking half of the difference. So in all three cases, a basic calculation will give you all three angles and enough information to find the third side. This may involve trigonometry, but the question is *whether*, not how, it can be done.

31. (C)

The measure of an arc is double its inscribed angle. If $\angle A = 40°$, then $\overset{\frown}{BC} = 80°$, and since $\overset{\frown}{ACB} = 180°$ (because it is a semicircle), $\overset{\frown}{AC} = 100°$. Although $\overset{\frown}{ABC} = 260°$, remember that if there are two arcs with the same endpoints, the major arc must be named by inserting an intermediate point, so $\overset{\frown}{AC} \neq \overset{\frown}{ABC}$.

32. (B)

Answer choice (A) is false because even if you knew the measure of $\angle C$, with two known sides you need to know the angle *between* them to determine the size of a triangle. Answer choice (B) is true because if you know the lengths of three sides of a triangle, Heron's formula gives the area. Answer choice (C) is false because you don't have the length of the third side. Answer choice (D) is false because the two triangles formed are not proportional.

33. (C)

The triangles are congruent because the three sides of one are equal to the corresponding three sides of the other, or SSS.

34. (B)

Sketch the circle, if necessary.

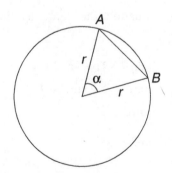

Since all radii of a circle are equal, the triangle formed is an isosceles triangle. Without knowing the

central angle α, we do not know anything about chord AB, so we cannot say that it is an equilateral triangle.

35. (C)

$\angle GKH$ is an interior angle formed by two chords, so its measure is half the sum of the intercepted arcs between the chords.

$$\angle GKH = \frac{1}{2}\left(\overset{\frown}{GH} + \overset{\frown}{JI}\right) = \frac{1}{2}(15° + 75°) = 45°$$

36. (B)

When two parallel lines are crossed by a transversal, the resulting angles are either equal or supplementary. Angle 10 is equal to angles 2, 4, 6, 8, 10, 12, 14, and 16, which all are corresponding angles and therefore equal to each other. Of course, equal angles do not have to be adjacent.

37. (A)

A three-sided figure (triangle) is formed. The triangle will be isosceles because the diagonal that was cut forms two equal sides of the triangle.

38. (B)

Alternate interior angles are on alternate sides of the transversal and are interior to the two intersected lines. A transversal is a line that intersects two coplanar lines at two different points; the lines don't have to be parallel.

39. (A)

The total angle measure in a triangle is 180°, so the equation for three angles with a ratio of 2 : 3 : 4 is $2x + 3x + 4x = 180°$. Solving for x yields $x = 20°$ but the question asks for the smallest angle, which is $2x = 40°$.

40. (A)

Sketch the figure.

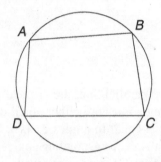

Each inscribed angle is equal to half the intercepted arc. Opposite angles intercept two arcs that together form the whole circle, so their sum is equal to half the whole circle. In this circle, for example, $\angle ABC + \angle CDA = \frac{1}{2}(\overset{\frown}{CDA}) + \frac{1}{2}(\overset{\frown}{ABC}) = \frac{1}{2}$ (whole circle) = 180°.

41. (B)

A rhombus has the following properties: (1) all four sides are equal, (2) opposite angles are equal, (3) consecutive angles are supplementary. Therefore, to construct a rhombus you only have to know one side and one angle, and all the other measures can be figured out.

42. (D)

The question doesn't specify where the plane cuts the figure. All of the solid figures mentioned are symmetrical with respect to a plane through the center of the figure and centers of the bases.

43. (B)

"An arithmetic progression with a common difference of 2 feet" means the three sides have a dimensional difference of 2. Assuming the shortest side is x, then the volume of the cube is $x(x + 2)(x + 4) = 48$ cubic feet. Substituting the answer choices into this equation, only $x = 2$ is a solution.

44. (C)

$$A = \sqrt{s(s - a)(s - b)(s - c)}$$
$$= \sqrt{28(28 - 7)(28 - 24)(28 - 25)}$$
$$= \sqrt{28(21)(4)(3)} = \sqrt{7056} = 84 \text{ square units}$$

The calculation is done quickly on the calculator. It is not necessary to use Heron's formula, however, because this is a right triangle ($7^2 + 24^2 = 25^2$, so the area is half the product of the legs: $\left(\frac{1}{2}(7)(24)\right) = 84$, an easier calculation, if you check first to see whether the given triangle is a right triangle (or recognize it as a Pythagorean triple or one of its multiples).

45. (B)

There is no xy term in the general equation for conics, which is $Ax^2 + Cy^2 + Dx + Ey + F = 0$.

46. (B)

Treat this equation the same as the quadratic $3(s + 1) = s + 4$:

$$3(\sin\theta + 1) = \sin\theta + 4$$
$$3\sin\theta + 3 = \sin\theta + 4$$
$$2\sin\theta = 1$$
$$\sin\theta = \frac{1}{2}$$

Then $\theta = 30°$.

47. (C)

The basic graph of a sin curve is $y = A \sin B(x - C) + D$, with $A + B + C + D = 1$. Each of these variables has an effect on the basic graph. Specifically, B, the coefficient of x, changes the period by a factor of $\frac{1}{B}$, and D is a vertical shift that raises the graph by D units if $D > 0$. Here, B is 2 so the period is halved, and D equals π, even though it is an unusual value for the y-axis. Without parentheses, π is not a phase shift, as it would have been if the graph were $y = \sin(2x + \pi)$.

48. (A)

If the function of one acute angle equals the cofunction of another acute angle, the two angles are complementary. Therefore, $\angle A$ and $\angle B$ are complementary, and

$$\angle A + \angle B = \angle A + (\angle A + 30°) = 90°$$

$$2\angle A + 30° = 90°$$

$$2\angle A = 60°$$

$$\angle A = 30°$$

49. (D)

You should recognize the Pythagorean identity, $\sin^2 x + \cos^2 x = 1$. If you don't recognize the identity, use $\sin 30° = \frac{1}{2}$ and $\cos 30° = \frac{\sqrt{3}}{2}$ (the 30°-60°-90°, or $1 - 2 - \sqrt{3}$ triangle), to get $\left(\frac{1}{2}\right)^2 + \left(\frac{\sqrt{3}}{2}\right)^2 = \frac{1}{4} + \frac{3}{4} = 1$. The answer is always 1, which is why it is called an identity.

50. (B)

cot A is the reciprocal of tan A.

$$\cot A = \frac{1}{\tan A} = \frac{1}{\frac{12}{5}} = \frac{5}{12}.$$

51. (C)

The fact that makes answer choice (C) false is that the curve never touches the x-axis. The x-axis is an asymptote.

52. (A)

The median is the value for which the number of data points above it is equal to the number of data points below it. In this dot plot, 5 data points are above the value of 12, and 5 are below it. Note that the median does not have to be a member of the set of values.

53. (B)

To get the average, add the 17 numbers and divide by 17 to get 2.88, which rounds to 3 days. Even though some of the numbers were 0, they still get included in the count of 17.

54. (D)

This is the area under the graph one standard deviation below to one standard deviation above the mean. It is $2 \times (34.1\%) = 68.2\%$.

55. (B)

The average cost equals $\dfrac{\text{Total cost}}{\text{Total number of books}} = \dfrac{(18 \times \$40) + (54 \times \$50)}{(18 + 54)}$. Use the calculator, or because every term is divisible by 18, the problem reduces to $\dfrac{\$40 + (3 \times \$50)}{1 + 3} = \dfrac{\$190}{4} = \$47.50$. Clearly, answer choices (C) and (D) are wrong because the average cost of the total cannot be higher than the individual costs.

56. (A)

The mode shows the value with the maximum number of data points. Answer choice (A) has three modes (5, 6, and 8), each with a frequency of 2; for answer choices (B), (C), and (D), the modes each clearly have a frequency of 3, even though the modes are not the same.

57. (C)

Recognizing that these are all the possibilities, the probability is 1, or 100%. Or, by calculating this, the probability of tossing any particular number on a die (as long as the number is 1 through 6) is $\frac{1}{6}$. Each number has a probability of $\frac{1}{6}$, and this is an "or" situation, so we add the probabilities: Pr(1 or 2 or 3 or 4 or 5 or 6) = Pr(1) + Pr(2) + Pr(3) + Pr(4) + Pr(5) + Pr(6) = $\frac{1}{6} + \frac{1}{6} + \frac{1}{6} + \frac{1}{6} + \frac{1}{6} + \frac{1}{6} = 1$.

58. (C)

Since the limit of a sum equals the sum of the limits, and the limit of a product equals the product of the limits, we have (since $\lim_{x \to -1} 2 = 2$),

$$\lim_{x \to -1}\left(f(x) + 2g(x)\right) = \lim_{x \to -1}\left(f(x)\right) + \lim_{x \to -1}\left(2g(x)\right)$$
$$= \lim_{x \to -1}\left(f(x)\right) + 2\lim_{x \to -1}\left(g(x)\right)$$

Now find $f(x)$ and $g(x)$ for $x = -1$ from the given table to get

$$\lim_{x \to -1}\left(f(x)\right) + 2\lim_{x \to -1}\left(g(x)\right) = f(-1) + 2g(-1)$$
$$= 5 + 2(-7) = -9.$$

59. (D)

Keep in mind that velocity is the first derivative of the position function, so it is the change in position with time, and likewise, acceleration is the change in velocity with time. A negative velocity indicates that the parti-cle is moving in the opposite direction (backward), and a negative acceleration is acceleration in the opposite direction (backward as well), which is actually speeding up the particle since the acceleration is increasing the velocity in the direction it was going (here, backward). (Note that if acceleration is opposite to velocity, the particle is slowed down.)

60. (A)

To use the special limit, the denominator x must be the same as the argument of the cosine function (which is $3x$), so just multiply the limit by $\frac{3}{3}$, which equals 1 and doesn't change the value. Then we have

$$\lim_{x \to 0}\frac{\cos 3x - 1}{x} = \lim_{x \to 0}\left(\frac{3}{3}\right)\left(\frac{\cos 3x - 1}{x}\right)$$
$$= 3\lim_{x \to 0}\left(\frac{\cos 3x - 1}{3x}\right) = 3(0) = 0.$$

61. (B)

When acceleration is zero $s''(t) = 0$. From the position function, velocity is $s' = 6t^2 - 12t + 20$ and acceleration is $s''(t) = 12t - 12$. If acceleration is zero, then $12t - 12 = 0$ and $t = 1$. Then evaluate the velocity at $t = 1$: $s' = 6t^2 - 12t + 20 = 6 - 12 + 20 = 14$.

62. (B)

The logarithm of the quotient of two numbers is equal to the logarithm of the dividend minus the logarithm of the divisor. Since $\tan x = \frac{\sin x}{\cos x}$, $\log \tan x = \log \sin x - \log \cos x$.

63. (C)

Since the degree of the numerator is smaller than that of the denominator, the limit is 0. The rule applies whether x approaches $+\infty$ or $-\infty$.

64. (A)

The first derivative is $y' = \dfrac{dy}{dx} = 4x^3 + 15x^2$, and the second derivative is then $y'' = \dfrac{d^2y}{dx^2} = 12x^2 + 30x$. Thus, at $x = -2$, $y'' = 12(-2)^2 + 30(-2) = -12$.

65. (C)

The argument is not valid because the conclusion does not follow from the premises, even though both premises are true.

66. (C)

One more piece of information, such as the length or width, is needed.

67. (A)

Note that the inverse doesn't have to be true, even though the original statement is true. Here it is true, though. Note that (D) is just a repeat of the original conditional statement.

68. (D) All of the above.

69. (B)

Not only will the teacher be able to clarify the concepts, any misunderstandings will be corrected with oral exercises. Of course, the presentation of these exercises has to be done in a manner that will encourage other students to participate and not be afraid to ask questions.

70. (D)

Word problems can pose a problem for students, but by showing their usefulness in everyday life situations and approaching word problems as a puzzle to be solved, teachers can overcome students' resistance to this method of questioning.

71. (A)

Much of the review in math "comes with the territory" in that, for example, a student cannot do division without a knowledge of subtraction. The logical progression of math topics incorporates prior knowledge at all levels.

72. (D)

Perhaps the most popular manipulative for the high school student is the graphing calculator, which can analyze graphs of functions. Answer choice (A) is wrong because manipulatives are also offered virtually. Answer choices (B) and (C) are incorrect because manipulatives can be effective at any grade level or cognitive level, although more manipulatives are available at the lower levels.

73. (D)

The reason for the excess erasures can be due to any of the explanations above, among others, such as sloppy work.

74. (B)

The use of an abacus is recommended for grades K–3. By sixth grade, the students have the idea of "carrying" in addition of columns of numbers. Even though that is not the only advantage of using the abacus, it is significant.

75. (D)

Understanding the how and why of each nuance within a topic and staying on track allows one to make the connections required to understand the topic. Although answer choice (A) brings up an important skill, the question isn't asking about communication, just understanding. These connections may be, and usually are, at a low level, so answer choice (B) isn't correct, and recitation doesn't necessitate understanding, so answer choice (C) is wrong.

Practice Test 1 Competency Coverage

The list below identifies which FTCE Math competencies the questions on Practice Test 1 address. Use this list to focus on those topics where you need more review.

Basic Math Review

Questions 1, 2, 3, 4, 5, 14

Algebra

Questions 2, 6, 7, 8, 9, 10, 11, 12, 13, 14, 15, 17, 19, 20, 22, 29, 39, 44

Advanced Algebra

Questions 16, 17, 18, 19, 20, 21, 23, 43, 62

Functions

Questions 24, 25, 26, 27, 28, 29

Geometry

Questions 26, 30, 31, 32, 33, 34, 35, 36, 37, 38, 39, 40, 41, 42, 43, 44, 66

Coordinate Geometry

Questions 32, 44, 45

Trigonometry

Questions 46, 47, 48, 49, 50, 62

Statistics and Probability

Questions 51, 52, 53, 54, 55, 56, 57

Calculus

Questions 29, 58, 59, 60, 61, 63, 64

Mathematical Reasoning

Questions 65, 66, 67, 72

Instruction and Assessment

Questions 37, 41, 66, 68, 69, 70, 71, 72, 73, 74, 75

Note that the solutions to some problems involve more than one competency. The topic labeled "Basic Math Review" is not an FTCE-listed competency.

FTCE Mathematics 6–12
Practice Test 2

FTCE Mathematics 6–12
Practice Test 2 Answer Sheet

1. (A) (B) (C) (D)
2. (A) (B) (C) (D)
3. (A) (B) (C) (D)
4. (A) (B) (C) (D)
5. (A) (B) (C) (D)
6. (A) (B) (C) (D)
7. (A) (B) (C) (D)
8. (A) (B) (C) (D)
9. (A) (B) (C) (D)
10. (A) (B) (C) (D)
11. (A) (B) (C) (D)
12. (A) (B) (C) (D)
13. (A) (B) (C) (D)
14. (A) (B) (C) (D)
15. (A) (B) (C) (D)
16. (A) (B) (C) (D)
17. (A) (B) (C) (D)
18. (A) (B) (C) (D)
19. (A) (B) (C) (D)
20. (A) (B) (C) (D)
21. (A) (B) (C) (D)
22. (A) (B) (C) (D)
23. (A) (B) (C) (D)
24. (A) (B) (C) (D)
25. (A) (B) (C) (D)

26. (A) (B) (C) (D)
27. (A) (B) (C) (D)
28. (A) (B) (C) (D)
29. (A) (B) (C) (D)
30. (A) (B) (C) (D)
31. (A) (B) (C) (D)
32. (A) (B) (C) (D)
33. (A) (B) (C) (D)
34. (A) (B) (C) (D)
35. (A) (B) (C) (D)
36. (A) (B) (C) (D)
37. (A) (B) (C) (D)
38. (A) (B) (C) (D)
39. (A) (B) (C) (D)
40. (A) (B) (C) (D)
41. (A) (B) (C) (D)
42. (A) (B) (C) (D)
43. (A) (B) (C) (D)
44. (A) (B) (C) (D)
45. (A) (B) (C) (D)
46. (A) (B) (C) (D)
47. (A) (B) (C) (D)
48. (A) (B) (C) (D)
49. (A) (B) (C) (D)
50. (A) (B) (C) (D)

51. (A) (B) (C) (D)
52. (A) (B) (C) (D)
53. (A) (B) (C) (D)
54. (A) (B) (C) (D)
55. (A) (B) (C) (D)
56. (A) (B) (C) (D)
57. (A) (B) (C) (D)
58. (A) (B) (C) (D)
59. (A) (B) (C) (D)
60. (A) (B) (C) (D)
61. (A) (B) (C) (D)
62. (A) (B) (C) (D)
63. (A) (B) (C) (D)
64. (A) (B) (C) (D)
65. (A) (B) (C) (D)
66. (A) (B) (C) (D)
67. (A) (B) (C) (D)
68. (A) (B) (C) (D)
69. (A) (B) (C) (D)
70. (A) (B) (C) (D)
71. (A) (B) (C) (D)
72. (A) (B) (C) (D)
73. (A) (B) (C) (D)
74. (A) (B) (C) (D)
75. (A) (B) (C) (D)

FTCE Mathematics 6–12 Practice Test 2

TIME: 150 minutes (2 hours and 30 minutes)
75 questions

> **Directions: Read each item and select the best response.**

1. The zeros of a quadratic equation are

   (A) the points where the graph of the equation crosses the x axis.

   (B) the y values for which the quadratic equation has a value of 0.

   (C) the x values for which the quadratic equation has a value of 0.

   (D) None of the above.

2. A well-known geometry equation shows that the volume of a cylinder (V), varies jointly with the height (h) of the cylinder and the square of its radius (r^2). If the volume of a cylinder that is 15 cm high with a radius of 10 cm is 1500π cm^3, what is the height of a 750π-cm^3 cylinder with a 10-cm radius?

   (A) 15 cm

   (B) 10 cm

   (C) 7.5 cm

   (D) 5 cm

3. All three sets of rational numbers shown below do NOT have which property?

   $$A = \{0,1\}, B = \{-1,0,+1\}, C = \left\{-\frac{1}{2}, \frac{0}{2}, +\frac{1}{2}\right\}$$

   (A) Closure property of addition

   (B) Commutative property of addition

   (C) Associative property of addition

   (D) Identity property of addition

4. A water tank is holding 215 gallons of water. It has two outlets: one has a flow rate of 5 gallons per minute, and the other has a flow rate of 8 gallons per minute. How many minutes would it take to empty the tank if both outlets are open? (Round your answer to the nearest tenth of a minute.)

   (A) 43.0

   (B) 26.9

   (C) 16.5

   (D) 69.6

5. A scout troop hiked 10 miles in 5 hours. If they hiked at a steady pace, approximately how many kilometers had they traveled after the first 4 hours? (1 km = 0.62 mi)

    (A) 12.9 km

    (B) 8.0 km

    (C) 6.2 km

    (D) 5.0 km

6. Find the equation of the line passing through (2, 0) with a slope of –2.

    (A) $y = -2x + 2$

    (B) $y = 4x - 2$

    (C) $y = 2x + 4$

    (D) $y = -2x + 4$

7. The volume V of a right circular cylinder is given by $V = \pi r^2 h$, where r is the radius of the base and h is the height. Rewrite this as a formula for h.

    (A) $h = V + \pi r^2$

    (B) $r = \sqrt{\dfrac{V}{\pi h}}$

    (C) $h = \dfrac{V}{\pi r^2}$

    (D) $h = V - \pi r^2$

8. A positive integer power of the imaginary unit i can have the value of

    (A) -1

    (B) $-i$

    (C) 1

    (D) All of the above.

9. Which of the following lines are perpendicular to $3y = 8x - 6$?

    (A) $8y = -3x + 16$

    (B) $8y = 3x - 16$

    (C) $3y = -8x + 6$

    (D) $6y = 16x - 12$

10. The product of two consecutive positive odd integers is 195. What equation could give the answer?

    (A) $x^2 - 2x = -195$

    (B) $x^2 - x = 195$

    (C) $x^2 + 2x = 195$

    (D) $x^2 + x = 195$

11. Simplify $\ln\left(\dfrac{1}{e^x}\right)$.

    (A) e^x

    (B) e^{-x}

    (C) x

    (D) $-x$

12. Evaluate $\log_8 \sqrt{8}$.

    (A) $-\dfrac{1}{2}$

    (B) $\dfrac{1}{2}$

    (C) $-\dfrac{1}{8}$

    (D) $\dfrac{1}{8}$

13. The complex fraction $\dfrac{a^2 - \frac{1}{a}}{a + \frac{1}{a} + 1}$ simplifies in lowest terms to

   (A) $\dfrac{\frac{a^3-1}{a}}{\frac{a^2+1+a}{a}}$.

   (B) $\dfrac{a^3 - 1}{a + \frac{1}{a} + 1}$.

   (C) $a - 1$.

   (D) It is already in lowest terms.

14. Admission into an exhibit is restricted to children at least 11 years old and at most 15 years old. Which of the following mathematical descriptions states the age requirement for admission?

   (A) $x \geq 11$

   (B) $x \leq 15$

   (C) $x \geq 11$ or $x \leq 15$

   (D) $x \geq 11$ and $x \leq 15$

15. Solve for x: $\sqrt{x + 6} = x + 4$.

   (A) $-2, -5$

   (B) -2

   (C) $-2, 5$

   (D) -5

16. Which operation is NOT possible when $R = \begin{bmatrix} a & b \\ c & d \end{bmatrix}$, $S = \begin{bmatrix} e & f \\ g & h \end{bmatrix}$, and $T = \begin{bmatrix} i & j & k \\ l & m & n \end{bmatrix}$?

   (A) $R + S$

   (B) $S + R$

   (C) $R \times T$

   (D) $T \times R$

17. If $\log x^2 = 0.6522$, then $\log 10x$ is

   (A) 1.3261.

   (B) 3.2610.

   (C) 2.3044.

   (D) 1.3044.

18. Simplify $10^{\log(5x^2)}$.

   (A) $5x^2$

   (B) $10(5x^2)$

   (C) $\log(5x^2)$

   (D) 10^{5x^2}

19. For the function $y = f(x) = \log_4(x + 1)$, what is the asymptote of the graph?

   (A) $x = 0$

   (B) $y = 0$

   (C) $x = -1$

   (D) $y = -1$

20. Which type of graph describes the following set of points?

   $$\left\{ (1,\ 9),\ (2,\ 3),\ (3,\ 1),\ \left(4, \frac{1}{3}\right),\ \left(5, \frac{1}{9}\right),\ \left(6, \frac{1}{27}\right) \right\}$$

   (A) Linear

   (B) Exponential

   (C) Quadratic

   (D) Cannot tell

21. The statement, "when x is less than six, y is half of x; when x is in the range from six to ten, y is twice x; and when x is greater than ten, y is two more than x," can be written for y as a function of x as:

(A) $y = f(x) = \begin{cases} \frac{1}{2}x & \text{if } x < 6 \\ 2x & \text{if } 6 \le x \le 10 \\ x+2 & \text{if } x > 10 \end{cases}$

(B) $y = f(x) = \begin{cases} \frac{1}{2}x & \text{if } x < 6 \\ 2x & \text{if } 6 < x < 10 \\ x+2 & \text{if } x > 10 \end{cases}$

(C) $y = f(x) = \begin{cases} 2x & \text{if } x < 6 \\ \frac{1}{2}x & \text{if } 6 \le x \le 10 \\ x+2 & \text{if } x > 10 \end{cases}$

(D) $y = f(x) = \begin{cases} \frac{1}{2}x & \text{if } x \le 6 \\ 2x & \text{if } 6 \le x \le 10 \\ x+2 & \text{if } x \ge 10 \end{cases}$

22. Express the time T in hours required for a journey of 100 miles as a function of the speed x in miles per hour.

(A) $x = \dfrac{100}{T}$

(B) $f(x) = 100T$

(C) $T = f(x) = \dfrac{100}{x}$

(D) $T = f(x) = 100x$

23. Which of the following operations determines whether a function $g(x)$ is the inverse of $f(x)$?

(A) $f(x) \times g(x) = x$

(B) $f(x) + g(x) = x$

(C) $f(g(x)) = x$

(D) They both pass the vertical line test.

24. What is the equation for the transformation of $y = f(x) = x^2$ shown as a dashed curve below?

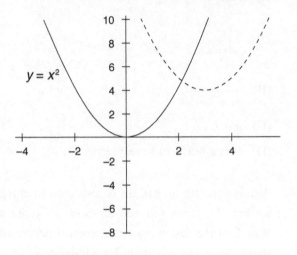

(A) $y + 4 = (x - 3)^2$

(B) $y = (x - 3)^2 + 4$

(C) $y = (x - 4)^2 + 3$

(D) $y = (x + 4)^2 + 3$

25. The upper curve in the graph below is a transformation of the lower graph for $f(x) = x^2$. What is its equation?

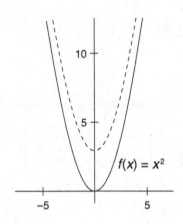

(A) $g(x) = 3x^2$

(B) $g(x) = \dfrac{1}{3}x^2$

(C) $g(x) = (x + 3)^2$

(D) $g(x) = x^2 + 3$

26. If you are given the measures of two sides of an isosceles triangle and one of the angles, what additional information is critical to determine all of the measures in the triangle?

   (A) Whether the angle is the vertex angle or a base angle

   (B) Whether the sides are the legs of the triangle

   (C) Both (A) and (B)

   (D) Neither (A) nor (B)

27. Triangle *ABC* is inscribed in a circle, whose diameter is *AB*. If $\angle A = 45°$, what is the measure of $\angle B$?

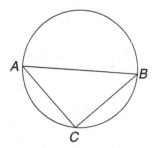

   (A) 90°

   (B) 45°

   (C) 135°

   (D) Not enough information given to answer the question.

28. In scalene $\triangle ABC$, $AB = 6$ and $BC = 10$. What are the restrictions on side AC?

   (A) $(AC)^2 = (AB)^2 + (BC)^2$

   (B) $AC > 4$

   (C) $AC < 16$

   (D) $4 < AC < 16$

29. Line *MP* joins the midpoints of two sides of $\triangle ABC$ and is parallel to *BC* as shown. Which of the following statements is FALSE. (Choose *all* that apply.)

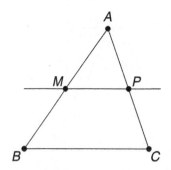

   (A) $\triangle AMP \sim \triangle ABC$

   (B) $\overline{MP} = \frac{1}{2}\overline{BC}$

   (C) $\overline{AP} = \overline{PC}$

   (D) $\triangle APM \sim \triangle ABC$

30. A triangle is drawn inside a circle with one vertex at the center and the other two vertices on the circle. If all three sides of the triangle are 8 units long, what is the central angle?

   (A) 30°

   (B) 45°

   (C) 60°

   (D) Cannot tell from the information given.

31. An equilateral triangle is drawn inside a circle with the center of the circle being one of the vertices, and the other vertices on the circle. Which statement is true?

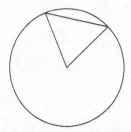

(A) The arcs formed are all equal.

(B) The arcs formed measure 60° and 300°.

(C) All three arcs formed are 120° each.

(D) The chord equals half a radius.

32. A regular polygon is composed of equilateral triangles. What kind of regular polygon can it be?

(A) Square

(B) Trapezoid

(C) Hexagon

(D) 13-sided polygon

33. Hector has a piece of leather with dimensions 14 inches by 30 inches. He wants to cut out a square 6 inches on a side and a circle as shown in the sketch. How much waste, in square inches, will he have? (Round your answer to the nearest whole number.)

(A) 36

(B) 154

(C) 230

(D) 420

34. Every side of a polygon inscribed in a circle must be a

(A) chord.

(B) radius.

(C) secant.

(D) tangent.

35.

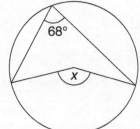

In the figure above, what is the value of x?

(A) 34°

(B) 68°

(C) 136°

(D) 180°

36. In the following figure, which shows two parallel lines cut by a transversal, what is the relationship between angles 2 and 7?

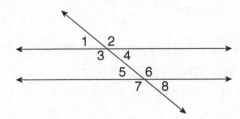

(A) Corresponding angles

(B) Alternate exterior angles

(C) Alternate interior angles

(D) Alterior external angles

37. What is the sum of the exterior angles of a nonagon?

    (A) 360°

    (B) 180°

    (C) 540°

    (D) 1260°

38. Which of the following equations is a hyperbola?

    (A) $x^2 + 2y^2 = a$

    (B) $y = ax^2 + b$

    (C) $x^2 - y^2 = a$

    (D) $x^2 + y^2 = a$

39. In which transformation can the original figure be made smaller?

    (A) Translation

    (B) Dilation

    (C) Rotation

    (D) Reflection

40. Sarah and Emily rode their bikes 10 miles west, then 4 miles south, and then 13 miles east. How far were they from their starting point?

    (A) 13 miles

    (B) 3 miles

    (C) 5 miles

    (D) 27 miles

41. In $\triangle ABC$ triangle below, point D is the midpoint of $\overline{AB}$, and point E is the midpoint of $\overline{AC}$. Also, $\triangle ADE \sim \triangle ABC$ and $\overline{DE} = \dfrac{1}{2}\overline{BC}$.

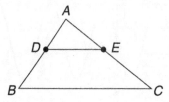

    If $\overline{AD} = 5$, $\overline{AE} = 6$, and $\overline{DE} = 6$, what are the lengths of the three sides of $\triangle ABC$?

    (A) 10, 12, 12

    (B) 10, 11, 12

    (C) 10, 10, 12

    (D) 5, 6, 6

42. When two dimensions of a cube are increased by 4 units and the third is decreased by 2 units, the resulting rectangular prism has a volume that is double the original volume of the cube. Which of the following equations determines x, the edge of the original cube?

    (A) $x^3 = (x + 4)(x + 4)(x - 2)$

    (B) $2x^3 = (x + 4)(x + 4)(x - 2)$

    (C) $x^3 = (x - 4)(x - 4)(x + 2)$

    (D) $2x^3 = (x - 4)(x - 4)(x + 2)$

43. Which of the following is the graph of
$y = 3\sin 2(x - \dfrac{\pi}{4}) + 1$?

(A)
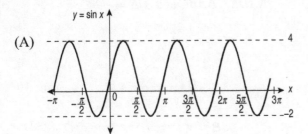

(B)
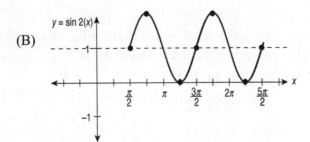

(C)
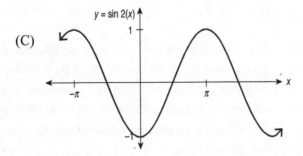

(D)
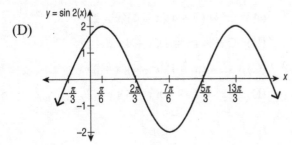

44. Express sin 75° as a function of an angle less than 45°.

(A) cos 15°

(B) csc 15°

(C) cos 75°

(D) sin(−75°)

45. Which of the following pairs of radian measures is NOT coterminal (doesn't have the same terminal ray)?

(A) $\dfrac{\pi}{3}$ and $\dfrac{7\pi}{3}$

(B) $\dfrac{4\pi}{3}$ and $\dfrac{\pi}{3}$

(C) 7π and π

(D) $-\dfrac{3\pi}{4}$ and $\dfrac{5\pi}{4}$

46. Rewrite sin 4x cos 3x using the product formula:
$\sin A \cos B = \dfrac{1}{2}\big[\sin(A + B) + \sin(A - B)\big]$.

(A) $\dfrac{1}{2}(\sin 8x)$

(B) $\dfrac{1}{2}(\sin 6x)$

(C) $\dfrac{1}{2}(\sin 7x + \sin x)$

(D) $\dfrac{1}{2}(\sin 7x - \sin x)$

47. Solve for θ in the first quadrant: $2\sin^2\theta = 1$.

(A) 0°

(B) 30°

(C) 45°

(D) 60°

48. Write as a single fraction: $\tan x + \cot x$.

(A) $\dfrac{\sin x}{\cos x} + \dfrac{\cos x}{\sin x}$

(B) $\dfrac{1}{\sin x \cos x}$

(C) $\dfrac{\tan x}{\cot x} + 1$

(D) $\dfrac{\sin x + \cos x}{\sin x \cos x}$

49. The principal of a new school wants to know what mascot the incoming students would prefer. She summons every student into her office and asks what the new mascot should be. What type of study is this?

    (A) Observational study

    (B) Sample survey

    (C) Experiment

    (D) Census

50. An example of ranked data is

    (A) the heights of students in the class taken as they enter the room.

    (B) all the whole numbers between 1 and 2.

    (C) all the numbers between 1 and 2.

    (D) strongly agree, agree, no opinion, disagree, strongly disagree.

51. Suppose the age of school principals in the United States approximates a normal distribution with a mean of 54 years old and a standard deviation of 7 years. Approximately what percentage of these principals are younger than 47 years old?

    (A) 15.9%

    (B) 34.1%

    (C) 50%

    (D) 84.1%

52. The letters of the set $\{A, B, C, D, E, F, G\}$ can be arranged to form ordered codes of three letters in $_7P_3 = \dfrac{7!}{(7-3)!}$ ways. Evaluate $_7P_3$.

    (A) 21

    (B) 35

    (C) 210

    (D) 840

53. Alan proposes a game of chance to Maddie. He tells her to draw one card from a standard deck of playing cards. If Maddie picks a spade, Alan will give her $10. If Maddie picks a face card that isn't a spade, she will get $8. If Maddie picks any other card, she will have to pay Alan $6. Should Maddie play?

    (A) Yes, Maddie should expect to win.

    (B) No, the odds are that Maddie will lose.

    (C) No, chances are that Maddie will just break even.

    (D) It depends on how many times Maddie draws a card.

54. Which pair of data plots are mutually exclusive?

    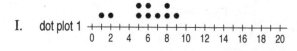
    I. dot plot 1

    II. dot plot 2

    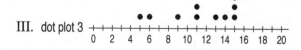
    III. dot plot 3

    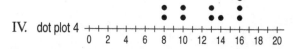
    IV. dot plot 4

    (A) I and II

    (B) II and III

    (C) III and IV

    (D) None of the above.

55. What is the probability of getting a 1 and a 6, in that order, on two tosses of one die?

   (A) $\dfrac{1}{6}$

   (B) $\dfrac{1}{36}$

   (C) $\dfrac{1}{3}$

   (D) $\dfrac{2}{3}$

56. What type of event is being the third of three people chosen one at a time for a committee out of a group of fifty?

   (A) Independent

   (B) Dependent

   (C) Overlapping

   (D) Impossible

57. Evaluate $\lim\limits_{x \to 2} f(x)$ for the piecewise function

$$f(x) = \begin{cases} 8, & x \le -1 \\ 4 - x^3, & -1 < x < 2 \\ 6 - 5x, & x \ge 2 \end{cases}$$

   (A) –4

   (B) 4

   (C) 2

   (D) The limit doesn't exist for this piecewise function.

58. Find $\dfrac{d}{dx}\sin 2x$. (Hint: Use the Chain Rule.)

   (A) $2\cos(2x)$

   (B) $\dfrac{1}{2}x(\cos 2x)$

   (C) $2\sin x$

   (D) $\cos(2x)$

59. What is the volume of a solid formed by taking a right triangle with a 3-unit leg along the x-axis and a 4-unit leg along the y-axis and rotating it around the y-axis?

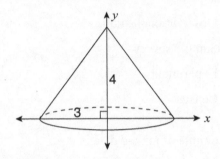

   (A) 16π

   (B) 12π

   (C) 9π

   (D) 4π

60. For position function $s = 3t^2 - 2t + 4$, what is the acceleration?

   (A) Cannot tell if a particular time isn't given

   (B) $6t - 2$

   (C) 0

   (D) 6

61. Find $\dfrac{d}{dx}\log(x^2 + 3x + 1)$. (Hint: Use the Chain Rule with $u = x^2 + 3x + 1$.)

   (A) $\dfrac{1}{x^2 + 3x + 1}$

   (B) $\dfrac{x}{x^2 + 3x + 1}$

   (C) $\dfrac{2x + 3}{x^2 + 3x + 1}$

   (D) $(2x + 3)(\log(x^2 + 3x + 1))$

62. Find the value of the indefinite integral $\int (11x^2 + 9\sqrt{x})\,dx$.

    (A) $11x^3 + 9x^{\frac{3}{2}} + C$

    (B) $\frac{11}{3}x^3 + 6x^{\frac{3}{2}} + C$

    (C) $33x^3 + \frac{27}{2}x^{\frac{3}{2}} + C$

    (D) $\frac{11}{3}x^3 + 6x^{\frac{3}{2}}$

63. Which of the following statements is NOT always true for a valid argument?

    (A) True premises guarantee a true conclusion.

    (B) The reasoning is sound.

    (C) The propositions are true.

    (D) A conclusion cannot be false if all the premises are true.

64. A $P \to Q$ conditional statement is false if

    (A) P is true and Q is false.

    (B) P is true and Q is true.

    (C) P is false and Q is false.

    (D) P is false and Q is true.

65. Provide a counterexample for the following conjecture: "For all real numbers n, $n^2 \geq n$."

    (A) $n = 0$

    (B) $0 < n < 1$

    (C) $n < 0$

    (D) $n = 1$

66. Direct geometry proofs consist of Statements and Reasons. Which of the following is NOT true of a direct geometry proof?

    (A) The conclusion is shown to be true as a result of the given information.

    (B) Statements flow from one statement to the next.

    (C) Reasons validate the truth of the associated Statements.

    (D) Justifications used in Reasons include definitions, conjectures, and theorems.

67. The availability of computers and other technology-rich advances has important results in the classroom. Which of the following is the most important of these classroom results?

    (A) Communication from student to student.

    (B) Communication between the school and parents.

    (C) Technological advances are available to teachers.

    (D) Students receive immediate feedback, resulting in active learning situations.

68. A fact about the set of rational numbers is that

    (A) it is a set of numbers with specific properties that are an extension of the number sets the students already know (e.g., integers).

    (B) $\frac{4}{1}$ and 4 are just different representations of the same number.

    (C) "rational" is related to the word "ratio," not to "being reasonable."

    (D) All of the above.

69. Students often confuse drawing, sketching, and constructing figures. How should the difference be explained?

    (A) Drawing is more precise than sketching.

    (B) Sketching is freehand, whereas drawing uses measurement, even if just estimated.

    (C) Construction uses a compass and straight-edge and is precise.

    (D) All of the above.

70. Which of the following algebraic identities should the teacher use to illustrate the best method to multiply (998)(1,002) without a calculator?

    (A) $(a - b)^2 = a^2 - 2ab + b^2$

    (B) $(a - b)(a + b) = a^2 - b^2$

    (C) $(a + b)^2 = a^2 + 2ab + b^2$

    (D) None of the above.

71. Manipulatives do NOT

    (A) aid directly in the cognitive process.

    (B) engage students.

    (C) increase interest in and enjoyment of math.

    (D) represent a new teaching method.

72. A student wrote that {natural numbers < 0} = {living humans more than 2000 years old}. When asked, the student said they are equal because they both have 0 members. How do you explain why this is wrong?

    (A) Natural numbers are not the same as human beings.

    (B) Only sets with identical elements can be equal.

    (C) The student is saying that both sets are equal to {0}.

    (D) Explain what the null set is and how it differs from the set {0}.

73. Students who are using their calculators to do complicated problems that require the answer to be rounded to a certain value are getting answers that are close to but not equal to the answer given on the answer sheet. The teacher should first check the most likely reason:

    (A) Entering the wrong numbers

    (B) Rounding too early in the calculation

    (C) Entering the wrong operation

    (D) Using the subtraction key instead of the negative key for a negative number

74. To teach the concept of raising the product of two numbers to a given power is the same as raising each of them to that power and then multiplying the result. Which of the following examples demonstrates this point?

    (A) $2^3 \times 2^2 = 2^5$

    (B) $(2 \times 3)^3 = 2^3 \times 3^3$

    (C) $3^5 \times 5^3 = 5^3 \times 3^5$

    (D) $5^2 \times (2^3 + 3^4) = (5^2 \times 2^3) + (5^2 \times 3^4)$

75. Which of the following data sets is the best feasible example that a teacher should choose to illustrate a normal curve?

    (A) The shoes sizes of the 15 students in the class

    (B) The height of all the 17-year-olds in the state

    (C) The number of times that a penny flipped 20 times will land heads-up

    (D) The weight of all the students in the school

FTCE Mathematics 6–12
Practice Test 2 Answer Key

1.	(C)	26.	(A)	51.	(A)
2.	(C)	27.	(B)	52.	(C)
3.	(A)	28.	(D)	53.	(A)
4.	(C)	29.	(D)	54.	(A)
5.	(A)	30.	(C)	55.	(B)
6.	(D)	31.	(B)	56.	(B)
7.	(C)	32.	(C)	57.	(A)
8.	(D)	33.	(C)	58.	(A)
9.	(A)	34.	(A)	59.	(B)
10.	(C)	35.	(C)	60.	(D)
11.	(D)	36.	(B)	61.	(C)
12.	(B)	37.	(A)	62.	(B)
13.	(C)	38.	(C)	63.	(C)
14.	(D)	39.	(B)	64.	(A)
15.	(B)	40.	(C)	65.	(B)
16.	(D)	41.	(A)	66.	(D)
17.	(A)	42.	(B)	67.	(D)
18.	(A)	43.	(A)	68.	(D)
19.	(C)	44.	(A)	69.	(D)
20.	(B)	45.	(B)	70.	(B)
21.	(A)	46.	(C)	71.	(D)
22.	(C)	47.	(C)	72.	(D)
23.	(C)	48.	(B)	73.	(B)
24.	(B)	49.	(D)	74.	(B)
25.	(D)	50.	(D)	75.	(D)

1. (C)

By definition, the zeros of a quadratic equation are the x values at which $y = 0$, where y is the quadratic equation. Answer (A) is incorrect because for complex roots, the graph of the equation does not cross the x-axis.

2. (C)

The easy way to answer this problem is to realize that the second cylinder has half the volume of the first cylinder, so with the same radius, the height should be halved.

But you don't have to know geometry to do this problem. The first sentence says that the volume varies jointly with height and radius squared. Therefore, this is a joint variation problem of general form $a = kbc$, and we must find k to substitute into the same equation for the second cylinder.

Substitute the given values into $V = kr^2h$ to find k.

$$k = \frac{V}{r^2h} = \frac{1500\pi}{(10)^2(15)} = \pi$$

Then for a 750π-cm^3 cylinder,

$$750\pi = \pi \times h \times (10)^2$$
$$h = \frac{750\pi}{100\pi} = 7.5$$

3. (A)

A set has closure under addition if adding numbers in the set always produces a member of the same set. For set A, $1 + 1 = 2$, which is not in the set, so no closure. For set B, $+1 + (+1) = 2$, so no closure, and for set C, $\frac{1}{2} + \frac{1}{2} = 1$, so no closure. For each of the remaining answer choices, there is at least one set for which the property holds.

4. (C)

If both outlets are open, the tank is losing 13 gallons per minute, so it will take $(215 \div 13) = 16.5$ minutes to empty the tank.

5. (A)

The first ratio is to find out how many miles they traveled: $\frac{10 \text{ miles}}{5 \text{ hours}} = \frac{x \text{ miles}}{4 \text{ hours}}$, or by cross-multiplication, $5x = 40$, or 8 miles. The second ratio is to find out how many kilometers are in 8 miles: $\frac{1 \text{ km}}{0.62 \text{ miles}} = \frac{x \text{ km}}{8 \text{ miles}}$, or $0.62x = 8$, so $x = \frac{8}{0.62} = 12.9$ km.

6. (D)

The quickest way to do this problem is by elimination. The slopes of answer choices (B) and (C) are not -2. Then substitute $(2, 0)$ into answer choices (A) and (D) to see which is the correct answer. If you don't recognize that elimination will work to find the equation of a line given the slope, you need just one point on the line, preferably the y-intercept. Here we are given the slope and the x-intercept, so we must find the y-intercept. A simple sketch will show that it is $(0, 4)$, and the equation in slope intercept form is $y = mx + b = -2x + 4$, which is answer choice (D). Even without a sketch, the y-intercept can be found by the definition of slope: $m = -2 = \frac{y - y_1}{x - x_1} = \frac{y - 0}{x - 2}$, which yields $-2x = y + 4$, or $y = -2x + 4$.

7. (C)

You don't have to know geometry to do this problem, which is just asking for a transformation of a formula to one particular letter in terms of the others. Since in the original $V = \pi r^2 h$, h is multiplied by πr^2, both sides of the formula must be divided by that same quantity to get h alone.

8. (D)

$i = \sqrt{-1}$; $i^2 = \left(\sqrt{-1}\right)^2 = -1$; $i^3 = i^2 \cdot i = (-1)i$
$= -i$; $i^4 = i^2 \cdot i^2 = (-1)(-1) = 1$.

9. (A)

The slopes of two perpendicular lines are negative reciprocals of each other. The given line is $3y = 8x - 6$, which in slope-intercept form is $y = \dfrac{8}{3}x - 2$, so the slope is $\dfrac{8}{3}$. Therefore, a perpendicular to that line must have a slope of $-\dfrac{3}{8}$, and answer choice (A) is the only choice with that slope.

10. (C)

The two consecutive positive odd integers can be represented by x and $x \pm 2$. (Notice that even though the numbers are odd, if they are consecutive odd, they are two digits apart.) Then the statement, "product of two consecutive positive odd integers is 195," translates to $x(x \pm 2) = 195$. This is $x^2 + 2x = 195$, which is the same as answer choice (C), or $x^2 - 2x = 195$, which is not an answer choice in this problem.

11. (D

$\ln\left(\dfrac{1}{e^x}\right) = \ln e^{-x}$, and ln and e are inverse functions, so $\ln e^{-x} = -x$.

12. (B)

From the definition of log as an exponent, we are looking for the power we would need to raise 8 to get $\sqrt{8}$. Thus, $\log_8 \sqrt{8} = x$, which is asking to find x for $8^x = \sqrt{8}$. $x = \dfrac{1}{2}$.

13. (C)

The reduction follows: $\dfrac{a^2 - \frac{1}{a}}{a + \frac{1}{a} + 1} = \dfrac{\frac{a^3-1}{a}}{\frac{a^2+1+a}{a}} =$
$\dfrac{(a-1)(a^2 + a + 1)}{\cancel{a}} \cdot \dfrac{\cancel{a}}{(a^2 + a + 1)} = a - 1$. The key here is knowing that $a^3 - 1 = (a-1)(a^2 + a + 1)$.

14. (D)

The word "and" joining two open inequalities means the solution is true for both of the inequalities (answer choice (D)). (Compare to "or" (answer choice (C), which means either but not both must be true.) Answer choices (A) and (B) do not convey the age restrictions.

15. (B)

The easiest and quickest way to answer a simple radical equation is just to check each answer choice. For answer choice (A), –2 yields 2 = 2, and –5 yields 1 = –1, so (A) is not correct. From the check on (A), we know that (B) is correct and (D) is incorrect, so we have the check only the 5 in answer choice (C), which yields $\sqrt{11} = 9$, incorrect, so the only correct answer is answer choice (B), –2.

16. (D)

Matrices R and S are 2×2 matrices, and matrix T is a 3×2 matrix. Addition and subtraction of matrices is possible only if the matrices are the same size, so answer choices (A) and (B) are possible. Multiplication of matrices is possible if the number of columns of the first matrix equals the number of rows of the second matrix. This is true for answer choice (C), but not for answer choice (D).

17. (A)

Use the rules for logs: Log of a power: $\log x^2 = 2(\log x) = 0.6522$, so $\log x = \dfrac{0.6522}{2} = 0.3261$. Log of a product: $\log 10x = \log 10 + \log x = 1 + .3261 = 1.3261$.

18. (A)

Since log has a base of 10, this is the same as asking the log of what number is $\log(5x^2)$, which, of course, is $5x^2$.

19. (C)

There are several ways to find the answer to this question.

- Graphs of the $\log_b x$ format always have an x asymptote at $x = 0$. Since x is increased by 1 in $\log(x + 1)$, the graph is moved one unit to the left, so the new asymptote is $x = -1$.

- Make a table of values by writing the function in exponential form: $\log_4(x + 1)$ is $4^y = x + 1$, or $x = 4^y - 1$. Assign values to y in this case and solve for x. It is obvious that as y goes toward $-\infty$, x gets close to -1 but never crosses it (definition of an asymptote).

y	2	1	0	-1	-3	-5
$x = 4^y - 1$	15	3	0	$-\dfrac{3}{4}$	$-\dfrac{63}{64}$	$-\dfrac{1023}{1024}$

20. (B)

We can recognize an exponential function from several points by noticing that as one unknown varies by a constant term, the other variable varies by a constant factor. Here, as the values of x increase by a constant term 1, the values of y decrease by a constant *factor* of $\dfrac{1}{3}$. That eliminates a linear model, in which the variables will increase or decrease by constant terms, not factors. A quadratic is eliminated because the change in y for a modest change in x is dramatic.

21. (A)

Answer choice (A) is the only choice that has all six parts translated correctly:

y is half of x	$\dfrac{1}{2}x$	when (if) x is less than six	if $x < 6$
y is twice x	$2x$	when (if) x is in the range from six to ten	if $6 \leq x \leq 10$
y is two more than x	$x + 2$	when (if) x is greater than ten	if $x > 10$

22. (C)

First, find the equation that connects T and x from the given information. Even if you don't remember the distance formula, $d = rt$ (distance = rate × time), you should be able to come up with $x = \dfrac{100}{T}$ because x is in miles per hour. Then to write time T as a function of x, just solve for T: $T = \dfrac{100}{x}$.

23. (C)

Multiplying or adding two functions or whether they pass the vertical line test tells nothing about any *relationship* between the functions. However, if a composite of two functions (answer choice (C)) leaves the variable x unchanged, then they are inverses, defined as each function "undoing" the other function.

24. (B)

The curve is shifted 4 units up so add 4 to the original equation, and it is shifted 3 units to the right, so subtract 3 from x. The shape is the same, so no other transformations are needed.

25. (D)

This is the same graph as the original raised 3 units, so just add 3 to $f(x)$. The graph may look narrower, but it is identical, so answer choice (A) is incorrect (besides, a coefficient of 3 would make it much narrower), and answer choice (B) would make it much wider. Answer choice (C) is for a graph that has been moved 3 units to the left.

26. (A)

Since it is an isosceles triangle, to determine all of the angles and all of the sides, you just need to know which angle is given. If it is a base angle, then you can determine the other two angles (one will be the same and the other will make the sum of the angles 180°). If it is the vertex angle, you can determine the base angles by subtracting it from 180° and dividing by 2. From the measures of the sides that are given, if they are equal they are the legs, and you can determine the base by drawing the altitude to the base and using trigonometry. If they are unequal, using the fact that the largest side is opposite the largest angle, you can determine which one is the base, and the legs are equal and no trigonometry is needed. Answer (B) isn't critical because you can figure it out from the information given. The question is *whether*, not how, it can be done.

27. (B)

A triangle inscribed in a circle with the diameter as one of its sides is a right triangle. Here, $\angle C = 90$. If $\angle A = 45°$, that leaves $180° - 90° = 45°$ for $\angle B$.

28. (D)

Answer choice (A) is valid only for a right triangle, and there is no indication that this is a right triangle, so we cannot assume it is. Although answer choices (B) and (C) are partially correct, side AC must be *between* the sum and difference of the lengths of the other two sides, so answer choice (D) is the only true restriction.

29. (D)

The two triangles in the figure are similar because their corresponding angles are equal and corresponding sides are proportional. All of the answer choices are true except (D), which is false because the order in which the letters of a triangle are written for similar (and congruent) triangles makes a difference. This statement implies that $\overline{AP}$ and $\overline{AB}$ are the corresponding sides, which is false.

30. (C)

Any triangle with all sides equal is an equilateral triangle with three 60° angles.

31. (B)

The figure is a circle with a 60° sector, which, by definition, intercepts a 60° minor arc and a 300° major arc since the whole circle is 360°. Two, not three, arcs are formed. The chord is a side of the equilateral triangle, and since the other two sides are radii, the chord equals a radius, not half of it.

32. (C)

This answer is best derived by elimination. If you draw the diagonal of a square, the triangles formed are right triangles, so answer choice (A) is incorrect. Answer choice (B) isn't a regular polygon. Answer choice (C) does, in fact, contain six equilateral triangles. Answer choice (D) is incorrect because a sketch will show that the greater the number of sides, the more "pointy" the top angle is for each triangle.

33. (C)

The area of the leather rectangle is $A = lw = 14 \times 30 = 420$ square inches. The area of the square is $A = s^2 = 6^2 = 36$ square inches, and the area of the circle is $A = \pi r^2 = (\pi)(7)^2 = 49\pi$ square inches. Therefore, the amount of waste is the original size minus the square and circle, or $420 - (36 + 49\pi) = 230.06196$, or 230 square inches to the nearest whole number. Notice that rounding is not done until the last calculation to avoid rounding errors, although in this case it wouldn't make a difference.

34. (A)

The vertices of the polygon have to be on the circle, and the lines that connect two points on a circle are chords.

35. (C)

The given angle is an inscribed angle and is equal to half the intercepted arc, so the arc measures 136°. Angle x is a central angle that intercepts the same arc, and a central angle has the same measure as the arc it intercepts, so $x = 136°$.

36. (B)

The two angles are on alternate sides of the transversal and are exterior to the two parallel lines, thus the name alternate exterior angles. Answer choice (D) is thrown in there to remind you to read every word and every answer choice. "Alterior" is not a word, much less a kind of angle. Incidentally, answer choices (A), (B), and (C) name angle relationships that are equal angles.

37. (A)

The sum of the *exterior* angles of any polygon is 360°, no matter how many sides. A nonagon has nine sides, and the sum of its *interior* angles is $(9 - 2)180° = 1260°$.

38. (C)

For any conic equation in general form, you have to look **only** at the x^2 and y^2 terms to determine the type of conic. If only one of the variables is squared, the conic is a parabola. If both variables are squared, the kind of conic depends on whether they have the same signs. If not, the equation is a hyperbola. (If they have different signs, the coefficients tell what kind of conic it is: if they have the same coefficients, it is a circle, and if the coefficients are different, it is an ellipse.)

39. (B)

The figure just changes orientation on the coordinate system in all answer choices except (B), dilation, in which the figure is reduced or enlarged.

40. (C)

Sketch the problem. The girls traveled three sides of a trapezoid (from A to B to C to D), as shown:

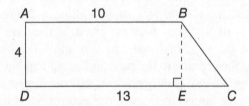

The distance from their starting point is the length of BC, which is the hypotenuse of $\triangle AED$, a 3-4-5 right triangle. The answer is 5 miles.

41. (A)

If $\overline{AD} = 5$, then $\overline{AB} = 10$. If $\overline{AE} = 6$, then $\overline{AC} = 12$. Finally, since the two triangles are similar, $\overline{DE}$ is equal to half of $\overline{BC}$, so $\overline{BC} = 12$.

42. (B)

Assume the original volume of the cube is x^3. Then the volume of the rectangular prism is $2x^3$. The formula for the volume of a rectangular prism is length × width × height, or $(x + 4)(x + 4)(x - 2)$. Therefore, answer choice (B) equates these two representations of the new figure.

43. (A)

Answer choice (A) is the only curve that triples the amplitude. Curves (B) and (C) have amplitude 1, and curve (D) has amplitude 2.

44. (A)

The complement of 75° is 90° − 75° = 15°. Since the function of an acute angle is equal to the cofunction of its complementary angle, sin 75° = cos 15°.

45. (B)

Two radian measures are coterminal only if their difference is a multiple of 2π. The difference between $\dfrac{4\pi}{3}$ and $\dfrac{\pi}{3}$ is π.

46. (C)

Using the given formula with $A = 4x$ and $B = 3x$, the calculation is

$$\sin 4x \cos 3x = \frac{1}{2}[\sin(4x + 3x) + \sin(4x - 3x)]$$
$$= \frac{1}{2}(\sin 7x + \sin x).$$

47. (C)

Rewrite the equation as $\sin^2 \theta = \dfrac{1}{2}$, or $\sin\theta = \dfrac{1}{\sqrt{2}}$, which is true for $\theta = 45°$ (try the 1–1-$\sqrt{2}$ triangle whenever you see $\sqrt{2}$ in trigonometry).

48. (B)

Convert the expression to one in sine and cosine and find an LCD.

$$\tan x + \cot x = \frac{\sin x}{\cos x} + \frac{\cos x}{\sin x} = \frac{\sin x}{\cos x}\left(\frac{\sin x}{\sin x}\right) + \frac{\cos x}{\sin x}\left(\frac{\cos x}{\cos x}\right)$$
$$= \frac{\sin^2 x + \cos^2 x}{\sin x \cos x} = \frac{1}{\sin x \cos x}$$

Note that answer choices (A) and (C) can be eliminated right away because the question asks for a single fraction.

49. (D)

The principal has collected data from every individual in the population, in this case, the population of all school students. If the principal had asked only some of the students, chosen randomly, this would have been a sample survey.

50. (D)

This is a ranking of categorical data. Answer choice (A) would be correct if the heights were sorted, but the answer indicates that they are not.

51. (A)

The phrase "younger than 47" translates to "is less than 1 standard deviation below the mean" (or $z = -1$), since the mean (54) minus one standard deviation (7) equals 47. So this problem is asking for the area under the normal curve to the left of −1 standard deviation. Use the fact that the area from the mean to 1 standard deviation = 34.1% and from the mean to either end of the curve is 50% of the total area, so subtract them (.50 − 34.1) = 15.9%. Alternatively, sketch the distribution and look at the answer choices and eliminate anything more than (.50 − 34.1) ≈ 16% as being too high.

52. (C)

Use your calculator for a quick answer: For $_7P_3$, press $\boxed{7}$ $\boxed{\text{PRB}}$ then choose $_nP_r$ and enter $\boxed{\text{ENTER}}$ $\boxed{3}$ $\boxed{=}$ to get 120. Or use

$$_7P_3 = \frac{7!}{(7-3)!} = \frac{7!}{4!} = \frac{7 \times 6 \times 5 \times \cancel{4 \times 3 \times 2 \times 1}}{\cancel{4 \times 3 \times 2 \times 1}} = 210.$$

53. (A)

Figure the expected value, and if it is positive, Maddie should expect to win. The probabilities of the winnings are $10 for a spade, $8 for a non-spade face card, and –$6 ($6 loss) for all the other cards, or $+10\left(\dfrac{13}{52}\right), +8\left(\dfrac{9}{52}\right),$ and $-6\left(\dfrac{30}{52}\right)$, respectively. This calculates to $\dfrac{130}{52} + \dfrac{72}{52} - \dfrac{180}{52} = \dfrac{22}{52} = \$0.42$. Since the expected value of the game is positive although small (approximately 42 cents), it is to Maddie's advantage to play the game. Answer choice (D) is wrong because if the cards are replaced in the deck, each draw is an independent event.

54. (A)

Mutually exclusive means there are no data points in common. That is true only for plots I and II.

55. (B)

Since these are independent events, each has a probability of $\dfrac{1}{6}$. $\Pr(1 \text{ and } 6) = \Pr(1) \times \Pr(6) = \dfrac{1}{6} \times \dfrac{1}{6} = \dfrac{1}{36}$.

56. (B)

The probability changes once the first and second people are chosen because the population changes from 50 to 49 to 48, respectively.

57. (A)

The piecewise function changes at $x = 2$, so we must evaluate and compare the limits coming from the left and the right of $x = 2$. The left-hand limit is $\lim\limits_{x \to 2^-} f(x) = 4 - (2)^3 = 4 - 8 = -4$, and the right-hand limit is $\lim\limits_{x \to 2^+} f(x) = 6 - 5(2) = 6 - 10 = -4$. Since the two limits are equal, the general limit exists and is $\lim\limits_{x \to 2} = -4$.

58. (A)

Use the Chain Rule with $y = \sin t$ and $t = 2x$. Then $\dfrac{dy}{dx} = \dfrac{dy}{dt}\dfrac{dt}{dx} = (\cos t)(2) = 2\cos(2x)$.

59. (B)

The triangle rotated around the y-axis has the shape of a cone with radius $r = 3$ and height $h = 4$. The equation for the volume of a cone with radius 3 and height 4 is $V_{\text{cone}} = \dfrac{1}{3}\pi r^2 h = \dfrac{1}{3}\pi(3)^2(4) = 12\pi$.

60. (D)

The equation is a parabola, so the acceleration is constant. It is equal to the second derivative of the position function. (Answer (B) is the first derivative, or the velocity function.)

61. (C)

Use the Chain Rule with $y = \log u$ and $u = (x^2 + 3x + 1)$. Then $\dfrac{d}{dx}(\log u) = \dfrac{d(\log u)}{du}\dfrac{d(x^2 + 3x + 1)}{dx} = \left(\dfrac{1}{u}\right)(2x + 3) = \dfrac{2x + 3}{x^2 + 3x + 1}$.

62. (B)

Separate the integral into two integrals:

$$11\int x^2\,dx + 9\int \sqrt{x}\,dx = 11\left(\frac{1}{3}x^3\right) + C + 9\left(\frac{2}{3}x^{\frac{3}{2}}\right) + C$$

$$= \frac{11}{3}x^3 + 6x^{\frac{3}{2}} + C.$$

Answer choice (D) is incorrect because it does not include the variable C, which is necessary in evaluating indefinite integrals.

63. (C)

Validity pertains to reasoning, not propositions, so the truth of propositions doesn't guarantee that the reasoning will be valid. Answer choices (A) and (D) are saying the same true statement.

64. (A)

A conditional statement is true whenever Q is true and if P and Q are both false. It is false when the hypothesis P is true and the conclusion Q is false.

65. (B)

Any real fraction between 0 and 1 is a counter-example. For example $\left(\frac{1}{2}\right)^2 < \frac{1}{2}$. The numbers 0 and 1 cannot be included because they are equal to their squares, and the sign is greater than *or equal to*.

66. (D)

Conjectures are "best guesses" that use inductive reasoning based on a pattern. They are not proven rules, so they shouldn't be used as proofs.

67. (D)

Technology-rich environments allow not only active student learning and immediate feedback, but also a collaborative environment and authentic information.

68. (D) All of the above.

69. (D)

Drawing or sketching can be used to picture a problem. Construction, on the other hand, has value because it reinforces the geometric properties of sets of points rather than the properties of measurement.

70. (B)

The teacher should emphasize that when it is obvious that two numbers to be multiplied are above and below another number by the same amount, using the difference of two squares is a useful shortcut. Here, the two numbers differ by 2 from 1,000, so a is 1,000 and b is 2. Therefore, $(a-b)(a+b) = a^2 - b^2 = 1,000^2 - 2^2 = 9,999,996$, a calculation that often can be done mentally.

71. (D)

In fact, the history of using manipulatives to teach math goes back at least 200 years. Manipulatives were used by such historical educational icons as Montessori and Piaget in the early twentieth century.

72. (D)

Apparently, the student is confusing the set {0}, which has one member, the number 0, with the empty set (∅), also called the null set, which contains no members.

73. (B)

Although all answer choices are common errors, options (A), (C), and (D) would get answers that are *not* close to the answer sheet value. If the answer is close, the reason is most likely rounding numbers during the calculation instead of waiting to the final answer to do the rounding. A possible solution is to have the student keep the intermediate calculations in the calculator's memory without rounding. Rounding π to 3.14 early in the calculation rather than using the value of π in the calculator's memory (use the π key) can make a large difference in the final answer. An example of rounding errors too early in the calculation happens in calculating compound interest—if the interest is rounded at each calculation, the difference can be considerable.

74. (B)

Answer choice (B) is the only example that has the product of two numbers raised to single power. Although all of the answer choices are true examples, only (B) satisfies the criteria of the problem.

75. (D)

The key words here are "best feasible example." The sample sizes in answer choices (A) and (C) are too small to show a normal curve (usually more than 30 data points are needed to approximate a normal curve). Answer choice (B), although it would show a bell-shaped curve, is not a feasible example because those data are not readily available. For this problem, it is assumed that there are more than 30 students in the school, based on the fact 15 students are in this math class, and that represents only one grade.

Practice Test 2 Competency Coverage

The list below identifies which FTCE Math competencies the questions on Practice Test 2 address. Use this list to focus on those topics where you need more review.

Basic Math Review

Questions 3, 20, 68

Algebra

Questions 1, 5, 6, 8, 10, 13, 14, 15, 16, 41, 48

Advanced Algebra

Questions 2, 4, 7, 11, 12, 13, 16, 17, 18, 20, 42

Functions

Questions 19, 20, 21, 22, 23, 24, 25, 39, 57

Geometry

Questions 2, 4, 7, 9, 28, 29, 30, 31, 32, 33, 34, 66

Coordinate Geometry

Questions 26, 27, 38, 40

Trigonometry

Questions 43, 44, 45, 46, 47, 48

Statistics and Probability

Questions 49, 50, 51, 52, 53, 54, 55, 56

Calculus

Questions 57, 58, 59, 60, 61, 62

Mathematical Reasoning

Questions 63, 64, 65, 66

Instruction and Assessment

Questions 67, 68, 69, 70, 71, 72, 73, 74, 75

Note that the solutions to some problems involve more than one competency. The topic labeled "Basic Math Review" is not an FTCE-listed competency.

INDEX

A

a–b–C formula, 271
absolute value, 35–36, 63–64
absolute value function, 141–143
acceleration function, 355–358
accumulation, 367, 374
accuracy, ensuring, 398, 404–405
acute angle, 164
acute triangle, 171, 175
addition properties, 25–26
addition rule of probability, 318
   overlapping cases, 324
additive identity, 26
additive inverse, 26
adjacent angles, 164
algebra, with trigonometric functions, 264–266
algebraic expressions, 51–53
alternate exterior angles, 165
alternate interior angles, 165
altitude
   of an equilateral triangle, 175
   of a triangle, 175
   of a two-dimensional figure, 166
amplitude, of a periodic function, 267
angle–angle–side (AAS), 177
angle–side–angle (ASA), 177
   and law of sines, 273–273
angles, 163–165
   adjacent, 164
   bisecting, 202
   complementary, 164
   exterior to circle, 199
   greater than 360° (2π), 263
   inscribed in circle, 197–199
   relationships between, 164
   supplementary, 164
   types, 164

vertical, 165
antiderivative, 361–362, 365–366. *See also* integrals.
apothem, defined, 188–189
approximation, of radicals, 39
area
   circle, 155
   parallelogram, 182
   quadrilateral, 180
   rectangle, 184
   rhombus, 145
   square, 185
   trapezoid, 180
   polygon, 188–189
area of a triangle, 175–176
   by *a–b–C* formula, 271
   by Heron's formula, 225–226
   by Pythagorean Theorem, 175
   by using coordinates, 225–226
area under a curve, 366–373
arc of a circle, 195–199
argument
   deductive, 387–388
   inductive, 387–388
   in logic, 381–382
arithmetic progression. *See* arithmetic sequence.
arithmetic sequence, 118–120
arithmetic series, 120–121
assessment, forms of, 403–405
associative property of addition, 26
associative property of multiplication, 26
asymptote, 138–139, 335–337
average, statistical, 282. *See also* mean.
average rate of change, 342
average velocity, 355
axes
   Cartesian coordinate system, 57
   of an ellipse, 233

of a hyperbola, 232–233
in three dimensions, 205
axis of symmetry
   absolute value function, 142
   parabola, 40, 232

B

bar graph, 286–288, 290
base
   of an isosceles trapezoid, 181
   of an isosceles triangle, 175
   of a logarithm, 103
   of a number to a power, 34, 101
   of a periodic function, 144
   of a three-dimensional figure, 206
   of a triangle, 175
base angles
   of an isosceles triangle, 171
   of an isosceles trapezoid, 181
base 2 system, 42–43
bell-shaped curve, 297–298, 302.
      See also normal curve; normal
      distribution.
bias, in sampling, 280–281
binary system, 42–43
binomial expansion, 112–113
binomial formula, 82
binomial theorem, 82
binomials, 79
   conjugate of, 79
   F–O–I–L method of multiplication,
      80–81, 99
   multiplying, 79–82
   Pascal's triangle, 111–113
bisecting an angle, 202
bisecting a line segment, 203
bivariate data, 324
box-and-whiskers plot, 296–297

C

calculator, 8–13
  angle modes, 9
  basic functions, 10
  combinations, 12
  fractions, 10–11
  keypad, 9
  logarithms, 13
  manual for, 9
  permutations, 12
  2nd key, 9
  trigonometry, 11–12
cancellation, 30–32
capacity, 41, 206
categorical data
  bar graph, 286–288, 290
  defined 281
  pie chart, 288–289, 291–292
  presentation, 286–292
  table for, 286, 290
causation, 308
census, 280
center
  of a circle, 191
  of an ellipse, 233
  of a hyperbola, 233
central angle, of a circle, 195
central tendency, 282
chain rule, 348
characteristic, of a log, 105
chord, of a circle, 191–192
circle, 191–200, 229–230, 234–235
  angles, 197–199
  area, 193–194
  circumference, 192–193
  center, 191, 234
  as a conic section, 229–230
  eccentricity, 234
  general equation, 230
  parts of, 191–192, 234
  real-world applications, 234
  standard form of equation, 234
circle graph. See pie chart.
circumference, of a circle, 192–193
closed figures, defined, 169
closure, 25
coefficients, defined, 52
cofunctions, 257
cognitive development, 395

collinear points, 162
columns of a matrix, 70–72, 125–127
combinations, 315–318
common denominator, 33
  lowest, 33
common difference, arithmetic
    sequence, 118–120, 125
common factor, 30–32
common log, defined, 102
common ratio, geometric sequence,
    121–122, 124–125
commutative property of addition, real
    numbers, 53–54
commutative property of multiplication,
    25–26
compass, for constructions, 202–205
complementary angles, 164
complementary events, defined, 312
completing the square, 86
complex conjugates, 81–82, 88, 96, 99,
    108
  graphing, 100
  multiplying, 81–82
complex numbers, 23–24, 88
  addition and subtraction, 98–99
  graphing, 100
  multiplication and division, 99
  operations, 98–100
complex roots, 88, 107
composite figures, 201
composite function, 147–150
  domain, 238–239
composite numbers, 58
composition of functions, 147–150
compound events, 318–319
compound interest, 123–124
compression 152. See also dilation.
concave polygon, 190
concavity of a curve, 351, 355
conceptual misunderstanding strategies,
    401–403
Concrete–Representational–Abstract
    (CRA) instructional model,
    396–397
conclusion, in logic, 382
conditional probability, 324
conditional statements, 384–385
cone, 214–215
congruence of triangles, 176–178
conic sections, 228–239

  eccentricity, 231
  general form of equations, 229–231
  real-world applications, 235–239
  standard form for, 231
  summary, 235
  See also specific conic sections.
conjecture, 381–382
conjugate axis of a hyperbola, 232–233,
    235
conjugate method with limits, 340–341
conjugates, 78–79
  complex, 81–82, 88, 96, 99, 108
consistent equations, 66–72
constant difference, arithmetic
    sequence, 118
constant
  of integration, 362
  of proportionality, 75
  of variation, 75–76
constraints
  absolute value, 63–64
  in inequalities, 54, 60–63
constructions, 202–205
contingency table, 308–311
continuity, 337–339, 350
  graph, 138, 140
  relation to differentiability, 350
  piecewise function, 140
continuous function, 138, 141
contrapositive, conditional statement,
    385–386
converse, conditional statement,
    385–386
convex polygon, 190
coordinate plane
  Cartesian, 57
  complex, 100
  in geometry, 223
  graphing on, 57–59
  transformations, 240–246
coplanar, 163
corner, on a graph, 350
correlation, 305–311
correlation coefficient, 305–306
corresponding angles, 165
cosecant function, 252–253
cosine function, 252
cotangent function, 252–253
coterminal angles, 263–264
counterexample, 25, 382

Barnes & Noble Booksellers #2878
5701 Sunset Drive Suite 196
South Miami, FL 33143
305-662-4770

STR:2878 REG:001 TRN:1965 CSHR:Andres R

FTCE Mathematics 6-12 (026) 3rd Ed., Boo
9780738612409   T1
(1 @ 39.95)   39.95

Subtotal   39.95
Sales Tax T1 (7.000%)   2.80
TOTAL   42.75
AMEX   42.75
  Card#: XXXXXXXXXXXX2008
  Expdate: XX/XX
  Auth: 884914
  Entry Method: Chip Read

  Application Label: AMERICAN EXPRESS
  AID: a000000025010801
  TVR: 0000008000
  TSI: f800

A MEMBER WOULD HAVE SAVED   4.00

Thanks for shopping at
Barnes & Noble

051.04C   08/13/2019 06:56PM

CUSTOMER COPY

seller's return policy. Magazines, newspapers, eBooks, digital downloads, and used books are not returnable or exchangeable. Defective NOOKs may be exchanged at the store in accordance with the applicable warranty.

Returns or exchanges will not be permitted (i) after 14 days or without receipt or (ii) for product not carried by Barnes & Noble or Barnes & Noble.com.

Policy on receipt may appear in two sections.

Return Policy

With a sales receipt or Barnes & Noble.com packing slip, a full refund in the original form of payment will be issued from any Barnes & Noble Booksellers store for returns of undamaged NOOKs, new and unread books, and unopened and undamaged music CDs, DVDs, vinyl records, toys/games and audio books made within 14 days of purchase from a Barnes & Noble Booksellers store or Barnes & Noble.com with the below exceptions:

A store credit for the purchase price will be issued (i) for purchases made by check less than 7 days prior to the date of return, (ii) when a gift receipt is presented within 60 days of purchase, (iii) for textbooks, (iv) when the original tender is PayPal, or (v) for products purchased at Barnes & Noble College bookstores that are listed for sale in the Barnes & Noble Booksellers inventory management system.

Opened music CDs, DVDs, vinyl records, audio books may not be returned, and can be exchanged only for the same title and only if defective. NOOKs purchased from other retailers or sellers are returnable only to the retailer or seller from which they are purchased, pursuant to such retailer's or seller's return policy. Magazines, newspapers, eBooks, digital downloads, and used books are not returnable or exchangeable. Defective NOOKs may be exchanged at the store in accordance with the applicable warranty.

Returns or exchanges will not be permitted (i) after 14 days or without receipt or (ii) for product not carried by Barnes & Noble or Barnes & Noble.com.

Policy on receipt may appear in two sections.

Return Policy

With a sales receipt or Barnes & Noble.com packing slip, a full refund in the original form of payment will be issued from any Barnes & Noble Booksellers store for returns of undamaged NOOKs, new and unread books, and unopened

counting numbers, 23, 28. *See also* natural numbers.
counting principle, 313–315
Cramer's Rule, 72
critical point, 351
critical value, 372
cross-multiplication, 74
cross-section method, to find volume, 374–375
cube, 209
cubed powers, 34, 63
curve, area under, 366–373
cusp, on a graph, 350
customary system of units, 40–41
cycle, defined, 254
cyclic functions. *See* periodic functions
cylinder, 210–211

D

data
  analysis, 279, 281–285
  categorical, 281–282, 286–272
  collection, 279–281
  interpretation, 279, 297–305
  presentation, 311, 317–323
  quantitative, 281–285, 292–297
  raw, 281
data sets, comparing, 305–311
  correlation, 305
  linear regression, 306–308
  scatter plots, 305–306
deceleration, 357
decimals, 29–31
  conversion to fractions, 30
  conversion to or from percentages, 30
  nonrepeating, 23
  repeating, 29
  terminating, 29
deductive argument, 387–388
definite integral, 361, 364–365
degrees, conversion to radians, 253
denominator, 29–33
  common, 33
  lowest common, 33
dependent equations, 66
derivatives
  first, 344, 351, 353–358
  graphing, 353–355

limit definition, 343–344
notation, 344
logarithmic functions, 349
second, 352–353
trigonometric functions, 349
Descartes Rule of Signs, 108, 137
determinant of a matrix, 70–72, 125–126
diagnostic assessments, 403
diagonals
  of isosceles trapezoid, 181
  of right prism, 208
diameter, 191
difference of two squares, 83
differentiability, 350
differentiation, 344
  chain rule, 348
  power rule, 344–348
  product rule, 346–348
  quotient rule, 259
  rules for various functions, 363–364
dilation, 245–246
  in the coordinate plane, 245–246
  of graph of a function, 152–153, 155, 267–268
dimension
  of a matrix, 125
  three-dimensional figures, 206–207
dimensional analysis, 39–40
direct reasoning, 386–387
direct variation, 75
direction of a vector, 113–114
discontinuity, 337
discriminant, 87
displacement-time graph, 355–358
distance
  between two points, 223–224
  from a point to a line, 224–225
  versus displacement, 359
distributive property of multiplication over addition, 27
divisibility rules, 383–384
division
  of fractions, 32
  of polynomials, 109–110
  of real numbers, 27
  by zero, 29
domain, 133
  of a composite function, 149
  of parabola, 135

of polynomial function, 137
of a relation, 133
of trigonometric function graphs, 257
dot plot, 295
double roots, 88

E

eccentricity
  of conic sections, 231
  of an ellipse, 234
edges, three-dimensional figures, 206
element
  of a matrix, 125
  of a relation, 133
ellipse, 229–230, 233–234
  real-world applications, 239
empirical probability, 312
endpoint, 162
equations
  consistent, 66–72
  creating from expressions, 51–53
  dependent, 66
  definition, 51
  exponential, 100–102
  inconsistent, 66
  logarithmic, 102–106
  quadratic, 79–91
  radical, 78–79, 100
  rational, 77–79
  simultaneous, 66–72
  systems of, 66–72
  using inverses in solution, 53
equiangular triangle, 171–175
equilateral triangle, 171–175
estimation, 44
Euler's number, 106
even function, 150–151
even numbers, 24–25
expected value, 329–330
experimental probability, 280–281, 312
experimental study, 280
exponential decay, 106
exponential equations, 100–102
exponential function, 144
exponential growth, 106
exponents, 34–35
  fractional, 37
  negative, 35, 101
expressions, algebraic, 51–53

exterior angles
    formed by parallel lines and a
        transversal, 165
    of a polygon, 180, 186–187
extrapolation, 307
extrema of a graph, 351
extremes of a proportion, 74–75

F

faces
    right prism, 207
    three-dimensional figures, 206
Factor Theorem, 108–109
factorials, 315–317
factoring quadratic equations, 83–87
factors
    of a number, 28
    of a quadratic, 83–85
fair, defined, 313
fallacy, 389
first derivative, 344, 351
    graph of, 353–355
    position-time graph, 355–358
first fundamental theorem of calculus,
    362, 364
focus
    of an ellipse, 233
    of a hyperbola, 233
    of a parabola, 232
F–O–I–L method of multiplying
    binomials, 80–81, 99
formative assessments, 404
fractional exponent, 37
fractions, 29–31
    addition, 33
    converting from decimals, 29–31
    converting to or from percentages,
        30–31
    division, 32
    improper, 32
    multiplication, 31–32
    reducible, 30
    simplifying, 31–32
    subtraction, 33
frequencies, 308–311
    count, 309
    joint, 309–311
    marginal, 309–311
    relative, 309–311

frequency curve, 299. *See also* normal
    distribution
frequency table, two-way, 308–311
function of a function, 147–150
functions
    absolute value, 141–143
    composition of, 147–150
    continuous, 138, 141
    defined, 133
    even, 150–151
    exponential, 144
    inverse, 145–147
    invertible, 143
    linear, 135
    neither even nor odd, 150–151
    odd, 150–151
    one–to–one, 143
    periodic, 143
    piecewise, 140
    polynomial, 137
    quadratic, 135
    step, 141
    symmetric, 150–151
    transformations, 150–155
Fundamental Counting Principle,
    313–315
Fundamental Theorem of Algebra, 107
Fundamental Theorem of Calculus,
    361–362, 364

G

geometric progression. *See* geometric
    sequence.
geometric sequence, 118, 121–123
    common ratio, 121
geometric series, 118, 123–125
    infinite, 123
graph
    corner, 350
    critical points, 351
    cusp, 350
    decreasing at a point, 351
    extrema, 351
    of first derivative, 344, 351, 353–354
    increasing at a point, 351
    inequalities, 60
    linear equations, 57–60
    maximum, 351
    minimum, 351
    of second derivative, 352–355

graphical representation, 397–398

H

height. *See* altitude.
Heron's formula, 225–226, 271
histogram, 292–293
hole in graph, 138
horizontal asymptote, 138–139,
    335–337
horizontal line test, 145
horizontal translation of periodic
    function, 268–269
hyperbola, 229–230, 232–233
    real-world applications, 238
hyperbolic paraboloid, 23
hypotenuse, 135, 188–189
hypotenuse-leg (HL) congruent
    triangles, 178

I

identity element
    for addition, 26
    for multiplication, 27
identity property
    addition of real numbers, 26
    multiplication of real numbers, 27
if–then statement, 382, 384–385
imaginary numbers, 23–24, 37, 88
imaginary roots, 88, 107
implication, in logic, 384
improper fractions, 32
inconsistent equations, 66
increasing curve, 351
indefinite integral, 361–364
independent events, 318–323
indeterminate, 34, 340
index, on a radical sign, 37
indirect reasoning, 386–387
inductive reasoning, 387–388
inequalities
    creating from expressions, 51–52
    linear, 72–73
    nonlinear, 97–98
infinite geometric series, 123
inscribed angles, 197–198
inscribed polygons, 199–200
instantaneous rate of change, 343
instantaneous velocity, 355

integers, 23–25, 28, 30
integrals, 361–376
    definite, 361, 364–366
    indefinite, 361–364
integration, 361–376
    by parts, 365–366
    constant, 362
    rules for various functions,
        363–364
intercepted arcs, 197–199
interior angles
    quadrilateral, 180
    triangles, 170
International System of Units, 40
interpolation, 307
interval notation, 54, 134
invalid argument, 388–389
inverse
    of conditional statement, 385–386
    of a function, 145–147
    of an operation, 26–27
inverse functions, 145–147
    of exponents, 37
    trigonometric, 259
inverse properties
    in algebra, 56
    real numbers, 26, 27
inverse variation, 76
invertible function, 143
invertible matrix, 72
irrational number, 23, 25, 39, 88, 193
isosceles trapezoid, 181
isosceles triangle, 170–171, 175

J

joint frequency, 309–311
joint variation, 76–77
journals, 405

K

kite, 179

L

law of cosines, 272
law of sines, 272–273
least common multiple (LCM), 77–78
legend, on bar graph, 287

legs
    of a right triangle, 172
    of an isosceles triangle, 175
length, units, 41–42
lessons, sequencing, 396–397
like terms, 52, 80
limits, 335–341
    definition of derivatives, 343–344
    finding by conjugate method,
        340–341
    finding by factoring, 339–340
    finding by substitution, 338–339
    indeterminate, 340
    notation for, 335
    operations on, 338
line, 162, 165–169
line graph, 293–294
line of best fit, 306
line segment, 162
    bisecting, 203
    division into equal parts, 168
    division into proportional parts,
        168–169
linear equations, 56–73
    slope-intercept form, 58–59
    standard form, 64
    systems, 66–72
linear functions, 135
linear inequalities, 72–73
lines
    parallel, 165–167
    perpendicular, 166–168
locus, defined, 228
logarithm, defined, 102
logarithmic equations, 102–106
logarithms, 102, 105
    characteristic, 105
    common, 102
    mantissa, 105
    natural, 106
    properties of, 102
logic, terminology, 381–382
long division of polynomials, 109
lower limit, definite integral, 366–368
lowest common denominator (LCD), 33

M

magnitude of a vector, 113–114
major arc of a circle, 195

mantissa of a log, 125
mapping, 240. *See also* transformations.
marginal frequency, 309–311
mathematical induction, 387–388
mathematical reasoning, 389
matrices. *See* matrix.
matrix, 70–73, 125–127
    addition and subtraction, 126
    invertible, 72
    multiplication, 126–127
    multiplication by a scalar, 126
    to solve systems of equations,
        70–72, 125
    square, 70
    value, 70–72
matrix mathematics, applications, 127
mean
    of a proportion, 74
    statistical, 202
Mean Value Theorem, 256
Mean Value Theorem for integration,
    368
means, of a proportion, 86
measurement, 40–42
median, statistical, 282–283, 295–296
metric system of units, 40–42
midpoint, of a line segment, 168, 225
    constructing, 203
midpoint rule, 368
minor arc, of a circle, 95
mixed number, 30
    conversion to improper fraction, 32
    multiplication, 32
mnemonic
    defined, 28
    F–O–I–L, 80
    PEMDAS, 28
mode, statistical, 282
modular congruence, 377–378
modular mathematics, 376–381
modulus, 376–381
multiples
    common, 77
    of a number, 28
multiplication of fractions, 31–32
multiplication properties, 26–276
multiplication rule of probability, 318
multiplicative identity, 27
mutually exclusive events, 319, 322–
    323

N

natural logarithm, 106
natural numbers, 23, 28, 387–388
non-mutually exclusive events. *See*
    overlapping events.
nonrepeating decimals, 123
normal curve, 297
normal distribution, 297–300
    applications, 304–305
    percentages, 300–301, 303
    raw scores, 302
    standard, 302
    z–scores, 302–303
number line, 22–23, 29
number systems, 22–27
    base 2, 42–43
numerator, 29
numerical data, 281. *See* quantitative
    data
numerical representations, 397–398

O

oblique asymptote. *See* slant asymptote.
oblique prism, 207
observational study, 280–281
obtuse angle, 164, 171
obtuse triangle, 171, 173
odd function, 150–151
odd numbers, 24
one-to-one functions. *See* inverse
    functions.
one-way frequency table. *See* bar graph;
    categorical data; pie chart.
optimization, 358–359
order of magnitude, 35–37
order of operations, 27–28
ordered pairs, 57, 66, 133, 161
origin, Cartesian coordinate system, 57
overlapping events, 319, 323–324

P

parabola, 89–90, 228, 232
    axis of symmetry, 90, 232
    directrix, 232
    domain, 135
    eccentricity, 232
    focus, 232

general equation, 89–90, 229
    real-world applications, 236–237
    standard form of equation, 232
    vertex, 232
    x-intercept, 136
    y-intercept, 136
parallel lines, 165–167
    constructing, 205
    distance between, 226–228
    slopes, 167
parallelogram, 179, 181–182
Pascal's triangle, 111–113
PEMDAS, 27–28
percentages, 29, 31
    converting to decimals, 31
    converting to fractions, 31
perfect squares, 37
performance task, 405
perimeter
    circle (circumference), 192–193
    polygon, 188
    quadrilateral, 130
    semicircle, 194
    triangle, 174–175
periodic functions, 143, 254
    period of, 254, 268
    real-world examples, 270
permutation, 315–318
perpendicular lines, 166–168
    construction of, 203–204
    slopes, 167
phase shift, of sine curve, 268
pi (π), defined, 193
pictograph, 296
pie chart, 288–289
piecewise function, 140
plane, 162–163
point, collinear, 162
    defined, 161–162
point of inflection, 351
polygons
    apothem, 188–189
    area, 188
    concave, 199
    congruent, 190–191
    convex, 190
    diagonals, 189–190
    inscribed, 199–200
    perimeter, 188
    regular, 187

    similar, 190–191
    sum of exterior angles, 186–187
    sum of interior angles, 186–187
polyhedrons, 207
polynomial function, 137
polynomials, 106–113
    complex roots, 108
    degree, 106
    division, 109
    domain, 137
    general shape of graph, 137
    identities, 107
    real roots, 108, 137
    roots, 107–111
    y-intercept, 137
population, statistical, 280
portfolios, 405
position function, 355–358, 373
    integration, 373
position–time graph, 355–358, 373
power rule of differentiation, 344–348
powers, 34–35
prefixes, in metric measurement, 41
premises, in logic, 382
prime factorization, 29
prime numbers, 28
    twin primes, 382
prisms, 207–208
probability
    addition rule, 318
    conditional, 324
    defined, 312
    distribution. *See* normal distribution.
    empirical, 312
    experimental, 312
    multiplication rule, 318
    summary of types, 326
    theoretical, 312
problem solving, 40
    skills, 398–401
    strategies, 399–400
product rule of differentiation, 346–348
properties, of number systems, 25–27
proportions, 74–77
pyramid, 212–214
Pythagorean formula, 173. *See*
    Pythagorean Theorem.
Pythagorean identities, 255
Pythagorean Theorem, 172–174
    converse, 172

to find distance between two points, 224

to find third side of a triangle, 272

to find area of a triangle, 175

Pythagorean triples, 173

Q

quadrants
Cartesian coordinate system, 57
unit circle, 260–263

quadratic equations, 79–91
algebraic solutions, 83–87
factoring, 83–87
graphic solutions, 89–90
real-word examples, 91
roots, 89
zeros of, 89

quadratic formula, 87–89

quadratic functions, 135

quadrilaterals, 179–186
area, 180
perimeter, 180
sum of angles, 180
See also specific quadrilaterals

qualitative data. See categorical data.

quantitative data, 282–285
box-and-whiskers plot, 296–297
defined, 281
dot plot, 295
histogram, 292–293
line graph, 293–294
pictograph, 296
presentation, 292–297
stem-and-leaf plot, 294–295

quantitative reasoning, 40

quantity, 39–44

quotient rule of differentiation, 346–348

R

radians, 253–254

radical equations, 78–79, 100

radical expressions, simplifying, 38–39

radical sign, 37

radicals, 37
approximating, 39
properties, 38

radicand, 37

radius, 191

random sampling, 280

range, 133
of a relation, 133
polynomial function, 137
statistical, 283

rate of change
average, 342
defined, 58
instantaneous, 343

ratio, 73
common, geometry sequence, 121

rational equations, 77–79

rational expressions, 53

rational functions, 138–139
asymptotes, 138–139
differentiation rules, 363–364
integration rules, 363–364

rational numbers, 23, 98
closure, 25
properties, 25–27

rationalizing a fraction, 79

raw data, 281

raw score, defined, 302

ray, 162

real numbers, 23
properties, 25–27

real-world applications
ellipse, 289
hyperbola, 238
parabola, 91, 236–237

reciprocal, 32

rectangle, 179, 183–184
area, 184
diagonals, 183
perimeter, 184

rectangular coordinates. See Cartesian coordinates.

rectangular solid, 206

reducible fractions, 30

reference angles, 260–263

reflection, 153–155
in the coordinate plane, 242–243

reflex angle, 164

regression line, 306–307

regular pyramid, 212–214

related rates, 359–361

relation, defined, 133

relative frequency, 309–311

remainder, 110

Remainder Theorem, 110

replacement, in conditional probability, 324–325

representations in classroom, 397–398

representative data, 279

reasoning, mathematical, 386–387

resources, educational, 377

rhombus, 179, 182–183

Riemann sums, 367–368

right angle, defined, 164

right circular cone, 214–215
surface area, 182
volume, 182–183

right prism, 176–178

right rectangular prism, 207

right regular pyramid, 212–214

right triangle, 171–174.
ratio of sides, 173–174, 256–257

roots, 34, 37
of polynomial, 137
of quadratic equation, 89

rotation, 154
in the coordinate plane, 240, 243–245

rotation method, to find volume, 375–376

rounding, 43–44

rounding error, 44, 225

rows of a matrix, 70–72, 125

S

sample
defined, 280
size, 280
space, 312
survey, 280

sampling, 280–281

scalar quantities, 113

scale, bar graph, 286

scale factor, 179, 245

scalene triangle, 171

scatter plot, 305

scientific notation, 35–37

secant, of a circle, 154

secant function, 252–253

second derivative, 352–353
graph, 354–355

second-degree equation, 79, 228–229.
See also conic sections, quadratic equation

second fundamental theorem of
     calculus, 364, 366
sector of a circle, 195–196
semicircle, 156
semi-perimeter, 225
sequences
     arithmetic, 118–120
     defined, 118–122
     geometric, 121–123
series, 118–125
     arithmetic, 120–121
     geometric, 123–125
shape of a curve, 137
side–angle–side (SAS) congruency,
     178, 271–272
     and area of triangle, 271–272
     and law of cosines, 272
side–side–side (SSS), 177
significance, statistical, 278
similar, defined, 178
similar triangles, 178–179
     corresponding parts, 178
     proportions in, 178–179
     scale factors, 179
simple interest, 120, 123
simplifying a fraction, 31–32
simultaneous equations, 66–72
     solution by addition or subtraction,
          68–69
     solution by graphing, 69–70
     solution by substitution, 66–68
     solution by using matrices, 70–72
sine function, defined, 252
     transformations, 267–270
size transformation. *See* dilation.
skew, 163, 283
slant asymptote, 138–139, 335–336
slant height, 213
slicing, plane and cone, 228–229
slope, 58–59, 63–68, 118, 306
     of tangents to a curve, 341–344,
          350–357
     of parallel lines, 167–168, 227
     of perpendicular lines, 167–168, 227
slope-intercept form, 58–59, 64, 167,
     227
solids of revolution, volumes of,
     375–376
speed, defined, 355
sphere, 215–216

spread of data, 283
square, 179, 184–186
     area, 185
     diagonals, 185
     perimeter, 185–186
     properties, 185
square matrix, 70
squared power, 34
standard deviation, 299
standard form
     of linear equation for conics, 64–65
standard normal distribution. *See*
     standard deviation.
standard score. *See z*–score.
statistics, defined, 279
stem-and-leaf plot, 294–295
step function, 141
straight angle, 164
Study Center, REA, 2
study schedule, 6–7
substitution to solve systems of
     equations, 66
subtraction of fractions, 33
subtraction properties, 26
summative assessments, 405
supplementary angles, 164–165
surface area. *See particular figures.*
symbolic representations, 397–398
symmetric functions, 150–151
synthetic division, 109–110
systems of linear equations, 66–72
     solution by addition or subtraction,
          68–69
     solution by graphing, 69–70
     solution by substitution, 66–68
     solution by using matrices, 70–72

T

table of values, 60–62
tallying, 282, 289, 295, 309
tangent
     of a circle, 191–192
     to a curve, 341
     point of tangency, 88
tangent function, 252–253
terminal ray, unit circle, 255–256
terminating decimals, 29
terms
     defined, 52

like, 52, 80
test overview, 3–6, 13–15
theorem, defined, 382
theoretical probability, 312
three-dimensional figures, 205–216
     relation to two dimensions, 206
transformations, 151–155
     in the coordinate plane, 240–246
     of geometric functions, 240–246
     of trigonometric functions,
          266–269
transitive property, 25
translation, 151–152
     in the coordinate plane, 240–242
     of graph of a function, 152
     of sine function, 268–269
     of words into algebra, 51–53
transversal, 165
trapezoid, 179–180
     isosceles, 179, 181
trapezoid rule, 368
tree diagram, 313–314
trend estimation, 307
triangles, 169–179
     acute, 171, 175
     altitude, 175
     area, 175–176
     base, 175–176
     congruent, 176–178
     equilateral, 171, 175
     finding area by using coordinates,
          225–226
     finding area by using trigonometry,
          270–273
     isosceles, 170–171, 175
     labeling, 170
     obtuse, 171, 175
     perimeter, 174–175
     properties, 169–170
     right, 171–175
     rigidity, 169, 177
     scalene, 171
trigonometric functions, 252
     derivatives, 349
     graphs, 257–258
     inverse, 259–260
     relationships, 252–253
     signs in quadrants, 261
     transformations of graphs,
          266–269

using algebra with, 264–266
trinomial, 80
truth of premises, 384
two-way frequency table, 327–330

U

unit circle, 255–256
  and Pythagorean identity, 255–256
unit conversion, 39–40
unit prefixes, 41
units, 39
universe of a Venn diagram, 327
upper limit, definite integral, 366–368
US standard system of units, 40–41

V

validity, of argument, 384
value of a definite integral, 364–365
variance, 299
variation, 75–77
vectors, 113–118
  addition of, 114–116
  graphing, 114
  multiplication by a scalar, 117
  subtraction of, 116–117

velocity
  average, 355
  instantaneous, 355
velocity function, 355–358
  integration, 373
velocity-time curve, 355–358, 373
Venn diagrams, 327–329
verbal representations, 397–398
vertex, *See* vertices.
vertical angles, 164–165
vertical asymptotes, 138–139, 258,
  335–337
vertical line test, 134–135, 149, 154,
  259
vertical shift sine curve, 269
vertex
  of absolute value function, 141–142
  of an angle, 163
  of an ellipse, 233
  of a hyperbola, 232–236
  of a parabola, 90, 135, 232
  of a polygon, 186–187
  of three-dimensional figures, 175
volume, 206–216
  of a cube, 209
  of a cylinder, 211
  by integration, 374–376

of a pyramid, 213
of a right circular cone, 214–215
of a right prism, 208
of a sphere, 216
units, 41–42

W

weight, units, 41–42
weighted means, 295
whole numbers, 23, 30

X

x-intercept, conic sections, 136, 229

Y

y-intercept
  absolute value function, 142
  conic sections, 136, 229
  linear equation, 58–59

Z

zeros of quadratic function, 136, 371
z-scores, 302–303